FREUD ON SUBLIMATION

✳   ✳   ✳

SUNY Series in Religious Studies
Harold Coward, editor

FREUD ON SUBLIMATION

✳   ✳   ✳

RECONSIDERATIONS

Volney P. Gay

✳   ✳   ✳

State University of New York Press

Published by
State University of New York Press, Albany

© 1992 State University of New York

For information, address State University of New York Press,
State University Plaza, N.Y., 12246

Production by Marilyn P. Semerad
Marketing by Theresa A. Swierzowski

Library of Congress Cataloging-in-Publication Data

Gay, Volney Patrick,
    Freud on sublimation : reconsiderations / Volney P. Gay.
        p. cm. — (SUNY series in Religious Studies)
    Includes bibliographical references and index.
    ISBN 0-7914-1183-4. — ISBN 0-7914-1184-2 (pbk.)
    1. Sublimation.   2. Psychoanalysis and the arts.
    3. Psychoanalysis and literature.   4. Freud, Sigmund, 1856–1939.
    I. Title.   II. Series.
BF175.5.S92G39   1992   91-47540
154.2'4—dc20   CIP

10   9   8   7   6   5   4   3   2   1

iv

For Laura

CONTENTS

ACKNOWLEDGMENTS

Grateful acknowledgement is made for permission to reprint the following:

Lines from "The Lifeguard" by James Dickey, originally printed in *The New Yorker*, reprinted in *Drowning with Others*, ©by James Dickey and Wesleyan University Press, 1961.

Lines from *The Odyssey*, translated by Robert Fitzgerald, ©Random House, Inc., originally published by Doubleday and Company, Garden City, N.J. in 1961.

A table "A feature by feature consonant matrix," designed by Sadanand Singh and Kala S. Singh, ©by Pro-Ed, Inc., Austin, TX, originally published by University Park Press, Baltimore, in 1976. Poem, "To stand by the window...," by Pierre Lecuire, originally appearing in *World Literature Today*, Winter, 1988, p. 18.

Parts of my original article, "Freud, Sublimation, and the Mystery of Transformation," originally appearing in *Thought*, vol. LXI, No. 240, March 1986.

A still from the motion picture, "Citizen Kane," ©1941 RKO Pictures, Inc. All Rights Reserved. Three pictures from William Hauptman, "Ingres and Photographic Vision," © *History of Photography: An International Quarterly*, January, 1977, no. 2, pp. 124–125.

This book was written with the kind support of the University Research Council of Vanderbilt University and the College of Arts and Sciences, Vanderbilt.

I wish to thank also Ms. Marilyn P. Semerad of SUNY Press and Ms. Joyce Arnold, and especially Ms. Evon Flesberg of Vanderbilt University, Department of Graduate Studies.

INTRODUCTION

Art and Public Morality

In the 1950s it was hard to find pictures of naked people. One searched in magazines that floated through the school or in art books, heavy volumes with clay paper, gold lettering, and tiny print. The magazine, an object creased by a hundred hands, was dirty, while the art book, stationed in the public library and in better homes, was clean. If I had known what "anomalous" meant at the age of ten, I would have said that this was anomalous. *Vogue* and *National Geographic* magazines could publish pictures of half-naked women, but *Life* magazine could not. This was confusing. What distinguishes dirty magazines, hidden in a book bag, from the art book displayed next to the oversized ashtray?

Similar problems emerged when I studied the history of art in college. On many great sculptures fig leaves covered the genital region. Like the shrouds that covered nudes in Renaissance paintings, these fig leaves covered up what artists like Michelangelo felt should be revealed. Because an adolescent identifies with an artist like Michelangelo, and not a prudish curator, this also puzzled me. Was Michelangelo wrong? Was the church correct? In hiding the genitals behind a fig leaf, the censors made the genital region all the more the focal point of the statue. Was even the "greatest" art subject to the moralizing that condemned some magazines but spared other representations?

The seminude illustrations of Christ, God himself, according to the Church, were also puzzling. In a Catholic girl's bedroom was the crucifix. On it a naked Christ stretched out on a cross, positioned so that Christ could see the girl and she could see Him. Parents who arranged this no doubt wished to remind their daughter of Christ's death; just before her eyes closed she could meditate on that event. Yet, many features of Christ's story, for example, His birth and healing His flock, would be equally good topics for bedtime reflection.

Tradition has made the crucifix a common object, displayed everywhere. (But replicas of Jesus in the act of breaking bread would also be important.) Unconscious reasons for hanging the crucifix over a daughter's bed are many and not available to us without a bona fide patient's associations. Yet, without clinical validations, we can note that Christ, his genital region wrapped in a tiny cloth, is a near-naked man. But consider the "Virgin and Child with Angels," (figure 1) a painting by Bernaert van Orley done around 1513. It shows Mary, Jesus, and Angels adoring the baby. As in many similar paintings, Mary fondles the baby's penis. Leo Steinberg (1983) says of this religious artifact, "How should this curiosity be perceived? Shall we hurry past it with stifled titters, or condemn it as scandalous?" (p. 6). The artist forces our attention upon the baby's penis and upon Mary's manipulation of it. Steinberg rediscovered the ubiquity of such representations of Christ. He terms these paintings *ostentatio genitalium*, the showing of the Christ Child's genitals, and likens it to another Christian formula, *ostentatio vulnerum*, the showing of the wounds of the Crucified One.

According to Steinberg, this visual formula occurs throughout Renaissance portrayals of Christ for some two hundred years. Then, the motif died out and hundreds of masterpieces became liable to censorship, destruction, or cover up. How did esteemed religious art that typifies one period of reflection upon the meaning of Christ become a scandal in the epochs that followed it? How did "art" turn into "non-art"? Do these paintings illustrate the culture's valuation of infants? Of course, this infant is the Christ Himself; we cannot deduce that parents valued all children this way. Yet, they celebrated the infant —not the young man Jesus, for example.[1]

Steinberg describes "...a Western artist nurtured in Catholic orthodoxy—for him the objective was not so much to proclaim the divinity of the babe as to declare the *humanation* of God" (p. 9).[2] Like the preachers of that period, artists did not doubt the truth of the Gospels, nor did they doubt the Church's duty to protect and to declare those truths. The divinity, the godlike qualities of Jesus, was unquestionable. Rather, His human nature and human qualities required amplification.

Steinberg analyzes hundreds of these paintings and shows how the artists declare the specific human maleness of Christ. These paintings announce that this God is fully human, alike in all respects to other men: "To us, the intent of these paintings is assured by their formal austerity and moral certitude. Their goal is pre-fixed, their aim steady: tirelessly, they confess the dual nature of Christ, and the leasing of his humanity to mortal suffering" (pp. 41–42).[3]

By celebrating Christ's sexual nature such art elevates human sex-

ual life to a station near God and other members of the Trinity. John W. O'Malley (1979) illustrates what such nearness and identification with God meant to Renaissance Christians. O'Malley summarizes years of careful scholarship on more than 160 sermons preached between 1450 and 1521 to the Pope in the Sistine Chapel and in Saint Peter's basilica. These sermons exhort faithful listeners to examine the beauty of God's world. We are to contemplate God's gifts: *contemplari*, not in the sense of think or meditate, but always "to gaze upon" (O'Malley 1979, p. 63). We are to see, look, view, find, and admire the goodness of God's manifest work and plans for us. Another preacher compares Christ, preaching the Sermon on the Mount, to a great painter: "Christ speaks like 'an expert in the art of painting,' who in that marvelous Sermon restored the true image of our souls as if with a new portrait" (1979, p. 65).[4]

The chief aim of these sermons is praise. Their chief mood is celebration. The preacher is to inculcate through his language a picture, as vivid as possible, of God's glory and the absolute treasure of the Incarnated Son. The "style must bring about seeing through hearing," O'Malley says, quoting an ancient master of rhetoric (see p. 79 in O'Malley). At the center of creation is mankind. At the center of human being is the body: "the beauty of the contours, the artful disposition of the members, the order of the whole" (1979, p. 133). The mystery that preoccupied these preachers was the Incarnation. When Mary received the Holy Spirit she made all creation new; all humans, dignified by God's descent, were lifted up to a new plane of beauty. The preachers adored this doctrine. They assimilated it into the tragedy of the Crucifixion: "The Incarnation joined God to man, the Redemption joins man to God. The two mysteries fuse, becoming almost indistinguishable" (1979, p. 146).

These features of Renaissance thought support Steinberg's discussion of the *ostentatio genitalium*, which he has retrieved after hundreds of years of repression. Steinberg and O'Malley assert that in these displays of Christ's sexuality is the affirmation of the beauty of the human body "lifted up" by God's Incarnation. Hence Renaissance paintings show an *uncircumcised* Christ Child," at an age well past the eighth day" (p. 159) when scripture states that He was circumcised. This brings us back to the difference between dirty art, or "mere graffiti," and real art, sublimated artifacts. The reconciliation of God with human beings, and the divinity of Christ's sexuality, make possible religious art that is also sexual. This is the idea I examine in this work.

An Ordered and Safeguarded Universe

Steinberg illuminates a period of Christian history that lasted al-most two hundred years. In it artists dedicated to the propagation of the true faith celebrated male sexuality. Steinberg roots these paintings in the religious sensibility of the period, in its positive valuation of the human body and the artistic representation of that body. Following Steinberg's lead, I have used O'Malley's summary of the sermons preached to the Pope during this period.

How do these sermons help us explain the appearance of such art? What makes such art celebrated in one religious epoch and rejected in another? Note that this question is analogous to the vexing issue of defining pornography: what makes one nude pornographic and another "high art"? These paintings depict Christ's sexuality. Some allude to erections. These are serious works of art, not salacious. It is easy to agree with this sentiment; the dozens of paintings of Madonna and Child, for example, are vivid pieces.

Yet, if these values are "in" the paintings, why would later author-ities subsequently repress these representations, with all their religious seriousness, and deny their obvious intent? These authorities were raised in institutions that esteemed these works of art. Why would they fail to see in them what their parents and grandparents saw, which Steinberg has recovered? One answer is that these paintings were always pornographic and "dirty," and that later authorities saw this obvious moral fact. Against this simplistic answer is the weight of two hundred years of tradition, spread throughout Europe, and upheld by the moral authorities of the period.

Perhaps aesthetic taste develops over time? Perhaps later ages have insight into "clean" art that earlier ages did not? Against these answers is evidence that while values shift over time no one can show a steady progress in the development of values. Were late Roman taste and values "higher" than classical Greek taste and values? More plaus-ible is that later authorities repressed these paintings because their sense of human being differed completely from that of the artists'. Lacking such understanding, those who wielded power in the next epoch interpreted the exhibition of Christ's genitals in a secular context of ordinary propriety and decorum. This seems clear and uncontrovert-ible. Less clear and more difficult to assess is the source of these changes in world view and valuation of the human (male and female) body.[5]

Assumptions that match this view of Christ's body, alongside the doctrine of the Incarnation, form a coherent world view which we glimpse by turning, again, to O'Malley's analysis of the Renaissance ser-mons delivered in Rome. O'Malley isolates nine assumptions "...so deeply imbedded in the preacher's consciousness that there was no clear perception that there might be alternatives to them" (1979, p. 125).

These assumptions attest that the mundane world reflects the structure of the divine world. I cite O'Malley's summary in full. It is lucid and bears an uncanny likeness to psychological claims and assumptions that underlie the notion of sublimation I put forth in chapter 1. From his analysis of these sermons O'Malley derives nine assumptions:

1. Reality is ordered;
2. reality is, consequently, coherent, and its parts interlock to form an harmonious totality;
3. the order and coherence of reality are discoverable, at least partially, by the human mind;
4. the discovery of order and coherence in its earthly expression discloses a divine exemplar that has impressed its own order and coherence upon earthly reality;
5. the order and coherence of earthly reality—the intelligibility of reality—reflects the exemplar, as that exemplar is made known through a study of its earthly reflection and through the exemplar's direct revelation of itself. (p. 125)

From these five assumptions, O'Malley says, the preachers derived four additional truths:

6. Thus, a study of the exemplar compels, in turn, a study of the reality of the world;
7. earthly reality in fact participates in certain qualities of the exemplar;
8. besides the qualities of order and coherence in which earthly reality participates, the divine exemplar's quality of stability or immutability is of particular importance;
9. the order, coherence, and stability discovered in the universe have aesthetic implications, since they are the components of that aspect of reality known as beauty. (p. 125)

Did these assumptions permit the artists of this epoch to portray Christ's sexual nature with so little shame? Christian sexual art challenges Freud's view of religion and the theory of "sublimation." For as I show in chapters 2, 3, and 4, Freud did not share the world view of the Roman preachers. Rather, he rejects assumption no. 6, which claims there is a linkage between the divine realm and the mundane realm. Therefore, he rejects assumptions 7, 8, and 9 based upon it.

Freud and the Problem of Sublimation

Like the Roman preachers, Freud assumes that the real world is coherent and knowable by the human mind. Freud denies that a divine Exemplar guarantees the coherence of this world and makes permanent the bond between us and itself. Freud denies that the apparent world of qualitative experience is the fundamental reality encompassing all human experience. Rather, he locates qualitative experience of all types in the mind of the subject: it is we, as subjects, who assign qualitative differences to the "mere quantities" that are "in" the world. In affirming this claim about the "real," Freud opposed the preachers whom O'Malley describes. From his beliefs, Freud constructed a theory of art contrary to the aesthetics of the preachers.

The preachers believed that they "lived in a reconciled universe" (O'Malley 1979, p. 145). Freud did not believe this, nor did he believe that there could be complete harmony between individuals and their civilization. Civilization and individuals, from the beginning, contend with one another because civilization taxes the libidinal energies given to individuals alone. In response to this burden, to this tax upon their libidinal economies, most people submit. Some people rebel, others become sick (the neurotics).

A few find ways to retain their libidinal energies, especially their "pregenital" libidinal drives, through a process Freud termed "sublimation." Some artists find ways to express their libidinal drives in ways that do not threaten the dominant culture. How such persons manage to escape detection became a key problem for the theory of sublimation. For the most part, Freud says, religion serves the interest of culture by helping those in authority dominate the libidinal lives of its members. Freud could have said that religion serves those in power who use it to dominate others under the guise of "cultural requirement," but he does not pursue this Marxist explanation of the use of religion. He says religion ameliorates conflicts between self-centeredness and the selflessness which culture requires.

Because sexuality is a focus of self-centeredness, religions control sexual life in all its forms, from behavior to thought to expression in the arts. Hence, the theory of sublimation predicts the existence of prudish, antisexual, Christian art. For such art would serve to repress sexuality at the behest of religious authorities who act as agents of the state. Sublimation theory predicts that atheistic, bohemian artists will be sexual or hypersexual, while devout persons will be antisexual and repressive. Against this view are hundreds of paintings documented in Steinberg's book which are both Christian and sexual. Do these paintings show "sublimation" in the way that Freud's theory requires? To say that an object represents the effects of sublimation is to say that a "lower" form of behavior has been transformed into a "higher" form. An example is the claim that the child's impulse to smear its poop may be "sublimated" into the artist's desire to smear and shape gooey clay. Clinical evidence of such transformation supports these claims, sometimes.

In hundreds of paintings Christian artists expose Christ's genitals with care; they do not cover them up, nor "transform" them. It is Christ's sexual, genital nature that is thus highlighted. His masculine, sexual nature, which one might consider "lower," because it refers to his mere body, was not transformed into higher forms of representation. Freud explains why later church authorities suppressed these paintings. He does not explain why earlier church authorities commissoned them.

The ontology O'Malley elucidates gives us a way to recast Freud's theory of sublimation. For, in a simple sense, that theory cannot account for such art, at least for such religious art. I follow Steinberg, who explains this sexual art as the product of views about God and human beings announced in the sermons of the epoch. These sermons declare that the "qualities" of earthly reality, including sexuality, extend beyond human beings. Rather, their origin in the Divine Will guarantees these qualities: human desires may later misshape such qualities into negative consequences.

For example, people may distort human sexuality into perversions. Human beings may respond differently to the actual qualities and intensities of sexuality. Yet, these qualities, their intensity and pleasure are permanent features of reality. They are not imposed upon it. Renaissance preachers and artists view the world as "pre-Kantians." Their notion of what is "real" and true contradicts Immanuel Kant. Kant's task was to preserve the possibility of religious faith, like that of the Renaissance preachers, by showing how the natural sciences could not invalidate it. Kant rejected naive belief that aesthetic qualities reflected reality in itself.

Kant located the source of experience within the human subject; Renaissance thinkers located qualities outside the human subject. I do not pretend to know which ontology, that of Freud or that of the preachers, is the better of the two. I do not know to what degree Renaissance ontology, as espoused by the preachers, depends upon a theological claim about God's existence and God's goodness. This book is not a study of theology nor is it a study in theology.

Rather, I propose to show how Freud's ontological commitments determined his theory of sublimation. Those ontological commitments were not to a theory of heaven of the divine but to a theory of the origins of the self. Using theological terms, the Renaissance preachers proclaim that the human self is, from the beginning, bounded in relationship to a divine other, a loving God. Using psychological terms, Freud claims that the human self is, from the beginning, unattached to an Other. Slowly, over time, the neonate comes to fit into a relationship to its mother and breaks free of "primary narcissism." In forsaking this urge to remain separate the child responds to the claims of others and experiences the world of qualitative differences.

This sense of a world of qualities is an illusion necessary for human beings to survive in this universe. From this theory of the illusory status of qualitative experience, Freud derived his theory of sublimation. From that theory of sublimation he derived a theory of aesthetic expression.

After I evaluate Freud's "classical" theory of sublimation, I propose ways to rethink the concept without abandoning it. I show that the issue of the location of "quality" is central to Freud's notion of sublimation. I show that an alternative psychoanalytic view, similar to that of the preachers, provides a more complete theory of sublimation. If I accomplish that task then this chapter may become a useful addition to a more complete psychoanalytic aesthetic.[6]

The Book in Brief

Psychoanalytic aesthetics depends upon Freud's understanding of where "values" and "qualities" are located. These terms are members of two distinct philosophic pairs: values versus facts and qualities versus quantities. Typically they are held to be exclusive: what is a fact cannot be a value and what is a quality cannot be a quantity. Freud agreed with this philosophy of science, as did most psychologists and scientists of his time. This distinction creates a gap between value judgments and factual judgments and between the perception of quantities and the experience of qualities. To overcome this gap many persons have employed many distinct methods. I consider two of them at length in this book, structuralism and phenomenology. For all their many virtues, neither seems adequate to the needs of a psychoanalytic aesthetics.

Structuralism does not permit us to examine and savor the qualities of a unique experience; phenomenology does. Phenomenology does not permit us to make direct, nonsubjective, claims about the actual nature of the object in question. It is always the object's pertinence to us that is important. I put this more baldly than members of either group would. Structuralist methods abjure the surface in favor of underlying and common structures. Phenomenology adores the surface and abjures making claims about "ontological" features of the object under investigation. Both methods attempt to locate the redundant features of an object and, through a formula, isolate it. In this way structuralists and phenomenologists reason as do other scientists: they look for ways to explain the complexities of the surface. There is no reason to suppose this is an impossible task. Sophisticated work done by structuralists on genres and that done by phenomenologists of religion is proof to the contrary.[7]

More important is that Freud's enterprise is not a linguistic one, while those of structuralism and phenomenology are. The existence of many brilliant treatises, like those of Jacque Lacan and his followers, may seem ample enough refutation of this claim. I do not believe this is so. Lacan does not convince me to reject Heinz Hartmann and his collaborators who argued that the ego is a biopsychological concept, not a linguistic entity. I do not deny Lacan's originality but I do not think it is adequate to the task of forging a new metapsychology out of linguistics proper. In chapters 4 and 5 I argue that there remains a radical gap between linguistic modes of representation (or signification) and non-linguistic modes. Consequently, there is a radical gap between intellectual analyses of linguistic artifacts, like poetry, and psychoanalytic events, like transference and neurotic symptoms.

This difference makes a science of psychoanalysis possible. The hysteric uses his or her body *as if it were* sending messages, but those messages are not structured like ordinary linguistic productions. Hysteria is like a kind of language, just as it is like a kind of dementia, and, indeed, like a kind of spiritual possession. However, hysteria is not identical to any of these behaviors. In more technical terms, hysteria employs iconic modes of expression, while language proper does not and cannot be reduced to mere iconicity.

I argue against Freud's conclusion that the process of valuation is private and restricted to the state of the organism's libidinal state. I think we can keep Freud's theory of primary process thought and argue for the objective existence of values. In order to accomplish these ends I first show where the usual psychoanalytic theory of value leaves us. We can affirm Freud's agnosticism about aesthetics. Or we can affirm the thought of the later David Winnicott, a British child psychoanalyst, who placed values within an imagined space suffused with illusions.

In contrast to both of these positions I argue for a new theory of the concept of sublimation. I summarize my technical arguments at the end of chapter 1.

CHAPTER ONE

ART AND THE ORGANIZATION OF THE SELF

In this book I pursue three aims. The first is to examine Freud's core concept *sublimation*. The second is to suggest ways that contemporary analytic reflections on the self might help us revive the concept of sublimation. My third aim is to show how this revised theory of sublimation might contribute to the larger tasks identified as "Psychoanalytic Aesthetics." This title names two vast areas, the study of the unconscious mind and the study of art and human experience. Many psychoanalytic authors have turned their attention to aesthetic experience. I refer to these contemporary studies throughout this essay. I do not see my study as proving the superiority of one mode of analytic reasoning or analytic theory over another. Analytic theories are many; ways to validate them are few. Given this limitation, an author can hope to articulate a treatise with as much clarity as possible.

Similarities and Differences: Symptoms and Work of Art

Regarding the childhood experience of the artist, Phyllis Greenacre writes: "[The artist's] unusual capacity for awareness of relations between various stimuli must involve sensibility of subtle similarities and differences, an earlier and greater reactivity to form and a greater sense of actual or potential organization, perhaps a greater sense of the gestalt" (Greenacre 1957, p. 53).

If psychoanalysis is a valid science, it has much to say about the production and enjoyment of art. This seems true of narrative arts, like the novel, which are often similar to dreams and other psychological acts that Freud first investigated. I believe psychoanalysis is valid science and relevant to the narrative and nonnarrative arts. Freud's insights into the "Opedipal" features of childhood, for example, reflect upon the original Oedipal drama, Sophocles's play, written in the fifth century, BCE. In using the name of Oedipus, Freud declared his debt to

Sophocles and other poets. Freud suggested that Sophocles's plays expressed psychological truths that he reclaimed for science, stated without the illusions of art. The notion that art only expresses unconcsious motives reduces art to a neurosis and pseudotherapy. Through art, feelings emerge and suffering decreases. The work of art is not different from symptoms and defenses against symptoms which are compromises that also express and conceal forbidden wishes.

Psychoanalysts learn to recognize and heal psychological disease. They use the theories derived from this work to investigate nonclinical entities, like works of art. A danger is that the analyst will treat the work of art as if it were a symptom or an artifact of the therapy. Both evaporate when the analysis concludes. However, the danger of the analyst destroying the artwork is slight. Many sympathetic studies of artists by psychoanalysts are available. Also, many art critics read Freud and apply his insights to particular artists.

Charles Bernheimer (1987) describes the difference between Degas's portraits of prostitutes and mere pornography: "Pornographic imagery is constructed to suggest woman's desire to submit pleasurably to phallic power. She is seen as guilty in the display of her sexuality" (p. 175). In contrast, Degas shows women masturbating with complete lack of regard for the viewer (or voyeur). They remain independent of the male's insistence upon the priority of the phallus.

Bernheimer does not absolve Degas of all voyeuristic urges; nor does he claim that Degas's paintings repeal male ideologies and repressions. Degas conveys complex views of male sexuality: "The small dimensions of the monotype, allowing it to be easily held in the hand, further suggest that these are fetishistic images made for a connoisseur's private enjoyment. But it is precisely the fantasy potential of these images of available female sexuality that Degas suppresses" (p. 172). Degas portrays both pornographic images and pornographic morality. By placing the viewer in the same space as the male whose money alone makes him significant, Degas reveals our own inferiority. Like him we are substitutable.[1]

Given these psychoanalytic contributions to critical theory, basic problems with psychoanalytic aesthetics remain, especially with the "art as expression" view. While the dream and a novel may share psychological themes, the novel is richer, more detailed, and better structured than the dream. Novels reveal a degree of organization and thought far beyond that of the dream. In contemporary terms, the novel, or any other complex artifact, exhibits more information per unit than does the dream. Hence, dreams by themselves cannot produce novels: "noise cannot generate information." A group of monkeys could write a Shakespeare play if they had a very long time, say half of an infinity. Even then, the so-called play would be an accidental event, the product of random typing.

A psychoanalytic critique of the art-as-expression view occurs in Greenacre's astute comments, summarized in the above quotation. Greenacre says that art is more than conflicts produced by invisible psychological processes. On the contrary, Greenacre says that the work of art is an organized and organizing achievement in which creative persons find within sensual experience moments in which the world and the self cohere. This is an active, constructive aspect of the artistic process and it is an active, constructive potential within the artifact itself. In this way, artistic artifacts are the opposite of neurotic symptoms.

The following, from Walt Whitman's masterpiece *Leaves of Grass* illustrates this idea. Whitman marvels at the complexity of his body which mirrors the complexity of the natural and social worlds. Whitman's poetry is a "song of himself." He sings the body electric, "the narrowest hinge in my hand puts to scorn all machinery" (*Song of Myself*, line 667).

> Space and Time! now I see it is true, what I guess'd at
> What I guess'd when I loaf'd on the grass,
> What I guess'd while I lay alone in my bed,
> And again as I walk'd the beach under the paling stars of
> the morning.
> My ties and ballasts leave me, my elbows rest in sea-gaps, I skirt
> sierras, my palms cover continents,
> I am afoot with my vision
>
> *Song of Myself*, pp. 710–716

Encompassing the universe of experience, Whitman responds to the gestalt of this world's emotional economy. He feels inflated, united from his ballast like a balloon untied from its guylines. Is this a pathological inflation born out of the narcissistic activity called "poetry"? The poem may well have a root in Whitman's pathology, but the poem is more than a symptom.

Inflation afflicts a person. It is a painful psychological state, and, like other symptoms, it is usually hidden, disavowed, and private. When symptoms become sexual, like compulsive masturbation, they become shameful and disorganizing. Academics often point out the dangers of psychoanalytic reductionism. They rarely point out the more serious danger: that presented by art to psychoanalysis and recognized by Freud when he looked back to Sophocles. In choosing the name Oedipus, Freud testified that psychoanalysis depended upon the poets for its validation. This is not rhetoric on Freud's part. "Applied analysis," using clinical theory to talk about nonclinical artifacts, as Freud practiced it, validated discoveries made in the analytic hour by showing their prototypes in religion and works of fiction, especially tragedy. Freud did not view these cultural artifacts as practice targets. He did not plunder works of art and reduce them to pathology.

A second reason Freud valued art is the need to distinguish between maturity and neurosis; between health and disease. Analysis and analysts need a bench mark of human achievements and human capacities. Great works of art provide these bench marks. If Bernheimer falis to show how Degas's monotypes are more than fetish objects, he fails to show how Degas's works retain value. If they can never distinguish between fetish and the work of art, then psychoanalysts have no way to distinguish art from pornography. Yet, that would mean that no work of art could transform us. Art would always remain entertainment or, in more cold-blooded terms, supplies for masturbatory fantasies.

A third reason psychoanalysts ought to consider art is to challenge the romanticism inherent in psychoanalysis. Out of deference to the "creative" aspects of the artist's life, many authors refuse to assess the concrete events that precipitate the work of art. There is a romantic tradition within aesthetic traditions and within psychology of art that portrays "creativity" as a "magic synthesis" (Silvano Arieti 1976). Legends that Mozart could compose a symphony in his head and then write it down, note perfect, retain a popular appeal. They reappear in the film *Amadeus*. Such legends elevate Mozart beyond the ken of mere humans and so make his achievements opaque.

A fourth reason analysts should examine art is that art cannot be controlled by forces exterior to the personality of the artist. Genuine art requires the participation of the artist's self, and that cannot be coerced by either church or party bosses. In this sense, within art lie new possibilities of human freedom. These possibilities resonate also in the value Freud placed upon the individual's capacity to become a self. For these reasons the science of analysis needs to consider in depth the nature of artistic achievements.

Yet, many problems confront the analyst who ventures forth into the fields of art. One is that the psychoanalytic theory of art inherited from Freud revolves around the concept of sublimation. This concept arose when Freud could not account for works of art whose content paralleled dreams and symptoms but whose forms did not. The concept of sublimation was Freud's effort to respond to this gap in the psychoanalytic theory of culture. It is a term with an odd heritage and even odder place in psychoanalytic theory.

A second problem is to say how the work of art differs from its siblings, dreams and neurotic symptoms. Related to this demand is another task: how can we account for the truth value in art? How can psychoanalysis account for works of art, rooted in infantile complexes, that are valid accounts of human life? Psychoanalysis can reveal the hidden connections that link the artist's childhood with the artist's adult achievements. Such links always exist, for upon whose life experience can the authentic artist draw if not the artist's own? The most complete theory of sexuality should say something about *The Scarlet Letter*, a book about a woman whose sexual power terrifies a minister. In style and content some works of art parallel psychoneurotic events. An obvious example of this parallel between art and symptom are movies and their similarity to dreams and the similarity of dreams to religious myths. Movies display naked eroticism, all possible perversions, and naked aggression. Film style often parallels primary process thinking.

Recent American "slasher" films, in which rampaging maniacs cut and slice the flesh of young persons, have a huge audience of adolescent devotees. Some of these films, like the cult standard *The Rocky Horror Picture Show*, become centers of adolescent worship complete with ritual time and ritual activity. The adolescent struggle to form a sexual identity and to forsake their parents' protection animates the film.[2] It portrays a young couple who, on the verge of marriage, enter a strange castle, see sexualized dancing, and meet Dr. Frank N. Furter. He sings "I'm just a sweet transvestite from Transsexual Transylvania" (Twitchell 1985, p. 198). Dr. Furter reveals his Frankenstein monster, named Rocky Horror. Dr. F. then kills the delivery boy who had supplied the life force necessary for Rocky and, finally, seduces both the virginal girl and the virginal boy.

American adolescents adore the movie. For it exhibits their anxieties and then denies them through its self-conscious art. Its campiness says, "this is a movie, not reality." The film is shown only at midnight (the magic hour) and now has a cult standing unattached to any other film. Some estimates suggest that *The Rocky Horror Picture Show* has grossed more than $430 million dollars (Twitchell 1985, p. 303, n.1). It is difficult to imagine films that could illustrate better the vitality of classical Freudian theory than these contemporary favorites where adolescent sexual anxieties, the upsurge of oedipal conflict, dominate the story.

Psychoanalysis and Psychic Pain

The loveliest of goddesses replied:
"Son of Laertes and the gods of old,
Odysseus, master mariner and soldier,
you shall not stay here longer against your will;
but home you may not go
unless you take a strange way round and come
to the cold homes of Death and pale Persephone.
You shall hear prophecy from the rapt shade
of blind Teiresias of Thebes..."
At this I felt a weight like stone within me,
and, moaning, pressed my length against the bed,
with no desire to see the daylight more.
                              The Odyssey, Book Ten
                         Trans. Robert Fitzgerald, 1961.

Psychoanalysis is a science and a clinical method. It attempts to explain and alleviate psychological suffering. There are many ways to suffer such pain. We can suffer guilt, shame, loneliness, embarrassment, and other suffering that color each human life. Novelists and poets have long reflected upon the texture of such suffering. When Odysseus says he feels a weight on his chest, we understand: he has to stand and face the dead.[3] In ordinary life we sometimes recognize what causes a particular moment of psychic pain. For example, when a loved one leaves us we feel bad and we know why. To go to the other extreme, when our favorite team loses we feel diminished.

Other forms of psychological pain are as intense as ordinary sufferings but their origins are unknown. This form of psychic pain one might term "neurotic disease." It is difficult to find an instance of neurotic disease in Homer; in modern literature examples abound:

But to enter the Church in such an unscholarly way that he could not in any probability rise to a higher grade through all his career than that of a humble curate wearing his life out in an obscure village or city slum— that might have a touch of goodness and greatness in it; that might be true religion, and a purgatorial course worthy of being followed by a remorseful man....He did nothing, however. (Thomas Hardy, *Jude the Obscure,* 1895, p. 103)

Jude Hawely contemplates the only chance he has to enter the university, which has been his singular ideal since boyhood. Alongside the fact that the church would pay his fees, is Jude's insight that this might be a noble pathway. It would make him superior to others in his humility and good will. Yet, Jude hesitates and in that hesitation makes likely the tragedies that befall him. Psychoneurotic pain hurts like hell but cannot be located within a part of the body nor traced to an event in one's past. (If the pain is the result of physical dysfunction, then this counts as located in the body and distinguishes it from psychoneurotic pain.) Many depressed persons cannot say why they feel that way. If they give some reason for their depression, it is a minor source of suffering and cannot account for the severity of pain. Here the psychological mystery begins. The therapist becomes a troubleshooter, searching for events whic precipitated psychological distress.

Psychic Pain and Two Types of Troubleshooting

We can describe two types of troubleshooting: straightforward and roundabout. The straightforward type is the kind performed by expert diagnosticians, such as skilled mechanics. The roundabout is the type performed by clinicians, both physiological and psychological. One way to illustrate the difference between straightforward and roundabout troubleshooting is to compare troubleshooting a faulty automobile with troubleshooting psychoneurotic pain. Troubleshooting a faulty car is easy. The car was designed to run properly—at least for a few years. Troubleshooting psychoneurotic suffering is more difficult because no one knows how human beings were designed. It is hard to distinguish between a mere problem in human living, which requires no treatment, and a pathological event which does. To illustrate the difference, let us compare two patients: your new car and Freud's patient, the "Rat Man." I use the Rat Man case because it is well known and filled with insights.[4] We can then compare the two patients with one another and the troubleshooting procedures used to treat each.

I have arranged these two charts so that they appear similar to one another. What the term *transference* means is the subject of debate within psychoanalytic circles. All agree that transference is the patient's unconscious expectation that the analyst will behave like important persons in the patient's past. Beyond this common definition are issues of technique. Whether one sees a particular action as "pure transference" or as a reality-based response to the analyst, alters the therapist's interventions. Robert Langs (1985) has shown that analysts often misidentify a patient's criticisms as "negative transference," these criticisms reflect accurately the therapist's errors and the therapist's own pathology.

Your Car	Freud's patient, the Rat Man
1. Your car's complaints: coughs in the a.m.; Engine stalls; stops on freeways.	1. His complaints: severe obsessions, fears, wasted much of his life.
2. Isolate problem: history of troubles, when, how, with what effects, etc.	2. Isolate the set of pathogenic ideas and images: *not* through formal inquiry but by asking him to speak "freely."
3. Examine flow chart of *designed systems:* fuel, etc. Exclude those one knows are irrelevant.	3. Record the flow and pattern of his complex narratives.
4. Test relevant systems.	4. Uncover the pathogenic ideas: follow resistances, locate transferences.
5. Make repairs.	5. Establish, monitor, dissolve the transferences in sequence. (S. Freud 1912 a, b, c.)

For these reasons, psychoanalytic problem solving, portrayed in the second column, is a set of tasks that has no definitive ending. Psychoanalysis cures, but how it cures and what constitutes "complete" cure remain problems. There is, for example, the issue of intersubjectivity in the analytic relationship. The analyst must interpret the meaning of the patient's behaviors, then gauge how the analyst instigated them. These are not new problems. They may illustrate the subtlety and difficulty of analytic work.

The first type of problem solving is desirable; the second type is what is available to the psychoanalyst. An edition of the *Diagnostic and Statistical Manual,* (American Psychiatric Association 1980) contains decision trees arranged much like the flow chart on the left. DSM III charts summarize the rules that dictate how one is to apply diagnostic labels to patient behaviors. This is an important task since it makes possible a shared vocabulary for clinicians and researchers. These rules for the use of diagnostic terms are not equivalent to theories of the cause of these disorders. For example, the decision tree for using the label "Academic or Learning Difficulties" requires one to note "patterns" of behavior related to school. It does not explain why these patterns occur.

Theorists hope to describe complex systems using the first kind of flow chart for it permits one to diagnose and then fix the disorder discovered. When Freud first set out to describe the complex structures of the mind, he hoped to establish theories compatible with this kind of flow chart. His earliest essays reflect this hope: to establish the theory of neurosis upon scientific, that is, causal and rational grounds.

When Freud failed to do this, he adopted theories that fit the second kind of chart. This is evident in his initial reflections on the causes of hysteria. Freud used neurological theories which portrayed the mind as a machine. Machines require organization of parts and a supply of energy. It followed that the mental apparatus, the mental machine, required the same things. The mind requires energy: "we may say that hysteria is an anomaly of the nervous system which is based on a different distribution of excitations, probably accompanied by a surplus of stimuli in the organ of the mind" (Freud 1888b, p. 57).

An immediate difficulty quashed Freud's hope to secure a biological theory of mind. Unlike machines of the nineteenth century, the mind operates with entities, called "thoughts," not raw energies. To reflect this fact Freud proposed that pools of energy (or excitations) are "distributed by means of conscious and unconscious ideas" (p. 57). Another problem arises: the problem of consciousness, a problem any theory of mind must address. Freud confronted this issue: "We possess no criterion which enables us to distinguish exactly between a psychical process and a physiological one...; for 'consciousness' whatever that may be, is not attached to every activity of the cerebral cortex, nor is it always attached in equal degree to any particular one of its activities; it is not a thing which is bound up with any locality in the nervous system" (1888b, p. 84).

The mystery deepened for Freud noted that: "in its paralyses and other manifestations hysteria behaves as though anatomy did not exist or as though it had no knowledge of it" ("Organic and Hysterical Paralyses" 1893c, p. 169). Therefore, if organic lesions cause hysteria, these lesions depend upon the patient's representations of the patient's body. To retain his physiological commitments, Freud claims that these lesions must be the result of the upsurge in a surplus of excitations. And, therefore, psychotherapy must be the "abreaction of these surpluses" (1893c, p. 172).

Critics have noted that Freud's case histories became more complex and novelistic than typical in good science. Freud's case histories are literary (Patrick Mahoney 1982) but they became so only because Freud found it impossible to capture his patients' essential pathology without telling their stories in depth. This requirement alone is responsible for part of the expanded length of Freud's case histories. Another dynamic reason is that Freud discovered his patients never told their stories in a simple, linear fashion. He had to investigate key events many times: first, from the patient's conscious memories; later, from points of view made available through the psychoanalytic process. As we will see in chapter 2, psychoneurotic stories are complex and contradictory. It takes time to set them out.

For some critics of psychoanalysis, this luxuriance of narrations signifies the errors entombed in the theories themselves. Using Occam's razor, one can cut away the narrative aspects of analytic theory, return to pre-Freudian days, and look for single-valued causes of symptoms. Many nonpsychoanalytic theories of psychological suffering attempt to change the second form of troubleshooting, typical of psychiatry, into the first. A theory of depression that explains it as a deficit of brain chemicals permits one to troubleshoot depression in the way one troubleshoots a misbehaving car. This may seem a prejudicial metaphor. One could use another metaphor and say that a biochemical theory of depression treats it as a physiological disease produced by dysfunctions in many systems.

Returning to Freud's efforts to troubleshoot the Rat Man, whom we know as Dr. Lorenz, we agree that his account is novelistic and complex. The amount of complexity ought not to count against a theory. We see that the complexity of Freud's account mirrors the complexity of his patient's self-understanding. The Rat Man's self-understanding is complex because it reflects contradictory self-representations, many of which are unconscious. A lovely instance is Freud's analysis of a typical obsession. Dr. Lorenz's fiancee had left him to nurse her grandmother. During her absence, he suddenly gave himself the command to kill himself; then he thought, "No, it's not so simple as that. You must go and kill the old woman" (1909d, p. 187). Freud demonstrates that his patient had reversed the temporal order of events. With much labor he reconstructs the actual sequence: the young man longed for his fiancee. She was with her grandmother. That enraged the patient. He wished the old woman dead, and that wish made him punish himself for such an evil impulse.

Even in less obsessive patients we must struggle to understand them. Each presents the task of comprehending the intricacies of a unique story. So, we turn to examine what makes up self-understanding. Here the oddities of psychoneurosis appear. For patients' self-representations contradict one another, contradict how society sees them, and contradict how we see them.

For example, consider a hypothetical patient who feels criticized by his boss and then feels "short." At other times, this patient may feel underweight. Is this the result of a perceptual experience? The crucial term is *perception*. If perception occurs within the networks of the visual apparatus, then most neurotic patients do not misperceive themselves. A patient who feels "short" does not report that his trousers were suddenly too long or that his wife had to bend down to kiss him when, in the past, she had always stood on tiptoe. The patient's experience of feeling "short" is an authentic experience; it is not a hallucination. Yet neither is it a perception. The man's feeling short reflects feelings evoked by the word *short,* just as other patients describe feeling "empty," or "hungry," when they leave some analytic hours.

We recognize that these people are talking about a sense of themselves using the metaphorical richness of our common language. What is true of self-representations is true also of object representations. Just as we have many conscious and unconscious representations of ourselves, so too, we have many conscious and unconscious representations of others. An illustration of such representations is the number of artistic renditions of the nude human being, especially nude females.

Ingres and Photography: Two Kinds of Representation

Everyone knows that psychoanalysts think a lot about sex and its role in human life. Since human beings are mammals on the verge of constant rut, it seems obvious that pictures of naked people would find a ready audience. And they do. Since up to this century all human beings nursed at a woman's breast, it seems reasonable that that part of the female body would be admired. It is. So it is not surprising that Western art has innumerable portraits of adult women whose breasts are celebrated. For example, in the paintings of Jean-Auguste-Dominique Ingres (1780–1867), we see detailed renditions of naked women whose breasts are often a prominent feature of the work. [See figures 1, 2, and 3.]

Ingres is a painter with a photographic sense of accuracy and realism. If painting reproduces visual experience, then this is a high compliment: Ingres's paintings are almost as good as photographs, that is, mechanical reproductions. This would also mean that with the discovery of mechanical reproductions painting should wither away. William Hauptman (1977) cites Paul Delaroche, who responded to the advent of photography by uttering: "From today, painting is dead" (p. 117).

Of course, painting did not die. Why not? Or, to return to Ingres, what makes his paintings of nude women more valuable than photographs of the same nude women? Ingres lived during the advent of

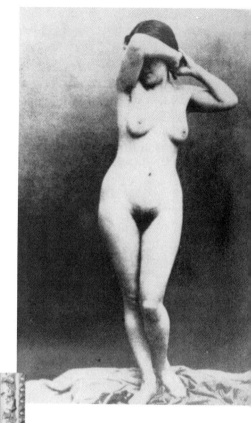

photography. There is some evidence that photographers influenced him: there is ample evidence that he influenced photographers. If painting were a second-best attempt to render visual experience, then Ingres's nudes should not retain their preeminence.

Yet they have and, hence, we conclude that Ingres's paintings are more than reproductions of what Ingres saw. For, assuming he had normal eyesight, Ingres saw what the camera saw: a pattern of light and shadow cast by rather heavyset, adult females. Ingres's paintings are, therefore, more than renditions of the visual events that occurred to him. Rather, they render what Ingres experienced as he responded to the naked women in front of him.

What Ingres thought about the female body includes his sense of ideal form. Ingres's intense eroticism is famous. To convey eroticism is more difficult than to paint naked women. Ingres's nudes are stylized representations of women; they are not remotely realistic. When he paints the female breast, for example, Ingres often gives it an arc which is more geometric than it is anatomically correct. Ingres employed his models to serve as windows through which he could realize his own reflections about femaleness. It is those reflections and thoughts, not the mere visual data, that Ingres records in his paintings and which continue to fascinate viewers.

Early photographers captured the light emanating from the bodies of nude models. Ingres captured the outline of the ideas emanating from his inner world. Is this true of the pictures of sexual organs sketched on bathroom walls? Yes. Why deny the title of art to these crude sketches? They often represent very strong wishes and human desires. True, most are poorly drawn renditions of sexual and scatological actions. Yet these sketches do not differ intrinsically from Picasso's celebrated sketches, done in his late seventies. A better contrast between art and non-art is compare these bathroom drawings with the "true to life" anatomical illustrations in medical textbooks. While these pictures may be "lifelike" in their exactness, they are not appealing and not artistic.

Problems with Psychoanalytic Aesthetics

Psychoanalytic aesthetics confronts a particular problem. For example, Susanne Langer says, in an influential study: "But [psychoanalytic criticism] makes no distinction between good and bad art" (quoted in Noy 1979, p. 229). Some psychoanalysts make no distinction between excellence and mediocrity because they seek to find wishes that are "latent," which lie beneath the manifest "surface." But it is on the surface that art demonstrates its vitality. Nuances of shade, color, balance, tonality, and other formal elements distinguish good art from bad. Cézanne's famous paintings of apples are revered for their formal qualities, not as "lifelike" illustrations of ripe fruit. One may see more accurate renditions of apples on the side of produce cans in the super-market. Some apples may represent the mother's breast. That does not explain why Cézanne's apples are better than apples pictured on cans of applesauce.

The second problem facing the psychoanalytic critic is the problem of evidence. This is a problem on two fronts. First, in the analysis of long-dead artists, we have no access to the thousands of observations that make up a real analysis. Without access to the details of an analysis, accrued over hundreds of hours, one cannot offer valid clinical inter-pretations.

Second, without the benefit of the relationship between patient and analyst, no transference can unfold and therefore the sine qua non of analysis is absent. In its absence that which makes psychoanalysis an empirical, objective event is also absent (Brian Bird 1972).

Many scholars recognize the first problem and respond by using diaries, the opinions of contemporaries, and other written materials to supply information about their subject. Yet, even diaries written for the benefit of the subject alone cannot equal psychoanalytic data, for writing implies the existence of an audience. Diaries are still manifest thoughts about subject's self. They are like self-analysis and other forms of therapy that do not recognize the transference.

The second problem has received less attention, for transference events are unconscious reenactments that portray in the here-and-now relationship to the analyst repressed memories and fantasies which have no other route of expression. It is to those repressed fantasies and archaic ego states (to use one contemporary set of terms) that the analyst must penetrate. Any analysis that fails to do so is superficial. Transference is the heart of the analytic process. It is wrong to suppose that transference means merely reenactments of childhood relation-ships that remain in conflict. While the patient associates the analyst with a specific person, like a parent, in the patient's past, this does not exhaust the transference itself.

Otto Fenichel (1945) says the term *transference* pertains also to the ways in which the analyst serves ego functions which are not within the patient's power or control. Bird (1972) makes the same point: "There [in the transference neurosis] the patient includes me somehow in the structure, or part structure, of his neurosis.... The identity difference between him and me is lost, and for the moment and for the particular area affected by the transference neurosis, I come to represent *the patient himself.* I come to represent some complex of the patient's neurosis or some element of his ego, superego, drives, defenses, etc., which has become part of his neurosis" (p. 281, emphasis in original).[5]

When analytic critics use clinical generalizations, their evaluations, may be useful but they have no merit as psychoanalytic data. Such evaluations are speculations about an artifact. There is nothing wrong with this. The results of such applied studies can be illuminating. Harm occurs if nonclinicians read such studies and conclude that such speculation typifies psychoanalysis, including the clinical work. For without transference reenactment and interpretation, all such speculations are intellectual constructs and have little empirical weight. To many nonclinicians psychoanalytic criticism seems odd, if not bizarre. Many scholars who read psychoanalysis conclude that psychoanalytic interpretations are like literary speculations. They cannot be justified with clinical evidence, only replaced by other speculations drawn from other intellectual disciplines, like literary criticism. Yet to justify interpretations of a dream, for example, one must give detailed accounts of the events that constitute the analytic process. To illustrate a typical encounter I offer the following ordinary clinical event. It will not persuade the skeptic, but it does illustrate an ordinary clinical encounter and how one form of psychoanalytic thinking takes place.

Say you are a therapist. A new patient, a young man, begins intensive psychotherapy with you. Weeks later, your patient mentions that he told a friend to call you, for this friend needs a good therapist. The question the analyst, you, must raise is, why now? That is, why is this new patient so willing to share you with a friend? Your patient adds, parenthetically, that should you have insufficient hours, then he stands willing to share his hour with his friend. For, it turns out, this friend is far needier than himself. In the interest of using a brilliant color to the utmost, he—the original patient—would consider forfeiting his hour, should external events require that sacrifice. While there is no disputing the accuracy of the patient's assessment of your clinical skills, one might ponder, for a moment, what all this means.

Under most circumstances a therapist would not accept this referral. At this moment, the therapist distinguishes herself or himself from other professionals who would accept such referrals with no questions asked. Why must we go to this length? Why not just ask the patient why he chooses to refer his friend to you? Here the much misunderstood concept of the "unconscious" makes its appearance; for if motives are unconscious they are not available to your patient's conscious mind. If they are not available, he cannot answer your questions directly. Since the patient's referral of his friend was an action involving his therapeutic relationship, its meanings cannot be present to him. If your patient cannot say what these actions mean, how can you assert what his "unconscious" motives are?

Freud's discoveries come to your aid. You attend to the patient's entire presentation of himself. Eight decades of clinical experience and theory tell us that all such actions occur in response to the patient's anxieties mobilized by treatment. In other words, something about therapy scares your patient and drives him to find another person to take his place and that would let him off the hook. His friend would enter therapy. You would suffer no drop in income, and he would not feel those moments of dread as he approached your office. What moments of dread? For has not your patient said that he admired your skill, your office, and your person? Again, theory tells us that the actual source of your patient's panic is not conscious. Hence, you cannot accept as complete your patient's protestations of admiration for you.

To figure out what your patient fears, you turn again to observe his actions, not just what he says. We rely upon Freud's insights into the nature of dreams and symptom formation. We assume that the patient cannot say what frightens him. But his associations about his decision to gather another patient for you will tell us what scares him (Langs 1985).

Now you listen for clues to what scares your patient. Following the recitation of your many talents, he goes on to think of nothing in particular, except a movie he has seen. In the movie a young woman, living alone in a large city, is attacked by a half-machine and half-human monster. This man-machine is ineluctable and unstoppable. He has one goal: to destroy this young woman. Once the man-machine scents his victim he will not give up the chase. Only his death of that of his victim will stop the pursuit. The man-machine, we learn, kills his victims by sneaking up behind them and then crushing them in his arms, from behind. The young woman's only chance is to flee from the monster.

Rambling on, your patient recalls reading science fiction in the family basement. These were enjoyable retreats, usually, since they permitted him to escape from his parents who fought constantly. He had thought about writing science fiction once, but he could never overcome his writer's block. That, in turn, reminds him of other things he does not complete. There are tasks in his job which he could perform but never gets to. There is cutthroat competition in his office. He feels he can trust no one, especially his superiors who are judging him behind his back. What occurs in the mind of his superiors anyway? It enrages him, sometimes, to think of how arbitrary they are and how much power they have over his life. This reminds him of being short in high school. He is suprised to find that he is taller than his boss, he concludes, who says all the right things but is completely untrustworthy.

This is a concocted hour and has no validity as an empirical moment in actual therapy session. Most clinicians will recognize this as a typical sequence of free associations. Taken as a set of reflections upon his referral of his friend to you, they provide insights into this patient's current state of mind. Clinical theory tells us to treat everything the patient does as reflections upon therapy. The more "free and spontaneous" the patient's speech the more valuable are his thoughts. Your patient's associations suggest what he fears: that his therapist will become a powerful, machinelike monster who will crush him from behind.

In a real case we would note this patient's identification with females, his feeling that his body is short, and his relationship to his father. Regarding his father we note the theme of being crushed from behind plays a role. Also, this patient uses literature to escape bad moods, feels frustrated with his current work, and has many inhibitions. His defensive style shows a propensity to take action when he feels anxious, to use his friends as go-betweens, and to praise people he fears. In a good case-conference with other clinicians one could deduce many other features of this man's life, even from the little material given above.

Having established that the patient fears you we can ask where did this idea come from? Does it represent an experience in the patient's past and a current wish? Mindful of these insights you can respond to this patient's story in many ways. One way is silence: let him continue to talk. You might also choose to interpret why you think he wishes to substitute his friend for himself. You could say, "The idea of referring your friend to me arose when you began to feel afraid of me. You see me as a monstrous person who will crush you just as the machine-man crushed the young woman in the movie."

Of course, you may be wrong—though I have stacked the deck. How do clinicians know when they are wrong? For do not "Freudian patients" have Freudian dreams, and "Jungian patients" have Jungian dreams? Well sometimes, but in day-to-day practice one offers an interpretation and then assesses its validity in a variety of ways. First, does the patient add confirming evidence spontaneously? Second, does the patient's total response to the therapist deepen the transference? Are specific neurotic symptoms relieved? Does the patient act differently in the patient's external life? Do formerly disparate threads of the patient's story begin to come together? Are there additional confirming memories from childhood? (See also Bird 1972.)

It is wrong to say that the single idea "crush me like the machine-man crushed the woman" is the entire structure present in this man's unconscious; this does not recognize that ideas are never the content of the unconscious. If ideas were the source of neurosis, then a patient's assent to the analyst's insights would bring about cure in record time. Intellectual patients and mental health professionals who read Freud would require no treatment. They would achieve self-cure through self-analysis. Since Freud's first remarks on the subject, we know that the process of psychoanalytic therapy requires the patient and analyst to engage emotionally with one another. The transference neurosis must be an authentic experience, not intellectualized reflection.

All therapists should use empathic interventions. Yet in making interventions like the one above, we are telling the patient that he does not know why he acts the way he does. This is a criticism of the patient. We do not intend to be cruel or patronizing. We offer it in the patient's interests. Yet, very sensitive patients recognize that all such interventions are slight wounds. For as we make such interventions we are also saying that the patient does not have complete control over himself; he is not, at that moment, the master of his actions and thoughts. He is not fully known to himself. Worst of all, the therapist, for a moment, knows more about the patient's motives that the patient does.

Interpretations, no matter how well formulated, are in this way narcissistic wounds because they challenge the patient's sense of narcissistic completeness and wholeness. These wounds are not, we hope, overwhelming. They may be minor for many patients. In such interventions we show that the patient does not know completely what the patient is talking about—even when speaking about long-held secrets. In a full-fledged analysis, interpretations like these may be shortened or become "family jokes" (Heinz Kohut 1984). The painfulness of therapy has lessened and the patient can hear interpretations without disruption and even with some humor. These moments of humor can soothe the narcissistic hurt.

Eventually, the patient will not need our presence and therapy will come to an end. We hope that our patients internalize our therapeutic intent. When they leave they should respond to themselves with the tact and empathy we strive to show toward them. However, even in these moments of self-interpretation the process is painful, for it requires us to overcome a similar quality of narcissistic hurt. Insights into oneself counter one's wishful images. We learn that we are not masters of ourselves; some of our secret ambitions crash upon the rocks of actuality.

An Ordinary Aesthetic Event: Responding to a Poem

To contrast the patient who feared being crushed from behind consider a poem, "The Lifeguard," by James Dickey (1958). Dickey describes the thoughts of a young lifeguard who had failed to save a young boy from drowning. The last stanza is:

> I wash the black mud from my hands.
> On a light given off by the grave
> I kneel in the quick of the moon
> At the heart of a distant forest
> And hold in my arms a child
> Of water, water, water.

I suggest some points about the aesthetic moment. First, we cannot plunge from the surface of this poem to an interpretation of its unconscious roots without losing sight of the poem. Second, the old saw "To be a translator, is to be a traitor" remains true. The idea of life slipping through one's fingers occurs in the image of the child made of water, a liquid that has no autonomous form. The Greeks employed this image when they said that a woman's anger is written in water, which disappears as it is written. In Dickey's poem we understand that the lifeguard never grasped the boy the way he wished, but only water. Now he asks the substance that killed the boy to assume the boy's form. The strident rhythm of the last line "Of water, water, water" catches us on the verge of speech and nonspeech. It is a chant; like "the Wa, Wa, Wa" the sounds an infant makes when it seeks the safety of its parent.

Freud discovered that we can decode the manifest content of a patient's narration and find in it latent memories and desires. "Life is but a dream." Freud shows us how self-understanding is the product of condensation, displacement, and symbolic thinking. In the "Golden Age" of psychoanalytic discovery Freud and his followers applied this discovery to the great works of Western culture. Freud delved into Shakespeare, Sophocles, Michaelangelo, Leonardo, Goethe, and Moses. Ernest Jones examined fairy tales, religion, and culture. Hans Sachs, Carl Jung, and Alfred Adler examined the whole of society. Each realized that their efforts to decode an artistic product, say a statue by Michaelangelo, told us nothing about the formal qualities of the work.

The Sensuous Surface and Deep Structure

The sensuous surface of things is an inexhaustible source of aesthetic pleasure. I believe this sentence is true but ugly. It sounds like a string of slurred "s" announced by a loud drunk. Of course, I can re-write the first sentence. As a scholar, all I care about is the abstract truth value of my propositions. The following may be less ugly: "We find in the surface of things a constant source of new pleasures." If this fails to capture every nuance of the logic of the first sentence, I can revise it also, and other sentences. Eventually I can make my claim clear and even defensible. As I carry out this standard activity called "academic discourse," I am aware that no one will confuse it with poetry or "literature."

Why not? Because the sensuous surface of my prose is not an in-exhaustible source of pleasure—a fact I have now demonstrated. I can put this claim more formally. Compare the ease with which I can restate my claims against the difficulty one has revising a poem. To rephrase Dickey's stanza about the lifeguard is to destroy the poem. This is a crude example. It illustrates my simple point: that it is easy to ruin a piece of art by treating it like an abstract proposition. Literary critics have, of course, known this for as long as there have been literary critics. They have created elaborate and subtle vocabularies of techni-cal terms to describe the rhythms, shading, meter, etc., of prose and poetry.

The Sensuous Surface vs. Abstract Propositions

Scientific prose ought to be clear, unambiguous, and translatable; for these reasons one finds that scientists strive to make their proposi-tions reducible to mathematical propositions. For mathematical propo-sitions are clear, unambiguous, and translatable. We realize this from the simplest rules of grade school mathematics. For example, the fol-lowing statements in parentheses are all true and translatable:

$$(1/2 \times 2/1) = (27/54 \times 666/999) = (.50 \times .6666666666)$$

A moment's reflection tells us that there is no significant differ-ence between these three propositions. True, the beginner may find the third version more difficult than the first. The expert will find no differ-ence between them. Within the rules of a mathematical system, the "surface" features of a proposition have no relevance to our ease in employing it. Because these are identical propositions, we can substi-tute them at will for each other in any well-formed set of propositions. We could also use different number systems, say hexadecimal, to ex-press the same mathematical truth and, again, experience no aesthetic shock. Scientific prose aims for this kind of formal "translatability." An English-speaking chemist strives to write in such a way that her article can be translated into Chinese or Russian.

So too, a German-speaking psychologist aims to write such that his claims about neural functioning can be translated into English. The obvious way to increase the likelihood of translatability is to us propositions that are unambiguous and clear, that is, mathematical formulae. A quick glance at a Russian physics journal reveals a large number of mathematical propositions which require no translation. It is easier to read a foreign-language science article than it is to read a humanities article. It is easier to read a humanities article than an article in the popular press.

Art and the Evocation of Primary Self-Experiencing

Art evokes and contains primary self-experiencing, that which pertains to each level of self-experience, especially to the preverbal and "primordial." Artists may use language to do this. They use language to construct opportunities for self-experiences that are nonverbal. The novel and the poem are, in this sense, shaped and molded as are the marble and clay objects worked by the sculptor.

Some works of art evoke recollections of self-experiences not previously available to us. These self-experiences may be unavailable because of repression. Themes of incest may be so taboo that they appear only in disguised representations in the theatre. These self-experiences are unavailable to us because we lack the capacity to perceive our concrete, sensual experience. Lacking that awareness, we also lack the ability to perceive the organizing power of natural objects, a power that helps organize the self in return. To put this another way, when neurotic mechanisms inhibit our capacity to enjoy the sensuous surface of things we are cut off from perceiving and therefore enjoying the intricate patterning effects of nature. Nature, in all its infinite variety within simplicity, cannot soothe us. If this is so, it is interesting to ask why. Why does it take more effort to read poetry than watch television? If we were afraid of sexual themes we would not watch thousands of movies that celebrate murder, revenge, and sexual variations of every kind. I agree with Greenacre that bona fide art can organize the self. Our reluctance to confront art is analogous to our reluctance to undergo challenges to the organization of ourselves.

In this way, our common avoidance of art is analogous to the avoidance of self-analysis: it requires too much work and generates too much discomfort. Watching revenge movies, especially those with special effects, requires no such reorganization because such movies are false to the core. They are pure wish fulfillments. They are structured, not by insights into actual living, but by fantasy that organizes each element into a dream, repeated endlessly.

This is not true of works of art. The bona fide work of art requires one to take a chance on a new experience, just as the good analytic hour does. It also requires us to tolerate leaving our customary sense of ourselves and assume a distance from those tensions. In Freud's early language, the work of art requires us to postpone discharge of psychic tension. This is already a burden. The work of art induces new tensions in us. Temporarily we give the artist some control over ourselves, just as the patient gives the analyst some control over the patient's ego. This is a source of resistance in the opening phase of an analysis. For to enter into an analysis is to enter into a transference neurosis with the analyst. We need another person to take care of us in ways we cannot.

To give over to the analyst that kind of responsibility is to feel again as exposed and as fragile as we did as children. While analysis promises to help us feel happier, patients dread the process because it requires us to return to fight the old dragons of childhood, including those dragons that are inside of us and our minds. This threatens the self we have organized. The analytic process requires us to become disorganized in depth. We give the analyst power to maintain our very being, a task we had assigned to ourselves alone. Even if we have done a poor job of that task, we know the area well and it feels like home to us. Our resistance to analysis is a resistance to suffering the agonies of childhood repeated within the analytic hour (Pietro Castelnuovo-Tedesco 1984).

When authentic art promises a similar form of reorganization of the self, it rouses similar resistance. Two more examples will illustrate this point. The first is from Whitman:

Cavalry Crossing a Ford

A line in long array where they wind betwixt green islands.
They take a serpentine course, their arms flash in the sun—hark
    to the musical clank,
Behold the silvery river, in it the splashing horses loitering stop
    to drink.
Behold the brown-faced men, each group, each person a picture,
    The negligent rest on the saddles,
Some emerge on the opposite bank, others are just entering the
    ford—while,
Scarlet and blue and snowy white,
The guidon flags flutter gayly in the wind.

Whitman asks us to imagine the vista he describes. He uses paint-
erly terms, like *line* and *color*, to construct a semblance of this scene.
But he also evokes other senses: we hear the weapons clank, the horse
hooves splash, and the flags flutter. The poem is a captured moment, a
precise unit of experience, recorded and preserved against loss by
Whitman's capacity to organize himself. Through the poem he organizes our experience now, some 120 years after this particular cavalry
group has passed.

It is tempting to say that this poem is like a snapshot, handed down
to us by a keen observer. This is not an adequate rendition of the poem.
First, it may be that Whitman wrote the poem out of many experiences
of seeing cavalry, water, and sunlight. This single poem is not an actual
historical recollection. Second, a snapshot is not the product of a
human mind, distilling an original artifact from interior events. That is,
snapshots tend to have no artistic merit because they are snapped, and
not the product of artistic reflection and judgment. Third, the colors
and feelings the poem evoke in me are not identical to those Whitman
experienced when he composes it.

This poem is not Whitman's sensation or thought transferred
magically to my mind. Rather, the poem is an organized, highly structured artifact with its own qualities and contours which make insight
into my self-experience possible. Whitman does not give me his experience. He lets me match the pleasures he achieved in composing the
poem to a similar set of pleasures I achieve in confronting it. These
pleasures are similar; both are produced by organizing self-experience
into a coherent whole. Does such pleasure derive from the inner world
alone or from the outer world too? Are the pleasures I assign to this
poem imagined, or are the poem and my pleasure an accurate por-
trayal of the world? Greenacre says that they derive from the outer
world. The artist captures in the artistic work a portion of the organized
world itself.

This may seem to be pure wish-fulfillment. Freud said that our
sense that the world is full of qualities is an illusion we foist upon ourselves. If this is so, then all the arts would be the products of similar
illusions and projections. This metapsychological issue is serious and I
describe it at length in chapters 2 and 3. I note a major problem with an
extreme version of this claim. If our experience of an organized world is
the product of projection, then the projecting device, our mind, contains the organizing principles and qualities we think we perceive. This
means that our "unconscious" mind is full of well-developed, organized, and detailed structures. This view of the "unconscious" directly
contradicts Freud's views of this portion of the psyche. To say that it is

an illusion to believe that the external world is a rich and organized environment does away with the possibility of bona fide science; for scientists seek to discover the order of the universe, shorn of illusions and projections.

To preserve the possibility of science Freud cannot affirm the radical claim that human beings always project order onto the external world. Freud affirms the possibility of science, including a science of the unconscious mind; he believes that some human beings accurately perceive the external world. Sometimes ordinary human beings can know the truth about their external world the way scientists know the truth. Can artists also? Can some artists at some time be correct in their judgments about the "world," both the external and internal portions of it? Consider another poem, by Pierre Lecuire, which describes the French suburb Menerbes:

> To stand by the window, to lean out, experience the air. The moment hesitates between start and finish. To look without strain. The sun drinks all things, one only has to draw them to oneself. A natural order transports a sea of miracles, of which the smallest and the greatest shine and darken only their assigned place. All has been born. The flood effacing the traces of day is not deep. The top of the tree, held up like a mute flower, enlivens less the sky than it marks a slight step backward. It is cold without leaves, speed goes unchecked.... A hedge, a stone wall face this faceless being, hardly blond, the blond breath that will end the flow. Later, the profile of the afternoon wastes away at the horizon. (*World Literature Today*, Winter 1988, p. 18)

I take this to be the product of Lecuire's reflections upon the experience of air on a hot afternoon. The poem describes the organization of light, shadow, and time in this world, a world of "natural order." One might conclude that this is gross anthropomorphization, since the poem seems to assign a wish and psychological process to the sun itself. Or one might say that the poem is theological: it ascribes intentionality and order to nature, shaped by a divine hand.

These readings overlook the poet's insight that the sun gives to each object a predictable amount of light and to each shadow a predictable shape. Painters who work from memory may err when they try to reproduce the light and shade of daylight. They may forget to illuminate this rock or that tree. Working from imagination, painters cannot perceive the infinite amount of information and organization present in nature. To call the afternoon a blond, faceless being evokes memories of looking at the sun, face to face: it reflects the poet's feelings about the afternoon as it turns into dusk and dusk turns into night.

Freud's Solution: Recollecting Libido Theory

Freud's solution to the problem of art was to recall the basic premises of libido theory. Libido theory accounted for the hypersexualiza-
tion of neurotic actions by linking them to universal, unconscious
wishes. These wishes, in turn, Freud linked to sexual body zones, present in all human beings and manifest in all human cultures. When
applied to the field of art, libido theory could easily account for the
ubiquity of sexual themes in the arts. When sexual themes were not
manifest, libido theory required one to explain where they were hiding.
One had to explain how an original sexual wish, for example, anal
wishes to smear, were transformed into nonsexual activities, like
painting.

Freud named this process of transformation "sublimation." There
are many positive features to this concept. First, it arises out of Freud's
most rigorous theory, the theory of the instincts, and so preserves the
integrity of that major research program. Second, it links the theory of
art to the theory of neurosis and so seems to preserve the folk psychological understanding that creativity and neurosis are similar. Third,
sublimation captures many artists' sense that making art is an erotic
activity.

More common associations between creativity and sexuality are
the genital and reproductive images that occur continuously in artists'
self-descriptions. Both male and female artists "give birth" to poems,
novels, and the like. A less public association links creativity and anality,
specifically, the product of the mind with the product of the anus. Many
artists describe feeling uptight, or "blocked," or walled off from their
usual sense of "flowing," releasing, and exuding experience. Other
artists express their feelings of their bowels. Leonard Shengold (1988)
describes healthy anality and its relationship to creativity in detail. He
emphasizes the child's experience of making (or in Greek, *poesis*) when
the child realizes that its urine and feces are both uncanny products.
Parents often ritualize going to the bathroom. Also the passage of
waste, from inside the body to outside the body, evokes pleasure.[6]

For example, Shengold describes Flaubert's spirited sense of anal
and phallic creativity. He cites Flaubert's letter to his mother: "When I
think of my future...when I ask myself: 'What shall I do when I return?
What path shall I follow?' and the like, I am full of doubts and indecis-
ions....I live like a plant, suffusing myself with sun and light, with colors
and fresh air. I keep eating, so to speak; afterwards the digesting will
have to be done, then the shitting: and the shit better be good! That's the
important thing" (1988, p. 47).[7]

In contrast to this portrait of anality in the service of creativity is the regressive use of anality. Janine Chasseguet-Smirgel (1984) notes how the Marquis de Sade represents the anal sadistic urge to destroy differences and undo organization. His helter-skelter coupling of sister and brother, parent and child, etc., is done not merely to satisfy forbidden incestuous wishes. Rather, incest is "linked with the abolition of 'children' as a category and 'parents' as a category" (1984, p. 3). Sade wished to destroy the actual world of differences, of categories, of stations, and to create an "anal universe where all differences are abolished" (1984, p. 3).

Like Shengold, Chasseguet-Smirgel wishes to distinguish anal regression from anal creativity. To do so each adopts Freud's original concept of sublimation. That concept links the two forms of anality by way of the theory of the instincts. Shengold notes, "Sublimation of anality (the ability to turn from direct discharge of the anal-sadistic drives to adaptive and creative 'making') implies 'healthy anality'" (1988, p. 49). Chasseguet-Smirgel extends this claim into a theory of perversion and its source in relationships between mother and child (1984, pp. 89–100). I find her account persuasive, though expounded in the part-instinct theory of Freud's early work. I attempt to rework her account in my summary, below, where I match it to an account based on the theory of the self.

Problems with the Concept Sublimation

There are also major problems with the concept. I explain this in more detail in the next chapter. Here we can note four major problems with the notion of sublimation as a theory of art.

First, it does not arise from clinical observations or clinical theory. The concept reflects the need to account for the difference between perversion and creativity. It does not arise from the study of creativity itself. Nor, for that matter, are there many direct clinical illustrations of the process of sublimation observed within the analytic setting. Second, the concept of sublimation is taken whole cloth from mystical traditions in which a magical process occurs such that one substance is transformed into another. This heritage makes the concept odd compared to other psychoanalytic concepts, like repression and defense, which originate from daily clinical work. Third, it does not increase our understanding of a particular work of art to learn that it is the product of a sublimatory process. Fourth, the concept often overlaps the clinical concepts of displacement and disguise.

Carol J. Clover (1987) says "Pornography thus engages directly (in

pleasurable terms) what horror movies explore at one remove (in painful terms) and legitimate film at two or more [removes]" (p. 189). She
illustrates this brilliant point by reference to the presence of the male
oedipal theme in movies. She describes denial that ranges from high-
cultural films, like *The Graduate* (in which a young man is seduced by
his girlfriend's mother), to films like *Psycho* (where the young man has
an abnormal attachment to his own mother), to outright pornography,
"like the porn film *Taboo*, in which the son simply has sex with his
mother ("Mom, am I better than Dad?")" (1987, p. 189). If sublimation
refers to the degree of disguise, then there is no need for the term since
the clinical concepts *displacement* and *condensation* accomplish this
task.

Energy Metaphors in Place of a Theory of Information

Freud's solution to the problems inherent in the notion of sublimation was to use libido theory. In doing so he overlooked the substantial superstructure of theory contained in his original metapsychology,
the theory section of *The Interpretation of Dreams* (1900a). There Freud
contended with the same scientific puzzle. How could he account for
the differences in the *quality of thinking* which appears in dreams and
the "more advanced" thinking that characterizes reasoning? I think he
arrived at an elegant solution, contained in chapter 7, but he lacked a
theory of information. It would be another fifty years before scientists
like Claude Shannon and Warren Weaver (1949), formulated a more
adequate theory of information.

Lacking such a theory, Freud had to make do with the conceptual
tools of his day. The most advanced concepts of the time included
theories about the conservation of energy and theories about human
evolution. Using his insights into neural functioning, Freud created his
edifice: the economis-structural theory of the "Project." Its published
version is chapter 7 of *The Interpretation of Dreams* (1900a).

Because he had to use energy metaphors to describe mental processes, Freud sometimes confused level of energy with level of organization. To use Information Theory terms, he confused the amount of
force evident in an instinctual wish with the amount of information
available within a mental representation.

I wish to mate instinct theory, exemplified in Shengold and
Chasseguet-Smirgel's discussions, with contemporary theories of the
self and its genesis, especially the work of Heniz Kohut. I examine the
theory of sublimation, show its origins in Freud's thought, and show
why it requires replacement. In the second half of this book I suggest
how we might think about that replacement. To do that I rely upon

work by child psychoanalysts, works in cognitive theory, communication theory, and clinical psychoanalysis, especially the essays of Christopher Bollas (1987). To make my discussion as clear as possible, I outline the major assumptions and major claims I make in this essay.

The Argument in Brief: Art and Self-Organization

We find either that individuals live creatively and feel that life is worth living or else that they cannot live creatively and are doubtful about the value of living. This variable is directly related to the quality and quantity of environmental provision at the beginning or in the early phases of each baby's experience. (David Winnicott 1971, p. 71)

The following points summarize the major claims I wish to advance in this book. Each pertains to this quotation from Winnicott's essay "Creativity and Its Origins." I record these points below only to give the reader a clear sense of what I wish to put forth in more detail later. When I introduce a technical term, like *RIG*, or *the unthought unknown* (Christopher Bollas 1987), I define it briefly here. I redefine it at length in its proper place in the chapters that follow.

1. The foundational drive to all ego strivings is the drive to retain a coherent sense of the self and its ongoingness.

2. Early traumata to the preverbal child are the result of failure in the infant-caretaker environment. When caretakers fail to help the infant regulate its sense of self-coherence, continuity, aliveness, etc., the infant becomes disorganized. (Cf. Kohut 1984.)

3. The sense of self includes the four types elucidated in Stern (1985): that of an emergent self, a core self, a subjective self, and a verbal self. There is an abundance of sources of invariance in the healthy infant's physical environment. The constancy of touch and the many invariants of perceptual experience amidst change are invariants. (See J.J. Gibson 1979.) Even the neonate has many opportunities to form a "core sense of self," as long as the infant's caretakers respond appropriately to it.

4. In response to external, interpersonal events, the infant creates RIGs (Representations of Interactions that have been Generalized) and EC (Evoked Companions). RIGs and EC incorporate these sets of self-with-other representations. In traditional language, the child internalizes the way its parents regulate these self experiences, e.g., the parent's response to the infant's mood states. (See Roy Schafer's useful definition of internalization 1968.)

5. Self- and object representations arise in the crucial period *before the development of language.* They are therefore (1) not structured like a language, and (2) not organized in memory solely by language-based processes. As representations (RIGs and EC), they are more than static elements: they are partly abstracted sets of expectations. Compare "transference" testing when the patient examines the analyst's claims to represent people who will not be seduced and ruined the way previous persons were.

The "structure" of these unconscious, nonlinguistic, memorial entities is the key issue in the analysis of unconscious forms. (See studies that address these issues; for example, see the concept *passive repression* in Freud 1926d, *passive primal repression* in Frank 1969, and *the unthought known* in Bollas 1987.) Many artistic pieces, like the poems cited above and Ingres's paintings, are metaphorical representations of both RIGs and ECs. Both kinds of artifacts represent the possibility of reorganizing and reordering the self through the work of producing and responding to art. Such art connects internal (unconscious) events with the organizing and organized process that occur externally in nature.

The work of art makes me feel alive because it reveals new linkages between myself and others and myself and the world. The authentic work of art cannot be reduced to any verbal interpretation, no matter how subtle. The work itself pertains to and reflects the preverbal aspects of self-experience that continue to undergrid our lives. To recall William James, the work of art is the meal, the interpretation is the menu. In this sense, the authentic work of art is more than reparative. Art can be more than response to infantile traumata. It may also be original and innovative, revolutionary and insightful.

6. In order for psychopathology to occur, the infant's caretakers must actively interfere with the infant's development. In order to produce infantile behavior that Freud said was universal, the infant's caretakers must obstruct the infant's natural aptitude to find organization. Freud said primary autism only gradually gives way to relatedness (based on painful failures). Contrary to Freud, Daniel Stern (1985) says primary relatedness turns into autism when parents attack the infant's urge to seek contact with other human beings.

A common source of such parental attack is the parent's unconscious set of activated memories about "child rearing" which dominate that parent's response to its child. The sins of the grandparents are visited upon the grandchildren.[7]

7. But these RIGs and ECs, based upon generations of parental attacks,

are faulty. Because the infant has been punished when it strives to find
constancy with its parents, it fails to achieve "object constancy" in the
psychoanalytic sense. "The most qualitatively special things to infants
are the social behaviors of persons that are eliciting of and expressive
of human vitality affects and regular emotions" (Stern 1985, p. 122, no.
8). Even objects can be imbued with mother's affect: "Once she has so
imbued an object and withdraws, the infant is likely to continue to
explore it alone, so long as it has the afterglow of personification" (1985,
p. 122).

8. Malignant RIGs and ECs fail to promote affect attunement between
infant and baby and therefore between self and others in later life.
When parents fail to regulate the infant, the infant turns toward its set
of inherently organized behaviors, the instinctual drives. Deficits in the
self and self-object milieu encourage the sexualization of ego functioning because the drives are organized and therefore provide a semblance of ego organization. According to this reading, it is a mistake to
see culture as the triumph of ego over perversions, to explain art as
sublimated sexualizations. Rather Daniel Stern and David Winnicott
(and Heinz Kohut) argue that perversions occur in the absence of culture, in the sense of a supporting, active, self-object milieu. Divisions
within the self and divisions between self and others produce behaviors
we term "pathological." Numerous reports illustrate the outcomes of
poor parenting. Kohut's works illustrate a similar set of insights, especially in his detailed account of therapy with Mr. Z (Heinz Kohut, 1979).

9. Disjunctures between the infant's needs for regulation by the "invisible" other and the infant's parents who attack these needs, create
infantile neurosis. Concerning self-representations, such disjunctures
force the infant or child to depend upon its interior resources. (See
"hallucination of the breast" in Freud 1895.) But, on turning to its own
resources the infant does two things. First, the infant loses access to
actual, real, external objects which ought to have regulated it. Therefore the infant loses touch with concrete, specific objects whose existence and permanence are guaranteed by their being actual entities.
Second, the infant attempts to capture and fix these internal RIG and
"object imagoes" by using its symbolic mechanisms, especially those
which employ primary process modes.

10. The infant now faces a double loss: permanency of the self and constancy of the object (the other) are no longer guaranteed by an empathic Other. Hence, the infant must create replacement representations out of its own relatively poor internal world. The infant (or child or
adult) therefore searches among the psychosexual zones for alterna-

tive sources of self-organization. Attached to these zones are self- and object representations, stemming from all periods of life. But these representations never have the required structural and structuralizing richness because, unlike actual objects, these intrapsychic representations do not provide new perceptual experiences. These internal replacements (unconscious fantasies) are one-dimensional ideas about reality, not reality itself. The menu has no food value.

11. In response to these environmental deficits, the infant effects several defenses. The most severe traumata, such as those inflicted by a psychotic parent who tortures the infant, produce massive splits in self-representations. The natural unity of the sense of self is destroyed and a "multiple personality" results (Bennet Braun 1986). In response to less severe traumata the infant retains a mixed set of self- and object representations. Where the original unitary sense of the physical self remains intact, now the sense of a verbal self and a self with others (Stern 1985) is liable to disruption. In response, the infant uses its symbolic mechanisms which, in this mode of operation, create personal myths and personal rituals. Both serve to maintain a sense of coherence and stability attacked by its caretakers.[8]

12. These private myths are not merely passive "memories." Rather, they are substitute structures that function in place of poorly evolved ego processes. These private myths do not have "meaning" per se. When patients attach "meanings" to them, they do so in a mythical way (Dan Sperber 1974). That is, they tell endless stories about what are actually nonsemantic structures. Hence, while the patient's accounts are presented using language, and may involve detailed memories about actual or imagined experiences, the referent is neither linguistic nor a memorial process.

13. Conscious fantasies and neurotic symptoms are the ego's attempt to work over and contain these private myths. (In terms drawn from ego psychology, such symptoms may be seen as secondary defensive responses to primary defensive mechanisms.) Neurotic fantasies are "compulsive" because the ego no longer can rely upon the underlying uniformity present in actual objects. Hence, lacking that form of interpersonal constancy, the ego automatically reverts to repetition, that is, to "repetition compulsion," which, in turn, reflects the drives.

14. These private myths are "transcendent": they refer to imaginary beings and they reflect a mythical structure. They may give the appearance of "reasoning." Because these myths are expressed in language and because they employ apparently well-formed patterns, they may

appear reasonable. But this reasoning is Distinctive Feature (DF) processing.

15. DF processing is a form of thought analogous to primary process thinking. DF processing shows these characteristics: water-tight logic; paranoid system qualities; and unconscious fantasies that revolve endlessly upon the destruction and repair of the self through pregenital traumata.[9]

16. Some works of art, like the shaman's mask, may reflect entirely their origin in DF systems. In these cases, they function as magical objects. When such artifacts are analyzed, they reveal their neurotic origins just as symptoms reveal their origins when they are fully analyzed.

17. Sublimation is an ego achievement that reflects the person's capacity to break free of repetition compulsion and to transcend the formal restraints of DF processing. Hence, while the contents of DF fantasy and an artistic product may be identical, their forms differ radically. It is the form of the artifact that conveys qualitative differences, and it is the qualitative differences that convey aesthetic values. Sublimation refers to the overall aesthetic achievement wrought by the person in the person's total effort to comprehend human conflicts. Sublimation is to unconscious wishes what dream interpretation is to latent dream thoughts.

The Problem of Validation: Utility?

The above is not sufficient a set of concepts, for concepts are nothing more than tools. As such, they ought to be examined for their utility as tools, wielded in the tasks for which they were designed. One may look back on early psychoanalytic papers and note how odd it now sounds to speak of "hypercathexes." Yet, at that time they served important functions, just as currently outmoded medical techniques were valuable at one time.

Because I propose to recast the psychoanalytic concept of sublimation, which has a long history, I ought to say why this is a good thing to do. I attempt to do it in more detail in chapters 2 and 3, where I work through all major psychoanalytic versions of the concept. I suggest the following tests are appropriate for such a revised theory:

1. The old concept is not very useful.
2. The old concept vitiates other portions of psychoanalytic theory.
3. The new concept repairs these faults and adds no new errors.

4. The new concept unites previously unassimilated clinical observations and clinical truths.
5. The new concept expands the range of subjects suitable for psychoanalytic inquiry.
6. The concept is testable both within a clinical environment and within the applied fields to which it is relevant.

This is a demanding list. Yet there are new concepts which, I think, one can argue fulfill these six criteria. For example, Kohut's basic insights about narcissistic transferences and the concept of "self-object" have provided major reorientations within clinical psychoanalysis and to applied studies (V.P. Gay 1989). I do not claim this degree of success. I do claim to show that the concept of sublimation should be revised and that a revision should follow along the lines I set out in this study. Validation of these more extended claims is an ideal that remains on the horizon.[10]

CHAPTER TWO

FREUD AND THE LOCATION OF VALUES

> The place where cultural experience is located is in
> the potential space between the individual and the
> environment (originally the object). The same can be
> said of playing. Cultural experience begins with crea-
> tive living first manifested in play.
> —David Winnicott 1971a, p. 100

The Location of Values and Aesthetics

I take my chapter title and this quotation from Winnicott's essay,
"The Location of Cultural Experience," where he describes his work
with psychotic persons. Neurotic patients seek relief from conflicts;
psychotic persons often seek relief from the struggle to feel alive (or
whole, or real, or complete). Psychotic persons fasten onto a religious
tradition or a therapist and demand proof that their life is worth living.
Winnicott is sympathetic to these kinds of distress, but he does not
champion these forms of external solutions. Rather, he says that these
severe forms of psychopathology occur because of failures in mother-
infant interation.

Winnicott makes a causal claim: psychological suffering damages
the child's ability to develop a strong self. In the jargon of psychoanalysis, early traumata impede ego structuralization. The child cannot
retain a sense of being alive: "primitive defenses now become organized to defend against repetition of 'unthinkable anxiety' or a return to
the acute confusional state that belongs to disintegration of nascent
ego structure" (p. 97). Parents must relieve the infant's distress. "If the
mother is away more than x minutes, then the imago [image of the
mother] fades, and along with this the baby's capacity to use the symbol
of union ceases" (p. 97).

Winnicott says that a traumatized baby can no longer use such
symbols and so it invokes primitive defenses which, in turn, develop

into behaviors termed "psychotic." Symbols of reunion with mother are originally idiosyncratic and personal; this blanket and that toy are concrete linkages to mother (the mothering person). The fortunate child who escapes trauma can use these idiosyncratic symbols to recover the safety of its mother's presence. Later, the same child can make use of cultural symbols, including religion, which occupy the same transitional space between the child's inner needs and the external world. For this reason, Winnicott esteems religion and other cultural forms because they can remind healthy persons of their original, positive linkages to good-enough parents. Implicit in Winnicott's work is a theory of sublimation compatible with the one I stated at the end of chapter 1. Sublimation occurs when a healthy person withstands the drives and discovers new routes toward relationship with others and with parts of the self. Freud did not affirm this notion of sublimation, because he did not share Winnicott's belief that one can locate qualitative experiences external to the perceiving subject. Freud was no fool; he recognized that we all experience qualities in the world and in other persons. He does not deny this; he denies that these experiences are valid. His disagreement with Winnicott and with the Renaissance preachers is a philosophic one for his theory of knowledge, his epistemology, differs from that of both the preachers and Winnicott. One might conclude that this difference is minor and irrelevant to psychoanalysis and aesthetics. I do not accept this conclusion. First, it is interesting to see how Freud's philosophy influenced his theory of art. Second, it is useful to show the consequences of clinical work these assumptions produce.

Where does Freud place or locate values? By values I mean those general qualities we hope to be true of ourselves and our environment. I identify "values" with "qualities." English speakers refer to the quality of light on a winter's day, moral qualities, like integrity, and aesthetic qualities, like grace and beauty. My naive question, then, reformulated is: Where does Freud locate values or qualities? If the world of experience includes persons who exist in a real world, then my question can have only three possible answers. Values exist:

1. in the mind of the perceiver alone (they are "subjective")
2. in the object alone (they are "objective")
3. midway between the two: in the relationship that exists between subject and object; e.g., between viewer and scenery, between patient and analyst.

These first two options are well known philosophic positions. Generations of brilliant thinkers have elaborated subtle versions of each. There is a wealth of sophisticated arguments for these positions. The issue of the location of values is similar to the problem of body-mind interactions. Both problems have only three solutions. One can argue that mind is distinct from body ("pure mentalism"), that body and mind are interdependent, or that the body controls the mind ("pure physicalism"). Few contemporary authors would identify themselves with either pure mentalism or pure physicalism. Yet Freud did for he never doubted the victory of biological reductionism, though he recognized psychoanalysis was not among the biological sciences. His epistemology was clear and unambigious: values (or qualities) exist in the mind of the perceiver alone.

Aesthetics and Epistemology

Of course, Freud never said this. He wrote no single treatise on aesthetics, nor did he write much about ethics, or other value-related questions. Many people hoped that so vigorous a mind would attend to these important problems and they faulted him for his neglect. Freud believed ethical issues could be settled by rational reflections on living.[1] Freud wrote no treatise on aesthetics because his reflections on artists and pieces of art derive from his clinical theory. His clinical theory was never a well-rounded system from which he could deduce a theory of art. Many of his essays on art are brilliant, others stand refuted by experts. Even when Freud goes wrong, as in his essay on Leonardo (1910c), he remains interesting. (See Gay 1989, pp. 270–271.) Freud's comments on the authorship of Shakespeare's plays fail to convince even psychoanalytic allies. Yet, for all that, they are worth considering, if not for the light they bring to Shakespeare, then for the insight they give to Freud's mind. Readers of Freud's exquisite essay on Jensen's novel, *Gradiva* (1907a), will know that no summary of Freud's aptitude as a critic is adequate.[2]

Art, Aesthetics, and Dualistic Pairs

Freud was never reluctant to admit that he had artistic precursors. On the contrary, they appear in all his writings, especially his popular lectures. There he calls upon Goethe, Shakespeare, and Sophocles to confirm his psychoanalytic claims. Yet, we ask: Why did Freud not maintain a consistent valuation of art and recognize it as a mode of knowledge? Why did he not maintain his admiration of its cognitive dimensions? He respects art deeply. He says great artists perfigured him in many ways but he does not grant art a status equal to that of science.

Freud's essays on art reveal what James Strachey calls "Freud's love of dualisms." Hans Sachs described: "The center...toward which every road and bypath turned, was the dualistic concept—first of the mind, then of life, and ultimately of the universe" (1945, p. 135). Sachs argues that the internal development of psychoanalysis is the "story of the broadening and deepening of this dualistic-dynamic concept" (1945, p. 136). Given Freud's focus upon conflict, he always seeks to delineate forces that oppose one another.

The way Freud employs these dualisms in his essays on cultural artifacts differs from the way he uses them in his case histories. Gordon Allport and other American psychologists have complained that Freud's case histories are nothing more than vehicles with which he expressed his preconceived theoretical opinions. This is incorrect. In his case histories like "Rat Man," (about a young man with a rat phobia), "Dora" (about a young woman), and "Wolf Man" (a young Russian aristocrat whose childhood dream of wolves terrified him) Freud follows the contours of his patients' associations and seeks their conflicted source. He is willing to abandon an interpretation if it is contradicted by his patient's behavior, including associations and transference manifestations.

An example occurs toward the end of the Wolf Man case history (1918b). Freud's patient recalls his fascination with butterflies: "Suddenly, when the butterfly had settled on a flower, he was seized with a dreadful fear of the creature, and ran away screaming. This memory recurred occasionally during the analysis, and called for an explanation..." (p. 89). Because his patient associates the insect with anxiety and a fear of females, Freud suggests the butterfly's stripes may have reminded the boy of stripes on women's underclothes. This persuaded neither of them. "*Many months later...* the patient remarked that the opening and shutting of the butterfly's wings while it was settled on the flower had given him an uncanny feeling" (p. 90, emphasis mine). It reminded him of a woman opening her legs like a Roman V. Freud says he himself could not have arrived at this association; children seem sensitive to similarities between motions and base their associations on them.

In this vignette we see a fascinating association and one of Freud's fascinating generalizations. The butterfly returns when Freud's patient recalls a nursery-maid, whose name, "Grusha," was identical to that of a large pear which had yellow stripes on its skin. Was it she whom the young boy had seen making the motion with her legs which later reminded him of the Roman V? His patient remembers a scene from his boyhood: a maid is scrubbing the floor with a broom, scolding him for something. As with other associations, the psychoanalytic task is to link it to disparate elements: a pear, a maid, and repressed anxieties. Months before, his patient had described falling in love with a peasant girl the had seen scrubbing in a similar manner. What was her name? The patient resists. Why?

> He asserted, however, that the reason for his being so much ashamed of mentioning the name was that it was a purely peasant name and that no girl of gentle birth could possibly be called by it. When eventually the name was produced, it turned out to be Matrona, which has a motherly ring about it. The shame was evidently displaced. He was not ashamed of the fact that these love-affairs were invariably concerned with girls of the humblest origin; he was ashamed only of the name. If it should turn out that the affair with Matrona had something in common with the Grusha scene, then the shame would have to be transferred back to that early episode. (p. 91)

To these memories Freud brings an additional element: his patient admired the story of the burning of John Huss, the fourteenth-century religious reformer. As he does with other patients, Freud assumes that the Wolf Man's strong feelings, especially those that are uncanny, link together in the unconscious.

> Now his sympathy for Huss created a perfectly definite suspicion in my mind, for I have often come upon this sympathy in youthful patients and I have always been able to explain it in the same way…. Huss perished by fire, and (like others who possess the same qualification) he becomes the hero of people who have at one time suffered from enuresis. My patient himself connected the bundles of firewood used for the execution of Huss with the nursery-maid's broom or bundle of twigs. (pp. 91–92)

Freud's conclusion is noteworthy; although his patient's thoughts seem odd, "This material fitted together spontaneously and served to fill in the gaps in the patient's memory of the scene with Grusha. When he saw the girl scrubbing the floor he had micturated in the room and she had rejoined, no doubt jokingly, with a threat of castration" (pp. 91–92). Another association concerns the German term *Wespe* which he "mutilates" into *Espe* which in turn he associates to with initials, *S.P.* (p. 94). Freud deduces none of these insights from his preconceived theories. He does look for instances of oedipal affection and finds them. Yet he also finds instances of pre-oedipal and negative oedipal feelings as well. His patient rejects interpretations and reconstructions which appear to him impossible. For example, Freud wavers about the existence of an actual "primal scene" in which the young boy saw his parents engaged in sexual intercourse. Perhaps his patient had merely added a fantasy of his later years onto an earlier memory of an "innocent enema" (p. 95)? "[B]ut the patient looked at me uncomprehendingly and a little contemptuously when I put this view before him, and he never reacted to it again" (p. 95).

None of these subtle discussions restates preformed views. Most of Freud's essays on culture differ from the clinical cases, where we tend to find dualisms, antithetical pairs, and labored reconstructions of archaic periods. In this way *Totem and Taboo* and *Moses and Monotheism* contrast sharply with the case histories. There are many good reasons for this: one is that the essays on culture are applied theory. The theory precedes the examination; therefore applied studies tend to become arguments by analogy. Freud himself distinguished these two broad groups of work, and there is no need to lambast him for doing what he promised. Most intellectuals read Freud's literary works, like *Civilization and Its Discontents*. This reinforces an image that Freud is didactic. Even for those scholars who go beyond the essays on culture to the true gold of the case histories and clinical papers, the yield is disappointingly small.

Hidden Truths and the Aesthetic Surface

[Psychoanalysis, Marxism, and Geology] showed that understanding consists in the reduction of one type of reality to another; that true reality is never the most obvious of realities, and that its nature is already apparent in the care which it takes to evade our detection. (Claude Lévi-Strauss, *Tristes Tropiques*, 1961, p. 61)

Among Freud's many intellectual virtues is love of the truth. Among his few faults is the pride that marked that love. Freud's discoveries far outweigh the idiosyncracies of his character. The science of psychoanalysis is long lived and greater than the character of its founder, no matter how fascinating and admirable we find the latter. The truth Freud seeks is truth that hides itself, that is furtive and elusive. It is like the truths that hid themselves from King Oedipus. To root them out, to let the light of day shine on them, Freud employed his ruthless intellect. Like Schilemann, who followed his boyish passion for the classics and dug up Troy, Freud retrieved truths that lay buried. The psychological truths Freud uncovered were not merely unavailable. They were hiding under false identities. The resisted the efforts of the authorities to discover them. Like the Rhinegold, they protected by awesome and unholy powers. Freud pictured himself a conquistador.

This fulfilled in part his boyhood wish to fight like Hannibal who sought to conquer an aging and totalitarian regime by cleverness and courage. Many commentators have noted Freud's passion for militraistic metaphors and other conflicted terminology. We recall that the central concept of *cathexis,* is his translator's pseudo-Greek rendition of the German, *Besetzung.* The English translation fails to capture the militaristic tone of the original. The German term refers to the "occupation" by enemy forces of a hostile country. Freud's character, plus the nature of repression, combined to give psychoanalysis the mark of action, of a struggle between patient and therapist.

Part of the vehemence with which Freud confronted his patients developed from his original therapeutic method. With Joseph Breuer, a physician senior in every way except genius, Freud discovered the talking cure. Talking to patients under hypnosis seemed to relieve them of pathological ideas. To explain the power of such talking each man offered a different theory. Breuer held that pathological ideas gained their power during self-induced hypnotic states, hence he termed this disease "hypnoid hysteria." Freud found no evidence for hypnoid hysteria. "Any that I took into my hands has turned into a defence hysteria" (1895d, p. 286). Breuer said hysteric symptoms, like Anna O's temporary blindness, were automatic repetitions of psychological dysfunctions formed in hypnogogic states. His treatment induced a controlled hypnotic state. This permitted the accumulated affect to discharge. The more severe the original trauma, the greater the accumulated affects, the longer such discharge took.

Breuer's technique required his patients to recall as much of their history as possible. Therapy was complete when the patient's memory reverted to its original state. No gaps should appear between what the patient recalled under hypnosis and what was available to the patient during ordinary consciousness. Breuer's hypnotic technique did not work for Freud. Freud's patients did not recognize, when awake, the "memories" they had reproduced while asleep. So Freud changed his technique:

> I now became insistent—if I assured them that they did know it, that it would appear to their minds—then, in the first cases, something did occur to them.... After this I became still more insistent; I told the patients to lie down and deliberately close their eyes in order to 'concentrate'.... I then found that without any hypnosis new recollections emerged which went further back and which probably related to our topic. Experiences like this made me think that it would in fact be possible for the pathogenic groups of ideas, that were after all certainly present, to be brought to light

by mere insistence; and since this insistence involved effort on my part
and so suggested the idea that I had to overcome a resistance, the situation led me at once to the theory *that by means of my psychical work I had
to overcome a psychical force in the patients which was opposed to the
pathogenic ideas becoming conscious (being remembered).* (1895d, p. 268,
emphasis his)

Freud reasoned that the force he exerted upon their foreheads
represented the force with which his patients resisted insight. That is,
the physical exertion he expended in uncovering the pathogenic ideas
measured the energy with which the truth hid itself. When Freud applied these principles to works of art, problems arose. The major one is
that Freud strove to confront the appearance of things in order to
uncover their inner and hidden nature. Like the pre-Socratics whom he
admired, Freud attacked the surface of things in order to combat a
universal tendency to repress the truth. Like Copernicus, another of his
heroes, Freud challenged the commonsense belief that we are in
command of ourselves. Just as the sun does not revolve around our
earth but we revolve around the sun, so too the unconscious "lives us."

Yet art is sensuous. Painting, music, poetry, and the other arts
produce tactile, visual, or auditory experience by creating superficial
textures and qualities. Many deep feelings reside in the "superficial"
qualities of ordinary objects. Proust's response to the taste of lime tea
and little cookies, and the revery they induced, is a glamorous example
of what everyone has experienced. Some Canadians grow sentimental
when they feel the bite of the first snow while Georgians fall homesick
when their foreheads are dampened by the first sultry wind. Yet it is
these kinds of nostalgic intensity which Freud most suspects. Like all
such feelings, especially the "oceanic feeling" Freud himself experienced, nostalgia too must be examined under the psychoanalytic
microscope. When we examine it, we find buried underneath a host of
repressed wishes for an infantile paradise.[3]

Freud says psychoanalysis cannot comprehend a problem unless
one discovers in it some hint of psychological conflict. When he discovered a conflict between the ego's defensive mechanisms and its
synthetic function, it became subject to psychoanalytic scrutiny. When
a patient (or an artifact) exhibits no psychological conflicts and gaps
within its makeup, it is not suitable for psychoanalytic work. It is the
hysteric's inability to tell her story in a coherent and complete way that
permits us to say her disease is psychological, not physical.[4]

According to this understanding, psychoanalysis works by provid-
ing a neutral time and space in which such conflicts can emerge with

full clarity and undiminished force. Some conflicts are permanent and unavoidable. Conflicts between individuals and between parts of the individual are unavoidable because the essential truth of the human condition is always hidden. Over the course of fifty years Freud assigned different names to this ultimate conflict. At first he explained it by the romantic notion that repressive societies unduly restricted the action of otherwise happy and contented persons. Eventually, he held that conflicts persist because the instincts that drive all living things oppose one another endlessly.

Because art is a part of culture it manifests the conflicts that animate all human institutions. Therefore, art is open to psychoanalytic inquiry. That inquiry is not identical to the usual forms of art criticism. Psychoanalytic criticism can never contribute to the official understanding of an institution, an artifact, or an artist. Open-minded scholars take up Freud only to toss him out when they discover how contentious his claims are.[5] They reject Freud because he requires one to assume that the true meaning of an artifact lies in the way it attempts to solve human conflicts. Fundamental of all such conflicts is that between the imperious drives (or primal instincts) and the person lived by them at the moment. When Freud interprets Dostoevski's novels (Freud, 1928b), he shows how Dostoevski attempted to bridge the gulf that separates blind instincts from self-understanding. Dostoevski failed to make this link and reverted, Freud says, to primitive forms of spiritualism and nationalism, philosophic positions which "lesser minds have reached with smaller effort" (1928b, p. 177). True to his central notion, that of quantitative versus qualitative forces, Freud says that the great Russian novelist suffered from an excess of instinctual forces (a quantitative factor) and an instinctual perversion (a qualitative factor). His great artistic gifts were not sufficient to prevent the resurgence of his neurosis, especially his adoption of an archaic religion. For this Freud condemned him: "The future of civilization will have little to thank him for" (1928b, p. 177).

Because we are nonlinguistic infants, fundamental values and meanings are nonlinguistic. Language arrives late on the scene, after the self has begun to take shape. "Sense" and "understanding" appear slowly as the child matures and assumes roles dictated by culture. Cultures, in response to the excessive length of human childhood, impose exorbitant costs upon the individual's freedom and pleasures. Cultures, Freud says again and again, derive the energy they need to operate by taxing the libidinal stores of individuals. Psychoanalytic interpretations cut through the propaganda which obscure this libidinal taxation. Psychoanalytic interpretations are, therefore, seditious.

The cultural tax on libido conflicts with the wishes of individuals. Psychoanalytic interpretations must reflect both sides of this conflict. Freud's radical interpretations of cultural artifacts do not merely report the discovery of certain sexual or aggressive "tendencies" within the piece in question. Rather, interpretations themselves manifest a mix of opposing tendencies, just as high-level ego defenses manifest conflicts imbedded in the conflicts between the instincts. (See David Rapaport 1960.)

Freud often says that psychoanalysis is like solving a crime or puzzle; yet, many psychoanalytic interpretations do not reveal a single solution. Rather, they capture, name, and state a conflict. They are like refinements of a musical theme or the resolution of a dramatic scene. They exemplify the deep conflicts within the artist's psyche. They do not pretend to dispose of one side of the conflict. Freud's fondness for representing such conflicts in all their complexity makes his texts opaque and subject to as much debate and interpretation as the theories he advanced within them. I discuss this issue at length in chapter 4. Freud recognized these limitations (he did not enjoy arcane arguments). He sought to overcome them by shaping his essays on culture around *causal* theorems. In most instances that meant he used the notion of the oedipal complex to provide a causal framework over which he could stretch his interpretations. Within the larger enterprise of offering a complete psychology of culture he elaborated the notion of sublimation. Sublimation linked his theory of knowledge both to his theory of personality and to his theory of culture.

Sublimation and Aesthetics

Freud perceived that there is a logical gap between biological forces and the ego, a psychological agency. An illustration of the mystery that surrounds the whole issue of humankind's bifurcated nature is verbal therapy. That persons get sick because they cannot live their lives as they wish is understandable. That they can get well merely talking about it is mysterious. The mystery of verbal therapy echoes the mystery of art; both art and psychoanalysis use symbols to effect real and sometimes permanent cures. While Freud was aware of this issue, he did not try to overcome it too quickly or too easily; he was not fond of synthesis. Because synthesis permits one to deny the actuality of conflict, it jeopardizes psychoanalytic insight.[6]

Other thinkers have confronted the same issue but arrived at different solutions. Two methods are important: one is structuralist method, the other is phenomenological method. Their practitioners have different aims but share a common ideal: philosophy will unite the realm of physical energy with the realm of human thought. This was not Freud's aim. His aesthetics is a subset of his theory of the neuroses. He never claimed to have exhausted issues of style and form central to a theory of art; he did not discover the artistic qualities that make some stories more "uncanny" than others (1919h). His aesthetics is a subset of his theory of the neuroses and suffers all the limitations of that theory. Chief of these is the disavowal of the importance of manifest content and his championing of latent, unconscious, and instinctual contents. Of course, this is also one of his principal strengths. Like Nietzsche and Darwin (and Augustine and Luther), Freud expended his intellectual capital upon an interrogation of the surface. It is worthwhile considering the fierceness of that attack and the costs psychoanalysis has had to pay to sustain it. It has forced psychoanalytic authors to undervalue the surface. Psychoanalytic concepts related to the metaphor of surface and depth, such as manifest/latent and conscious/unconscious, always favor depth over surface. Yet artistic objects reveal their values on their surfaces. More so, because these concepts form radical pairs, each member is the logical opposite of the other. Hence Freud tried to tie them together, using three distinct methods.

The first is through case histories. One uncovers truths that operate below the surface of awareness and that manufacture manifest content in order to hide themselves. Accordingly, surface features of an artifact or an institution are reducible to the operations of mechanisms that operate beneath consciousness. Freud used this method in *The Interpretation of Dreams* (1900a), in his case histories, and in his papers on technique. The second way is to compare the structure of manifest content of artifacts with neurotic symptoms, and those in turn with the structure of cultural institutions. One looks for shared abstract patterns (structures) and, having found them, argues that common patterns suggest common origins and common functions within the psychic economy. Freud carried out this method in *The Psychopathology of Everyday Life* (1901b), *Jokes and Their Relation to the Unconscious* (1905c), and his many essays on religion (1907b; 1912–13; 1927c; 1939a). A third way is to explore how surface features of an artifact reflect the shapes of drives, wishes, and feelings that are unavailable to consciousness. Freud employed these methods in his essays on Leonardo (1910c) and on Michaelangelo (1914b). Like most subsequent dynamic psychologists, Freud uses all three methods in varying degrees in each of his works.

The "Gold of Analysis" and the Analytic Relationship

The gold of analysis is the capacity for change and fundamental alteration of the personality through the joint labors of patient and analyst in the analytic relationship. It is not accidental that Freud uses an ironic mode to illustrate how the Wolf Man rejected his hypothesis about the source of his fantasies. When Freud criticized psychoanalytic claims, his patient rebuffed him. This confirmed Freud's technique: to follow out the analysis wherever it leads. The method guards against the stultification of theory because analysis is an activity never fully exhausted by words. This truism allows us to see why applied psychoanalysis is often not satisfying. A little diagram may help summarize my suggestion. By correlating the patient with the work of art we can say that psychoanalytic aesthetics must explicate the following relationships:

(1) Analyst   Patient
(2) Analyst   Work of Art

Patient and therapist are human beings who interact and whose interaction produces new insights and new discoveries. This is not true of the second relationship, analyst and work of art. The work of art does not respond to its interpreter; hence there can be no mutual discovery between the novel and the analyst as there is between the patient and the analyst. The work of art cannot regard the critic with contempt; of course, its creator can and often does.

Even if educated in their discipline's history, artists have no privileged status as critics. Unless the work of art is merely an "expression," its creator has no special claim to know its meaning. The analytic critic may be armed with hypotheses with which to confront the work. Yet the analytic critic also focuses upon narrative content. "Analytic" themes of sexuality and aggression, oedipal issues, self representations, etc., are rarely intrinsic to the work itself.

Early psychoanalytic critics did not usually go beyond asserting the existence of such parallels. They had few ways to reduce the novel, say, to the dimensions of the case history. Rather, psychoanalytic criticism, like Freud's on *Gradiva* (1907a), for all their brilliance, reveals how similar themes appear in both neurotic symptoms and the work under investigation. This is a fascinating element that nonanalytic critics have taken up too. Yet it does not explain how the work of art differs; how it reaches the status of a public artifact more important than any symptom.

An alternative approach, and one used by both analyst and non-analyst alike, is to judge the work of art, in part, by its effects upon oneself. While the work cannot react as a real human does to our presence, we can report our reaction to it. In psychoanalytic applications, Norman Holland's many valuable comments on the effect of the text carry out his enterprise. In *Five Readers Reading* (1975) he judges a text by its effects upon five students who report their fantasies about it.

Art designed to affect human beings (although some medieval sculptures were placed to be seen by God alone). The undeniable limitation to this method is that it does not include a theory of taste. It does not permit one to assess the value of the work itself, apart from its popularity at the moment. Some great art, like Beethoven's late quintets, or Wallace Steven's poetry, or James Joyce's *Ulysses*, rarely becomes popular.

Against this obvious limitation—that popularity is not a measure of intrinsic values—is a more obscure one. Its polar alternative, that the elite set the tone and value, is unattractive. No matter how refined and distinguished the critic, we do not want to give up all claims to disagreement. When T. S. Eliot proclaims that *Hamlet* is a deficient play we rebel and reassess our previous enthusiasm for Eliot.

A third alternative is to judge the work of art as a real thing which is pertinent to particular human needs. This is the thesis I pursue in this book.

The Work of Art as a Location of Values

For the nonanalytic reader this third alternative will not appear revolutionary. One might find it obvious and another example of psychoanalytic authors reporting what everyone else already knew. Erich Fromm proffered a similar remark in his attack on the usefulness of ego psychology (Fromm 1959). Given the abuse which Fromm received from some analytic circles, his bitterness is understandable. Fromm feels that the individual sciences, including psychology and psychoanalysis, ought to progress more or less as a whole. Discoveries in one field or subfield should be reflected in all others. In that way a general advance will occur. Hence Fromm felt justified in combining Marxism and psychoanalysis to synthesize a general critical theory. Other neo-Freudians, like H. S. Sullivan, gravitated toward eclecticism. All eclectic thinkers believe that science advances from truth to truth, discards what is contentious, and upholds the majority's opinions.

However, eclecticism has peculiar difficulties, as Herbert Marcuse argued in his attack upon Freudian "revisionism" (1955). American psychiatry and psychology appear dominated by eclectic theoreticians

(Darrell Smith 1982). Eclectic authors may feel free to reject portions of a theory they consider outmoded or distasteful, yet they must do so on some grounds. It is not fair to reject a theory because it violates received opinion.

Science is often counterintuitive. Since most psychologists take the natural sciences to be paradigmatic of real science, they ought to examine how progress occurs there too. Imre Lakatos and his students have argued that science progresses within specific research programs (1976; 1978). These programs are evolved methods generated by many investigators pursuing the same problems. In a research program anomalies are set aside in favor of the dictates of the central program.

Lakatos is no lover of psychoanalysis but his favorite concept of research program describes Freud's career, Freud's ability to tolerate anomalies, and Freud's ability to face bitter criticism. Heinz Kohut's works on narcissism are well within that psychoanalytic tradition, even though Kohut came to reject nearly every aspect of Freud's philosophy and metapsychology. Kohut's adherence to the psychoanalytic attitude—the empathic exploration of a human being's life—let him make new discoveries.

In this book I show that the concept of sublimation is enmeshed in outmoded theories of perception. This enmeshment limits the usefulness of the concept. Here I follow Robert Waelder's distinction between metapsychological speculations and clinical theory (1960). For example, no one can doubt that human beings "repress" ideas and feelings that are painful and distressing. Is repression the transfer of "binding" energy from one site to another in the brain where it serves to inhibit a flowing cathetic current?

Theory of Sublimation and Theory of Perception

Freud's notion of sublimation is more precise than this. No matter which principles he used, the term relies upon the fundamental concept of *regression*, which relies upon the theory of developmental stages. This theory, in turn, relies upon Freud's theory of perception. I criticize Freud's metapsychological explanation of the concept of sublimation. I do not deny that there is some relation between instinctual needs and artistic artifacts. To investigate the possibility of psychoanalytic aesthetics we consider Freud's theory of perception. That theory located values and all qualities within the perceiving subject. An intrinsic element in Freud's theory is that hallucination is the primary state of the infant's perceiving apparatus. Primary process thinking occurs when illusions or hallucinations predominate: in dreams, in acute psychotic episodes, and in some forms of religious ecstasy. Like the infant's hallucination of the breast, each of these processes demonstrates the power of wishful thinking to overwhelm reality testing. Such processes are primary because, Freud says, they preceded the establishment of reality testing, a major component of secondary process thinking.[7]

Given this Freudian claim, a new task arises. In order to argue for a coherent theory of sublimation, which is part of general psychoanalytic aesthetics, one must assess the psychoanalytic theory of perception. This task is unexpected and difficult. There is no single accepted theory of preception in psychoanalysis.

Usual Complaints about Freud's Theory of Values

The usual complaints are that Freud attacked common values and so undermined the effects of ethical training. More sophisticated persons complain that he avoided the question of value theory altogether. The first complaint has no basis in fact. Freud was strict toward himself and toward his patients. The second is more weighty. Indeed, Philip Rieff's book, *Freud: The Mind of the Moralist* (1959) is esteemed because Rieff takes seriously the ethical commitment that underlies the psychoanalytic enterprise. The commitment to cure and the affection for truth which permeate Freud's thought are values he held dear.

No doubt one could examine Freud's work and select from it a large set of such assumptions. Rather than do that, I refer to portions of Adrian Stokes's essay, *Greek Culture and the Ego* (1958). Stokes describes many of the basic Western ideals he and Freud found in the classical Greek period. Ideals of temperance, of balance between opposing forces in politics and opposing appetites within persons, of self-government in both realms, of the nobility of the individual, are all present in the analytic relationship.

Many commentators have noted similarities between the method and aims of analytic treatment and those Socrates pursued. The art of conversation, the celebration of speech, and the emphasis placed upon method, upon the way one speaks, that Socrates championed in his philosophic method are almost identical to those Freud elaborated in his psychological method. Socrates assumed that wisdom resides within the individual soul, so that even slaves may, with proper help, deduce the inherent truths of geometry. This finds a counterpart in the psychoanalytic belief that insight into the self is a chief good and a source of strength (Pedro Lain Entralgo 1970).

As Stokes points out, Freud and the Greeks esteem most that person who faces life and falls neither into despair nor relies upon transcendental solutions. Freud affirms this value in his bitter critiques of religion. It suffuses his ideal of analysis: to undo conflict and liberate a person to live without recourse to religious solutions that cost the ego its sovereignty. Analysis is much more than medical repair. The analyst aims not to reduce the individual's pleasures but to free the ego. Analysis is a process by which we discover where the ego made compromises that now cost it its power and authority over itself. The goal of analysis is liberation. One should be free to experience one's life in its richness without neurosis and without the sacrifice demanded by transcendental cures, like religion or the transference cures offered by hypnosis and similar methods.

Person, Perception, and Hallucination

Freud's affection for Greek values reflects similar affection for the Greeks that has dominated education since the Renaissance. In Western philosophy this affection links together authors who would otherwise be opponents; for example the atheist Freud versus the theist philosopher Immanuel Kant. Kant wished to defend Christian faith against the onslaught of Newton's revolutionary insights. Freud wished to be among Newton's successors.

Yet rejecting Kant's wishes to make faith possible, Freud adopted many of Kant's principal assumptions. In particular, Kant's vision of the status of the human being, an animal with transcendental yearnings, reappears in Freud's basic model of human existence. We can see this interesting linkage by referring to Kant's essay on anthropology. There the philosopher considers pleasure and pain in human life:

> Sensuous pleasure is the feeling of life being furthered, pain, that of life being hindered. Life (animal life), however, is, as the physicians have already noted, a continuous play played by the two antagonists, pleasure and pain. It follows that pain must precede every pleasure; pain always comes first. For the vital power, vitality, cannot grow beyond a certain degree. Hence what else would follow from feeding vitality continuously but a quick death from joy? (Kant 1798, pp. 60–67)

Kant does not describe anyone who died from too much joy. Folk Christian thought always claims that in heaven there will be continuous joy and, of course, no death. Kant makes these claims as a philosopher who wishes to deduce the necessity of pain in human life. In the same way, preachers deduce the necessity for shadow: without shadow there can be no experience of the light, etc.

But Kant is also wary of pleasure, especially "sensuous pleasure" (pp. 60–67). The translator of Kant's *Analytic of the Beautiful*, his treatise on sublime beauty, appended these remarks on pain and pleasure to that book. In both texts Kant attempts to describe the experience of beauty, a task much different than describing the logical structure of knowledge. We can clarify the difference by quoting again from the *Anthropology:* "Sensuous pleasure and pain are opposed to each other, not like lack and gain (0 and +), but like gain and loss (+ and –), that is to say, their oposition is not the logical opposition between contradictories ...but the real opposition of antagonists..." (p. 59). Kant's use of the term *antagonists* is not accidental. It comes from Greek drama in which noble characters engage in "agon," that is contests with one another and with gods. "Agon" captures the feeling of actual combat and struggle that Kant ascribes to human life.

This is Freud's view. The ubiquity of conflict in human life was a deep psychological puzzle (1950a) Freud wished to solve. Following usual Freudian scholarship, we can say that those explanations fall into four periods. The first is the composition of the "Project" of 1895 (which I discuss at length). The second is chapters 6 and 7 of *The Interpretation of Dreams* (1900a). The third is the metapsychological period (roughly 1911–1918). The last period is that of ego psychology (1918–1938).

In each epoch Freud reworked his theory to account for a primary fact: the persistence of conflict. Kant distinguishes between real antagonisms, like hate and love, and mere logical contraries. The former occurs in daily life; the latter are intellectual formulae. It is easy and sometimes useful to employ logical contraries as formulaic representatives of actual antagonisms. In Freud's metapsychological papers he says that invisible parts of the psyche that are in conflict produce visible (manifest) conflicted behaviors. In the last period, from 1918 to his death, Freud explained conflict behaviors as products of the interaction between contrary structures, the ego-superego versus the id. The distinction between these systems is not absolute and radical. On the contrary, in *The Ego and the Id* (1923b), he notes the ego's origins in the id, and the superego's intimate relationship to id contents.

Freud recognized that all abstract models of clinical phenomena are overly precise. Their terms are too distinct and too logical to serve as adequate referents of feelings, behaviors, and thoughts that are fused together in the furnace of intense, libidinal relationships. The major parts of Freud's texts are clinical observations and clinical generations. In cases like Rat Man (1909b) and Wolf Man (1918b), he breaks off a line explanation, a reconstruction, or an interpretation if his patient's behavior contradicts the explanation offered. In these cases Freud seeks validation of clinical discoveries by seeking to find contradictions to his clinical theories. This willingness to be invalidated by clinical data does not appear in his comments upon general questions of epistemology. In his texts on epistemology Freud analyzes semantic relationships between logical contraries, like Eros and destructiveness: he does not analyze the nature of actual antagonisms. Since mythical thought is also about logical contradictions, it is not surprising that Freud's epistemology manifests a mythical structure.

The Official Theory of Perception

The official psychoanalytic theory of perception, at least in the authors with whom I am familiar, rests upon an unexamined thesis that is mythic, not empirical. That thesis is: there are two distinct worlds, the world of bare quantities that impinge upon the personality (ego apparatus, or self) and the world of qualities. This second world is coextensive with the internal world (self-consciousness, or ego awareness). The problem of perception includes the question of how external forces (bare quantities) are transformed into internal qualities of conscious experience.

The official theory, which is richer than my summary, always includes this thesis, usually unstated and subsumed under issues of mental representation; that is, memory. In terms of information science, the official theory says that human perception occurs when an internal system (the ego) adds new information to the bare quantities impinging upon it.

These enchanced "data" can then achieve a state of meaning, that is, bare quantities manifest sensorial qualities, like touch, taste, and warmth. The following is an excellent statement of this position:

> the tremendous amount of information pouring into the apparatus is incessantly meaningless to the receiver until the data are processed and organized into meaningful schemata which can be identified by matching them up against corresponding schemata stored in memory. Almost any one of the various mental functions, such as *perception,* memory, orientation, or assimilation, can be carried out only after the raw data of input have been organized into some kind of meaningful and identifiable schemata. (Noy 1973, p. 127, emphasis mine)

Noy explains his view of perception when he speaks of the "human computer" which manipulates raw data into complex representations according to its internal programs. Noy is consistent; he refers to a phenomenological maxim, "Keine Gestalt ohne Gestalter." We may translate this German maxim as "No pattern without a patterner." If true, then Noy and Freud correctly assign to the ego the responsibility to add "qualitative" features to the bare sense data that impinge upon human beings. If Noy and Freud are wrong, then the Freudian notion of sublimation is also incorrect. I suggest that another theory of perception, that proposed by J. J. Gibson, is more persuasive than that of Freud and Noy. I try to show why in chapter 6.

In this chapter I reveal how Noy's claims have their origins in Freud's epistemology. I discuss the philosophic context of Freud's theory of perception. Then I discuss his theory of psychic pain and its relationship to his theory of perception. I show why he concluded that hallucination was the primary state of perception. Finally, I show how these assumptions produce paradoxical claims about artistic creativity and the mysterious process of sublimation.[8]

Philosophic Context of Freud's Theory of Perception

> The intention is to furnish a psychology that shall be a natural science: that is, to represent psychical processes as quantitatively determinate states of specifiable material particles. (Freud 1895a, p. 295)

With these famous words Freud initiated his most sustained piece of pure reasoning, the "Project" of 1895. The one hundred or so pages of handwritten text, untitled and not intended for publication, set forth a brilliant materialist theory of mind. That theory and its relationship to Freud's later theories and its origin in his neurological training have been discussed at length (e.g., Karl Pribram and Merton Gill 1976; Peter Amacher 1965; Henri Ellenberger 1970). In most of these discussions the author, whether pro- or anti-Freudian, accepts Freud's orientation toward an intrapsychic point of view. Thus even Paul Ricoeur (1965), who rejects Freud's dismissal of religion, agrees with his general understanding of the ego's status.

The ego's status is problematic. According to European philosophy, it is situated midway between the real, external world and an inner world whose structures lie beneath conscious awareness. Ricoeur traces this general idea to Kant, though David Hume's role is also significant. Because he also shares that tradition, Ricoeur does not criticize Freud's reliance upon it. Of course, Freud and Ricoeur differ about which parts of Kant are important. Freud understood the main features of Kant's *Critique of Pure Reason* written in 1781. Freud accepted most of Kant's criticisms of previous philosophers, especially Kant's arguments against metaphysical deductions. He rejected most of Kant's constructive efforts, including Kant's attempt to make room for religious faith. To see which parts of Kant Freud accepted and which he rejected we visit Locke, Hume and Kant.

Locke, Kant, and Qualities

A key to Freud's epistemology is the term *quantity.* Why must scientific accounts be quantitative? If quantities are the "real," where do qualtities come from? Where do qualities originate? Freud answers: "Not in the external world. For out there, according to the view of our natural science, to which psychology too must be subjected here, there are only masses in motion and nothing else" (1895a p. 308).

Most people think that terms like *self, pain,* and *empathy* refer to distinct qualities of experience, e.g., I feel sad because they laughed at my haircut. If there are only masses in motion, how can psychology explain our belief that we in a world filled with infinite qualities? The problem of qualities has a long and noble lineage. Kant's attempts to answer it depended upon the tradition of English rationalism, especially the treaties of John Locke and David Hume; for they located the problem of epistemology in the theory of the experiencing subject. They bound up the theory of knowledge with the problems of philosophical psychology.

Locke made this clear when he argued for his famous distinction between primary and secondary qualities. Primary qualities are those essential features of an object such that we cannot imagine them absent, e.g., extension, mass, and duration. Locke sometimes calls them "powers" (1690, Book 2, chapter 8, pp. 169–170). Secondary qualities are those features of an entity that we directly experience, e.g., its taste, texture, or color. These secondary qualities may vary over time. Given so radical a distinction, it is not difficult to predict the next question: How do primary qualities influence or "give rise to" secondary qualities? For Locke, Hume, and Kant this was the question of perception. It is tied to the classical problem of deception of the senses. Such events, a straight edge appears crooked when half immersed in water, seem clear cases of a perceptual error in which the mind misconstrues secondary qualities. Locke explained how such errors could occur by imagining there were sense data:

> [S]ince the extension, figures, number and motion of bodies of an observable bigness, may be perceived at a distance by the sight, it is evident some singly imperceptible bodies must come from them to the eyes, and thereby convey to the brain some motion; which produces these ideas which we have of them in us. After the same manner that the ideas of these *original qualities* are produced in us, we may conceive that the ideas of *sec-*

ondary qualities are also produced, viz. by the operation of insensible particles on our senses. (1690, p. 172)

The latter particles are insensible because they are so small that we cannot see them. They are real and, according to Locke, must have, therefore, all the primary qualities. Now another problem arises. What determines the way we perceive these secondary qualities? There are two extreme answers: there is a one-to-one correlation between our experience and the actual disposition of the insensible particles or there is no correlation. Neither of these is adequate: the first rules out the possibility of error; the second rules out the possibility of correct perception. Locke seems to choose a middle ground. Reflecting upon sensations, like warmth, which is a secondary quality, we note that the same water may feel cold to one person yet warm to another. Neither the water, nor any of its qualities, has changed. It must be the physical state of the perceiving organ that varies, such that at one time the "motion in the minute particles of our nerves" gives rise to warmth while a slower motion gives rise to feelings of cold (p. 177).

Almost two hundred years later Kant addressed himself to the same problem. His "experiment" in the *Critique of Pure Reason* refers to the same problem, but Kant begins with a revolutionary assumption. He shares Locke's belief that the perceiving subject is somewhere in the middle of a flow of sense data or "stream of imperceptible particles" emitted by real objects. He reverses Locke's claim that we experience such particles passively. His Copernican Revolution (1781, p. xvii) amounted to this reversal: "If intuition must conform to the constitution of the objects, I do not see how we could know anything of the latter a priori; but if the object (as object of the sense) must conform to the constitution of our faculty of intuition, I have no difficulty of conceiving of such a possibility" (p. 22). This experimental shift (p. 23) allows Kant to account for the otherwise mysterious fact that we mortals have some forms of a priori knowledge, that is knowledge not based on direct experience. For example, the most excellent of the sciences, Newton's physics, deals with space, time, number, and causation without experimentation. The *Critique* was to establish, by philosophic argument, that these primary categories are themselves prior to all human experience. Therefore these principles constrain all human experience.

Locke said that primary qualities adhere in all real objects. Hume seemed to refute this view, especially the notion of causation. Kant, accepting Hume's refutation, replaced primary qualities with primary categories. It is not things that have duration but we human beings who have the a priori notion of duration and who ascribe that "primary quality" to them. This radical shift in the evaluation of primary qualities meant that their near cousins, secondary qualities, were even more split off from a direct, one-to-one relationship to real objects. Kant claimed to have charted the limits of pure reason: we cannot go behind the operations of our mental apparatus. Since it is our own equipment that conditions all experiencing, "we are brought to the conclusion that we can never transcend the limits of possible knowledge" (p. 24).

Locke and Kant on the Identity of Persons

Locke's notion of primary qualities permitted him to define personal identity: "An animal is a living organized body; and consequently the same animal, as we have observed, is the same continued life communicated to different particles of matter, as they happen successfully to be united to that organized living body" (p. 445). He adds, "This also shows wherein the identity of the same man consists" (p. 444). Ordinary experience shows us, Locke says, that personal identity consists in the direct experience of self:

> When we see, hear, smell, taste, feel, meditate, or will anything, we know that we do so... and by this every one is to himself which he calls self... consciousness always accompanies thinking, and it is that which makes every one to be what he calls self, and thereby distinguishes himself from all other thinking things, in this alone consists personal identity, i.e., the sameness of a rational being. (p. 449)

Locke did not doubt the reality and limits of this self: "Self is that conscious thinking thing... which is conscious of pleasure and pain, capable of happiness or misery, and so is concerned for itself, as far as that consciousness extends" (pp. 458–459). Kant reduced primary qualities to primary concepts (to synthetic a priori judgments). This permitted him to account for the success Newton's physics enjoyed, for by nature, scientists discovered an ordered universe, available to human understanding because as human beings they employed a priori categories that imposed an unshakable order upon all experiencing.

This allowed Kant to make room for religious faith: Kant bowed to Hume's demonstration that matters of faith could not be validated through reason. Yet, Kant felt he had shown that neither could matters of faith be disproved. For faith is a set of convictions about noumenal reality, reality that lies beyond the world of phenomenal experience. In his "critique" of science, Kant felt he had shown its limits; the phenomenal domain of this ordinary world. Science could have no say about those realms that lay beyond its ken.

In preserving the possibility of faith Kant also dethroned consciousness as the deciding feature of self-understanding: consciousness could no longer serve as an adequate demarcation of the person, as object, or of self, as subject. Kant argued that scientific laws, like those Newton discovered, are founded upon synthetic a priori judgments which were necessarily true. These truths are limited to phenomenal experience, that is, experience subject to empirical inquiry. Since human beings are among the furniture of this phenomenal realm, their actions are also subject to causal inquiry. Kant's Copernican hypothesis—that we impose the order we discover in experience—assumes that all objects, including human beings, must be understood in two senses.

Human beings are phenomena determined by the laws of Nature. They are also noumena, things-in-themselves, not subject to those laws "*and therefore free*" (p. 28, emphasis his). This move allowed Kant to preserve the possibility of freedom and, hence, of morality, because the noumenal self is by definition beyond the bounds of the inexorable clockwork of causation: "But though I cannot *know*, I can yet *think* freedom" (p. 28, emphasis in original).

Yet this move also had the unavoidable consequence of making the notion of person obscure. Since persons are, like all other real entities, things-in-themselves, their actual nature is beyond the reach of empirical (phenomenal) methods. In addition, as Locke had noted, persons are self-conscious and capable of comprehending limits to their empirical knowledge, including self-knowledge. That means one cannot know or understand these primary features of oneself, including the feeling of personal freedom and personal identity. What Kant says about freedom applies to all aspects of one's deepest feelings about self: "Morality does not, indeed, require that freedom should be *understood*, but only that it should not contradict itself, and so should at least allow of being *thought*" (p. 29, emphasis mine).

The German, later American, theologian Paul Tillich says that Kant's doctrine of the a priori categories is "a doctrine of human finitude" (1951, p. 82, n.7). It also reemerges in Freud's conception of the ego.

The Place of the Ego in Kant and Freud

Paul Ricoeur's "third reading" of Freud (1965) is a constructive attempt to bring phenomenological rigor to Freud's critique of religious thought. As such, it argues from an examination of consciousness as intentional action. This is un-Freudian (but not uninteresting). Freud rejected the phenomenological route because he rejected a psychology based on the examination of consciousness. This rejection is based upon his inability to solve the problem of quantity and quality. This is most evident in Freud's treatment of the problem of consciousness. His answer to that problem is to dismiss it. His dismissal results from his fundamental assumption that the real, external world consists only of masses in motion, that is quantitative factors.

Philosophers like Ricoeur see their task as the explication of consciousness: Freud turns round the other way. As Ricoeur puts it, Freud is an antiphenomenologist (1965, pp. 117–122, 424–425). Ricoeur limits Freud's antiphenomenology to the analysis of the unconscious in the metapsychological papers. It was present, in a more direct way, in the "Project" of 1895a: "[E]very psychological theory…must fulfill yet another major requirement. It should explain to us what we are aware of, the most puzzling fashion, through our 'consciousness'" (Freud 1895a, p. 307). This theorem is compatible with general phenomenological concerns. Freud's concluding clauses are not: "and since this consciousness knows nothing of what we have so far been assuming— quantities and neurones—it [the Project] should explain this lack of knowledge to us as well" (p. 308, my emphasis).

Science cannot rely upon examinations of consciousness for they can provide "neither complete nor trustworthy knowledge of the neuronal processes" (p. 308). Hence we must assume that basic psychological processes are not conscious. The grandest process of all, how quantities become qualities, remains mysterious. Our ordinary experience of self-awareness and the reflections of consciousness upon itself are misleading. Science must now explain how the conscious ego so often fails to perceive the "real world" of masses in motion. This assumption, and not ingrained pessimism, underlie Freud's portrait of phenomenal realms, especially those of culture, as illusory.

The following scheme represents similarities and differences between Kant and Freud on the status of the experienceing ego. These tables are simplified pictures of complex ideas. Yet they have one virtue. They show graphically that where Kant located the possibility of reason, within the realm of critical thought, Freud locates the possibility of reason in the body-ego. He says in *The Ego and the Id:* "If we come back once more to our scale of values, we shall have to say that not only what is lowest [the drives] but also what is highest [superego morality] in the ego can be unconscious. It is as if we were thus supplied with a proof of what we have just asserted of the conscious ego: that it is first and foremost a body-ego" (1923b, p. 27).

Ricoeur inspiredme to compose these tables. He claims that

The Status of the Ego
According to Kant

Actual world of things in themselves, hidden from direct human knowldege.	Objects, "the world," subject to the laws of science (*Pure Reason*).	Objects, "the world," subject to Transcendental Reason (realm of philosophy).
Noumena	*Phenomena:* persons as objects in space and time; rule of causality.	*Noumena:* persons as reasoning agents; as immortal souls; as known only to God.
	The *experiencing ego*, the self that is known.	The *transcendental ego*, the self that comprehends the ideas of Self, Duty, Immortality, Freedom, and God.

The Status of the Ego
According to Freud

Actual world Bare quantities that obey the thermodynamic laws.	*World of Experience* Awareness of qualities in consciousness (csc.); ego is a part of culture, tries to obey the reality principle.	*Inner World* Bare quantities within the brain/mind arena obey thermodynamic laws.
	Superego = voice of conscience, parents, religious authority.	Set of drives Ego/id matrix obeys the pleasure principle.
		Superego = voice of the id

Freud's instincts are like the Kantian thing-in-itself. Kant said we cannot know things-in-themselves because they are "never attained except in that which stands for and represents them" (Ricoeur 1965, p. 116). But Freud believed that the instincts were already known, indirectly, as the effects of hormonal quantities. He believed that they would become better known as physiology and neurology proceeded to explain the body-ego. Unlike things-in-themselves the instincts are knowable in principle. This allows one to hope for a scientific psychology: one can hope to know directly the springs of human action. Freud has a working knowledge of Kant's basic argument about the "unknowability" of things-in-themselves. He believed that his own discoveries contradicted Kant's argument: "There is nothing in the id that could be compared with negation; and we perceive with surprise an exception to the philosophical theorem that space and time are necessary forms of our mental acts" (1933a, p. 74).

The Status and Unity of the Self

We can see why Freud neither promoted a theory of the self nor ascribed value to the quest for a "unified self." (He also destroyed his metapsychological paper on consciousness.) Freud never doubted that the real world was one of quantities while our conscious experience is one of qualities. Among those conscious experiences is our notion of self. This notion can have no more status than any other idea or any other particular contents of consciousness. Consciousness is misleading. It presents a picture of unified self-experience that cannot be accurate.

Ricoeur is committed to philosophical beliefs that are opposed to Freud's. In Ricoeur's phenomenological-idealist orientation, the self is a primary object of investigation. Self-analysis and reflection is a royal method of inquiry. This orientation permits him to affirm claims made for religious faith and it grants a supreme ontological status to the self. By locating the self in the noumenal realm, Kant and Ricoeur justify speaking of an immortal soul, an entity that exhibits the essence of a person.

Freud does not. Freud rejected the traditional claims made for the primacy of consciousness. In rejecting this traditional starting point, ordinary issues of perception, reality testing, and the experience of psychic pain became obscure: for each of these complex behaviors requires the perception of qualities, and qualities are, by definition, the products of consciousness. Freud's focus upon unconscious mental life made it hard to account for conscious pain, an obvious task for a theory that claims to be therapeutic. After discussing Freud's comments on psychic pain, we can turn to the more basic epistemological issue: How does the ego manufacture qualitative experience out of quantitative stimuli? This question dominated Freud's unpublished masterpiece, the "Project" of 1895.

The Location and Alleviation of Psychic Pain

[T]he psychology of consciousness was no better capable of understanding the normal functioning of the mind than of understanding dreams. The data of conscious self-perception, which alone were at its disposal, have proved in every respect inadequate to fathom the profusion and complexity of the processes of the mind.... The hypothesis we have adopted of a psychical apparatus extended in space ... which gives rise to the phenomenon of consciousness only at one particular point and under certain conditions—his hypothesis has put us in a position to establish psychology on foundations similar to those of any other science, such as, for instance, physics. (Freud 1940a, pp. 195–196)

Freud hoped to alleviate psychic pain, but neither his general nor clinical theories explain it. He devoted a section of the "Project" to the problem of pain, but there and elsewhere he made only brief comments about it. This is not surprising. As the quotation above demonstrates, Freud never abandoned his assumption that the mental mechanism operates unconsciously. Only occasionally does it give rise to conscious experience, that is, to qualities. Because of this assumption. Freud's vocabulary of terms for emotions, both pleasant and unpleasant, is surprisingly small. He uses few terms other than *anxiety, mourning, depression, rage, guilt,* and *shame.* These concepts, usually defined in metapsychological terms, may designate unconscious affects of feelings.

These terms do not give one a rich description of the experience of shame, for example. Rather, Freud conceives of feelings as additional quantitative factors that may contribute inerita to other drive-based wishes. When Freud's patient, Dora, slapped Herr K for making a sexual advance, she did so because, "Wounded pride added to jealousy and to the conscious motives of common sense—it was too much" (1905b, p. 106).

The source of this relative lack of a theory of emotions is not hard to find. In his essays on hysteria Freud does not grant to conscious emotions causal efficacy: "Indeed, it is perhaps wrong to say that hysteria creates sensations by symbolization. It may be that *it does not take linguistic usage as its model at all, but that both hysteria and linguistic usage alike draw their material from a common source*" (1895d, p. 181, emphasis mine).

Phenomenologists investigate the qualitative structure of emotions (or as phenomenologists say, the structure of the appearance of emotions). They do so by examining their own (conscious) experiences and by examining ordinary terms for various emotions. Freud does not pursue this form of analysis. Rather, he sought to uncover the basic symbolizing process that produces *both* linguistic expressions of emotions and nonlinguistic expressions of emotions, such as hysterical symptoms. That basic symbolizing process occurs, of course, within the unconscious sectors of the mental mechanism, that is, within the inner world. Emotions experienced and emotions expressed are but signs of an internal state: "Instincts are forces that originate in the organism, and enter consciousness only through their quantitative and ideational representations. The "affect charge" is the quantitative representative of the instinct... feeling as well as emotion—peripheral discharge—are but manifestations of it" (Rapaport 1950, p. 168).

A complete psychoanalytic explanation of an emotion, therefore, reveals how the manifest experience is the product of latent and unconscious instinctual conflicts. Given this strict requirement, Freud's extraordinary statement about instinctual anxiety, that we cannot understand it, makes sense. In the structural theory Freud pictured the ego confronting three different opponents: the outside world, the id, and the demands of the superego. Since the ego struggles on all three fronts, we may say that it experiences three kinds of anxiety, because anxiety is "the expression of a retreat from danger" (1923b, p. 56). The external world threatens castration; the superego threatens to impose a sentence of guilt; but what can the ego fear from instinctual upsurge? "We know that the fear is of being overwhelmed or annihilated, but it cannot be grasped analytically" (1923b, p. 57). It cannot be grasped analytically because the fear of instinctual upsurge is the fear of losing control of one's consciousness, as is the fear of death. Freud's effort to explain both types of fear (e.g., pp. 57–59) is a measure of his commitment to his initial model of the mental apparatus. Hence he concludes that the fear of death is a response to the superego (a "real" primary structure), not to the loss of the self (a secondary content).

Psychic Pain, Self, and Empathy

A further consequence of Freud's orientation is that classical psychoanalytic theory has few treatises on either psychic pain or the self. (Again, by classical I mean before recent developments in "Self Psychology" and other contemporary schools.) When theoreticians addressed the problem of pain, they were forced to speak of a self. "The self, in contrast to the many cathexes of the self-presentations, is the result of the ego's pooling of an averaging of these cathexes to form a single overall constant cathexis" (L. H. Spiegel 1966, p. 76).

In the same way, Freud never uses the term *empathy* in anything other than a simple sense of imagining the "amount of innervation" a particular thought requires. For example, in his treatise on jokes (1905c), he says that humor and its expression, laughter, must be understood in terms of the discharge of psychic tension. Caricatures are funny because: "I am being spared the increased expenditure of the solemn restraint. The difference between the two states is a quantitative one, and the 'release' of that difference issues in laughter" (1905c, pp. 200–201).

The inadequacies of this point of view (based on classical libido theory) are obvious and well documented. It leaves mysterious the gap between the domain of force and the domain of language. It ascribes personalities to subsystems of the individual. It perpetuates an abreaction model of insight (e.g., B. Apfelbaum 1965; Don Swanson 1977; Roy Schafer 1976).

Freud's economic theory of psychic pain does not permit one to conceive of a psychoanalytic theory of the self. Kohut's efforts to meld his clinical theory of self-pathology with the economic point of view in his *The Analysis of the Self* (1971) were finally unsuccessful. Hence in his next major text, *The Restoration of the Self* (1977), he abandoned the economic formulations presented in his earlier book. Like Kurt Goldstein (1957), Kohut elaborated a phenomenological description of psychic pain, especially narcissistic injuries, and he emphasized the role of empathy in development and treatment.

These differences between Kohut and Freud are not accidental; nor are the philosophical differences between Freud and the others accidental. Ricoeur says that Freud believes the real world is a world shorn of God. It is shorn of all qualities, including those elemental ones of warmth, color, and smell that dominate the infant's earliest relationship to the world. Of course, Freud believes that there must be some relationship between the structure of the real world and our perception of it. The nature of this correspondence remains unknowable. He repeated these claims almost unchanged from their original form in the "Project" in his last theoretical statement:

> [B]ehind the attributes (qualities) of the object under examination which are presented directly to our perception, we have to discover something else which is more independent of the particular receptive capacity of our sense organs and which approximates more closely to what may be supposed to be the real state of affairs. *We have no hope of being able to reach the latter itself, since it is evident that everything new that we have inferred must nevertheless be translated back into the language of our perceptions.* (1940a, p. 196, emphasis mine)

But is this true? Does it make sense to speak of a part of nature (and a part of ourselves) that we can never reach directly? The theory of perception that Freud prosecuted in the 1895 treatise is here reasserted with even more authority. Consciousness is inherently limited. It is we who impose upon bare quantities the range of qualities exhibited in conscious experience.

Freud on the Primacy of Hallucination

Freud's attempt to adapt Kant's philosophy to empirical psychology was not unique. Like many other scientists, Freud obeyed Kant's strictures on the possibility of transcendental knowledge. Freud was perpared to admit that human beings could not escape "constructing" some aspects of their experience as Kant explained in his *Critique of Pure Reason*. Of more importance was Freud's decision to employ the neurological speculations of his teachers and fellow researchers in Brücke's Institute (Peter Amacher 1965, passim). In his "Project" of 1895 we see Freud state metapsychological principles that underlie all his later speculations. The most pertinent of these is his account of the nursing infant. (This topic came to dominate psychoanalytic speculations, particularly those of the English school.) Following Meynert's neurological theory, Freud tried to explain how the infant learns to recognize its mother and to distinguish her presence from remembered "representations" of her. The infant accomplishes this first step in reality testing by discovering that wishful representations of mother do not satisfy its hunger pains. The pains persist and this persistence of pain becomes the first signal that representations in memory differ from actual perceptions. Pain drives the infant to search for differences between its wishful ideas and its percepts.

Otto Fenichel repeated this basic theorem in his textbook on psychoanalytic theory (1945, pp. 16–17). Robert Holt (1976) shares Fenichel's opinion but laments the notion of "immaculate perception" that this theorem entails. Holt believes that Freud's theory of perception is too close to Cartesian metaphysics and too far away from a "constructionist one" (see J. G. Schimek 1975; M. Feffer 1982). These authors reject Freud's minimal emphasis upon the ego's role in constructing representations of the external world. They prefer the constructionism of Piaget and phenomenological psychologists who assert that the ego constructs aspects of what we believe is the "really out there real." For example, Robert Holt rejects Freud's assumption that there can be unconstructed perception of reality as it is. He complains that Freud accepted the nineteenth-century version of naive realism which holds that perception is not a conflicted behavior. One perceives what is there. Holt disagrees: "But Freud, unlike Piaget, treated perception as invariant, undergoing no such successive developmental changes as memory" (p. 79). Among Freud's implicit assumptions, Holt says, is that all "percipient organisms naturally and easily form phenomenal copies of external reality merely by being exposed to it, though young human beings, at least, also tend to distort the veridical imput," (p. 81) and "the assumption of a single kind of reality, namely the kind Freud himself and his mentors reported—a notably Euclidean, Appollonian world of pellucid air, clean sunlight, and crisply articulated, differentiated forms moving against stable backgrounds in which the real always had the property of simple location, and object constancy was complete and reliable" (p. 81).

Why Holt Cannot Be Entirely Correct

I think Holt's criticism is well taken and highlights an important aspect of Freud's thought. His complaint is misplaced. He should complain that Freud did not maintain his naive realism at sufficient length. Instead, Freud gives very little room to the veridical in perception. He assumes that the "inner world" dominates perception. My difference with Holt is not about Freud's theory of perception but about Holt's replacement. Holt ascribes too much authority and too much weight to wishful thinking when he asserts that wishful thinking can easily override perceptual processes. This presumes the issue at hand: that wishes can easily override perception. If "object constancy" refers to the reliability of human beings to anticipate our needs and be there when we want them, then this term has little to do with perception.

The Camera Theory of Perception

Holt's complaint is accurate in the sense that Freud does hold the usual "camera" theory of verdical perception, as did most scientists of his time. Freud's version of this theory is more subtle than most. He asserts that human infants initially cannot distinguish wishes from perceptions, ideas from reality, and memory from observation. This is not a Kantian proposition. Kant said that one can perceive qualities in the phenomenal world because human cognition is constrained by the inexorable workings of the a priori categories, e.g., space, time, and causality. This is not a state of hallucination; it is ignorance of ultimate causes and our ultimate nature. Kant says *we can know* our proximate nature, just as *we can know* the proximate causes of our behavior. By assuming an intrapsychic point of view, Freud made the proximate causes of behavior themselves suspect. For example, our conscious motives as proximate causes of our actions are knowable, but they are products of causes and distant motives that stretch back into the unknowable unconscious.

From Hallucination to Frustration to the Chastised Ego

Before Freud, authorities attempted to explain hallucinatory experience, including dreams and psychosis, as deviations from normal processes of accurate perceptions of reality. Freud reversed this usual explanation. Hallucinations, he says, are primary both in the development of the individual from infancy to adulthood, and structurally, in the development from the ego-id matrix to full ego maturation. The accurate perception of reality occurred later, and then, only in part, and only in the strongest of persons. Freud explained the ubiquity of religious illusions by the ubiquity of persons who obey their original impulse to hallucinate the presence of needed objects.

Freud's shortest and most complete account of this theory is in sections 10–13 of the "Project" of 1895.[9] In those sections we learn that the primitive ego, a mass of highly cathected neurones, occupies a place midway between two equally dangerous forces. These dangerous forces correspond to upsurges in energy, which Freud names "Q," using the Greek letter to represent quantity and "$Q\acute{\eta}$" to represent raw energy transformed into bound psychical energy. I use "Q" to designate quantity and "Qh" to designate transformed energy.

The ego must battle against influxes "Q" from both external and internal sources. We can diagram the ego's location between these two sources as follows:

External World   *Inner World*

Primitive Ego Apparatus

Source of external stimuli that impinge upon the person, then upon the ego.	Set of neurones filled with energy (Q) changed into psychic energy (Qh).	Body is source of internal Quantity or "Q" that impinge upon the ego.

According to this chart, the primitive ego cannot distinguish the source of raw quality (Q) that impinges upon it. Influxes of Q from either the external world, such as extreme cold, or the body, such as drive upsurges, threaten the ego with identical dangers. Both kinds of upsurge threaten the delicate equilibrium established within the primitive ego.

Initially, the organism attempts to remove itself from the increase in tension (caused by an influx of "raw Q") by the usual expedients: flight or fight. This may work sometimes with external stimuli; it does not affect those coming from the inner world. The ego's inability to escape Q arising from the internal world, compared with its usual ability to escape Q arising from the external world, makes primitive reality testing possible. If I cannot escape the danger it must be an internal one. (If I cannot flee the danger with muscular exertion then it must arise from the inner world.)

To combat this rise in internal Q the ego happens upon the mechanism of repression. Repression is an archaic form of flight where representations of internal stimuli are denied access to motility and to consciousness. Hallucination became a key concept in this initial metapsychological theory because it represents the immediate consequence of the primitive ego's reflexive response to internal needs.

Freud reasons that following an "experience of satisfaction," like nursing, the infantile ego learns to associate the pain-pleasure sequence with a mnemonic representation of the breast. When similar needs occur they cause the level of Q to rise; this produces a rise in Qh felt as hunger pains. These currents of Qh retrace the routes of facilitation that now exist between similar memories of "hunger" and representations of the object that satisfied them, the breast: "Now, when the state of urgency or wishing reappears, the cathexis [Qh] will also pass over on to the two memories, and will activate them. Probably the mnemic image of the object will be the first to be affected by the *wishful activation*" (1895a, p. 319, emphasis in original).

This formulation serves Freud well. He uses it in his book on dreams where he explains why even normal persons believe in the hallucinations that animate dreams (chapter 7, 1900a). Freud's conclusion is momentous: "I do not doubt that in the first instance this wishful activation will produce the same thing as a perception—namely a *hallucination*" (p. 319, emphasis in original). Freud was very fond of this theory of hallucination. While it is clear and distinct, depending as it does upon the notion of a reflex arc, it is also revolutionary.

Pavlov had used classical conditioning to shape his dogs' normal reflexes: smelling meat gives rise to salivation. Freud describes an internal state in which hunger, appetite, representation of food, and hallucination are equivalent behaviors. In other words, the theory of primary process thinking holds that "thinking" and "hallucination" are of the same stuff and operate in the same manner as other, overt behaviors. This notion is as radical as Watsonian behaviorism.

Hallucination and Pain as Education to Reality

Freud pursued these thoughts to their logical conclusion. If hallucination is the original state of human being, then "reality testing," the ability to distinguish hallucinations from perceptions, is a secondary achievement. To acquire it one must pass through a lengthy education to reality in which one suffers a series of disillusionments. If hallucination is the primary state, it follows that the infant's initial experiences are painful: "[I]f, while it is in a *wishful state*, it newly cathects the memory of an object and then sets discharge in action; in that case satisfaction must fail to occur, because the object is not real but is present only as an imaginary idea" (1895a, pp. 324–325, emphasis in original). To avoid the "immense unpleasure" that such behavior would bring, the organism must learn to distinguish two kinds of stimuli, those arising from the correct perception of the breast and those arising from wishful representations of it. In the same way, the organism must learn to distinguish perceiving a "hostile" object from imagining it to be present.

Omega Neurones and Indications of Reality

How does the infant's rudimentary ego accomplish this task of discrimination? To explain this ability in detail Freud elaborated a three-level model of the mind with which he attempted to account for all psychological functioning. This model is based on Freud's neurological training and his own speculations.

The following summarizes Freud's model of the mental mechanism elaborated in the "Project." The arrows represent the direction of incoming stimuli (Q) that impinge upon the ego system. The "Phi" neurones correspond to receptor cells, like those of the tongue, or skin, which accept and then transmit sensations to the next set of nervous structure, the "Psi" system which corresponds to memory cells that "store" some part of this excitation. The final set of cells, the "omega" or "w" cells, correspond to memory cells that give rise to qualitative, conscious experience.

Stimuli impinging upon	Phi System	Psi System	Omega System
Q from the body and the external world. ⟶	Admits Q into the mental apparatus; = the processes of ⟶ perception.	Hinder Q: store Qh in the mind = the processes of ⟶ memory and recollection.	Not premeable to Qh; respond only to period motion; ⟶ seat of consciousness.

In general, the intensity of stimuli decreases as they pass through the first two neural "sieves," the phi and psi systems. Although Freud revised this schema (1895a, p. 310, n. 3), it reflects his general claim that as neural structures become more and more like a mind, they require less and less energy (less Qh). This model anticipates the general theorem in information sciences which says that high information systems may use low energy to do what high energy and low information systems accomplish with more labor.

Freud explained reality testing by referring to the structure of the "omega" (w) neurones. Reality testing names the ego's ability to distinguish actual perceptions of external objects from merely imagined objects. In the language of the "Project," this ability must derive from an actual difference in the type of stimuli that impinge ultimately *upon and from* the seat of consciousness, the "w" neurones. He reasoned that if all external perceptions excite these "w" neurones, but internal representations, even if hallucinated, do *not*, then "The information of the discharge from w is thus the indication of quality of the reality for [Psi]" (p. 325, emphasis in original).

Freud remains true to his quantitative thesis by explaining that internal discharge of Q could cause the w neurones to discharge if the initial quantity is *large enough* to pass through the first two layers of the cortical mass. It is only the gradual structuralization of the ego, its ability to bring about inhibition of the intensity of internal quantities, that prevents these initial representations from gaining energy sufficient to discharge the w neurones: "It is accordingly inhibition by the ego which makes possible a criterion for distinguishing between perception and memory" (p. 326, emphasis in original).

This additional theorem allows Freud to give an elegant account of the hallucinatory quality of dreams, and other states, like severe intoxication, where a wounded or constrained ego seems incapable of carrying out its usual inhibition of internal quantities (pp. 335–343). Hallucinations occur in these states because the w neurones are subject to excessive stimuli and thus discharge, the latter being the sign or indication of reality (p. 327).

Freud makes these distinctions with vigor; as he said to his confidante, Fliess, the whole argument of the "Project" sometimes seems to walk by itself, so persuasive are Freud's conjectures. Yet two questions force themselves upon one. Is the doctrine of the neurones coherent? Is it a plausible account of perception? These are not small questions, nor will I answer them completely. But, by examining Freud's reasoning about these important elements, we can gain some ground on the less complex problem of the primacy of hallucination.

What the w Neurones Contribute to the System: Periodic Oscillations

What the w neurones contribute to Freud's model of the mind is nothing less than the capacity for qualitative experience. Freud never abandoned his belief that the real, external world was one of bare quantities set in perpetual motion, obeying the immutable laws of the physical universe. The world of human experience, the world we all believe is real, is full of qualitative encounters. We enjoy warm baths but not hot weather, cool drinks but not cold days, vigorous exercise but not arduous labor.

We live within the bounds of numerous occasions in which the qualities of pain and pleasure intermingle, as Kant said in his *Anthropology*. Freud attempts to link his speculations on the mechanics of the brain with our immediate knowledge of the sensuous surface of human life. This forced him to create a concept that would bridge the gap that exists between these two distinct realms. He assigned this considerable task to the w neurones. What they contribute, therefore, to Freud's model of the mind is their ability to make his neurological theory relevant to ordinary experience. What they contribute to the psychological system (which is equivalent to what he later terms the ego) is periodic oscillations.

Further, Freud holds that even internal Q (actually Qh) may cause the w system to discharge if the ego (the psi system) fails to restrict the total amount of Qh "free" in the system at any one time (see Holt 1962). How do the w neurones accomplish their crucial task? To answer this question Freud adds another assumption:

> I can see only one way out of this difficulty: a revision of our fundamental hypothesis about the passage of Qh. So far I have regarded it only as the transference of Qh from one neurone to another. But it must have still another characteristic, a temporal nature....I speak of this as period for short. Thus I shall assume that all the resistance of the contact-barriers applies only to the transference of Q, but that the period of the neuronal motion in transmitted without inhibition in all directions, as though it were a process of induction. (p. 310)

What is the source of these periods? "Everything points to the sense organs, whose qualities seem to be represented precisely by different periods of neuronal motion" (p. 310). "Periodic motion" seems to correspond to something like the rhythm, tone, or characteristic oscillation of the neural wave. As such, it is another dimension of the actual energy pattern that impinges upon the system. The sense organs receive such patterns from internal surfaces, the body, as well as external ones. It follows that proprioception, sensations of one's interior body, includes the registration of periodic motions as well.

In order to keep his periodic theory intact, Freud has to add the proviso that periodic motions (what I term "polytonal excitations") *cannot be stored* in any part of the system: "The transmission of quality is not durable; it leaves no traces behind and cannot be reproduced" (p. 310). He must say this or forfeit the single criterion with which he distinguishes the perception of "actual events," of which we become aware through the operation of our sense organs and mere thought.

The w neurones and the period theory perform extended service in his subsequent account of consciousness; for consciousness is always a state of neural sensitivity to qualities (pp. 311–312). Indeed, as we saw above, it was the fact that *consciousness is the awareness of qualities,* and not quantities, that required scientific psychologists to abandon a phenomenological starting point. As we have seen, Freud's metaphysics required him to affirm that the real world is one of quantities, not qualities.

Returning to the Problem of Hallucination: Periods or Not?

Returning to the problem of hallucination we find a major difficulty. Does the experience of hallucination include the discharge of the w neurones, with their periodic stimuli? Freud's answer is both yes and no. First, yes: the experience of hallucination is one in which the ego believes that the ideas appearing before it indicate an actual perception, complete with subtle qualities. Since qualities and the like are the result of w discharge, and since w discharge is nothing less than the release of periodic, or polytonic, oscillations, it follows that hallucinations are the result of w discharge. But this cannot be so. First, hallucinations depend upon the functions of memory. Memory is the result of the storage of stimuli in the psi system in the form of traces on the neural substrate. For the w neurones to discharge while not in the presence of qualitative excitations, they must manifest the capacity to retain a "charge" of periodic oscillations. In other words, at least sometimes w neurones must be impermeable and hence able to record or register traces of earlier periodic waves. But Freud had already said this was not true of these neurones.

This is a costly contradiction, not remarked upon because Freud separates his account of the w neurones from his account of hallucination. Indeed, it is not accidental that in the latter discussion (pp. 317–324) he makes no mention of the whole period theorem. Instead, he only says that given sufficient intensity of Qh, and an ego that cannot inhibit them, the w system will be stimulated in turn, and this stimulation constitutes the biological signal of a perception.

Neither does Freud invoke the concept of periodic motion, nor the entire w system, in his account of hallucinations during sleep: "the primary memory of a perception is always a hallucination and ... only inhibition by the ego has taught us never to cathect a perceptual image in such a way that it is able to transfer [Qh] retrogressively to psi" (p. 339).

He says again that hallucinations (that carry with them indications of reality) occur whenever a sufficiently large amount of Qh (later termed "unbound cathexis") is loosed upon the dormant system. The perceptual neurones are cathected by the charge coming from the mnemonic neurones. In turn, the mnemonic neurones receive indications of quality from the discharge of perceptual neurones; hence hallucination. "This explanation is further supported by the circumstances that in dreams the vividness of the hallucination is directly proportionate to the importance—that is to the quantitative cathexis—of the idea concerned" (p. 339). Suddenly we are back to the original theorem of hallucination in which the w theory and periodic oscillations do not appear. Neither do they appear in Freud's later paper on hallucinations in dreams and overt pathological states (1917d).

Freud cannot have it both ways. The w neurones furnish indication of reality, that is, perceptions of quality, but the w neurones cannot store the periodic motions unique to them. Yet hallucinations occur when the w system is hypercathected by a powerful wish (as in hysteria) or when the ego system is at very low ebb (as in sleep or in psychotic states).

Freud's Revision: Hallucination Again

A few months after he had given the entire draft of the "Project" to his confidante, Wilhelm Fliess, Freud sent him a short revision (SE 1:388–391, *Origins*, pp. 140–145). In it he attempts to recast theory of hallucination, "whose explanation always raised difficulties" (p. 389) by reordering the sequence of the three neural strata and placing the omega neurones between the perceptual and the mnemonic neurones.

Freud also resorts to another stratagem. To account for the difference between quality and quantity, he supposes that there are two kinds of sense organs: "I start from the two kinds of nerve endings. The free ones receive only quantity and conduct it to psi by summation— that is, to affect w. In this connection the neuronal motion retains its genuine and monotonous qualitative characteristics" (p. 388). The other kinds of nerve ending "do not conduct quantity but the qualita-

tive peculiar to them; they add nothing to the amount in the psi neurones, but merely put these neurones into a state of excitation" (p. 388).
Freud illustrated the notion of two types of nerve endings when he wrote to Fliess. Regarding Fliess's nasal theories of disease, Freud says there must be two kinds of sense organs in the nose: "the *qualitative* organ for olfactory stimuli may be Schneider's membrane and the *quantitative* organ (distinct from this) may be the corpora cavernosa" (p. 390, emphasis mine).
The following represents Freud's revision of his neural theory:

	Sense Organs	Neural Systems
External stimuli impinge upon the mental apparatus.	1st Type: conduct Qh (monotonic sensations).	Phi Omega Psi Neurones
	2nd Type: conduct periods (polytonic sensations).	Phi Omega Psi Neurones

If this new diagram is accurate, the omega cells must respond to both types of stimuli: monotonic and polytonic; otherwise there is no way monotonic currents of Qh could induce consciousness, since consciousness is always the consciousness of qualities, a capacity of the omega system alone. Freud appears to agree for he says, "There are, so to say, three ways in which the neurones affect one another: (1) they transfer quantity to one another, (2) they transfer quality to one another, (3) they have an exciting effect on one another in accordance with certain rules" (pp. 388–389).
Of his many laconic accounts of complex processes this is among the most obscure. Freud appears to say that any of the three neural systems may affect any of its neighbors in these three ways. If this is so it allows him to account for perception: "the perceptual processes would eo ipso...involve consciousness" (p. 389) because they lie next door to the omega system. "The psi processes would in themselves be unconscious and would only subsequently acquire a secondary, artificial consciousness" (p. 389) because they stand last, after the omega system.
This new arrangement of the three neural systems allows Freud to give a new account of hallucinations. Hallucinations occur when a "backward movement of excitation" is transmitted to the omega system, not to psi. If this is so, then the psi system is capable of either (1) transferring "quality" (polytonic) excitations to the omega system, or

(2) exciting the omega system such that the latter responds, like a sounding board, with polytonic discharges. These, in turn, are perceived by the psi system as indications of perception of qualities and hence external reality. The second of these two propositions is impossible. Theory tells us that omega system cannot store polytonic excitations; it can only respond to their presence with discharge that functions as a signal to the psi system. If the omega system cannot store polytonic excitations, it follows that the monotonic excitations coming from psi *are transformed into polytonic ones* within the omega system. But this too seems impossible. For the monotonic chord, as it were, carries no information for such a leap in complexity (it also violates the second law of thermodynamics, which Freud himself had sworn to uphold [1918b, p. 116]). Consequently, if the psi system can excite the omega neurones to fire and so produce hallucinatory experiences, the psi system itself must be able to transmit polytonic excitations; that is qualities. This would seem to be Freud's reasoning when he says, above, that all neurones may transfer quality to one another.

But can the psi neurones transfer qualities, according to the rules by which Freud constructed the "Project"? Yes, they can transfer qualities, if by that one means that they might serve as conduits for the passage of such excitations *through* the system. But, in the case of hallucination, it is not merely a matter of transmitting actual polytonic excitations, it is also a matter of *storing* them; for by definition there are no actual polytonic excitations to be transmitted. The "Project" requires us to assume that hallucinations arise from within the system. But where?

By simple elimination we can prove that they must arise from within the psi system. For polytonic excitations arise from the phi system. First, the phi system is the most permeable of all the systems, and so it is least able to store information. Second, during sleep and other altered states, the phi neurones operate at very low levels. Third, hallucinations, again by definition, are not instigated by perceptions, but by ideas. Nor can hallucinations arise from within the omega system itself since, again, it cannot store excitations, nor could it excite itself. It follows that the psi system somehow stores a large measure of polytonic excitations, then transmits these excitations to the omega system. One might say that the psi system can store polytonic excitations, representations of quality, under extraordinary conditions which are yet to be understood. But this will not do either since Freud wishes to account for the normal and universal experience of hallucinations during dreams. (See the topographic accounts of this same problem in

Freud 1900a, chapter 7, and 1917d; see also Merton Gill 1963, chapter 4.) If hallucinations were atypical, then an atypical functioning of the neural systems might account for them. But hallucinations are common. Hence Freud must say that the psi system is capable of storing polytonic excitations normally and does so repeatedly in all well-functioning persons. This raises another problem. If the psi system stores polytonic excitations and these are indicators of reality (since they represent the influx of external stimuli into the mental apparatus), then every recollection should carry with it residues of perceptual—that is hallucinatory—experience. Freud cannot admit this, nor could he in his later topographic and structural theories in which he places consciousness and reality testing in systems distinct from those of memory and recollection. More so, as he says in the "Project," "Remembering brings about de norma nothing that has the peculiar character of perceptual quality" (pp. 308–309). Indeed, it was for this reason that he felt required to "summon up courage to assume that there is a third system of neurones—w" (p. 309).

I do not see how Freud can save the system. The tact that he abandoned it and actively suppressed knowledge of its existence suggests he did not feel it succeeded. Yet the "Project" was a valuable exercise. All Freud's later published works on metapsychology have their roots in this early treatise. Among the doctrines that survived was that of the primacy of hallucination. It survived, I believe, because while Freud gave up the attempt to forge a neurological model of perception, he retained his philosophical belief in the radical dichotomy between qualities and quantities.

This is the doctrine that Noy and Fenichel reaffirm in their descriptions of perception as a "constructive" process in which the mental apparatus adds data to incoming stimuli. They use different physical models of perception. Noy refers to computers, and Fenichel refers to a vague electrical machine. Both assume that perception is a mechanical process in which perceivers add information to the "bare sense data" striking their sense organs. Or as Noy says, "The mental apparatus, in its various cognitive functions...scarcely operates on the raw data of input, but rather with the various schemata *constructed by the organizing processes*" (p. 133, emphasis mine). The cost of maintaining these particular mechanical models of the mind is very high. One must perpetuate a distinction between qualities and quantities. This, in turn, hobbles attempts to construct a psychoanalytic aesthetics because it makes mysterious the external world of sensous surfaces. Indeed, it makes them products of an internal process of which we can have no direct knowledge.

Why These Assumptions Produce Mythical Prototypes

In addition, Freud's assumptions also produce what one might call "mythical prototypes." Why? That is, why does Freud's adherence to a well-conceived epistemology, founded upon the most advanced biology of his day, issue in the overt mythologies of his late texts on the primary instincts? I will state my answer here and argue for it below.

Freud's commitment to the quantity–quality distinction is a conceptual one, not one based upon a careful analysis of the actual experience of vision, or hearing, or any other sense. To revert back to Kant's discussion of actual antagonisms, Freud believed he was describing actual antagonists; I argue he was not. Freud believed he was describing a truth of nature when he distinguished between our experience of qualities and the "real world" of bare quantities. Actually, he was affirming a particular metaphysics just as the Renaissance preachers affirmed a particular metaphysics in their sermons to the Pope.

The pair of terms, *quality–quantity*, has numerous cousins. Similar pairs of terms are *light–dark, good–evil, person–god, beginning-of-time–end-of-time*, and *man–woman*. When used in these sets, each term is defined in opposition to the other. Each member of the pair is antithetical to the other; there is no shading of edges or shared boundaries. In Kant's terms, the pair *quantity–quality* does not designate an actual antagonism, like love and hate. Rather it designates logical contraries; quantity and quality are defined by their negation of each other.[10]

This is not true of the actual antagonisms Freud elucidated in his clinical papers: love and hate added together do not make nothing; they make ambivalence. To use yet another metaphor, true antagonisms, like love and hate, imply contrary actions while logical contraries imply contrary points of view. To love someone or something is to want to be near it, or if away, to approach it, to move into its orbit. As Buber says, when I love persons everything shines in their light. To hate someone or something is to want to be away from it, or if that is impossible, to isolate it and to destroy it. Love and hate are emotions; *they move* us to perform particular actions (cf. J. De Rivera 1977).

This is not true of conceptual antitheses. As we have seen in Freud, quantity and quality are, in part, the same phenomenon viewed from distinct points of view. Here we use point of view in an extended philosophic sense since there is no actual difference in perception, it being impossible to perceive "mere quantities." There is only a difference in conception: Freud's assumptions require him to assert that the "real world" is one of quantities, not qualities. What is true of qualities in not true of quantities. For example, according to Freud quantities are bare, monotonous, and primary, while qualities are rich, polytonic, and secondary. In itself there is nothing pernicious about this kind of theorizing. On the contrary, it would appear to be a universal mode of reflection. The French anthropologist, Claude Lévi-Strauss investigated antithetical pairs in many essays on binary thought patterns. He and his numerous followers have alerted us to the ubiquity of such thought.[11]

Robert Holt also noted that one can find similar conceptual antitheses throughout Freud's metapsychology: "As the tabulation grew, I began to feel that this simple scheme was in fact the principal latent structure of Freud's thought, an underlying state of ordered ideational conflicts with ramifications into almost all aspects of his intellectual life" (1978, p. 53). Holt's discovery is not surprising, nor is it distressing. When Freud wrote philosophical pieces, he wrote as a philosopher and used binary categories much as philosophers do.

An illustration of such binary pairs occurs in Friedrich Nietzche's famous essay on the origins of Greek drama, *The Birth of Tragedy* (1872). Nietzsche says Greek drama rose out of the union of two antithetical qualities in Greek culture: their insight into the terrors of nature and their love of reason. "The Greek knew and felt the terror and horror of existence. That he might endure this terror at all, he had to interpose between himself and life the radiant dream-birth of the Olympians. That overwhelming dismay in the face of the titanic powers of nature, the Moira enthroned inexorably over all knowledge ... all this was again and again overcome by the Greeks with the aid of the Olympian *middle world of art;* or at any rate it was veiled and withdrawn from sight" (emphasis his, 1872, p. 962). Like Winnicott, whom I cited above, Nietzsche also locates culture, the middle world of art, between two distinct ontological realms. Both authors elaborate a dualistic theory of poetry.

But these poetic claims, persuasive in their rhetorical power and passionate because of the intensity Nietzsche brings to them, are not good clinical theory. For clinical theory is similar to historical reconstruction: both require one to investigate the nitty gritty qualities of an actual moment in a patient's life. These actual moments, except in severe, compulsive, neurotic conditions, are never as single valued and simple as a binary theory would suggest.

In recognition of the subtlety and complexity of actual human experience, Freud advanced the notion of overdetermination, just as later analysts advanced similar concepts, like Waelder's notion of "multiple function" (1962). In these clinical instances Freud and

Waelder state that the analyst *cannot deduce* the meaning of a patient's dream, for example, by using metaphysical principles. Rather, analyst and patient attempt to see how each particular detail of the dream fits together with this patient's particular life at this particular moment. Freud did not follow these rules when he investigated cultural artifacts. Rather, in those cases where he wished to illustrate the validity of clinical discoveries, he "applied" deductive theory to the subject at hand. One of such applications in addition to those discussed above, is that mythical propositions (those which rely upon the prosecution of conceptual antitheses) cannot be validated—nor invalidated—because they have no direct reference to the actual world. In a strict sense, mythical propositions are irrefutable.

In addition, Freud's assumption of radical difference between two entities, qualities and quantities, makes it difficult to assess "mixed" cases, since by definition the two types of stimuli are unlike one another.

Irrefutable Claims

Lest the reader believe I now propose to reveal that all of Freud's propositions are nothing but mythical ideas masquerading as science, I note that we are discussing his epistemology, not his clinical theory. (See Freud's fondness for binary thinking in "Analysis Terminable and Interminable" [1937c].) Using Freud's terms, we criticize his metapsychology, not his psychology. The former, he termed his "witch," the latter we may term the "substance" of his scientific discoveries, e.g., the reality of repression, transference, infantile sexuality, the meaning of dreams, the place of fantasy in mental life, and the primacy of oedipal wishes. However, some of his metapsychological formulations are mythical, and it is those that underlie his theory of sublimation, and consequently his aesthetics.

Mythical utterances that are based upon a radical dichotomous set are irrefutable because they are covert tautologies. For example, when some Christians assert that Jesus was sinless and perfect they are not reporting the results of a battery of psychological tests; nor are they referring to a reading of the New Testament which substantiates their claims. Rather, because Jesus is the Son of God, He is blameless, perfect, and free from sin in every manner. His sinlessness is a characteristic of his nature; it is to be asserted and understood, not verified. A demand for verification implies one doubts the Gospel and that can only be the product of incomplete understanding. (Hence prayer and other acts of contrition may be necessary to receive extraordinary gifts of insight into His true nature.)

A tautology is necessarily true, if one understands the meaning of its terms. It is true, even if one does not believe that the terms, in themselves, refer to actual objects. For example, non-Christians can understand the meaning of the utterance: (1) Jesus was sinless. One can affirm the truth of this proposition even if one does not believe that Jesus was an actual person, nor that the term *sin* refers to actual events. Rather, as Dan Sperber (1974) points out, one affirms sentence (1) is true by affirming sentence (2), "Jesus was sinless is true." One can affirm (2) is true, given the usual meaning of the terms *Jesus* and *sinless*. For those who wish to understand how other people can believe proposition (1), the task becomes one of understanding what *sinless* means, that is, understanding sentence (2). This task evolves into the new task of understanding the diverse meanings of the word *sin* and its origins in Jewish and other Near Eastern religious traditions (see Ricoeur's attempt to do this [1967]).

But, even those people who have the talent and time to carry out such an investigation must arrive at a point where in order to affirm (1) they must affirm the existence of a radical gap between their ordinary experiences of temporally bound existence and the absolute claims asserted in sentence (1). All I know immediately, as a creature of this world, is myself bounded by ignorance. I can only affirm sentence (1) as a matter of faith. Sentence (1) is affirmed by persons who assume that there are two realms, one limited by time and space, the other a realm of possible experience that is antithetical to it. Hence Ricoeur says, in his own voyage of discovery, that the gap which separates ordinary goodness from sinlessness is a radical ontological gap in our very nature; "It can be said, in very general terms, that guilt designates the subjective moment in fault as sin is its ontological moment. Sin designates the real situation of man before God" (1967, p. 101).

Ricoeur is correct, whether one affirms Christian teachings or not. Like his predecessor, the great French philosopher and theologian Blaise Pascal (1623–1662), Ricoeur argues that the religious question always involves risking intellectual certainty to win emotional and existential goods. One can agree with this psychological proposition without agreeing to join him in the leap to the Christian shore. However, we do not wish scientific propositions to be issues of faith. Certainly Freud never suggested there was any need to perform a leap of faith in order to comprehend the values and truths of psychoanalytic discoveries. He says repeatedly that the ideal attitude for both students and patients is detached, but interested, skepticism. The gap between the true believer and the empirical investigator remains unbridgeable. Attempts to cross it by way of language always require one to use paradoxical formulations. It is not happenstance that at the heart of Jesus's teachings we find paradox upon paradox (He who does not lose his life cannot gain it), and parable upon parable (For it is only at the End of Time that the full meaning of his mission will be understood).

How to Generate a Paradox: Sublimation

In contrast to religious paradoxes, those that bedevil part of Freud's metapsychology are products of conceptual confusion. (Given the complexity of his tasks we ought not to be surprised that even a genius falls into errors.) Among these is the concept of sublimation, an element of the libido theory that remains one of the gaps in the metapsychology (J. Laplanche and J. B. Pontalis, 1967, p. 465). Sublimation is also one of Freud's paradoxes for it entails the proposition that libido can become desexualized. Since libido is by definition composed of sexual energies, a desexualized form of it would seem to be impossible.

A paradox occurs when true premises, arranged in a valid argument, produce a conclusion that is necessarily false. One example is a variation of the Liar's Paradox: (3) "This sentence is false." Assuming that statements may refer to themselves, it follows that if (3) is true it is false, and if it is false it is true. But it cannot be both true and false at the same time, hence it is necessarily false. Zeno's paradoxes about the impossibility of motion are longer but similar in their construction: one uses apparently incontrovertible premises to create a valid argument, the conclusion of which is necessarily false.

Paradoxes occur also in Freud's epistemology. Locke's question Where do qualities originate? reappeared in Kant's critiques of pure and practical reason and, again, in Freud's earliest attempt at an explanatory psychology, the "Project" of 1895a. Given Freud's assumptions and his commitment to materialist theory he had to place qualities within the "inner world" of the mental mechanism. For, again, his metaphysics told him that the real, external world could not be composed of qualities as we know them, but only of varying units of quantities careening through the void.

Yet aesthetic experience is qualitative experience. It is the sensuous surface of the painting or the sculpture that arouses our interest. It is not their "depth structure" that fascinates us. More so, artistic performances are often repetitions of earlier performances. Singers and other musicians may be accounted great artists yet, create no new artifacts, much less new artistic forms with distinctive depth structures.

Freud realized this was a problem with the notion of sublimation. He attempted to account for individual differences through a variety of subtle concepts, particularly the notion of ontogenesis. For all that, he did not or could not complete a theory of character, nor of style, for both are expressions of superficial differences. In this way the often oversimplified rejection of Freudian points of view as reductionist is understandable. Freud's drive to found a science of depth psychology, one which would eventually unite biology and physiology, made him abjure the surfaces of individuals, where differences reign, to explore the depths where we are identical. Like other thinkers of his time, Freud viewed science as the uncovering and delineation of global characteristics, not individual differences.

These are not the questions that animate most students of the arts and most students of culture. For them, both the depth structure and the superficial qualities of an artifact are important to its value. Like William James, they hold that one should judge, including human actions, by their fruits as well as by their roots. Freud was aware of these difficulties and he attempted to overcome them, in part, by way of the concept of sublimation. But that concept has its roots in the closed world of the quality–quantity distinction.

As in other mythical systems, boundary concepts, like boundary persons, become mysterious. Sublimation, the concept that was to link Freud's psychology to a theory of culture, did not escape this fate. Medieval alchemists used the term *sublimation* to describe their wishes to turn base metals into gold. This remarkable fact gives hints as to its role in Freud's thought.

CHAPTER THREE

SUBLIMATION AND THE MYSTERY OF TRANSFORMATION

> For the true sublime, by some virtue of its nature,
> elevates us: uplifted with a sense of proud posses-
> sion, we are filled with joyful pride, as if we had
> ourselves produced the very thing we heard.
> —Longinus, *On the Sublime*

The ideas of sublimation and the sublime are thousands of years older than the science of psychoanalysis. This passage from Longinus's essay *On the Sublime* ("Peri Hupsious") is one of many Greek discussions on the topic. Writing in the first century, Longinus emphasizes being "uplifted," and "filled with pride" that mark sublime experience. In these moments we resonate with our imagined sense of the artist's experience. When we hum along with the *Ode to Joy* from the Ninth Symphony, we share Beethoven's greatness. For that moment, his creative pleasures belong to us. Who has not turned up the stereo and poured out sounds not fit for mortal ears?

Longinus struggles to define what constitutes greatness in literature, his favorite example being Homer's *Iliad*. It is greater than the *Odyssey*, Longinus says, because its "consistent sublimity ... never sinks into flatness" (p. 153). By "flatness," Longinus means the lack of organized passion. He prefers the *Iliad*'s "flood of moving incidents in quick succession, the versatile rapidity and actuality, brimful of images drawn from real life" (p. 153). War does not make these passages sublime. Homer's ability to unite feeling with language is sublime as is Sappho's poems which display "a whole congress of emotions" (p. 157).

Sublime poetry and sublime thought have the power to transform us, to wrench us from our ordinary selves. We yearn to be transformed by literature, including philosophy. Longinus longs to be inspired by Plato and others from whom "there flows into the hearts of their admirers as it were an emanation from the mouth of holiness" (p. 167). This mouth is both the poet's and the rift in the earth. For out of both come the divine afflatus, the holy spirit, that "impregnates" with greatness those who absorb its power.

The Greek Old Testament, the *Septuagint,* employs the term *hupsos,* "sublime," that is, to refer to God's loftiness over human folly and lowliness. When the poor but righteous man, Job, challenged God to explain God's failure to keep God's bargain with him, a sublime rejoinder ensues:

> Then the Lord answered Job
>   out of the whirlwind:
> "Where were you when I laid the
>   foundation of the earth?
>   Tell me, if you have
>   understanding.
> Who determined its measurements
>   —surely you know!
>   Or who stretched the line upon it?
> On what were its bases sunk,
>   or who laid its cornerstone,
> when the morning stars sang
>   together,
>   and all the sons of God shouted
>   for joy?
>
> "Or who shut the sea with doors,
>   when it burst forth from the womb;
> when I made clouds its garment,
>   and thick darkness its swaddling
>   band,
> and prescribed bounds for it,
>   and set bars and doors,
> and said, 'Thus far shall you come,
>   and no farther,
>   and here your proud waves
>   be stayed'? (RSV,38:1–11)

Reading the book of Job in a poetic translation suggests that it meets all the tests of sublimity Longinus sets forth. To the question

Why do good people suffer? the author describes God's sublime majesty and God's ability to make order out of disorder. In responding to Job's challenge, God sometimes comes across like a bully; a huge God against a litte man worn away with suffering.[1]

Yet the book of Job is less about the justice of God's actions than it is about God's sublime nature and God's ability to constrain gigantic powers. The poem names these powers: the seas, the earth, the planets and the sun, as well as Behemoth, Leviathan, and other majestic animals. We see that God needs to constrain Job's grandiose yearnings, his incessant claims to dignity. God's task is to bind up those spiritual dangers as well; to restrain Job's narcissistic urges and therefore reduce Job's narcissistic terrors. God will save Job from himself by reminding Job of God's infinite ability to organize the natural and human worlds. God is the source and ruler of upwelling powers. God continues to speak to Job:

> "Is it by your wisdom that the hawk
>   soars,
>   and spreads his wings toward the
>   south?
>   Is it at your command that the eagle
>   mounts up
>   and makes his nest on high?
> On the rock he dwells and makes
>   his home
>   in the fastness of the rocky crag.
> Thence he spies out the prey;
>   his eyes behold it afar off;
> His young ones suck up blood;
>   and where the slain are, there is
>   he."   (39:26–29)

God empowers the eagle and the hawk and God also empowers similar urges toward soaring found in human beings. Because God empowers both human and animal nature, God can constrain both and so preserve human beings from the terror of unbounded grandiosity.

About nineteen hundred years after Longinus, Walt Whitman read that *Iliad* and struggled with his own anxiety when he compared himself to his poetic forbears:

The Iliad... I read first thoroughly on the peninsula of Orient, northeast end of Long Island, in a shelter'd hollow of rocks and sand, with the sea on each side. (I have wonder'd since why I was not overwhelm'd by those mighty masters. Likely because I read them, as described, in the full presence of Nature, under the sun, with the far-spreading landscape and vistas, or the sea rolling in.) (Prefatory Letter to the Reader, *Leaves of Grass*, 1889, p. 569)

In this apologetic way Whitman portrays himself on a par with the idealized, master poets who preceded him. To defend himself against the charge of grandiosity and to protect himself against feeling overwhelmed by his own "uplifting" pride, he locates the point of control *outside* of himself. He can challenge these masters because a force external to himself, majestic Nature, controls him; the sublime sky and ocean will guard him against narcissistic tensions that would otherwise inhibit his urge to contest with his poetic forebears.

The poet's search for a suitable, external object occurs in both Greek and romantic poetry. Sublime objects, especially vistas, lightening, thunder storms, and hidden valleys of all sorts, were counterparts to the sublime within human beings. Like other artists, poets were to reveal this central truth, obscured by city folk who had denied their kinship with the grandeur of nature. At a latent level, sublime objects, like grottos, safeguarded the poet against becoming emotionally unbound. Nature mirrors and objectifies the poet's need for an external object that can absorb yearnings for greatness. These sublime objects prevent collapse into grandiose delusions.

Contrary to this ancient tradition of viewing humans and nature as allies, is the equally venerable one of viewing nature and human beings as antagonists. In this tradition Nature resists and fights against the domination of humans, and human beings force Nature to reveal her secrets. To this tradition we may assign Aristotle, the alchemists, and most nineteenth-century scientists, including Goethe and Freud. For them the sublime is mysterious because unknown, dangerous because untamed, and attractive because knowledge of it promises dominion over nature itself.

Sigfried Bernfeld linked Freud, nature, and sublimation. He commented that Freud turned from dreams of power over men, to "the more sublime power over nature, through science" (Jones 1953, p. 30).[2] The dominion of nature figures in an essay ascribed to Goethe that Freud heard just before he decided to enter medical studies (Freud 1925d, p. 8). Yet this form of dominion could merge into extremes of emotionalism and therefore psychic dangers, where "untamed urges," might overwhelm a young man. Nature, as a personified force, usually female and maternal, could turn against the youthful investigator. Freud recorded his own sense of this danger in a complex dream about himself and his comrade, Wilhelm Fliess. In Freud's dream Goethe attacks an acquaintance, named Herr M. The dreamer struggles to figure out how this could have occurred since the great man had died in 1832, well before Herr M's birth. The dreamer calculates that Herr M must have been eighteen at that time.

To the dream text Freud adds, "Incidently, the attack was contained in Goethe's well-known essay on 'Nature'" (Freud 1900a, pp. 439–440). Freud recalls that Herr M had asked Freud to examine his older brother who was showing signs of general paralysis. This older brother spoke of the younger man's follies. Freud also recalls that he had just denounced the editor of a journal that ran a "crushing" criticism of Wilhelm Fliess's book. To protest this hostile action, Freud resigned from the journal. Yet he told the journal's editor that he hoped this political gesture in support of Fliess would not anger him. Freud adds another association to his dream: a patient had described her eighteen-year-old brother's mental illness: "he had broken out in a frenzy with cries of 'Nature! Nature!' The doctors believed that his exclamation came from his having read Goethe's striking essay on the subject. . . . I myself preferred to think of the sexual sense in which the word is used" (1900a, p. 440).

Freud's suspicion that "nature" refers to sexuality, is verified when he adds that this young man "subsequently mutilated his own genitals. He was eighteen at the time of his outbreak" (1900a, p. 440). At the time of the dream Fliess was pressuring Freud to accept Fliess's numerological theories of mental and physical diseases. After flirting with Fliess's theory and mirroring the latter's ambitions, Freud pulled back from his friend and colleague. Freud, two years older than Fliess, was the "older brother" of the pair and corresponds to his patient, the older brother, who criticized the younger brother for his indiscretions.

At the same time (1895-1900) Freud wrestled with *The Interpretation of Dreams*, in its scope and courage, the premier example of self-analysis. The courage Freud displays goes beyond moments of personal confession. Freud faced urges as frightening as those faced by the young man who, confronting similar demons, mutilated his genitals. Those demons must have included compulsive ideas of sexual actions, like incestuous rape. The young man countered with a cruel superego: an eye for an eye, a tooth for a tooth, castration for sexual sins.

The boy who mutilated himself failed to get beyond the power of sexuality, "Nature," in the sense of genital urges just as Freud's confidant, Fliess, had not gotten beyond grandiose scientism. Neither of these young men had sublimated their internal powers; therefore Nature subjugated each. In his dream, Freud uses Goethe to criticize Fliess in a poem, "On Nature" that had attracted Freud to medicine and from medicine Freud created psychoanalysis, which is the conquest of inner nature.

Fliess had not addressed that bit of "Nature" in himself that drove him on to his grandiose theorems. He had not attained the level of "sublimation" that Freud wished for himself. Instead Fliess developed elaborate, numerological theorems that took on wider and wider scope. In German-speaking countries Goethe stands as a supreme genius who is both artist and scientist; statesman and critic; poet and philosopher. His stature approaches that of Shakespeare and Darwin combined.

Freud's identification with Goethe reappears when he disowns his doubt about Fliess; he recalls another criticism ascribed to a reviewer of Fliess's book in which Fliess made numerological claims about the length of Goethe's life. Speaking of this "one wonders whether it is the author or oneself who is crazy" (Freud 1900a, p. 440). Fliess's claim has an occult dimension to it: "Goethe's life was a multiple of a number [of days] that has a significance in biology" (p. 440). Freud denies the manifest logic of his dream about Fliess: that the greatest person in German letters attacks Fliess's theory. Instead, Freud claims that this manifest element shows reversal and irony: "Goethe attacked the young man, which is absurd" (1900a, p. 440). This dream element is not absurd if Freud identifies himself with Goethe and lets the great man express his own forbidden thoughts. He can rely upon Goethe to distinguish his science, psychoanalysis, from Fliess's science, which Freud felt was not equal to his.

Romantics, like Whitman, viewed sublimation as an event that occurred in heightened moments of union between artists and nature. Scientific realists, like Freud, viewed sublimation as an internal process that occurred within the psyche. According to this second tradition, in sublimation one form of matter (or energy) was transformed into another, more valuable and more powerful. The alchemists said this transformation was the conversion of base metals into gold and the purchase of immortality.

Freud said the transformation was one in which private and antisocial instincts converted themselves into public interests and social labors. How this occurred, that is how private perversions turned into public works, was a mystery Freud tried to solve. The shape of this idea followed from his fundamental understanding of the ego's (self's) relationship to the external world. Although Freud's honesty is worthy of his character the concept of sublimation remains obscure. One source of his obscurity is Freud's fondness for dualistic modes of thought.

Dualisms and Antinomies in Freud's Thought

> The King has two Capacities, for he has two Bodies, the one whereof is a Body natural, consisting of natural Members as every other Man has, and in this is he subject to Passion and Death as other Men are; the other is a Body politic, and the Members thereof are his Subjects, and he and his Subjects together compose the Corporation...and he is the Head, and they are the Members...and this Body is not subject to Passions as the other is, nor to Death. (Justice Southcote, quoted in Kantorowicz 1957, p. 13)

This quotation is from a study of English laws of kingship. This particular law required one to believe that the King has two bodies. Although many people ridiculed the notion of the King's two bodies in the sixteenth century, it persisted well into modern times. Thus Parliment could execute Charles Stuart, the king, in 1649 in the King's name because it was the King's Name that Parliment owed allegiance and not the mortal person of a body natural. Learned jurors of the time perceived how awkward this idea appeared and they labored to overcome it. Justice Brown discussed the problem: "King is a Name of Continuance, which shall always endure as the Head and Governor of the People (as the Law presumes) as long as the People continue...; and in this Name the King never dies" (Kantorowicz, p. 23).

The English nation is immortal and so is its King and when the immortal King joins with an earthly being the King's two bodies are joined and remain united for the duration of the life of the natural body. At the latter's death the place and role of King continues, awaiting another occupant. The problem of continuity of the Kingship was neither easily stated nor easily solved for in the medieval and early modern periods theological questions of the eternity of the world and the divinity of the king's person were important. Kantorowicz observes that Grace, Justice, and Law are values that presuppose the idea of eternity (pp. 271–272).

None of these transcendent values could admit of a temporal or spatial limitation. By divine appointment the King represented these values. His continuity was of paramount importance. The doctrine of the King's two bodies was no mere quibble confined to logicians. Jurists and theologians recognized the parallels between this doctrine and the Christian doctrine of Jesus's two natures and the question of the triune god. The two-body issue was not inherently religious. Rather, the "...concept of the 'king's two bodies' camoflagued a problem of continuity" (p. 273), which remained contentious up to our times. In order to preserve the possibility of permanent justice and permanent grace, English jurists maintained the otherwise incoherent theorem of the king's dual nature.

This absurd doctrine reappears some two centuries later, in Kant's chapter, "The Antinomy of Pure Reason" (*Critique of Pure Reason*, pp. 396ff.). Kant wished to map the limits of pure reason, including metaphysical reason. He would demonstrate its illogical consequences: insolvable antinomies surrounding the crucial ideas of space, time, causality, and God. Kant preserved the possibility of moral action (and God's existence) by demonstrating that reason could neither prove or disprove transcendent claims. He shows the limits of reason by deducing valid arguments that support two opposing opinions. For example, he proves that time is both infinite and not infinite (pp. 396–402). If pure reason can do no better, then it cannot give us certain knowledge about freedom, the afterlife, and God.

Because Freud denies that qualities may adhere in the "external world" and he championed a quantitative psychology, he elaborated a similar duality. Where Kant located the transcendental ego, the ego which by definition has direct knowledge of transcendent issues, Freud located the body ego. Freud inverted Kant and upon that inversion formed his critique of consciousness. Freud could not escape Kant's fate: to erect a whole series of metapsychological concepts, brilliant in their symmetry, yet ultimately disappointing. These antithetical concepts fall into three sets: (1) neuroses versus cultural institutions, (2) thing versus word presentations, and (3) repression versus sublimation.

Neuroses as Negative Social Structures

> The neuroses exhibit on the one hand striking and far-reaching points of agreement with those great social institutions, art, religion and philosophy. But on the other hand they seem like distortions of them. It might be maintained that a case of hysteria is a caricature of a work of art, that an obsessional neurosis is a caricature of religion and that a paranoic delusion is a caricature of a philosophical system. (*Totem and Taboo*, 1912–13, SE 13:73)

A master of subtlety, Freud seems to suggest that the similarities he finds between neurotic forms and cultural institutions are interesting parallels. In *Totem and Taboo* he demonstrates that taboo behavior is obsessional neuroses on a large scale. Freud says one might call obsessional neurosis the "taboo illness," so similar are the two sets of behavior. In 1909d Freud completed his masterful treatise on obsessional illness (the Rat Man) and was in an excellent position to apply his clinical theories to the investigation of taboos.

Although he retains hold of the libido theory, it does not dominate Freud's discussion. Rather he says: "The asocial nature of the neuroses has its genetic origin in their most fundamental purpose, which is to take flight from an unsatisfying reality into a more pleasurable world of phantasy" (1912–1913, p. 74). External reality is, in part, the world under the "sway of human society and the institutions collectively created by it" (p. 74). Therefore the neuroses are asocial structures and inversions of their social counterparts.

More so, they are options one can choose to pursue. Instead of taking part in social institutions, the neurotic creates a counterinstitution. This antithetical mode is a caricature of social forms; "Psychoneuroses are, so to speak, the negative of perversions" ("Dora," 1905e, SE7:50). To use another metaphor, Freud pictures neuroses and their social counterparts as two branches of a tree: they share a single trunk, the human body, and they share common roots, instinctual forces. This is more than a metaphor, for Freud says that choosing religion precludes the development of its counterparts, the neuroses and health. As he says in *The Future of an Illusion* (1927c), true believers are spared the task of constructing personal obsessional systems because they partake in the universal one. Freud does not pursue the other two comparisons. I will.

Hysteria involves the repression of ideas tied to strong feelings. It employs the hysteric's body as a medium. It exhibits somatization, denial, conversion, and similar ego defenses, as well as the sexualization of thought, e.g., Dora's coughing. The plastic arts use external media (even dance uses the body in a stylized manner); they do not employ directed defenses. Rather, they aim to communicate and do not sexualize thought.

In its search for completeness and in its use of ideas as the sole vehicle of truth, paranoia parallels metaphysics. More so, both forms of thought use elaborate, sometimes ingenious, constructs to "explain" what everyone else takes for granted. Metaphysicians are superior: they seek "ultimate" truths, especially those not apparent to mere nonphilosophers. Freud's comparisons between neurotic form and cultural analogue are not accidental. Freud holds the thesis that neurotic behaviors are products of unconscious choices. The neurotic chooses to satisfy a universal need in an idiosyncratic manner. Freud described this structural relationship between neuroses and cultural institutions differently at different times: sometimes he spoke of them as mirror

images of one another, at other times he spoke of inversions, caricatures, and echoes (see 1919g, SE 17:260–261). In these accounts he
retained his central thesis: that individual neurotic structures parallel
in form cultural institutions.

In this sense Freud is a structuralist of the first order. His structuralism is not a linguistic one (Gay 1982). Lacan and some of his school
read Freud with passion and charm. Yet there remains the obstinate
problem that Freud's models are biological. He focuses upon the drives
and their somatic representatives, not upon linguistic theorems. Of
course a very clever reader could "reread" these texts and with a little
magic make Freud sound like Lacan.

This is not persuasive, for the drives are not linguistic forces. They
are fixed by biological constraints. They do not show linguistic arbitra-
riness. They are universal, not culturally specific; limited in number,
not potentially infinite in extension; in short, biological, not mental.
Although Freud used metaphors taken from linguistics, especially in
his essays on dreams, his models of the mental domain are biological
and, sometimes, geological. Hence, he says that the drives operate within the mental mechanism as streams of water that cut their own channels through a basin. Another French author seems to me more useful.
Emile Benveniste says that the "archaic level" of the mind is shaped by
powers "which deforms it or represses it" (quoted in Ricoeur 1965, p.
397).

This adds yet another metaphor, "deformation," to our already
large stock of metaphors of mind. It is useful for it suggests that repression shapes the drives, just as the drives shape behavior, for example,
compulsiveness. Deformed drive elements reflect the shape of the
deforming forces, as a dent in metal records the force with which the
hammer struck it. This violent deformation is structural, not linguistic.
Freud's relentless criticism of cultural morality and the lies of civilization records the horror with which he viewed the cost of civilization.
That cost is a real cost, born by most of us, and exacted with the
hammer blows of physical and psychological punishment. Dora's many
neurotic complaints were not intellectual options. Nor delicate "translations"; they were deformations caused, in part, by her father's lies and
her mother's inability to rescue her from the family's disease.

Freud might be wrong, but he is lucid; neuroses result from the
conflict, the deformation, of primary drives at the hands of external
demands, especially the family. Without conflict and without deformation, neuroses cannot form. All manner of perversions and psychopathy
might emerge, but they would not be neuroses. It is not thoughts that
make people neurotic, it is their conflict over those thoughts. The true

psychopath, like the true believer in witchcraft, behaves strangely. Neither person is in conflict (and neither would be a good subject for analytic work).   ·

True neurotics conflict with what they believe are social norms. That conflict itself is an expression of many years of deformation that creates the "negative social structures" we call the neuroses. Freud felt justified in writing about the "positive" social structures, including religion and government, because he had investigated their neurotic counterparts. His essays on culture are not merely "applied" speculations. His work with patients "pointed persistently in the direction of this new task [applied psychoanalysis], for it was obvious that the forms assumed by the different neuroses echoed the most highly admired productions of culture" (1919g, SE 17:260–261).

The forensic pathologist can reconstruct the approximate shape and weight of the hammer which shattered the victim's skull. So too Freud feels he can reconstruct the blows with which society deforms its children. Yet this is a mystery for, if neuroses are negative social structures, it follows that social structures must bear some formal relationship to the neuroses. They do, as Freud does not tire of asserting. The cultural institutions themselves must employ the same store of psychical energy (the drives and their products) which the neuroses feed upon. If repression is that intrapsychic process by which the ego carries out the behests of the group, then sublimation must be its inversion. It is, as we shall see in more detail below. Repression, the crucial factor in the genesis of neurosis, *is a quantitative process in which instinctual representatives are denied access to consciousness.* Then sublimation, too, must be *quantitative* process, as it were, going the other way.

Sublimation is not quantitative (in most formations) since it requires either the individual or the group to equate symbolically one kind of behavior, say masturbation, with another, say banjo playing. J. C. Flugel noted sublimation involves a "qualitative" factor as well as quantitative ones. He says, "... our goal is the discovery of a satisfactory compromise which will allow the instinct a maximum of satisfaction and give the repressing forces, as it were, minimum ground for complaint" (1942, p. 98). The symbolic equivalence between two otherwise distinct behaviors makes one the sublimated counterpart of the other (see Jones 1916, as well). Symbolic equivalences would appear to be matters of complex, qualitative reasoning. Sublimations would appear to be like jokes in which one thing can stand for another as in *pars pro toto*. The latter idea figures in Freud's discussion of primary process thought, e.g., the dream work. This would seem to be an attractive way out of our problem. For we do not want to say that sublimations are secondary process activities. That would imply one could redirect the instincts at will, an idea that is incompatible with sublimation being the counterpart of repression. Both processes are automatic and unconscious; they cannot be forced, nor directed by conscious effort. (Freud is adamant about this point as we shall see when we consider his essay on Leonardo da Vinci.) Yet sublimation cannot be a product of the primary processes for those are internal and typically unconscious. This is just the opposite of what we feel is true of sublimations. They are external, public, and conscious and fully esteemed as such.

So sublimation, that crucial process by which private wishes transform themselves into public achievements, cannot be a product of primary process nor secondary process thinking. More so, it may be conscious or unconscious, planned or unplanned. It is wholly quantitative, since it originates in responses to the pressure of the instincts yet it employs symbolism and other sophisticated qualitative modes for its expression. Many authors have noted these problems. Freud himself was aware of how troublesome the term was and in his many comments on it we find him uneasy. He did not develop the concept with the thoroughness which distinguishes his work on the related concepts of repression, defense, and identification. Why not? Why do we find, first, that this crucial term is full of contradictions and, second, that neither Freud nor his later followers developed it? The status of the concept sublimation has declined. In the early period Freud and Jones used it extensively. In the twenties Flugel gave it grudging approval. In recent times L. Kaywin (1966), Paul Ricoeur (1965), and others recommend dropping it from the psychoanalytic lexicon.

Physical versus Cultural Hierarchies

The central reason for the decline of the concept is its dependence upon the quantity–quality distinction. It was this distinction, discussed above, which Freud upheld consistently and which caused his predicament in his essays on culture. For culture, that realm of human action built upon sublimations, is a place of values, and values are nothing other than expressions of qualitative differences. The critic who compares a late Beethoven sonata to an earlier one uses qualitative criteria, most of which cannot be justified by quantitative arguments. Even if one adduced quantitative measures, say the balance between opening and closing tempi, other critics need not agree.

Critics defend their failure to use quantitative measures by arguing that they respond with both technical reasoning and "taste." They respond with a range of emotional and intellectual understandings of the music. Most humanists have no difficulty in accepting taste as a legitimate defense of critical methods, but Freud cannot. At least he cannot accept these claims and remain true to his metapsychological principles. The realm of illusion includes religion, with its obvious wish-fulfillments, and all the arts, for they too pretend to elucidate a reality made up of qualities and of good and evil. We know that reality is nothing more than the eternal fluctuation of quantities in motion.

Perhaps this does Freud an injustice? It might be that he accepts the implications of his metapsychology in the way a physicist understands the truth that a "solid" table includes molecules composed of "empty" space. Physicists do not hesitate to sit upon chairs, even if they are "empty." Freud often makes aesthetic judgments. When he does he alludes to an artifact whose most important features, its qualities, are present only in his experience. Physicists describe a continuum of physical structures. It stretches from the "empty" atoms to molecules, to wood tissues, to the "solid" surfaces which make up the chair. Although most of us do not care to make such an analysis, it is feasible. More than that, the ability to show this continuum is an essential part of the scientist's total explanation. A good theory ought not to leave gaps in its account of hierarchical structures. Natural scientists do not leave such lacunae in their accounts. If they do, they count them as problems they should solve as quickly as possible.

Freud's discussion of qualities and quantities is, ostensibly, like that of the physicist. Freud wished to show how biological drives produced psychological drives and, in turn, how these produced wishes, hopes, and yearnings. In the "Project," he attempts to portray this hierarchy of structures. His assumption that the "real world" is only quantities required him to show how these quantities produced qualities. I suggested Freud rearranged his model of the three neuronal systems in response to this deficit in his theory, but the deficit remained and the gap between qualities and quantities remained unbridged. He says little about how these invisible elements (quantities) give rise to the visible structures (qualities) of everyday life. Like the alchemists who wished to transform one substance into another, Freud can name this gap. With admirable honesty, he confesses that he cannot bridge it. Hence, sublimation becomes a mysterious process. Many of the "qualitative" features of the arts are unavailable to psychoanalytic inquiry and "creativity" often dissolves into "magical" properties.[3]

The physical sciences are not adequate models for the social sciences, in which I included psychoanalysis, for the former can carry out hierarchical analyses while the latter cannot. This is another way of upholding the quantity–quality distinction. Chemists may be able to explain why two substances taste the same but art historians cannot explain why one painting is in better taste than another. They can give arguments, pleas, and such, but their reasoning does not carry the force of their counterparts in the physical sciences. This is not a new point. Well-worn concepts like taste, style, interpretation, insight, and genius are all part of the language of aesthetics. Together they amount to a confession that the analysis of cultural forms differs from the analysis of physical ones.

The origins of the term *sublimation* point to this fact. For it designates processes in which a substance is transformed from a solid to a gas without passing through the liquid state. In other words, these are exceptional processes which violate the usual sequences of transformation. That violation, the absence of the usual middle stage, marked the existence of a "gap" in the ordinary world of common experience. Freud's many comments on sublimation and his many attempts to employ it reveal their roots in this magical image.

Sublimation in Popular Culture

> In many of his icons [Shiva] is ithyphallic; often he appears with his consort. At the same time he is the patron diety of the yogis.... This is not inconsistent with his sexual vitality. For the source of the yogi's power is his own divine sexuality, conserved and concentrated by asectisism. (Rawson, *Indian Sculpture*, p. 48)

When Christ was portrayed with an erection in the few paintings that survived, most viewers simply ignored this fact. If brought to their attention with too much clarity, the painting disappeared or gained a loincloth. When the Hindu god Shiva is portrayed with an erection, or as scholars say "ithyphallically," the icon remains public. Hindu philosophy links the god's body to Hindu psychology: by storing sexual tension the yogi stores spiritual power.

Most psychoanalytic concepts suffer when popularized. Anna Freud notes that the terms *trauma, transference,* and *acting out* lost their clinical meanings when employed in nonclinical contexts (Nagera 1970, pp. 10–11). This is not true of the term *sublimation,* a term which Freud used more than 100 times according to the concordance to the Standard Edition.[4] The wish to transform the power of sexuality into a "higher" kind is of ancient vintage. For example, the equation of semen with magical fluids and the idea of reigning in male potency are primary process concepts. It is a theme that permeates Indian thought. Semen is a substance associated with life, procreation, and ectasy, yet is "expended" in orgasm. Hence conserving it ought transfer those qualities of this "life force" to oneself, or so the yogis argue. Dramatic artists have not overlooked this folk wisdom. Some, like Thomas Hardy (1891), have portrayed its gruesome side. After seducing and ruining the gentle woman, Tess, Alec takes up charismatic preaching and so uses his old talents as a seducer in new ways. This change, this about-face, is a transfiguration. Hardy describes this false transformation in detail:

> It was less a reform than a transfiguration. The former curves of sen-
> suousness were now modulated to lines of devotional passion. The lip-
> shapes that had meant seductiveness were now made to express sup-
> plication; the glow on the cheek that yesterday could be translated as
> riotousness was evengelized to-day into the splendour of pious rhetoric;
> animalism had become fanaticism; Paganism Paulinism; the bold rolling
> eye that had flashed upon her form in the old time with such mastery now
> beamed with the rude energy of a theolatry that was almost ferocious.
> Those black angularities which his face had used to put on when his
> wishes were thwarted now did duty in picturing the incorrigible back-
> slider who would insist upon turning again to his wallowing in the mire.
> (*Tess of the d'Urbervilles*, 1891, p. 352)

Alec's change is a magical inversion, not a transformation. We are not surprised that Alec abandons his newfound vocation when he sees Tess once more. He falls into violent desires to have her again. John Updike (1979) describes the comic side of such efforts in his short story "Sublimating." After a sudden vow of celibacy, Mary and John Maple discover their efforts to sublimate their sexual life does not yield greater spiritual insights. Instead emerge depression, moodiness, and in John, the urge to chop down healthy trees. This causes both spouses to ponder whether or not the bloody crusades of the Middle Ages had been born in similar ill-chosen vows. Another example is Stephen Daedelus's rejection of the priesthood and celibacy in James Joyce's *Portrait of the Artist as a Young Man* (1916).

Folk wisdom has always linked creativity to sexual arousal and orgasm. For in both kinds of experience one acquiesces: "powers" be-yond the ego impinge upon it with great force. Poetry and erections are alike in that neither can be willed into existence. One must wait, wonder, and not worry. This deep and abiding similarity between the two forms of experience is a staple idea in romantic philosophies of art. It suffuses Whitman's hymns to sexuality and, in a more refined mode, appears throughout English romantic poetry, yet none of these often

beautiful evocations of the idealized power of sexuality is psychoana-
lytically valid. They are all prepsychoanalytic and usually adamant jus-
tifications of magical beliefs.

Freud's Use of the Term Sublimation

Many reviewers have surveyed the development of this psychoanalytic concept. I will refer to them in the next section yet none of
them shows that sublimation is a concept that bridges Freud's theory of
mind and his theory of culture. I discuss what they left out.

Freud apparently first used the term in a letter he sent to Fliess in
May of 1897 (SE 7:156, n). Freud evokes the notion of sublimation regarding fantasies young children have of parental intercourse. He notes
that such fantasies deny the memories of actual traumatic experience
and also distort them, by "refining the memories, of sublimating them"
(1905a, p. 197). This is an ordinary use of the German term *Sublimierung* which, like its English counterpart, derives from the Latin term,
sublimare. All three terms refer to the chemical process of refining and
purifying solid substances by "sublimating" them. This requires one to
apply enough heat to the solid form to vaporize it. When the vapor condenses back into a solid form, it is purified.

In his case history "Dora" (1905e) Freud uses the term at least
three times. He uses it in a nontechnical sense of the as-yet-unspecified
process by which undifferentiated instinctual drives are "turned"
toward socially useful works. This mysterious process causes actions
that are the opposite of perversions and "are destined to provide the
energy for a number of our cultural achievements" (p. 50). To this text,
Freud added a Postscript in which he discusses *transference*—an
important new technical term. Among the many types of transference
he counts those that have been subject to "a moderating influence—to
sublimation, as I call it" (p. 116). In these accounts, sublimation is an un-
specified mental process through which sexually perverse action is
avoided and a socially sanctioned one is performed. Freud employs the
term in a third sense in which sublimation connotes a sense of refine-
ment, akin to the sublime.

In *Three Essays on the Theory of Sexuality* (1905d) Freud expanded his use of the term. He reasserts that through sublimation cultural institutions tax the pregenital libido of individuals by the "diversion of sexual instinctual forces from sexual aims" (1905d, p. 178). He
adds to this notion a new claim that sublimation refers to a complex set
of defensive behaviors. Hence he says that sublimation and reaction
formation often overlap one another. Sublimation, though, can "also
take place by other and simpler mechanisms" (pp. 178–179). The con-

cept does not refer to a single mechanism but to an effect that may have distinct sources. He also adds another dimension to the term's meaning when he says that the "instinct" for knowledge is a sublimated derivation of scopophilia (p. 194). Again, he does not explain how this occurs. Later he considers how these events might occur and how he might account for them using metapsychological principles. He refers to vague "pathways" within the body. Freud makes the general claim that all human beings manifest pregenital impulses which have their own organization and aims. These impulses originated in the pregential zones. These zones, in turn, become the focal point of other drives, like hunger and elimination. We can "understand why there should be disorders of nutrition if the erotogenic functions of the common zone are disturbed" (p. 206).

To account for these common symptoms, Freud propounds a biological speculation. There must be pathways within the mind over which both sexual and nonsexual energies course: "The same pathways, however, along which sexual disturbances trench upon the other somatic functions might also perform another important function in normal health. They must serve as paths for the attraction of sexual instinctual forces to aims that are other than sexual, that is to say, for the sublimation of sexuality" (p. 206).

Freud was fond of the concept of "the attraction of the repressed." He confesses its inexactness and hypothetical nature. Yet he does not doubt that something like it is true: "these pathways...certainly exist and can probably be traversed in both directions" (p. 206). This concept appears first in the "Project," (1895a) in a section on the "cathected neurone." There Freud explained psychological habits (like perversions) and psychological learning using the neurone model.

The notion of the ego as the organ that inhibits discharge of wishful ideas developed from this early model. The ego is that structure within the mental apparatus characterized by highly cathected neurones (1895a, pp. 319ff.). Sublimation, according to this model, occurs when a pregential impulse is "deflected" from its aim, e.g., anal sadism, by an excessively cathected ego structure. This highly energized structure bends the original trajectory of the biological urge. Freud invokes a metaphor from astronomy. The hypercathected ego, like the hypercathected neurone, "attracts the pregenital impulse to itself the way the sun bends the pathway of comets" (see also 1908a [SE 9:161]; 1908b [SE 9:171]).

Although he repeats his formulation later in the text, Freud did not consider it a satisfactory explanation. He says the opposite: "No other influences on the course of sexual development can compare in im-

portance with releases of sexuality, waves of repression and sublimations—the latter two being processes *of which the inner causes are
quite unknown to us*" (p. 239, emphasis mine).

Sublimation as Innate Disposition: Physical Constitution

The concept of sublimation remains murky in three essays Freud
published in 1908 (1908a, 1908b, and 1908d). The last article's title,
"'Civilized' Sexual Morality and Modern Nervous Illness," with its sardonic quotation marks, conveys Freud's criticism of modern society.
Societal institutions require a store of energy. Therefore, individuals,
the only source of power, must forfeit some of their energy to the
group's demands. The unquenchable sexual appetites of human beings
"places extraordinarily large amounts of force at the disposal of civilized activity, and it does this in virtue of its especially marked characteristic of being able to displace its aim without materially diminishing
in intensity" (p. 287). This characteristic of human sexuality is what we
know as sublimation. It is characteristic of all persons and, like other
characteristics, it varies in intensity and degree: "Mastering... by sublimation, by deflecting the sexual instinctual forces away from their
sexual aim to higher cultural aims, can be achieved by a minority and
then only intermittently" (p. 193). Freud is using the term by this time
(SE 1:247n) in its psychoanalytic sense, a sense not very different from
that implied in the Hindu practice of conserving semen. For example,
Freud writes, "An abstinent artist is hardly conceivable; but an abstinent young savant is certainly no rarity. The latter can, by his self-
restraint, liberate forces for his studies" (p. 197).

This distinction between the unrepressed artist and the sublimated scholar is doubly confusing. First, Freud suggests that "self-will,"
that is, a conscious effort at "displacing" one's sexual energies, can alter
what he had just termed an "innate disposition." Second, Freud suggests that fully mature genital impulses may undergo such deflection.
These two claims contradict his statement in *Three Essays*, (1905d)
where he said that only pregenital impulses were susceptible to sublimation.

Not a year later Freud returned to the concept. In two case histories, Little Hans and Rat Man (1909b and 1909d), he states that sublimation is a process which occurs haphazardly. Sexual constitution
coupled with environmental changes account for the presence and
degree of sublimatory behavior (SE 10:138n, and SE 10:203). He recapitulates his general notion in the "Five Lectures" of 1910 (1910a). He
adds that "Premature repression makes the sublimation of the repressed instinct impossible; when the repression is lifted, the path to

sublimation becomes free once more" (p. 54). However, we cannot expect to tax these libidinal currents forever, any more than one can work a draft horse, with no concern for its needs. So also, too great a restriction upon direct sexual aims would "inevitably bring with it all the evils of soil-exhaustion" (p. 54).

Yet, it was the wholly abstinent artist, Leonardo da Vinci, to whom Freud turned for an example of a perfectly sublimated type. He is among the "rarest and most perfect" (1910c, p. 80) because most of his libidinal energies were sublimated from the beginning. Thus he could escape the common fate of repression, with its burdens of inhibition and control. Freud's language is ambiguous, especially when he says Leonardo "succeeded in sublimating the greater part of his libido into an urge for research" (pp. 80–81). One doubts the young child took upon himself a regimen of self-denial and asceticism. He must mean that Leonardo transformed the normal amount of infantile feelings, which are expended in transient moments of rage and affection, into talent. Geniuses are people who employ the energy of the powerful infantile drives and escape repression. Where most children must expend to control the upsurge of infantile (id) impulses, Leonardo escaped that fate. By sublimating rather than repressing his infantile urges he gained a double measure of creative energy.

In other words, Leonardo did not suffer from common, intrapsychic conflicts, neither did he bear their cost: repression. As we have seen, psychoanalysis is preeminently a psychology of intrapsychic conflict. It follows that psychoanalysis per se cannot provide a complete explanation of sublimated behaviors. They lie beyond its ken. Psychoanalysis is the scientific study of the transformation of instinctual drives, not of their transfiguration (see 1917c). To be transformed is to be changed from one form into another according to natural laws. To be transfigured is to be exalted, glorified, and raised from one state to a higher one.

Transfiguration is a spiritual transformation accomplished by the intervention of divine forces. Hardy, who was suspicious of Christian sentiments, says that the evil Alec was transfigured, not reformed. That is, his change from a violent sexual pursuer to a preacher did not reveal natural change. It was "miraculous" and therefore suspect, "animalism had become fanaticism." Yet, sublimation is a process of transfiguration, not transformation:

> Instincts and their transformations are at the limit of what is discernible by psycho-analysis. From that point it gives place to biological research. We are obliged to look for the source of the tendency to repression and

the capacity for sublimation in the organic foundations of character on which the mental structure is only afterwards erected. Since artistic talent and capacity are intimately connected with sublimation we must admit that the nature of the artistic function is also inaccessible to us along psycho-analytic lines. (1910c, p. 136)

These remarks, made at the end of his essay on Leonardo, exclude sublimation from those topics amenable to psychoanalytic explanation. When Freud uses the term in his later case histories, he does so in a descriptive sense which echoes concepts of transfiguration, magic, and spirituality. He says of the Wolf Man: "The chief motive force the influence of religion had on him was his identification with the figure of Christ, which came particularly easily to him owing to the accident of the date of his birth [December 25]. Along this path his extravagant love of his father, which had made the repression [of homosexual feelings] necessary, found its way at length to an ideal sublimation" [*ideale sublimierung*] (1918b, SE 17:115; GW 12:150).

Freud distinguishes repression from sublimation when he explains why the Wolf Man could not use the "incomparable sublimation" which the Passion of Christ offered him. First, there is a psychical inertia, similar to fixation, against which the urge toward sublimation had to struggle. Second, the Christian story retains ambivalent feelings about the Father. Hence it touched off the Wolf Man's own unrequited feelings of love and hatred. Third and most important, the presence of an earlier repression of strong homosexual and aggressive wishes prevented further sublimation.

The passage cannot be made more succinct:

The truth was that the mental current which impelled him to turn to men as sexual objects and which should have been sublimated by religion was no longer free; a portion of it was cut off by repression and so withdrawn from the possibility of sublimation and tied to its original sexual aim. In virtue of this state of things, the repressed portion kept making efforts to forge its way through to the sublimated portion or to drag down the latter to itself. The first ruminations which he wove round the figure of Christ already involved the question whether that sublime son could also fulfill the sexual relationship to his father which the patient had retained in his unconscious. The only result of his repudiation of these efforts was the production of apparently blasphemous obsessive thoughts, in which his physical affection for God asserted itself in the form of a debasement. A violent defensive struggle against these compromises then inevitably led to an obsessive exaggeration of all the activities which are prescribed for giving expression to piety and a pure love of God. Religion won in the end, but its instinctual foundations proved themselves to be incomparably stronger than the durability of the products of their sublimation. As soon as the course of events presented him with a new father-surrogate, who threw his weight into the scale against religion, it was dropped and replaced by something else. (pp. 116–117)

Repression prevents sublimation, is its opposite, because it "drags down" actions and thoughts associated with the forbidden topic into the unconscious. Using metaphors from the "Project" Freud ascribes to the unconscious the quality of uncanny attraction, linked in part with repetition compulsion. Like the dream work, unconscious attraction can manufacture linkages between forbidden thoughts and formerly innocent pleasures. In this beautiful and persuasive account Freud uses both terms in their clinical senses: *repression* denotes one type of behavior, *sublimation* another.

The Problem of Quality Returns: Infantile Sexual Aims

In his account of the Wolf Man's failure to employ religion, Freud used the theory of infantile sexuality elaborated in his *Three Essays* (1905d). When we examine that work we find, to our surprise, that the problem of quality (versus quantity) returns. In "The Sexual Aim of Infantile Sexuality" (SE 7:183ff.), Freud repeats his distinction between sexual aim, the release of tensions, and sexual object, the "target" toward which the organism turns. The sexual aim consists "in obtaining satisfaction by means of the appropriate stimulation of the erotogenic zone which has been selected in one way or another" (p. 184). That occurred when the infant learned that some actions, like rubbing its mouth, produced "a feeling of pleasure possessing a certain quality" (p. 183).

He does not claim these are metapsychological theorems, like those of the "Project." Yet Freud's concepts parallel them: "There can be no doubt that the stimuli which produce the pleasure are governed by special conditions, though we do not know what those are. A rhythmic character must play a part among them and the analogy of tickling is forced upon our notice" (p. 183). This "rhythmic tickling" is comparable to the periodic motions Freud ascribed to one form of stimuli impinging upon the mental apparatus. It was the rhythmic character transmitted by the sense organs which account for qualities in general and for pain and pleasure in particular. Where does the quality of sexual excitation come from?

We have seen that qualities, according to the "Project," arise within the organism. For they cannot arise from a correct perception of the "external" world since the latter is nothing more than mere quantities in endless motion. Freud agrees with this conclusion as he makes clear in a crucial section of the third essay on sexuality, "The Libido Theory" (pp. 217–219). There, in brief (1895a) comments, he distinguishes his metapsychological theory—the libido theory—from its lower-level cousins, the general clinical theory of the neuroses. The former, using as it does concepts and principles borrowed from the natural sciences, is to explain and order data derived from observation. The libido theory is a conceptual scaffolding upon which Freud hopes to hang the insights of psychoanalytic clinical theory: "We distinguish this libido in respect of its special origin from the energy which must be supposed to underlie mental processes in general, and we thus also attribute a qualitative character to it" (p. 217). What are these qualitative characteristics?

At first glance the notion of a "qualitative energy" is a contradiction in terms. Energy is an exceedingly abstract term. Like mass and velocity, its sister concepts in physics, it is purely quantitative and relative, not qualitative and particular. Yet libido has special negative qualities (need, displeasure, unlust) and special positive qualities (pleasure and satisfaction). More so, libido has special locations and origins. The pregential body zones have distinctive libidinal charges: hence Freud speaks of oral, anal, and phallic libidinal currents. Freud recognized these difficulties. He also recognized Jung's decision to "water down the meaning of the concept of libido itself by equating it with psychical instinctual force in general" (p. 218). Freud refused to abandon a concept, especially one as important as libido. (This is a hallmark of his philosophy of science; see his remarks on "progress in the sciences" in 1914c.)

For most rationalist philosophers of science the libido theory is inconsistent and often contradictory; for many clinicians it ties together observations which would otherwise remain disjointed. This is evident in Freud's essays on the relationship between anal eroticism and adult character traits. Anal qualities manifest in the infant's behavior are replicated in the obsessional actions of the adult. Freud's discoveries about the importance of anality in culture make it an ideal topic. In addition, the clinical theory of defenses against anality, reaction formations, and sublimations of anal interests gain support from many studies.

Anality and Its Sublimations

The disposition of human beings toward everything connected

with bodily wastes affirms Freud's judgment that human beings are anal erotics. In his prepsychoanalytic period (1905a), he observed that money, especially gold, was associated with feces. Like J. G. Bourke (1891) and Reginald Reynolds (1946), Freud described jokes, puns, stories, fairy tales, and the like that used anal themes as their most pungent resource. W. C. Menninger (1943) summed up many of the psychoanalytic discoveries about anality. Freud's paper "Character and Anal Eroticism" (1908b) develops these themes in detail. Because anal eroticism is abhorrent it is available for sublimation: "Now anal eroticism is one of the components of the [sexual] instinct which, in the course of development and in accordance with the education demanded by our present civilization, have become unserviceable for sexual aims. It is therefore plausible to suppose that these character-traits of orderliness, parsimony, and obstinacy, which are so often prominent in people who were formerly anal erotics, are to be regarded as the first and most constant results of the sublimation of anal eroticism" (p. 171).

These insights are the result of Freud's clinical experiences. Analyzing patients who liked anal stimulation, he discovered the historical connections between the two forms of behavior. The "intrinsic necessity" (p. 172) between a child's fondness for dirt and the adult's abhorrence of it is their mutual fascination with it. Ernest Jones (1955, pp. 295–296) reported that Freud's article outraged many, including psychiatrists. According to classical theory, the anal erotic part instinct is sublimated when it gains "expression" in behaviors that are socially acceptable, ego syntonic, and adaptive. Like Erikson whose epigenetic charts followed soon after, Menninger (1943) used a schema to make this idea clear. On the left side he maintains a general distinction between "autogenic" and "exogenic" events which arouse anal erotic feelings in the infant. These events, like pleasure in soiling and flatus, have "direct carry overs" in adult pleasures in defecating and the like. They have indirect carry overs in "sublimated" good habits, like neatness and handicrafts, especially sculpting. Finally, they may appear in symptomatic behaviors like reaction formations, neurotic, and psychotic symptoms, especially anal perversions and coprophagia.

The most fantastic and the most original of these claims is the linkage of authentic achievements, like sculpting, with an original anal erotism. The mose persuasive accounts are clinical vignettes in which a reaction formation dissolves into its earlier structure. Also persuasive are studies of children who use clay as a substitute vehicle for their anal expression (see Kris 1952).

What accounts for this continuity? Freud did not hesitate to answer: the persistence of the original anal instinct (drives) and its aim:

the excitation of the anal zone. The "anal qualities" of adult behaviors, including sublimated ones, are two dimensional. The first dimension is the historical linkage, discovered by analysis, between an original "naked" impulse and representations of it. From the child's pleasure in holding onto feces develops the adult pleasure in collecting butterflies. The second is symbolic: the metaphorical linkage between a pleasure in flatus and enjoying wind instruments; between feces and clay; between diarrhea and speechifying. At this point the concept becomes murky for Freud said originally that an instinct is like an itch. It provokes the organism into scratching, or rubbing, or some way stimulating part of its body. The frequency of scratching ought to reflect the frequency of itching. At the level of character traits this is not true. The frequency of sculpting is not determined, solely, by upsurges in anal erotism. Freud recognized this and therefore linked anal erotism to other part instincts, which in unison made up the motive forces that determined one's character. His notion of "pregenital organization" implies that the primary drives are only the motor aspects of a complex event. He held that changes in the mix of genital and pregenital instinctual forces altered overt behavior:"...after women have lost their genital function...they become quarrelsome, vexatious and overbearing, petty and stingy; that is to say, they exhibit typically sadistic and anal-erotic traits which they did not possess earlier, during their period of womanliness.... This alteration of character corresponds to a regression of sexual life to the pregenital sadistic and anal-erotic stage" (1913i, SE 2: 323–324).

I set aside the question of the adequacy of this as a contribution to female psychology. Freud says the original drives (or "part instincts") however numerous, persist throughout one's life and govern the "quality" of one's experience and one's character. The mature adult is peaceful when détente exists between competing drives ruled by the ego. Like Bismarck, the ego must labor tirelessly to forge overt and covert alliances between hostile factions, else it faces the danger of outright violence and perhaps general war. The loss of a countervailing power forces those that remain to reassert themselves and this drags the rest of the personality into the conflict that has now become unavoidable.

Sublimation is the fortunate alignment of a partial instinct and the claims of society. Instinct and society share a common aim. At first glance this form of theorizing is persuasive. It accounts for the undeniable importance of conflict, particularly in neurotics. Long before Freud, many noted how much of life's suffering consisted in being of two minds. Yet, balancing off this phenomenological acuteness, is the theory's undue reliance upon metaphor. The "socialized" view of the ego projects interpersonal conflicts back into the "mental theatre" of the individual. Unless there are little persons within one's mind, it does little good to describe overt neurotic difficulties as if there were. The social conflict and war imagery of which Freud was very fond highlights the experience of neuroses but does not explain their origins.

Freud was aware of these difficulties, and he avoided claiming too much for these phenomenological descriptions, except in his essays on culture. There he championed them with all his rhetorical skill. This is especially true of his essays on religion, where the analogies between intrapsychic and interpersonal processes take on explanatory weight. Contrary to many received opinions, there is nothing in *Totem and Taboo*, nor in *Moses and Monotheism*, which shows Freud avoiding explanatory claims. Rather he holds that his conclusions are about historical events, "In the beginning was the Deed" (1912–1913, p. 161), as he says of the original oedipal murder. In the Postscript to *Group Psychology and the Analysis of the Ego* (1921c), we learn that adult forms of affection are "sublimated" forms of sexual longing suppressed by the primal father. They in turn, suppressed their son's libidinal hopes, until a later generation learned to repress automatically these now-dangerous, incestuous impulses.

None of these powerful formulations is metaphorical. Although Freud cannot document his claims, since they are about the prehistory of the race, he does not doubt that such events must have occurred. In *Group Psychology* and *Moses and Monotheism*, Freud says actual deeds became symbolized later as neurotic fantasies. Like Heinrich Schliemann, the German archeologist whom he revered, Freud read texts as accounts of historical occurrences, not merely pleasantries spun for enjoyment. Schliemann asserted that the events recorded in the *Iliad* were real. He followed the Greek dramatists who explained the downfall of great families by reference to *real crimes*, like the murder of a father. Freud reflects a similar belief in the actuality of the crime when he says of the early Christian attacks upon the Jews, "It was as though Egypt was taking vengeance once more on the heirs of Akhenaten" (*Moses and Monotheism*, p. 136). Freud contends the Jews did not accept their real guilt for the murder of the original Moses. Christians accepted their guilt, but defended themselves by claiming that the Passion cleansed them.

This brings us back to the question of sublimation. The parallels Freud draws between individual and cultural forms, between types of neurosis and types of institutions, are not merely illustrative. They are essential parts of his general explanatory theory. He did not doubt there were physiological elements responsible for the formation of neurotic characters. Yet, Freud held that a psychoanalytic explanation of behavior required an account of the individual's interpersonal history. That interpersonal history influenced the intrapsychic structures which developed through the interaction between the "remorseless" instincts, the ego, and superior, external powers. This is a social model of the psyche, just as it is a psychological model of society.

Like all central psychoanalytic concepts, sublimation is ambiguous. It employs a social analogy (partial powers competing for dominance) to explain what is also an intrapsychic process. A psychoanalytic anthropologist, Geza Roheim made this explicit: "the specific features of mankind [culture] were developed in the same way as they are acquired to-day in every human individual as a sublimation or reaction-formation to infantile conflicts" (1941, p. 149). He adds, "If, as Freud has shown, neurosis is an archaism or infantilism…this amounts to the statement that neurosis is but an exaggerated form of culture" (1941, p. 154).

These are powerful claims: they unite individual and cultural forms. Freud and Roheim perpetuate a double mystery. Sublimation is not amenable to psychoanalytic insight and the *events* which produced culture occurred in the prehistory of the race and hence both processes are inaccessible to direct, scientific scrutiny.

Freud recognized these problems with the concept of sublimation and attempted to address them in his texts on the structural theory. After his death, ego psychologists used the notion of neutralization to refine the concept. These held sway until the middle 1960s when the entire libido theory suffered wholesale assault by theorists of every school.

Sublimation and the Transformation of Energy

Over and over again we find, when we are able to trace instinctual impulses back, that they reveal themselves as derivatives of Eros. If it were not for the considerations put forth in *Beyond the Pleasure Principle,* and ultimately for the sadistic constituents which have attached themselves to Eros, we should have difficulty in holding to our fundamental dualistic point of view. But since we cannot escape that view, we are driven to conclude that the death instincts are by their nature mute and that the clamour of life proceeds for the most part from Eros. (Freud, *The Ego and the Id,* 1923d, p. 46)

The Moerae were created as a result of a discovery that warned man that he too is a part of nature and therefore subject to the immutable law of death. Something in man was bound to struggle against this subjection. (Freud, "The Theme of the Three Caskets," 1913f, p. 299)

Many theoreticians have championed linguistics as the proper foundation of a valid metapsychology. There is no dearth of brilliant reconstructions of Freud that employ this as their ruling dictum. It is not difficult to understand why this linguistic turn is so attractive. Language is unique to humans for it is amenable to humanistic methods of study. It seems to be the dominant agent of change in psychoanalytic treatment. Without prejudicing this issue, I note that a linguistic reading of Freud avoids key elements in psychoanalytic practice. That unsettling aspect is their author's idealization of intellectualism. Jacque Lacan's students often reduce neurotic symptoms and dreams to puzzles and "texts."

One sign of this malaise is the effort required to read their explications; subtleties mount upon subtleties begetting affected and precious insights. For all the fire thus displayed we ought not to forget a simple fact: that self-analysis is almost always a failure. One can read and read Freud and remain ill; "Knowing" what Freud said, or what Lacan says, is not equivalent to understanding oneself. Or if it is then Freud was wrong in all his papers on technique. For he notes how much labor analyst and patient expend to counter resistances to change and to insight. No one believes this who has not suffered through his or her own analysis. Prospective patients, particularly academics, often believe the opposite. They want to be treated by the best-known analysts available. Aside from the narcissistic wishes this illustrates, it entails as well the belief that they will yield their secrets to the most subtle of minds. Their ideal analyst is a combination of Sherlock Holmes and Lewis Carroll. Besides idealizing intellectualism, this attitude ignores the elementary courage and goodwill analysis requires of patients and therapists.

Freud's remarks on abstinence and the value of truthfulness in analytic treatment are beautiful accounts of these two virtues. The transference and the status Freud accords it is an argument against the linguistic model of treatment. The transference is a safe form of repetition in the constraints of the treatment hour. It is a form of serious play that makes possible the transformation of a private neurosis into actual unhappiness. It permits patients to realize how they have been "lived" by forces and wishes outside their control. Patients are "driven to conclude" the truth of their pasts because they find themselves driven to carry out transference wishes.

These forces struggling against the work of treatment are not linguistic. Freud noted, as have others, that obsessives may express wishes and describe memories which are at the core of their disease. Only after the work of analysis has tied those intellectual elements to their original feelings does cure become possible. Freud does give language (speech) an exalted status. Word representations, psychic registrations of heard language, bind consciousness together. With them the ego constructs its legitimate rule over the id. What connects sublimation, which occurs apart from the ego, with the ego's ability to use words to tame the instincts?

Before answering this question we can see Freud's answer in the two quotations with which I began this chapter. In the first Freud's style, full of passive constructions, reinforces his message. We are forced, driven, compelled against our wishes to recognize the equal dignity of the death instincts. They are mute, they destroy language and the clamor of life. In the second he champions Greek thought as a heroic moment. They are great because they avoided both repression and religion. This permitted human beings to glimpse their true destiny, the silence of death. The muteness of death is so repellant and the death instincts so strict that most people tolerate them only with the aid of well-formed symbols.

While the Greeks saw time as irretrievable, Christianity promised to reverse the rush toward death because ritual correctness would conquer death and undo its dominion. Even Shakespeare used fairy tales to make palatable the awful truth that we cannot choose death for death always chooses us. It is not too farfetched to say one of Freud's goals was to retrieve the Greeks' capacity for tolerating these facts, for they transformed the Horae, who were beneficient deities, into the Moerae: they "who watch over the necessary ordering of human life as inexorably as do the Horae over the regular order of nature" (1913f, p. 298).

It was then that they "perceived the full seriousness of natural law when they had to submit their own selves to it" (p. 298). This something that struggles against insight, and which underlies the elaboration of both neuroses and cultural institutions, is not language nor is it linguistic. The life instincts struggle against the knowledge of death. We recall Prometheus who, because he loved humans, removed their ability to foresee their death. In the place of that knowledge he gave them the arts of seercraft and other hermeneutic methods. The culture hero gives us culture; and culture gives us a set of tools with which we first disguise the truth and later recover it.

Psychoanalysis is one of the arts of seercraft and, like them, a product of language. It employs language to reveal the intricacies of self-deception accomplished through the manipulation of language itself.

Having language is the mark of being human and the vehicle of self-deception and blind hopes. Hence repression serves the life instincts but at the cost of sacrificing our actual understanding of the other side, death. Death cannot speak, nor does it have to. It is like the character Aeschylus calls "Bia" ("Violence") in *Prometheus Bound,* a "muta persona," against whom the culture hero struggles.

Violence is a-logos, without words, ruthless, and, with force ("Kratos"), carries out God's punishment of Prometheus. Prometheus is guilty of not listening to the Father's words—a sin that has unimaginable consequences. That and his theft of fire contradict the edicts of the new ruler, Zeus, and his henchmen, who set out to destroy humanity. Even they are subject to Ananke, the single deity Freud found worthy of worship: force, guile, and torture will yield to necessity and the triple-formed Fates, the Moerae (II, 11.511–519).

Language is a tool, like other forms of culture, with which the human species creates a place for itself. It is not a vehicle of salvation because there is no salvation from the ultimate power of the Fates. This metaphysical assumption is an important feature of Freud's thought. In his comments on word representations in the psychic economy, Freud says that they work to the degree that they represent actions. Freud's view of language is much closer to the American behaviorists than it is to European linguists. As discussed later, his lifelong distinction between *thing representations* and *word representations* is not a distinction between body and mind or between behavior and thought, but between types of behavior. Word representations have an exalted status, because self-consciousness seems to require thinking with words. In turn, self-consciousness is tied intimately to motor actions of speaking and responding. Freud says that thinking is a kind of responding, that is, action. For it is nothing other than speaking at a very low level of enervation.

Of course, this distinction underlies the difference between fantasy and actions, between dreaming and criminal behavior. About language, we note that the gold of psychoanalytic treatment, transference, is a new form of behavior. Typical dreams of patients first entering into analysis often manifest themes of slipping beneath the water, or falling into the sea and being submerged. The anxiety they portray is of drowning in a foreign element, water, where one can neither breathe nor speak; one cannot cry out, nor call for help; prayer, propitiation, and promises are impossible when submerged beneath the waves.

In other words, one cannot rely upon the magic of language to cover up the gaps and tears in one's psyche. The therapist's "demand" for free association is contrary to ordinary speech, just as the patient's horizontal attitude is contrary to good taste and ordinary conversation. These factors induce regression which increases one's anxieties.

Sublimation in the Structural Theory of the Twenties

When Freud recast his model of the mind in *The Ego and the Id* (1923b), he also recast his explanation of sublimation. He did not reject the concept, he rejected the limited accounts he and others had given of it. Even contemporary theorists who reject the term *sublimation* altogether, retain the notion of "redirected" energies and the automatic transformation of goals, that is, sublimation. The structural theory improved upon Freud's earlier metapsychology. It gave to perception a dominant role in the formation and preservation of the ego. Freud now says there must be an autonomous ego that functions independently of the primary processes (the "id" of this essay). These innate ego functions may become sexualized (or aggressivized, that is, used to satisfy aggressive wishes) and so enter into neurotic distortions—but they are not born out of such conflicts. There are at least two kinds of energy: instinctual energies, derived from the id, and noninstinctual energies derived from the original ego.

Ego processes of perception, recognition, and other basic psychological functions may use noninstinctual energy (that is, the neutral energy indigenous to the ego). This change in theory means that hallucination—which occurs at the behest of upwelling instinctual energies—is not the norm. Rather, it is a deviant type of cognitive functioning. Hallucination occurs when an influx of unneutralized instinctual energy overwhelms the ego which distorts the ego's usual, conflict-free functioning, and so induces hallucinations and other distortions. It will be helpful to summarize the role of the perceptual system abbreviated as the system Pcpt.

Perception and Sublimation: Qualities Again

Freud says the ego is a coherent organization (1923b, p. 17) as opposed to its counterpart structures. Freud discovered that the ego has unconscious aspects "in the proper sense of the word" (p. 19) which make it amenable to psychoanalytic inquiry because psychoanalysis is the scientific study of the dynamic unconscious. The ego's unconscious functions include repression and defenses. The ego is not completely unconscious, nor is it born unconscious: "It starts out, as we see, from the system Pcpt. which is the nucleus" (1923b, p. 23). If we go back a few pages in his text we find that Freud has defined the system Pcpt. as (1) inherently tied to consciousness (the system Cs.), and (2) characterized by the experience of qualities. The ego is conscious and aware of qualitative differences, "All perceptions which received from without (sense perceptions) and from within (sensations and feelings) are Cs. from the start" (1923b, p. 19).

Consciousness is always the consciousness of something which has a qualitative character. Then, from the beginning, the ego must be able to record and remember qualities. This theorem amounts to a critique of the speculations of the "Project" 1895a. We can measure the extent of Freud's reversal by comparing this discussion with a similar discussion in his paper, "The Unconscious" (1915e). There he tackles the problem of the relationship between memories of words and memories of objects. In these discussions the old issue of the memory of qualities reappears disguised, though, under the rubric of "thing and word presentations." He refers to an account in *The Interpretation of Dreams* (1900a, p. 617). He argues that thought process cannot become conscious until linked to word presentations:

> Word-presentations... are derived from sense-perceptions in the same way as thing-presentations are; the question might therefore be raised why presentations of objects cannot become conscious through the medium of their own perceptual residues. Probably... thought proceeds in systems so far remote from the original perceptual residues that they have no longer retained anything of *the qualities of those residues,* and, in order to become conscious, need to be reinforced by *new qualities.* (SE 14:202, emphasis mine)

If we return to *The Interpretation of Dreams* we find that the problem of qualities is central. In chapter 7 of that book Freud recapitulates the "Projects" basic model of the mental mechanism. While the terms *quantity* and *quality* reappear, the question of their relationship to one another does not because Freud no longer worries how mere quantities change into qualities, the task he had assigned himself in the "Project."

The absence of such a concern in chapter 7 may not be a defect. It may be an admission that Freud could not solve the epistemological problems he had set out in his letters to Fliess. The likelihood that this is true increases when we compare the vocabularies of the two texts. In the "Project" Freud spoke of neural systems (the phi, psi, and omega systems) he hoped to locate in the actual body. For example, he suggested that the spinal cells correlated with phi and the brain's grey matter with psi.

In the dream book he speaks of abstract mental systems, designated by their functioning and not by their physical locale. In making this radical shift Freud created a psychology, not a physiology, and abandoned the question of how the physical world of "mere quantities" produced the world of qualitative experience. Therefore in the dream book he can describe the process of perception:

> Excitatory material flows into the *Cs.* [system Cs.] sense-organ from two directions: from the Pcpt. system, whose excitation, *determined by qualities*, is probably submitted to fresh revision before it becomes a conscious sensation, and from the interior of the apparatus itself, whose *quantitative processes* are felt *qualitatively* in the pleasure-unpleasure series. (1900a, p. 616, emphasis mine)

As in the "Project," Freud refuses to link the system responsible for perception with the system responsible for memory. The system Cs. is a sense organ that perceives psychical qualities but it is "incapable of retaining traces of alterations—that is to say...memory" (1900a, p. 615). Like the omega neurones, its distant cousins, the system Cs. can only respond to the influx of stimuli. It must remain permeable and therefore incapable of recording the passage of sensations. By distinguishing between memory and perception Freud explained why memories are more susceptible to distortion than are perceptions. Repression acts upon memories rather than upon perceptions, because "the former can receive no extra cathexis from the excitation of the psychical sense-organs [i.e., the system Cs.]" (p. 617).

The storage of qualities remains a problem; because the perceptual system (omega neurones or the system Cs.) cannot store qualities, there must be another system that carries out this task. The neurone theory faltered on this point. Freud did not grant the ability to store qualities to any neural system. He corrected this deficit in chapter 7 of *The Interpretation of Dreams*, "In order that thought-processes *may acquire quality*, they are associated in human beings with verbal memories, whose residues of quality are sufficient to draw the attention of consciousness to them and to endow the process of thinking with a new mobile cathexis from consciousness" (1900a, p. 617). Attention cathexes are what he later termed "the ego's neutral energy." Because humans can examine internal representations (memories) they gain an advantage over animals that lack language and therefore lack verbal residues. By using attention cathexis humans acquire a "new process of regulation" (p. 617). This new process is the capacity to think rather than to act.

It is difficult to overestimate the gravity of Freud's remarks about the place of language in human development. For with the capacity for language arrives the capacity for human beings to direct their consciousness. By thinking, humans use small amounts of psychical energy to model actions which would require large amounts of physical energy. The obverse is also important. Human beings may regulate themselves and control destructive impulses through thought alone. Freud quotes Plato, "the virtuous man is content to dream what a wicked man really does" (1900a, SE 5:620). Dreams are to individuals what myths are to society: arenas in which we express archaic impulses using symbolic media. This liberates the psychic energy that courses through such impulses and prevents disaster.

Word Presentations and the Recollection of Qualities

That we arrive back at Freud's view of the relationship between individual pathologies and cultural forms is no accident. For the dream is a temporary psychosis in which we hallucinate the presence of perceptual qualities which do not originate in the real, external world. This analogy is persuasive. It unites two mysterious phenomena by showing how each replicates the internal structure of the other. Yet it remains problematic for we still do not know how this central process—representation—occurs nor how memory retains "qualities."

Linking the memory of qualities to the memory of word presentation is a dazzling theoretical move on Freud's part. It lets him continue to speak about two distinct mental strata or parts: the archaic, preverbal part, operates upon thing presentations; the advanced, verbal part, operates upon word presentation. Yet he does not explain how word presentations retain qualities.

To understand this issue, we must consider Freud's earliest comments on word presentation. Those occur in his monograph *On Aphasia* (1891b) where, reviewing the neurology of speech disorders, Freud argues against the popular claim that brain lesions were the most important causes of pathology. Against this claim, he championed Hughlings Jackson's development theory. Jackson argued that neurological systems developed phylogenetically and ontogenetically. Functions acquired late are more susceptible to retrogression, or "disinvolution," than are ones acquired earlier (Freud 1891b, pp. 86–87).

As the editor to *On Aphasia* points out, this developmental claim became a principle in Freud's theory of emotional maturation. Freud always holds that early traumata are more damaging than later ones, therefore behaviors and skills acquired late are first to be impaired when the organism suffers duress. Among the traumata which may instigate such retrogressions (or regressions) Freud counts psychological ones, like terror in the face of life-threatening situations. Citing his own experience of near death, he felt "this is the end." At that moment his inner language regressed to indistinct sound images. He heard these words, uttered by himself, "as if somebody was shouting them into my ears, and at the same time I saw them as if they were printed on a piece of paper floating in the air" (p. 62).

In *On Aphasia* Freud analyzes the notion of word presentation in great detail. Aphasia has many distinct forms, e.g., some patients may speak, but with very few nouns; others cannot speak unless they hear another person speak first. Following Jackson, Freud argues we can distinguish between types of aphasia. We can distinguish the severity of traumata, not simply which brain areas they affect. This lets him explain why he found no linkage between specific lesions and specific language difficulties. There are speech areas responsible for language: "when learning [to speak], we are restricted by the hierarchy of the centres which started functioning at different times; the sensory-auditory first, then the motor, later the visual and lastly the graphic" (1891b, p. 42).

He amplifies this point when he uses a psychological schema rather than a neural mapping to sketch word representations (p. 77; SE 14:214). The major item in these sketches is the "sound image" to which he attaches the "visual images" for printed and handwritten scripts. Along a different line he attaches the "kinaesthetic image" to the sound image as well. Using this sketch and the quotation above we can say that normal linguistic development takes a fixed route. The "A" sequence names the neural centers; the "B" names the behaviors:

A. sensory-auditory-----motor---------visual--------- graphic
B. hearing-----------------speaking----- reading-------writing

Given this developmental sequence, severe traumata cause one to lose the advanced capacities first and the others more slowly. Since hearing is the primary modality by which we acquire language, hearing is the least likely to suffer impairment. Conversely, its impairment is a sign of the most severe regression. While Freud uses neurological metaphors, his idea is similar to Piaget's: advanced cognitive processing cannot occur unless its predecessors have occurred. Freud's is a neurological treatise not a psychological one. Apart from his bit of self-reporting, he does not connect this neurological schema with a theory of emotional development. That marriage took place four years later in his psychology for neurologists, the "Project." Returning to it we find that our old question How are qualities retained in memory? returns. We note that it touches upon the complex issues of word presentations and consciousness.

Thing Presentations in the "Project": Qualities Again

In the third part of the "Project" Freud addresses the questions How are qualities remembered? and Why are speech associations (hearing) primary? There he attempts to account for normal psychological processes (as opposed to pathological ones) by way of the neurone theory. Freud's exposition is laconic and difficult to condense further. He wishes to use a mechanical model (the phi, psi, and omega systems) to explain psychological processes (like perception, remembering, self-reflection, and planning).

He uses the basic premises of biological reductionism to constrain his theorems. Psychological processes tend to "release quantity" because an increase in quantity is painful (a psychological law) and contrary to the rule of entropy (a natural law). Freud's attempt to work out a developmental scheme and his habit of altering his model when he reaches an impasse complicates his discussion. These problems make it difficult to summarize his position. Yet quoting Freud at length does the reader no service. In this section I trace the way he links together the issues of word and thing presentations with the quality–quantity distinction.

Freud retains the developmental schema of *On Aphasia* but not as explicitly as one might wish. In the earlier text he took the point of view of the scientist examining the course of a disease category. In the "Project" he takes the Creator's view of the human mind. Given the constraints of physical laws and given the need to create human psychological behavior, how can a brain accomplish all these tasks? Freud says he cannot give a mechanical explanation of psychical attention: "For that reason I believe that it is biologically determined—that is, that it has been left over in the course of psychical evolution" (1895a, p 361). He then repeats his general theory. The ego must learn to distinguish between perceptions of objects and hallucinations: "... discharge [action] must be postponed till the indications of quality appear from the idea as a proof that the idea is now real, a perceptual cathexis" (p. 361).

"Idea" here is probably the German term *Vorstellung*, which is more accurately translated "representation" (cf. 1895a, p. 365, n. 2). "Attention" is a state of the ego in which it examines incoming perceptual stimuli and compares them to the particular idea uppermost at the moment. When it can match the wish (an internal *Vostellung*) against an external perception "identity is attained" (p. 361, emphasis his). This basic process constitutes the biologically determined process of learning.

We have already seen this thesis. Freud amplifies it when he explains that "observing thought" asks "what does this mean?" (p. 363). How does the ego manage to follow the right path among the thousands associated with the particular idea? Or as Freud puts it, "How...are the psychological neurones in the ego to know where the cathexis is to be directed?" (p. 364). He answers by linking the sensory–auditory system with the discharge of Qh (which constitutes the experience of qualities). Attention cathexes orient toward the flow of qualities because qualities indicate actual perceptions. How can observing thought find qualities within the apparatus itself? How can we recognize qualities in our thoughts when there is no "data" from external perceptions? As Freud notes:

> After all, indications of quality themselves are only information of discharge (of what kind [we may learn] later perhaps). Now it may happen that during the passage of Q a motor neurone is cathected as well, which then discharges Qh and furnishes indications of quality. It is a question, however, of receiving discharges of this kind from all cathexes. They are not all motor, and for this purpose, therefore, they must be brought into a secure facilitation with motor neurones. (1895a, p. 364, Strachey's interpolations)

In other words, to achieve self-consciousness the ego links ideas to the discharge of Qh because discharge of Qh characterizes indications of quality. "This purpose is fulfilled by *speech associations*. This consists in the linking of psychological neurones with neurones which serve sound-presentations and themselves have the closest association with motor-speech-images" (p. 365, emphasis his). To establish consciousness, which includes observing thought, the ego associates ideas with sound images, for sound images evoke motor word images, that is, speech which is a behavior and therefore has qualitative features. This is a major claim. It asserts that self-consciousness and problem solving occur only if the person has learned to hear and speak (and later read and write). This is also a behaviorist principle (supported both by the American psychologists John Watson and B. F. Skinner): thinking is a special form of speech. In Freud's language, self-conscious thinking requires facilitations between neurones associated with hearing, linked with the motor activity of vocalization, that is, speech. For the indications of speech-discharge help. They put thought processes on a level with perceptual processes and "lend them reality and make memory of them possible" (1895a, p. 366).

This point reappears in Freud's discussions of "thing and word presentations" in *The Interpretation of Dreams* and in his papers on metapsychology. Freud holds to the principle that consciousness is always the consciousness of qualities. Hence self-conscious thought, which includes all the higher thought processes, must use qualities in some manner. Humans acquired this capacity because they learned to associate ideas with sound images and sound images with motor images. They learned to associate ideas with hearing and hearing with speech. Although "we do not really speak, any more than we really move when we imagine a motor image" (1895a, p. 367), the movements differ quantitatively, not qualitatively.

Added to his neurological account, Freud considers the infant's capacity to communicate internal states to others: "The biological development of this extremely important [kind] of association also deserves consideration" (p. 366). He concludes consciousness springs from the infant's experience of unavoidable suffering. The memory of that experience, not the experience itself, makes consciousness possible. This occurs when the ego perceives similarities between an earlier event which issued in psychological pain and a new event.

We can state Freud's thesis in three propositions: (1) At first the baby screams automatically upon suffering; speech operates like a safety valve. (2) Then its screaming acquires a secondary function: it draws the helpful person to the infant. Hence, screaming serves as a rudimentary form of communication. (3) As the infant matures it comes to associate some objects with suffering and suffering with its own screaming. Even with no other information about the dangerous object, "information of one's own scream" serves to characterize it. This third process makes memories of unpleasure conscious and so "the first class of *conscious memories* has been created" (p. 367, emphasis his).

Unlike idealist philosophers and psychologists, Freud says the mind became complex because it faced the complex burden of protecting the human animal. Freud's famous aspersions upon the burdens of civilization are literary formulations of this thesis. To control itself and to use thought rather than action, the ego must increase its burden of bound cathexes. (Hence this problem dominates the rest of Freud's account, 1895a, pp. 367ff.)

Thing presentations (or ideas, in German, *Vorstellungen*) are those parts of the perceived image which are generic. For example, the child perceives its mother as a "thing" (object) which manifests characteristics typical of mature females. To perceive his mother the child must recognize her distinctive features, that is her distinctive qualities. As we have seen, this is the role of word presentations. Word presentations are linked biologically to speech and speech is a form of motor innervation. Therefore, word presentations can reinvoke qualities (representations of qualities) by using memory to compare pereptions with ideas. Freud argues that the capacity to employ word presentations underlies the mature ego's capacity to distinguish the particular from the generic.

Strachey notes that this obscure claim rests upon Freud's earlier discussion of the activity of judgment. There (1895a, pp. 328, 330–333) we learn that judgment requires the ego to scan perceptual images and to compare them against images called up by wishful thinking. If the ego discovers the perceptual image is not identical to the wishful one, it will not initate discharge automatically. The ego compares two images, one wishful, the other perceived, which are of similar things but have distinct predicates (p. 328). Hence the one-year-old who is hungry but realizes that this is not her mother does not attempt to nurse at a stranger's breast.

Primary process thought fails to carry out this delayed process of judgment. For primary process thought treats similar objects as if they were identical, and therefore the ego initiates discharge (action). The neonate nurses with any vaguely appropriate object. The dream considers babies, penises, and feces as interchangeable entities. An analytic patient deep in a transference neurosis responds to the analyst as if the analyst were mother. This distinction, and those like id and ego, that follow, do not oppose object presentations to word presentations. Freud does not say that the infant judges the perception of a breast against the word image "breast." The infant does not use language to distinguish safe objects from dangerous ones.

Rather, the child's capacity for language marks it as having achieved a level of secondary process functioning. This capacity distinguishes acting automatically upon the perception of objects similar to one's wishes and acting with rational judgment.

David Rapaport (1955, pp. 117–119) discusses the general problem of hierarchy in Freud's metapsychological speculations. He points out that Freud's notion of levels of functioning was more sophisticated than commonly understood. Freud draws no sharp boundaries between ego and id functioning, nor between ego and superego functioning for that matter. In the healthy individual we will not be able to find the seams between these three agencies since each harmonizes with the others. Just as one must suffer to "feel" where one's gall bladder resides, so too psychopathology reveals the borders between the mental agencies.

Among contemporary American theorists, John Gedo (Gedo and Goldberg 1973; Gedo 1979) has argued a similar thesis regarding the developmental hierarchy of all major psychological systems. Rapaport notes that when the ego defends itself against infantile drive elements it absorbs that conflict within itself. Even adaptive identifications absorb archaic conflicts. The ego ameliorates them but at the expense of internal peace, since it now suffers the lower level strife within itself (p. 118).

Freud amplified this point in the last pages of "The Unconscious" (1915e). He recapitulates *The Interpretation of Dreams* (1900a), "Moreover, by being linked with words, *cathexes can be provided with quality* even when they represent relations between presentations of objects and are thus unable to derive any quality from perceptions" (SE 14:202). Again, it is the ego's capacity to link together nonverbal presentations (images or representations) with a word (sound representation) that permits discharge of quality. This discharge of quality enables, but does not guarantee consciousness: "being linked with word-presentations [*Wortvorstellungen*] is not yet the same thing as becoming conscious" (SE 14:202–203; GW 10:301).

What consciousness is we cannot say, nor could Freud. He breaks off his exposition promising to revive it in a paper on consciousness—which he destroyed (see SE 14:203, n.). In the language of the topographic theory, word presentations occupy a stratum of mental functioning which is hierarchic to that occupied by thing presentations. Word presentations characterize the system Pcs., while thing presentations characterize the system Ucs. (SE 14:203).

Qualities and Sublimation

Before considering how Freud reformulated his thinking on word and thing presentations, it will pay to summarize what we have discovered so far. The usual understanding of sublimation overlooks Freud's distinction between the experience of qualities and their location. For example, Jones (1953) summarizes Freud's theory of the mental apparatus (before 1923): "the preconscious possessed *no qualitative attributes*, only quantitative ones. In that it differed from consciousness, which derives qualities from three sources: (1) the release of either pleasure or unpleasure, (2) from association with speech memories, which have a quality of their own, and (3) more directly, from perceptions. No consciousness can exist without some quality" (1953, p. 403).

While this describes Freud's claims, it does not convey his reasoning. Qualities are the result of periodic oscillations instigated by external quantities but which have their being only within the experiencing organism. This is true of the three sources of qualitative experience.

The organism's first response to the pleasure–unpleasure series is an internal affair: an event or stimulation that pleases one person may traumatize another. In *Studies on Hysteria* (1893–1895), a letter to Fliess (letter 46 of 30 May 1896), and in the "Project," Freud says that an early memory, say of witnessing parental intercourse, may become sexualized at puberty, *after* the original perception. This sexualization infuses the dormant memory with danger and produces the anxiety which "fires" the ego into recognizing the possibility of unpleasure. We recall, of course, that unpleasure is a quantitative event in which ego mechanisms are threatened with a surplus of excitation. The primitive ego's reliance upon the pleasure–unpleasure illustrates the organism's tendency to maintain equilibrium of the quantities operating within its boundaries.

Freud never gives us a psychological theory of pain; he always bases his discussions of it on its obvious biological functions. In *Inhibitions, Symptoms and Anxiety* (1926d) he revives his original notion that anxiety serves the biological purpose of signaling to the ego imminent dangers. Anxiety is a psychological version of the biological rule flight or fight. Its presence causes the animal to carry out one of these automatic defenses. The ego draws upon the pleasure–unpleasure series to evoke defenses like fight or flight.

The ego's ability to link thing presentations with word presentations permits it to rely upon behavioral clues. These linkages between words and actions are effective because they replicate the primary interaction between infantile hearing and infantile behavior. That is, the child learns how to speak and to match its expressive behavior to incoming stimuli. I find nothing in the arguments of *On Aphasia* or in the "Project" which suggest that words themselves convey qualities. Their linkage to vocal communication makes them eligible to connect disconnected thing presentations with consciousness. Freud says that self-conscious thought requires qualitative sensations: "A mechanism of attention ... presupposes ... *indications of quality*" (SE 1:364, emphasis mine).

Attention cathexes are drawn to indications of quality. These arise from silent speech (a form of behavior). Silent speech prefigures the ability to use words because word images are tied to the motor neurones used in producing speech. Word associations gain an exalted status in the psyche. For they derive from behavioral events which reproduce the condition of perception: the passage of a small amount of Qh in the form of quality. (See "Project," pp. 364ff.)

The three sources of quality Jones discusses are actually one: the ego's perception of quantitative variations within its environments. Is this not an unfair summary? Jones, like Freud and his commentators, says that perception yields the sensation of qualities, not quantities. This is accurate according to ordinary theories of perception. It cannot be valid according to Freud. It cannot be true if Freud's basic epistemology is correct. I have tried to show that Freud's fundamental understanding of the ego's relationship to the world is one of illusion. The natural sciences explain that ultimate reality is composed of quantities which obey the inexorable laws of thermodynamics. It follows that human experiences of qualities are illusory responses to impinging waves of quantitative particles.

The problem of qualities is tied to the question of consciousness: In what does it consist and what are its boundaries? Freud links the two problems, as do all those who follow his general line of thinking. Freud's rhetorical arguments are persuasive and restate traditional claims that each human being is unique. Yet they complicate rather than simplify both problems. If we cannot understand the nature of qualitative experience without first solving the problem of consciousness, and vice versa, we have little hope of doing either.

Reducing the problem of qualities to the problem of consciousness, a private, internal event, makes qualities unavailable to ordinary knowledge. It is similar to the problem of other minds: If I can know only my own internal thoughts, how can I be sure that other people are like me "in their souls"?

The Problem of Consciousness and Qualities

Freud's solution to the problem of consciousness is troublesome. It is not just other minds that become obscure; my own does as well. We saw this already in the way Freud employed Kant's *Critique*. Kant had said that the conscious ego can know only within the constraints it imposes upon sense experience. Freud made this a more radical doctrine. Since ultimate reality is quantitative and since the ego does not know this (its experiences are always qualitative), the ego is always ignorant. Hence phenomenological modes of investigation are misdirected. They presuppose as true what science tells us is false: the real world is one of qualities. To repeat Ricoeur's illuminating phrase, Freud is an antiphenomenologist.

Human experience is one of qualitative differences. One might subsume qualitative sensations, like warmth, tastes, wishes, and fears, under the rubrics of pleasure and unpleasure, as Freud does. But even then it makes little sense to say that these categories are exhaustive. There are many pleasures associated with viewing landscapes, none of which is identical to another. Hearing rain strike the trees is a different pleasure from seeing headlights sweep across the grass.

The Location of Qualities in The Ego and the Id

Freud responded to these difficulties in his texts on metapsychology. In *The Ego and the Id* (1923b) he reexamined the question of qualities using the new dual instinct theory (see 1920g). In these essays he examined his former explanations of the genesis of qualitative experience. In brief, he locates qualitative experience, particularly affective experiences, even deeper within the psyche than he had in the papers on metapsychology. Positive (libidinal) and negative (aggressive) wishes represent the operation of primal instincts. These primal instincts impart their qualities to their derivatives. Primary experiences of pleasure and pain derive from the operation of primary instincts whose effects are intrinsically pleasureable or intrinsically painful.

Qualities and Quantities in the Dual Instinct Theory

To illustrate Freud's new view of quantities and qualities compare what he says about the origin of pleasure and pain in texts from different periods. In the "Project" he argued that pain occurred when the quantity of stimuli reached a threshold beyond which the organism sought discharge. This gave him some trouble in describing the ego as an entity made up of highly charged neurones. He elaborated a notion of "bound energies" which the ego uses to carry out its duties. So he redefined pain: it occurred when a surplus of unbound energy was loosed within the mechanism. Even this failed to explain why sexuality, one of the primary pleasures, often used an increase in unbound excitation as a way to heighten pleasure:

> pleasure and unpleasure, therefore, cannot be referred to "an increase or decrease of a quantity (which we describe as 'tension due to stimulus')," although they have a great deal to do with that factor. It appears that they depend, *not on this quantitative factor,* but on some characteristic of it which we can only describe *as a qualitative one.* (1924c, SE 19:160, emphasis mine)

He adds that unknown qualitative factors may reflect the rhythm of the stimulus, which echoes the notion of periodic motion in the "Project." This argument, from "The Economic Problem of Masochism," completes a line of thought initiated in *Beyond the Pleasure Principle.*

There he stated that pleasure might be the result of a change in quantity over a particular period of time (1920g, SE 19:8). This permitted Freud to explain puzzling behaviors, like masochism, as products of the mixture of primal instincts. It is the admixture of the two primal instincts, eros and destructiveness, that produces neutralized energy made available to the ego. The urge toward destructiveness is tamed: "we can only assume that a very extensive fusion and amalgamation, in varying proportions, of the two classes of instincts takes place, so that we never have to deal with pure life instincts and pure death instincts" (1924c, SE 19:164). Given this, Freud explains perversions as the composite of primary instincts, fused and aimed at various targets, sometimes the self (masochism) and sometimes others (sadism).

True to his reasoning, Freud follows out the implications of the new instinct theory. If pleasure and pain express primary forces, then it makes sense to speak of unconscious feelings (1923b, SE 19:41,49; 1924c, SE 19:166–67). For unconscious feelings are, by definition, a state of the psyche in which a raw instinct, like destructiveness, dominates an unconscious complex. More important to our concern, Freud uses the dual instinct theory to reformulate his theory of sublimation. It appears he did so while composing *The Ego and the Id.* In encyclopedia articles written in the same year (1923a) he gives the old definition of sublimation alongside his new dual theory (SE 18:256–258). In any case, *The Ego and the Id* contains his most radical account of the process of sublimation.

The Transformation of Instincts: Desexualization

Even a patient reader of this chapter may have wondered when we would return to the question of sublimation. We can do so now. I have shown that the problem of qualities versus quantities reappears in the new dual instinct theory of the structural period. We can now see how the dual instinct theory resurrects the problem of sublimation. It does so by way of the ego, the theoretical entity which dominates Freud's later thought. In his earlier essays sublimation occurred at the behest of the partial instincts. Because they were denied immediate gratification, they sought it elsewhere via symbolic substitutions: in this sense sublimations are behavorial antitheses to the neuroses. Where neurotic symptoms are compromise formations engendered by conflict between conscious forces and unconscious ones, sublimation occurred "prior" to conflict. Hence, Freud concluded that he could not account for this mystery.

This all changes in *The Ego and the Id.* Instead of suffering, as it were, sublimatory events to occur sub rosa and unconsciously, the ego, according to the new theory, effects sublimations. It does so by altering the ratio of the two great classes of instincts. In the famous words of chapter 3, the ego is built up out of precipitates of abandoned object cathexes. Its character, what others call "personal identity," centers around a conglomeration of partial identifications. Although Freud vacillates about how much independence and strength to grant the ego vis-à-vis the id, he does not believe it can contradict the id's needs entirely.

The general term that accounts for the ego's adaptive response to its demands by way of internalization is *identification* (Roy Schafer, 1968). There are many kinds of identification. Freud includes pathological and adaptive forms under this single rubric. We recall that identification is also the process by which the ego "defuses" the primary instincts. It gains access to their primal energies: "The transformation of object-libido into narcissistic libido which thus takes place obviously implies an abandonment of sexual aims, a desexualization—a kind of sublimation, therefore. Indeed, the question arises…whether this in not the universal road to sublimation…which begins by changing sexual object-libido into narcissistic libido and then, perhaps, goes on to give it another aim" (1923b, p. 30).

The dual instinct theory let Freud make many of his most far-reaching claims, such as the aim of all life is death. It also had problems. The chief difficulty is that even when neutralized, instincts retain their original goals: either union or destruction. To explain conscious love and hate, and affection and disagreement, Freud links them with the primal instincts. Eros lies at the bottom of our conscious desires for union with others and unity with ourselves. Destructiveness lies at the bottom of our conscious efforts at discrimination. Though diffused, primary instincts do not lose their characteristic qualities.

We see this in Freud's discussion of the ego's neutral energy (1923b, pp. 44–47). He says that the ego appears to have a neutral energy at its disposal. With it the ego can "augment its total cathexis" (p. 44) and so counteract the effect of either too much eros or too much destructiveness. Where does this ego energy originate? The ego's tendency to unite disparate feelings and to solve conflicts manifests its drive toward unification. This is desexualized libido or "sublimated energy; for it would still retain the main purpose of Eros—that of uniting and binding—insofar as it helps towards establishing the unity, or tendency to unity, which is particularly characteristic of the ego" (1923b, p. 45).

Many people have criticized the deftness with which Freud mates abstract ideas with clinical observations and with his theory of narcissism and objects libido. (See Bibring 1941; Ricoeur 1965; Gill 1963; Barros 1973.) There is something heroic in Freud's language. For example, many lower animals die after completing the act of copulation "because, after Eros had been eliminated through the process of satisfaction, the death instinct has a free hand for accomplishing its purposes" (1923b, p. 47). This turn to metaphysics does not answer our original and less grand question: Where do qualities originate?

Or if it answers our question it does so in a way that is disappointing. We have followed Freud from his letters to Fliess, through his essays on sexuality, to these last works. The issue of qualities is more obscure than ever. Qualities must derive from the actions and interactions of the two great classes of instincts. It is these two great forms—Eros and destructiveness—which condition and dominate the quality of our conscious experiences. While we can answer our question, we are not happy with it. Qualities are echoes of the aims of the primal instincts. Their origin is, therefore, in those powers of which we are but one instance.

Following the publication of *The Ego and the Id* Freud used the term *sublimation* many times. In most instances he did not employ the new theorems regarding the fusion and diffusion of the primal instincts. Rather he recapitulated the earlier notion of displacement of aims and symbolic substitutions. Except for a brief comment (1925j, p. 257), the following characterizes his accounts: "The wish to get the longed-for penis...may contribute to the motives that drive a mature woman to analysis, and what she may reasonably expect from analysis —a capacity, for instance, to carry on an intellectual profession—may often be recognized as a sublimated modification of this repressed wish" (*New Introductory Lectures*, 1933a, SE 22:125).

Sublimation in Other Psychoanalytic Authors

In a review that remains valuable, Edward Glover (1931) distinguished the two ways in which Freud used the concept sublimation. He notes that sublimation must be more than another form of displacement and that if it is not we had better drop the term altogether. That other dimension is the forms of energy involved in sublimatory activities. Glover reflects uneasiness with the dual instinct theory. He says, "the old Freudian classification of instincts was in some respects more convenient than the recent antithesis of death and life instincts" (p. 294). For example, some "self-preservative instincts" are unalterable with respect to aim, while many pregenital sexual instincts (or part instincts) are capable of being "modified beyond recognition" (p. 294). Further, research into the sublimation of the death instincts themselves is much less advanced than research into the modification of the "life" instincts. Glover does not challenge the assumption of qualitative energies, the Life Forces, about which Nietzsche and Shaw had much to say.

In a similar vien, Glover does not believe the individual process or activity of sublimation reflect cultural forces and cultural expressions. This is contrary to my argument in chapter 2. There I tried to show that Freud is very much a "structuralist" in his consistent linkage of cultural forms with their individual (neurotic) counterparts. According to Glover the "introduction of ethical or cultural valuations" (p. 295) creates more confusion and trouble than they are worth. He suggests we restrict our investigations and examine the mechanisms by which sublimations effect a balance within the psyche. "According to the taste of the investigator, this function can be expressed in terms of the pleasure-reality principle, or in terms of illness (which includes maladaptation to existing social regulations)" (p. 295).

Is this so? The sublimation of anal eroticism into pottery, for example, does not carry with it an overwhelming quality of valuation. We would be happy to join Glover in his rejection of the "incubus of absolute values." Yet from an evolutionary and genetic point of view we must side with both Freud and later anthropologists who connect the two realms.

Freud's forays into the prehistory of the race, that of the Jews and Christians especially, were not an accidental application of the clinical theory for Freud felt bound to explore the other half of the genesis of neurosis: the individual's development. Roheim and Freud made this point many times: "The [human] organism can get rid of tensions only through another organism and therefore in a biological sense the infant is anaclitic" (Roheim 1941, p. 157). From its beginning the human being is a cultural being. It cannot survive without the presence of loving and actively involved mature human beings. Aside from stories of feral children, scientific evidence shows that human infants and children require interaction with adults. Roheim notes that a specific culture authorizes particular forms of sublimation and can "canalize the latent conflicts of its members" (p. 156). As Roheim says in a beautiful passage, "for a human being at the dawn of life environment is essentially another human being" (p. 161).

Glover's strictures on falling into moralism about a patient's behavior ought not to lead one to reject Roheim's point of view. "Values" are not mere matters of taste, used like perfumes or spices: they persist in their role as guides as long as they reflect the instincts which employ human beings for their expression. Following Glover's paper many people reviewed the concept; most found it wanting. Other analysts enriched the descriptive literature on sublimation. Heinz Hartmann and his collaborators attempted to reformulate the metapsychology. Ernst Kris began the task in his famous studies on regression in service of the ego (1952). Heinz Hartmann and Kris consolidated the general economic argument. It can be summarized as follows. We should distinguish behaviors which may be called "sublimations" (or displacements), and which resemble ego defenses, from the economic process of neutralization. Following Freud, Hartmann and his associates distinguished three kinds of energy: libidinal, aggressive, and neutral. The latter belongs to the ego from the beginning. Neutral energy constitutes the ego's original armament against the pressure of libidinal and aggressive energies. The ego increases its store of neutral energy by "neutralizing" the other two energies. This increases the ego's adaptive capacity and therefore its creative activities. Among the latter are behaviors termed sublimations.

Hartmann and Kris felt this explained the energic process that occurred within sublimation (Hartmann 1955, p. 239; Kris 1955, p. 30). We could investigate the mechanisms by which a part instinct achieved expression and the "energy" which the ego used to accomplish it. Edith Jacobson (1964) employed these economic formulations in her acclaimed treatise on self-identity. Like her colleagues, she asserted that the economic theory of transformation (desexualization and neutralization) can illuminate clinical observations. Thus she describes processes of resexualization, deaggressivization, and reaggressivization. Creative people who focus on a single problem exclusively must employ sublimated orality. This orality enables them to manifest "devouring" interests (pp. 80–81, n.4). She and Kris explain how some young children vacillate between sexualizing their paintings and using "neutralized energy" in their art.

For all the virtuosity of their authors, these formulations fail to convince critics of the economic point of views. I will not capitulate those arguments here, many of which seem to me well founded and unanswerable. I evaluate the claim that Hartmann and his critics make, though addressing values, culture, and conflict, psychoanalysis is a value-free mode of inquiry. Hartmann (1960) says psychoanalysis is a science and does not and should not champion one kind of values over another. Or, as he says in another context, "Psychoanalysis is…an inductive science of the connections between complex mental structures. Its propositions are obtained empirically and have to be verified empirically" (1927, p. 401).

As a rejection of moralizing about one's self or one's patients it seems true. As a description of analytic inquiry and treatment, it seems false. Jacob Arlow (1955) amplified Hartmann's opinion: "Those definitions of sublimation which stress the displacement of sexual drives from manifestly instinctual aims to aims of a higher order of social estimation obviously introduce an element of value judgment. Such valuation is a highly questionable procedure in a scientific investigation of mental processes" (1955, p. 515).

If Hartmann is correct, the concept has come full circle from its origins in Freud's letters to Fliess. There, we recall, it carried its usual preanalytic meaning of the (magical) transformation of sexual interests and energies into substitute behaviors. That magical transformation was what religious teachers, novelists, and other wise persons had described from ancient times. Plato's famous scale of the orders of love, from gross sensuality (heterosexual) through homoerotic affection, to the love of wisdom, predates Freud by two millennia. By rejecting this common understanding, Hartmann would appear to have given the concept a new, clearer, nay sublimated, status. It now is to refer to an intrapsychic, energic process that can be measured and assessed apart from issues of cultural or moral valuation.

Rapaport was quick to note that if Hartmann is correct, it makes little sense to retain the term in the scientific lexicon of psychoanalysis (1955, pp. 522–523). It is much closer to Erikson's notion of ego mode, that is, a behavioral repertoire based on activities of the primary zones. These are covert value judgments under the guise of psychosocial theorems about the interaction between infant and environment.

Another problem arises. Martin Wangh (in Arlow 1955, p. 524) notes that there appear to be gradients of sublimation such that some forms of sublimation like hobbies and the arts, especially dance, culminate in "orgastic climax" while others do not. Are we to say that the former are more "sublime" than the latter? Kris referred to the same problem under the heading of "distance from the drives," as does Kaywin (1966). It seems reasonable to say that the more "distant" the behavior the less physical, or sensual it appears. Yet the greatest amount of "orgastic" responses occur in highly structured and difficult arts, like ballet and theatre. Or are these only symbolically orgastic? Can one distinguish the actor's simulation of sexual hunger from a naive subject's experience of the same feeling?

This is not an easy question to answer. Many critics have pointed out the interesting paradox that people playing themselves are often less believable than actors playing similar roles. Kris used the notion of "adaptive regression" to account for this fact. He argues that an actor can "regressively" retrieve orgastic feelings (primary process feelings), then employ those feelings in art (a secondary process behavior). This seems plausible for many artists report similar feelings (though self-reports would not count against psychoanalytic claims since they are not derived from analytic work). Are such actors "closer" or "further away" from the drives? The answer is that the notion "distance from the drives" is a metaphorical one. It cannot explain all cases of sublimatory behavior.

Freud as Historian

In this chapter I have reviewed the range of psychoanalytic opinions on the process of sublimation. In his pre-1923 texts Freud's notion was the classical one of diversion of archaic ("lower") impulses into advanced ("higher") forms of activity. This always suggests a bit of magic, for the images associated with such transformations, like those drawn from alchemy, are ones of fantastic transfiguration. This is evident in archaic religious traditions in which the retention of semen, for example, is held to increase one's metaphysical potency.

While Freud was not as vulgar, his theoretical assertions about sublimation repeat the vulgar understanding of sublimation. We noted his comments on the unavoidable conflicts between the needs of culture and the privatization of sexuality. This was so because he had committed himself to explaining the diverse courses of the instincts. The instincts are by their nature nonpsychological forces which shape human life, as it were, from below the level of consciousness. Yet Freud did not abjure the analysis of culture itself.

His notorious books on religion and the history of the race are more than essays in applied analysis.[5] It is wrong to read these as mere illustrations or metaphorical musings. The relationship between religion and obsessional neurosis, for example, is not one of mere analogy. They are structural inversions of one another; as are art and hysteria, paranoia and philosophy, and others. Freud's thesis reappears when he claims that his reconstructions of the beginnings of the human race are historical, not metaphorical. He does not, of course, claim he can pinpoint when and where the first primal family acted out the oedipal tragedy. He does not doubt that such an event took place. We see this in his essay on Moses, *Moses and Monotheism*, (Freud 1939a). Freud's texts, like other "mythologies," manifest a love of dualisms. Freud makes these subservient to his historical claims. There were two Moses: the first was an Egyptian murdered by his followers then resurrected in the name and guise of a later, lesser Moses.

One might say that Freud's essays on culture are irrelevant to the true gold of his thought, his clinical reports and clinical theory. This is a suspicious move since it presumes to discard about one-third of the *Standard Edition*. Even if we grant it, concepts of the clinical theory are inherently social and historical. Transference includes the repetition of previous relationships in an automatic reenactment engendered by the artificial regression of the analytic encounter.

In his reformulation of the concept sublimation, Freud says it is through identification that the ego secures "neutral energy." While I have not followed this economic theorem, for reasons noted above, one cannot deny that identification is a crucial dimension in many sublimated behaviors. Identification cannot proceed without the presence of a loved, and perhaps feared, "external" object. What of the concept sublimation and its relationship to the critique of culture?

I see no way of understanding Freud's thinking on this topic other than saying he was inconsistent. First he tried to explain sublimation by reducing it to the drives. Later he tried to reduce it to the process of neutralization of the primal instincts. Both attempts led him back to the psyche and its interaction with the body (or the "id" in *The Ego and the Id*). Freud noted parallels between the neuroses and social institutions; he explained them with theories about energies that could not be measured, and processes that could not be observed.

Heinz Hartmann and his collaborators did much to clarify these later speculations.[6] Distinguishing between neutralization and displacement, did not explain sublimation. Elegant descriptions of hypothetical energies does not yield additional understanding. With the collapse of Hartmann's economic schemata, the concept of sublimation, now associated with desexualization, began to fade away as well. In recent reviews of the term authors as sophisticated as Louis Kaywin (1966) argued for its exclusion from the psychoanalytic lexicon.

I hope it may be retained. Many people transform what would be unacceptable or conflicted behavior into actions pleasing to them and beneficial to their society. Second, there is no doubt that behaviors and feelings associated with the pregenital zones are of special importance in these transformations. Third, there is some relationship between the forms of such individual sublimations and cultural constraints. Fourth, the notion of sublimation is, for better or worse, tied intimately to issues of values and valuation.

One way to make sense of the term is to reconsider Freud's reasons for making all processes of valuation intrapsychic. The "Project" reveals how closely tied are his theories of perception, of qualities and quantities, of valuation, and of sublimation. Having shown that, I suggest a different theory of perception can help us elaborate a distinct, psychoanalytic theory of values. I argue for this distinct orientation in the following chapters. I can summarize it as follows: perception is an activity in which the ego recognizes the array of qualities inherent in the world. I reject the official theory that qualities are added to quantities "in the mind." I believe this extreme thesis is wrong. I also reject its corollary, that processes of valuation are even more private and interior.

Regarding sublimation, I believe a revised theory of perception, and therefore of the location of qualities, forces us to agree with Whitman. Whitman could read the *Iliad* because he could count on the sublime power of the sea and land to balance Homer's sublime powers. For Whitman the sea and land are sublime. They have that quality inherently. We does not project our interior states onto them. In this I think he is correct.

CHAPTER FOUR

ORIGINS OF COMPLEX BEHAVIOR
AND SUBLIMATION

> I attempted to show that there is a steady tendency
> in the forms which are increasing in number and
> diverging in character, to supplant and exterminate
> the preceding, less divergent and less improved
> forms.
> —Charles Darwin, *The Origin of Species* 1859, p. 415

Herbert Simon, a philosopher, says science proceeds by finding
sameness in the midst of difference, by finding homogeneity in the
midst of heterogeneity (1969). Science aims to make simple what
appears to be complex. Rudolph Carnap (1955), another philosopher,
says in science there are no depths, all is on the surface where simple
forms obey simple laws. If Carnap is correct, complex artifacts should
reduce into simple rules. Freud said there are many theories of mind,
but one true neurology. Freud shares Simon's belief that good science
is simple and clear. That there are many psychologies means we know
little: where knowledge is sparse, theories abound. Freud aimed to discover how the biopsychological machinery (a singularity) created the
variety of psychological experiences (a multiplicity). How does a
common neural structure, governed by rigorous laws, produce diverse
symptoms, character, and cultural institutions?

The problem of sublimation reappears at this point. It is a theory
of how instinctive behaviors, the pregenital urges, evolve into complex
public institutions, remote from their origins. One can imagine three
types of answers. The first kind of answer is outright reductionism.
Like Carnap, one can try to show how cultural forms and institutions
are reducible to simple causes and simple forms. A second answer is
some form of essentialism. The "gap" between the psychological
machinery (instincts or brain or genes) and cultural institutions is

unbridgeable. According to this answer, cultural forms are in essence not reducible to their psychological origins. If science always shows causal origins of behavior, then there can be no scientific psychology for causes precede effects. Yet people order their lives according to future goals, not just previous causes.

A third answer is to respect the complexity of conscious behavior, but to account for it by evolutionary theory. This third answer permits one to respect the fact of complexity of cultural forms, like the arts, but to also remain scientific. We can accomplish this balancing act by way of developmental theory and show that complex behavior is the end product of simple laws and simple agencies operating over time. Darwin explains the complexity of the natural world by invoking the laws of "Natural Selection." Darwin seems to show that more complex and more developed entities have an advantage over their less complex cousins. Over a long enough stretch of time, natural law, not divine wisdom, encourages the evolution of more and more developed biological forms.

Complex Behavior and Evolution

Contemporary theories of personality development represent this third option. Freud's theory of psychosexual stages and Marx's theory of cultural stages are similar. Each says high energy, low information modes of production evolve into high information modes which use less energy (d'Aquili, et al 1979; Gay 1978). Developmental theory allows one to give simple (at least linear) explanations of complex phenomena without reducing advanced forms to their simpler precusors. (Such theories also use many charts.) Marx and Freud recognized this dimension of social theory and both rely upon developmental theorems to strengthen their explanatory theories.

Freud examined psychosexual development in which one form of libido superseded earlier modes; Marx examined historical sequences in which one mode of production superseded earlier modes. There is a major difference between their theories and the one I propose. It can be summarized by an axiom of information theory: noise cannot generate information (C. E. Shannon's Tenth Theorem [Shannon and Weaver 1949]). Like its cousin, the Second Law of Thermodynamics, this theorem holds only for a closed system, an event that never occurs in ordinary experience. Nevertheless, the Tenth Theorem is valuable because it shows that Freud's view of the mind as originally independent of external reality cannot be correct. For the infant's mind cannot contain sufficient information to create a semblance of the world. Rather, the surplus of information available in the external world organizes the mind. In organizing the mind, the external world also organizes the personality. Freud accounted for diverse individual behaviors by uncovering their origins in the individual's body, the set of instincts. Darwin accounted for diverse species and showed their origins in the *interactions between germ plasm and diverse external conditions*. Theologians had argued that the diversity of nature, with its "designed" entities, proved the existence of a Designer. To retrieve an earlier phrase, "no pattern without a patterner." Theologians mounted some of their strongest arguments for the existence of God by referring ot the fact of design throughout nature. Surely no one could deny that nature revealed designed flora and fauna, each fitted to one another with art and skill? Was not God the great Designer? Darwin weakened this argument when he showed that natural laws could account for diversity and therefore we need not assume a Designer. All nature required to turn simple forms into complex, "designed," forms was the operation of these natural laws through eons of time.

Was this true of complex human behaviors as well? No late nineteenth-century scientists could remain unimpressed by the sweep and power of Darwin's theory. Psychology could not claim a scope as grand as Darwin's yet psychologists would not propose theories that violated Darwin's discoveries nor contradicted the main tenets of his evolutionary theory. Freud recognized Darwin's achievements and did his best to mold his psychological theories to the constraints imposed by Darwin's central claims. Freud had "Lamarckian tendencies," (Jones 1955, pp. 194–195) and did accept Darwin's materialist solution to the puzzle of the diversity of species.

Yet Freud retained his claim that the real world is one of "quantities" alone. He restricted "qualities" to the operation of the mental agencies. In doing this he overlooked a key element in Darwin's thought. Because he lived before modern genetic sciences, Darwin could not name the internal elements (DNA) responsible for the preservation of diversity. He could name other sources of diversity in the external world, "As geology plainly proclaims that each land has undergone great physical changes, we might have expected to find that organic beings have varied under nature, in the same way as they have varied under domestication" (Darwin 1859, p. 466).

Darwin refers to the crucial discovery that species evolve because they face intense competition for each biological niche available. A geometrical increase in the numbers of each generation means that "More individuals are born that can possibly survive. A grain in the balance may determine which individuals shall live and which shall die" (p. 466). External forces amplify the value of any variation that favors one animal or plant over another. Each variation increases the survivability of the favored organism which means that these external forces control the structuralization of the favored members. In Information Theory terms, external forces reinforce the message, "make this kind of animal." External forces *add* important information to the ecosystem by shaping the behavior of hundreds of species, each struggling in a changing environment.

Freud recognized this environmental aspect of Darwin's theory. Pursuing his research program, he stressed the role internal forces, the instincts, play in shaping behavior. Here, Freud's interest in Lamarck's theory of transmissible adaptations reappears. Lamarck held that animals transmitted adaptations to the next generation through an unnamed mechanism of inheritance. We know such transmission occurs through teaching; Lamarck and Freud held that it also occurred through some unnamed biological process as well.

By adopting Lamarck's thesis, Freud could explain how unconscious ideas influenced somatic structures. Sandor Ferenczi, his Hungarian colleague, shared Freud's passion for evolutionary theory. With Ferenczi, Freud elaborated a comprehensive view of evolution that united psychoanalysis with biology. Freud described their goals in a letter in November 1917 to his colleague, Karl Abraham:

> Our intention is to place Lamarck entirely on our basis and to show that his "need" which creates and transforms organs is nothing other than the power of unconscious ideas over the body, of which we see relics in Hysteria: in short, the "omnipotence of thoughts." Purpose and usefulness would then be explained psychoanalytically; it would be the completion of psychoanalysis. (Quoted in Jones 1955, p. 195)

Antimaterialist theologians used the notion of "purpose" to argue that causal theories could not explain planned actions. In harmony with Kant's mission, the antimaterialists declared psychology off limits to the materialists. In biology the materialists were beating the vitalists who claimed that physical laws about "inert" entities did not rule living things. Freud recognized that the external world altered all species. "Two great principles of change or progress would emerge: one through (autoplastic) adaptation of one's own body, and a later (heteroplastic) one through transmuting the outer world" (p. 195). Yet he views the outer world mainly as a source of discomfort: the organism must respond either by changing itself or changing portions of the external world. This principle is identical to one elaborated in the "Project." If persons cannot avoid friction with the external world they first attempt to modify it. If that fails, they use dreams or religious solutions and other imaginative modes that ameliorate conflict. They produce illusions of control over the sources of pain and discomfort. Because people dislike death but find it impossible to escape, we create religion which explains death away. We do not die, according to some traditional Christian teachings. We are transformed from one state into another, a better one in which there is no death; the wounds inflicted by this world are healed by the loving powers that rule the next.

This traditional psychoanalytic account may well be accurate as a theory of religion. When carried to an extreme it overlooks the degree to which the external world not only impinges upon the organism but also provides to it information that helps the organism rearrange itself and so adapt. Freud felt compelled to argue that complex, high information systems are equivalent to simple, low information structures. This violates Shannon's Tenth Theorem, since it requires one to argue that low-information systems alone gave rise to high-information progeny.

The Structure of Objects, The Structure of Representations

All things have internal structure. Externally, a thing may have form, and possess considerable grace in the balance of its parts, but it cannot be said to have a style unless some aspect of the relationship of its parts appears in other objects and by its replication provides a basis for a perceptive eye to group them together. Original creations must inspire copies. Style is the recognition of a quality shared among many things; the quality, however, lies in a structure on a smaller scale than that of the things possessing the quality. (C. S. Smith 1978, p. 16)

I have tried to show that in its usual form the problem of sublimation is insoluble. Freud presupposes there is a "gap" which separates the drives from their eventual products, behavior. I have focused on the way in which this gap appears in Freud's labored discussions of the transition from quantities to qualities. I argued that Freud's epistemological dualisms led him into untenable, mythlike conclusions. As a result, the theory of sublimation failed to develop alongside the clinical theory. To the degree that sublimation is an aspect of psychoanalytic aesthetics, the latter has suffered as well.

The gap between quantities and qualities may be bridged in other ways. One is to use a linguistic metapsychology. A second way to bridge the gap is by phenomenology. Structuralism offers a third way. I examine each of these alternatives below. If psychoanalysis is a linguistic theory and a linguistic method, we can avoid the issue of quantities. Instead, we can focus exclusively upon issues of meaning. I have discussed this option above. I analyze this option at length in chapter 5.

Another way out is to conceive of psychoanalysis as a form of interpretation, what philosophers call "hermeneutics." Philosophers like Paul Ricoeur and Jurgen Habermas (1968), literary critics and some psychoanalysts, like Donald Spence (1987) have championed this gambit with much skill and erudition. Their primary orientation is phenomenological. According to these authors, we need not and cannot pretend to ground psychoanalysis upon objective, scientific claims. Psychoanalysis is a discipline that interprets intentional structures, like motives and wishes. In the lecture hall this claim seems valid. For does not analysis occur between two persons, both of whom speak to one another? Yet, in the analytic encounter, especially with erudite patients, one does much more than interpret the meaning of "symbols of the unconscious." The patient's actions become the focus of analytic scrutiny, not the patient's thoughts insolated from the patient's life.

Does phenomenology offer a way out? Among the many significant workers in that vineyard Paul Ricoeur (1965) proposes a comprehensive philosophy of interpretation. Ricoeur reflects a type of phenomenology as defined by Edmund Husserl. Ricoeur does not challenge the authority with which philosophers of science, even positivists, define what will count as valid scientific efforts. He grants to Freud's critics their most extreme rejections of Freud's claims to scientific method. Ricoeur disavows the possibiltiy of a "unified science." This means that he need not to *demonstrate* the difference between material hierarchies (investigated by natural scientists) and cultural hierarchies (investigated by humanists).

Kenneth Pike's (1954) "emic/etic" distinction addresses this difference. As one moves from the explanation of material hierarchies to the interpretation of cultural hierarchies, one must make more and more arbitrary rejections of "irrelevant" matter. What one gains in clarity and intellectual precision one loses in scope and accuracy.

Material vs. Linguistic Structures

Another route is that of general structuralism. Do general structuralist methods give us a way to create a unified science of natural and cultural forms? While the term *structuralism* has suffered the fate of popularization, structuralist perspectives permeate thinking in biology, psychology, anthropology, and other sciences. Structuralism is not atomism; neither is it materialism nor idealism. Structuralist analyses are propositions about the redundant features of the given system. C. S. Smith (1978) describes this in his essays on material hierarchies.

His essays are illuminating for those who identify structuralism only with the work of semiologists like de Saussure and Lacan. Semiologists focus their efforts upon linguistics. Because language is human behavior, semiological structuralism confines one to anthropocentric points of view. Smith discovers homologies between patterns in material objects, like soap bubbles, and patterns in artifacts, like Chinese landscape painting. This suggests a way out of such anthropocentrism:

> Nothing can be understood without at least a simplified glance at levels that are above and below the one of major interest. In both science and art the center of the limited perception of the human mind can be placed anywhere. The future seems to lie with a more extensive science, but it will have to be a multilevel science that, eschewing mysticism but not metaphor, will be able to pass continuously with a controllable focus and precision into the field of art. (C. S. Smith 1978, p. 51)

I use Smith's argument to show why there is no easy passage from the analysis of natural forms to the analysis of cultural forms. This does not mean one should cultivate mystification. It means a theory of culture cannot be deduced from a theory of nature. A multilevel science must include, at its higher levels, an awareness of this gap. A general structuralist theory assumes that both mind and matter are systems of interacting particles. Which came first? Evolutionary theory tells us that material forms and hence material patterns must have preceded the appearance of mental ones. To distinguish material things from one another we must locate distinctive qualitative differences between parts of the mass:

> The hierarchical alternation between an externally observable quality, property, or trait, and an internal structure which gives rise to it occurs at all levels and applies to all things. The interface, being both separation and junction, is always Janus-faced—that which is characterized as an entity is in some way more closely connected within than without. To define an entity, to separate it from the rest of the world, the interface closes upon itself, and hence in sum, but not necessarily everywhere, is concave inwards [sic]. (Smith 1978, p. 23)

This Janus-faced quality of all entities resembles Kenneth Pike's distinction between emic and etic units in descriptive linguistics (Pike 1954; 1962). "Emic" units (from the term *phoneme*) are entities constituted by more plentiful "etic" units (from the term *phonetic*). In turn, emic units constitute the minimal units of all linguistic behavior. Thus sets of phonemes constitute words. The emic/etic distinction is not another way of talking about "insider's" and "outsider's" points of view. It does not refer to subjective and objective approaches to human behavior. On the contrary, the emic/etic distinction is not that of material hierarchies. Then what is the difference?

Emic units, like phonemes, differ from the elements that make up material hierarchies. Smith hopes for a general structuralist analysis of art and nature. This assumes that the relationship between material forms and say, a Chinese painting, is one of continuous hierarchy. This is true of material structures. The microscope reveals finer and finer details of the subelements which make up printed color, for example. It does not reveal "left overs," subelements that do not enter into the structure's "style."

In Smith's terms, physical objects are "concave" inwards. One finds there are always more connections between surfaces and interiors than there are connections to external objects. Each subelement links to others and to the "surface." A "quality," like the smoothness of glass, depends upon the orchestration of subelements into a more or less fixed pattern which produces a consistent sensation. To return to the microscope; when we examine plate glass under sufficient magnification we see that its lower level elements are not "smooth." If, like the hero in *The Incredible Shrinking Man*, we were tiny, ordinary glass would not be "smooth." It would appear as jagged as a holly bush. This does not mean the quality of smoothness is illusory. It means that glass will not be smooth to creatures whose sensory equipment is finer than ours. The smoothness of glass is a function of the total organization of subelements in relationship to the sensory net that makes up our perceptual apparatus. The "smoothness" of plate glass is not illusory; it is determined by our perceptual apparatus.

Smith's materialist hopes require cultural forms, like myths, paintings, and stories, to exhibit "material" concavity. We should be able to analyze cultural forms the way we analyze the smoothness of glass. Other "qualities" of the artifact should yield to the same kind of analysis.

Human Languages Are Not Material Hierarchies

Human language is a redundant coding system that employs sounds which the human being can produce and distinguish easily. In any workable system, coding processes must be uniform and governed by a small number of rules. A language selects from numerous sound events, a small set of sounds which constitute its minimal units, the phoneme. A phonetic analysis of sounds shows them to be "concave" inwards. Sounds are made up of smaller units, individual vibrations. Vibrations are made up of even smaller physical events. Scientists can analyze the components of each item "down" to its smallest parts. Phonemes cannot be reduced this way. (See Zellig Harris 1951.)

A linguist learning a new language first assesses the range of sounds used by native speakers. This requires an etic analysis in which one uses physical measures to designate the material dimensions of something. One can make finer and finer etic judgments by using finer and finer instruments of analysis. The linguist can use better microphones and more sensitive instruments to gather finer etic measures of native sounds. A linguist could, like a metallurgist, make more and more etic distinctions, e.g., one could measure humidity levels in various locutions. Of course one rarely finds this kind of detail in most linguist's transcriptions.

Phonetic transcriptions usually reflect the ability of ordinary speakers to discriminate audible events. Because there are few ways the brain and sense organs can discriminate easily among humidity levels in vocalizations, one does not find humidity measures in the annals of descriptive linguistics. Once settled on a transcription device, the linguist seeks to discover sounds similar to one another and distributed in characteristic ways, e.g., complementary distribution (H. A. Gleason 1955).

Finding this class of sounds and discovering *the rules of their appearance* in native speech constitutes a phonemic analysis. Phonemes are sets of sounds restricted by specific rules. To analyze emic structure one first learns how native speakers divide the stream of etic units and from those divisions create a phonemic system. Emic entities exist within well-defined systems governed by well-defined rules. Emic units are distinguished according to systematic features, like voiced and unvoiced. The English phonemes /p/ and /t/ are distinguished by the presence of labiality in the former and its absence in the latter. The linguist cannot predict which sounds a particular language uses to constitute its phonemes. For example, the forty-five English phonemes do not include the tones that are essential to spoken Chinese. To the degree that his speech is unintelligible, a foreigner's accent is a mark of his inability to match our phonemic expectations.

Pike (1954) and Zellig Harris (1951) note that the emic/etic distinction does not assume that a particular phoneme "means" anything in itself. The English phoneme/p/ does not "mean" anything. When used in an English utterance along with another phoneme, e.g.,/ai/, one hears the word *pie*. Then, an English speaker may recognize a meaningful utterance about dessert, or the ratio between the diameter and circumference of a circle.

Scientists verify their hypotheses about a foreign emic system by testing them against a native informant. They cannot and usually do not ask their native informant to articulate their own phonemic analysis. Natives are necessary as colleagues to validate the emic researcher's guesses, but they can rarely elaborate an accurate description of their own emic system. Most native English speakers cannot begin to list the set of English phonemes.

Are Human Behaviors and Values Emic?

Can we use the emic/etic distinction to explain human behavior other than human language? Pike tried to do this when he divided human behavior into "actemes." He hoped to discover the syntactic and grammatical rules which governed actemes. "Actemes" linked to each other form "actions" (Pike 1954). Edmund Leach and other antropologists have proposed similar ideas. These applications have two problems. First, Pike assumes that there must be actemes. These must be logically arbitrary in the way phonemes are. If true, then actemes could not mean or refer to anything in themselves, in the same way that the English phoneme /p/ does not mean anything in itself. A code requires a grammar for a grammar and imposes restrictions on the use of emic entities. Emic entities are defined by their place in a rule bound system. A homely example is teaching a child how to create a simple "secret code" that uses numbers to identify English letters, e.g., A=1, B=2. The first rule is that one can select any letter to match with any number. The second rule is that afterwards you have to obey rule one. You must always assign the same letter to the same number. It happens I assigned A=1, and this is identical to the ordinal place that letter occupies in the English alphabet. I could just as well have assigned A=15.

The actions that make up social life, such as facial expressions, or other "actemes," are not arbitrary. They typically enjoy a "meaning" based on actual, nonlinguistic codes, for example, a loud, bellowing shout with snarled teeth tends to suggest anger. The "actemes" and "symbols" and "mythemes" that make up individual and social self understandings are not arbitrary. Not only are many, if not most, of these mythical elements nonarbitrary, they are universal. Even if one agrees with the standard anthropological challenge to Freud's claims that oedipal conflicts were universal, sexual themes and unconscious "ideas" are universal. Psychotherapists and novelists describe a litany of sexual and aggressive actemes throughout their informant's lives. Within psychoanalysis proper many of these themes have been codified. Freud and Karl Abraham (1927) could list the equation of "baby= penis=nipple" as an exemplary datum of psychoanalytic investigation. An explanation for this invariance is not hard to find. Human beings are mammals. Their images of themselves reflect issues of mammalian existence. Eating, defecating, being taken care of, fighting, copulating, and dying dominate mammalian life. Images of these actions dominate unconscious mental life. To return to our logical problem, these images are not emic. Their structure and their contents are not arbitrary. Symbols of loss, like the damaged body, and symbols of mother, like the salty ocean, function like icons not like "actemes." Icons, as we shall see, are not linguistic. Representations of the self and of other persons are usually iconic, not linguistic.

A second, major problem is that Pike's use of linguistics requires him to argue that actemes are structured like material particles. Pike's argument about the relationship between etic and emic strata parallels Smith's analysis of the style of material artifacts. This is contrary to my position.

Pike's Argument: Phonemes as Material Structures

Ordinary, solid objects, are composite structures which, like all structures, depend, "in the main on the repetition of relationships, there is always some hierarchical level in any natural, social, or aesthetic structure at which it can withstand the replacement of some of its parts by others" (Smith 1978, p. 23). Is a phoneme such a structure? One can find within a phoneme many phonetically distinct elements which are nevertheless treated as if they were equivalent. They are in free variation with one another. A native speaker can discover this fact only by rejecting his or her acquired ability to hear these variants as the same thing. To be fluent in a language is to hear different sounds as essentially one sound, the phoneme, and to reject all others (etic units) as meaningless.

In communication theory such nonphonemic etic elements constitute noise. Pike holds that emic entities and etic entities are ontologically alike, they are all types of sound or, he claims, types of action. These entities neither change nor occupy different ontological categories. It is I the interpreter who create order and so create emic entities. In this sense Pike maintains the usual understanding that phonemes are not "larger" than other sounds. Phonemes are classes of sounds treated as if they were identical.

Phonetic units and all etic units, like all material entities, are composed of smaller etic units. Any etic unit can be broken down further into even smaller etic particles. Pike says the reverse is also true: emic entities may become etic elements at a higher level:

> [E]tic and emic data do not constitute a rigid dichotomy of bits of data, but often represent the same data from two points of view.... the emic units of a language, once discovered by emic procedures, may be listed for comparative purposes with the similar emic units from other languages studied. The moment that this has been done, however, the emic units have changed into etic units. (Pike 1954, p. 41)[1]

An emic analysis cannot proceed without the proper attitude. One should be a few feet away from the painting. Emic analyses are more chancy than etic ones. Etic units are available before the work begins. The etic researcher need not worry about his or her "place" in the behavior of the system under investigation.

In contrast, theologians, literary critics, and anthropologists realize that meaning systems must be discovered at their level of operational existence. The art critic must discover how one should stand and how one should squint in order to "see" the picture upon a pointillist's canvas. Standing too far away one sees only splotches of color, too close and one sees only "meaningless" dots. Pike says one cannot defend an emic analysis without also defending one's choice of "attitude" or point of view.

Pike's arguments and conclusions are valid only if one agrees with him on two counts: that phonemes are identical to material structures and that human actions are structured like phonemes. He claims that once we learn the rules that govern phonemes we can treat them as if they were etic units. But "the emic units have changed into etic units" (Pike 1954, p. 41).

Pike's claim cannot be correct for if it were correct, then we could "analyze" language the way we can analyze material artifacts. We could work "top down" from macroscopic to microscopic levels. Smith says we can do this with material artifacts because they are stable wholes. For example, the human body is a material arranged in material and functional hierarchies. Cells make up tissue, tissues make up organ systems, organ systems make up major body systems.

In any hierarchical analysis of a material thing, one can treat the lower level system as "parts" of the higher. Tissues are to organs as organs are to the organism. When Pike says that phonemes turn into etic units he cannot mean that they cease to be phonemes. They have not lost their status within a particular language; /p/ remains an English phoneme even when set alongside a symbol for a Chinese phonemic tone. Pike says this amounts to treating /p/ in an etic way. By this he means we treat it as if it were a unit that could be employed by anyone, just as anyone can use a metric ruler. This is not equivalent. To mention the name /p/ is not equivalent to use /p/ as a phoneme. Mentioning Chinese phonemes is not equivalent to speaking Chinese. A bilingual person can do both: mention Chinese phonemes and use them as phonemes within the Chinese language. Pike misconstrues his distinction between the two kinds of units. Etic units measure physical characteristics. Emic units are arbitrarily defined and codified classes of sounds. Emic units cannot become etic at any level of use.

Consider Smith's discussion of Chinese painting. One could use finer and finer etic methods to measure the hue and intensity of the artist's name (assuming he or she signed the painting). Those measures would never permit one to read the name.

This simple but important difference between the two kinds of structures—a difference Pike did so much to clarify—is irreducible. To decipher unknown scripts we need contrasting texts which employ symbols determined by phonemic rules, and higher level codes as well. Experts can determine those rules if they are given enough examples. For all linguistic texts must reflect the small number of rules which constitute the syntax and grammar of that language. Every emic entity, like every phoneme, can be analyzed into its component etic units. Emic structures are not material things.

The difference between materially complex things, like mountains, and emically complex ones, like cocktail parties, does not lie in their constituent parts. It lies in the rules which govern their construction. The laws that describe the association of certain atoms with other atoms are not arbitrary. Chemists should be able to explain why a particular substance crystallized at a particular temperature. The laws of chemistry respect no national or ideological boundaries; water freezes at 0 Centigrade in Moscow and in Dallas. In contrast, the rules which govern the opeartion of emic system are idosyncratic to that system. One cannot predict which etic units will become the raw materials that will constitute the emic set.

This makes the task of interpretation difficult. To understand why let us consider the rudiments of communication processes, beginning with the simplest systems. We can define communication as a process in which an operator sends a message which effects a particular change in the environment. We can then say that rudimentary communication occurs at the level of molecular interaction.

Referring to A. G. Cairns-Smith (1971), Peter Calow (1976) suggests how the simplest biological processes might "communicate" meaning. The fit-fill schema of molecular replication illustrates a primitive feature of matter, shape: "Shape, then, is a property of all matter, from the simplest atom to the most complicated molecule and so is well-suited for a general solution of our problem" (p. 118). A protein can replicate itself because it is "able to select a particular molecule out of a mixture by virtue of the molecule fitting into the socket formed in the tertiary protein structure" (p. 118). This simplest level of replication corresponds to the message "copy me." At the next higher one the message requests the creation of dissimilar products. At this point we consider the emergence of biological forms where "we tend to talk more about the [genetic] code having meaning" (p. 120).

How this leap occurred, how a particular "great molecule" replicated its *arbitrary* code, remains a mystery. However, once it has occurred one may speak of a truly semantic code, for "there is no obvious reason why one base triplet should specify for one amino acid rather than another. It seems as if the genetic code is established by convention rather than by the laws of physics" (p. 120). The DNA code is arbitrary with respect to which particular sequence specifies which protein. The original gene depends upon the correct transmission of such messages. It must find ways to guarantee their accuracy. To say that the particular sequence of chemical bonds is arbitrary is to say that their dissociation is also a matter of chance. Therefore the new entity develops ways to protect the acquired code. Richard Dawkins (1976) says the original super-molecule, the primitive gene, must construct survival machines. Higher mammals give the germ plasm a chance in an environment dominated by natural selection and competitors.

Pike's argument helps us clarify one aspect of the interpretation of cultural artifacts. Psychoanalysis, a boundary discipline, is an excellent example of an interpretive science. Psychoanalytic theory is an account of biological forces (the instincts) and their relationship to material events (behavior), passed through the alembic of memory. Material events and physical or biological forces are not emically structured. They are structured the way Smith described Chinese paintings and soap bubbles. However, self-understandings and psychoanalytic interpretations are, *in part*, empically structured because they employ language to categorize representations of oneself and representations of others. Freud realized that his science, the critical examination of self-understanding, competed with the claims and perogratives of religion.

Self-representations are not simple products of arbitrary codes, religious or otherwise. In other words, they are not merely composite products of grammatical operators. Rather, self-representations are similar to natural objects because they incorporate iconic representations of the self and other objects. Self- and object representations have a dual parentage. They are partly iconic and partly codified. In other words, they have both etic and emic dimensions. They are partly perceptions of natural objects, one's self and other persons.

Responding to Art: Iconic Representations

Gregory Bateson (1972) says we can understand some artifacts without the need for translators because their message is prelinguistic, that is, iconic. He compares these iconic qualities of artifacts, like religious rituals, with what Freud termed "primary process thinking," such as dream thinking. Iconic representations bear a homologous relationship to the entities they represent. Funeral masks and rites of mourning are shaped both by somatic and cultural forms.

This is not true of higher level codes, like the sequences in genetic replication or the phonemic system. An iconic representation of the message, "It's raining" bears a formal relationship to the shape of falling rain while a linguistic message, like the German sentence, "Es regnet," need not. "This difference provides a near formal criterion to separate the 'arbitrary' and digital coding characteristics of the verbal part of language from the iconic coding of depiction" (Bateson, p. 133). To distinguish the two types of messages note that one could not deduce the meaning of my statement, "It's raining" without many behavioral (iconic) clues. I could mimic rain-falling with my hands.

Speakers may use both iconic and noniconic codes simultaneously. Like good actors, we can say one thing with one's hands, and another thing with one's speech. Nonverbal arts, religious rituals, and other artifacts appeal to different audiences. They can do because they convey iconic messages. Wittgenstein knew at once that a painting of men sitting in a bare room represented a dream.

Icons are not emic entities. Like all material things they are composed of smaller "etic" units. However, at the level of object perception and pattern recognition icons are "simple elements." They enter into patterns with similar elements and constitute ritual and mythic artifacts. Workers in many disciplines examine the nature of iconic representation. We have seen already how important the issue of icons is to anthropologists. Religionists also examine iconic images and their interpretation. Carl Jung's notion of the archetypes and Claude Lévi-Strauss's discovery of universal mythemes refer to iconic representations. Alongside these academic studies is the world of psychoanalytic inquiry and treatment.

Distinct problems emerge when investigating icons in these two distinct realms. In academic realms the problems are conceptual and logical. In the psychoanalytic realm the problems are emotional and biological. Neurotic persons are famous for being irrational and recognizing that they are irrational. Upon analysis these irrational attitudes always disclose a "reasoning" about the world based on infantile prototypes and because that reasoning takes place unconsciously it operates like a mental reflex. So, it takes hundreds of hours to discover the causes of the patient's irrational action or belief.

To interpret this hidden connection destroys the reflex and undoes the inhibition. Hundreds of instances of such uncovering, working through, and resolution occur in any long-term therapeutic encounter. For example, a man "accidently" forgot to add important calculations to a business report for his boss. If approved the report would have won him an important promotion. On reflection, he recalled similar moments of unconscious sabotage, actions that also took place in his analytic work. When analyzed they disappeared and ceased to dominate the patient's life. Moments of self-sabotage reappeared only during regressions in his analysis.

This patient discovered that he experienced his boss as if the boss were tall, muscular, and dangerous. My patient's iconic image of a "dangerous man," an image that was usually unconscious, emerged in dreams, in associations, and in transference responses to me. We discovered that this iconic image had its roots in the patient's boyhood. Compared with the little boy, his father was tall and muscular and seemed to know everything, including his son's sexual and aggressive fantasies. The patient's father often validated this frightening (iconic) image. So the young boy grew into a man whose self-sabotage protected him from appearing too aggressive toward "dangerous men."

This bit of case history is a typical instance of ordinary treatment. As the heirs of ninety years of psychoanalytic science, we may take such instances for granted. Freud taught us how to deal with unconscious "icons." The courage Freud manifested may be measured by reflecting how hard it is for most of us to deal with our unconscious anxieties. This courage is not merely one of baring one's private feelings and private life to another, although that is hard enough. Rather, it is the courage to confront powers lurking, waiting for us to make an error.

Public and cultural instances of such unconscious iconic representations appear throughout folk religion. Raffael Scheck recounts an example told by Ernst Bloch. In the early eighteenth century:

In a North German city a robber was sentenced to death on the wheel, but the local authorities gave him a chance to save himself. It was shortly before the "Walpurgisnacht," the night in which the devil and the witches are said to have their meeting on the Brocken mountain. The delinquent would have been released with a pension if he ascended the Brocken mountain during the "Walpurgisnacht" and reported afterwards what he had seen. The robber rejected the offer. He preferred the extremely terrible death on the wheel (people often lived up to nine days after the execution) to the possibility (or certainty in his eyes) that he would meet the devil and fall into eternal damnation after death. (1988, pp. 179–180)

I have no way to validate the accuracy of this story, but it is told in a literary way. Yet it is also believable. In our times many adults believe in devils, spirits, and possession in a culture dominated by science. That a poor robber might believe absolutely what everyone else did and that he chose correctly, given those beliefs, seems to me plausible. He was correct and not "irrational." Given the icon of the devil as "evil incarnate," the poor robber made the right choice.

Iconic representations can terrify or gratify. They can convey intense feelings directly. Many parents can "read" their child's emotional and physical condition by simply noting the child's posture and expression. Dramatic artists, psychotherapists, and other human-relations experts rely heavily upon their common ability to respond to nonverbal, iconic representations their patients use. Because this kind of sensitivity to iconic representations does not depend upon logical operations, conveying one's insights is especially difficult because "a great deal of conscious thought is structured in terms of the logic of language, [and therefore] the algorithms of the unconscious are doubly inaccessible" (Bateson 1972, p. 139).

Plato said the same thing in his attacks upon the mimetic arts which he feared becuse their origin was in iconic representation: "poetry, and in general the mimetic art, produces a product that is far removed from truth in the accomplishment of its task, and associates with the part in us that is remote from intelligence, and is its companion and friend for no sound and true purpose" (*Republic*, 603b). Like Plato, Freud says that human cognition and all the "higher" processes of mind rest upon a base of iconic representation. Human feelings are also tied to iconic forms. Linguistic forms, like poetry, which employ or create iconic structures, are more powerful emotionally than the most rigorous deductions of the strictest logicians. Those who wish to reform the emotional life of another person must analyze the person's old icons. Like artists, they must create better representations from the remains.

Psychotherapy, like religious conversions or politics, cannot proceed as a rational venture only (Castelnuovo-Tedesco, 1989).

Logical Difficulties

Iconic representations have many limitations. Because iconic communication requires a more or less homologous relationship with the object signified, and because it lacks the rule-bound rigor of an arbitrary code, it lacks logical operators. Iconic representations cannot enjoy the luxury of self-reference. Paintings cannot say that they are forgeries. Dreams cannot give their own "meaning." Dancers cannot "say" what their dance means, or else, as Isadora Duncan said, "Why dance it?" (Bateson 1972, p. 137). Research in sign language suggests a correlation between the degree of iconicity of a sign system and its grammatical features. Israeli sign language is very iconic and has very few grammatical operators. American Sign Language is the opposite (Cohen, Namir, and Schlesinger, 1977; Klimar, Bellugi, et. al, 1979). Expert charade players use icons to represent abstract ideas and a whole set of fixed signs to represent tense, number, and other grammatical features. Flipping the left hand behind one's ear means past tense. This is an arbitrary sign, not an iconic image.

What Freud called primary process ideation operates, as Bateson notes, like an iconic system. For primary process thought lacks the many virtues of logical operations, particularly structural redundancy and negation hence primary process messages must be repeated and elaborated to ensure accurate transmission. Dream thoughts are "overdetermined." The symbolic regalia of office typically repeat the assertion: "this is a person of power." The higher classes reinforce their status by drowning themselves in the conspicuous consumption of useless but costly goods. In short, iconic representations can be emotionally powerful. For emotions are strong feelings evoked by iconic memories and iconic wishes for the future. They are logically anemic; icons cry out for interpretation but provide the erstwhile interpreter no guidelines.

I have argued icons are not emic forms. Were they arbitrary, like phonemes, one could find or create a code which used them as its constituent parts. One could make a language composed entirely of symbols. Contrary to those who have composed dream books since the beginning of commerce, there are no such codes. Dan Sperber (1974) made this point when he criticized Jacque Lacan's particular credo that the "Unconscious is structured like a language." If unconscious ideation were linguistic it could be translated into any other language, like English. For all natural languages are translatable with all other natural languages. One can neither find nor create a language made up of unconscious thoughts or any other strictly iconic system.

Unconscious thought lacks logical necessities like grammar; one finds no consistency among various "translators." Each translator must comprehend how people employ icons and manufacture their group myths and their personal myths as well.

Psychoanalytic Interpretation is Not Hermeneutics

Before analytic training I viewed psychoanalytic work as the uncovering of hidden meanings. This is understandable for Freud said this was so. Also, it suggests that we investigate hidden meanings just as clinicians examine the dream. When one uses psychoanalytic ideas to interpret artistic objects, these ideas cease to be psychoanalytic. True, the "oedipus complex" when used by Freud and when used by a literary critic seem identical. In the clinical encounter the term designates *behavior* that occurs between patient and analyst. In the literary encounter the term *oedipus complex* designates *an idea* that may be used to categorize the writer's representations.

These are not equivalent uses of the term. The term *oedipus complex* is not a "lens," a "generalization," or a "working hypothesis." It cannot be exported whole from the clinical encounter to the classroom. To say that Freud advanced just another "view of human nature," denies that he made any real discoveries about the human mind. In particular, these standard academic references to Freud deny that there is such a thing as the "unconscious mind." For the "unconscious" mind is unconscious. Words do not capture it, even if the words emerge from concrete, clinical work with patients.

A simple but dramatic example of the reality of the unconscious is to examine one's nightmares. In the nightmare we are paralyzed with fear. We believe horrors await us just as the robber believed horrors waited for him on the Brocken mountains. Another way to sample the reality of the unconscious is to supervise another person's psychotherapy work with patients. Then one discovers that it is easy to "see" another person's struggle with unconscious anxieties and it is easy to point out to them. It is more difficult to see the identical anxiety in oneself. Doing therapy is like driving a car, or swimming the back stroke, or since there are at least two persons involved, dancing or playing. *These are all activities;* one learns them by trying, by failing many times, and by trying again. No coach has a vocabulary large enough to describe the muscular memory used in tennis or any other complex behavior.

Psychotherapy deals with the consequences of failures in the patient's previous realtionships, especially in early life. Transference is the patient's automatic repetition of these failed realtionships in the new encounter with the therapist. Progress occurs when the therapist makes similar, but not catastrophic, errors with the patient in the here and now. Together, patient and therapist can figure out where the failure occurred and how it could be corrected.

The therapist struggles to comprehend the patient's life as internal, self-conscious reality. A typical instance is the furious patient who acts enraged, but is aware only of being afraid of the therapist's response. To attend to the patient's speech alone, or to focus on the patient's self-understanding restricts the therapist forever to the surface of the patient's life. The unconscious is, after all, unconscious. By definition, it is never available to the patient's self-understanding (see Langs's many discussions of this issue, e.g., Langs 1985).

Logical Problems with the Interpretation of Icons

One wishes to "interpret" an iconic religious form or a patient's dream, establish their messages, and convey those messages using ordinary language. To do this one treats the formerly pristine myth or dream as an etic field out of which one can forge minimum units of meaning. These new units of meaning will be made up of new emic elements. Hence one treats the icon or the dream as if it were a linguistic element. This has two important consequences.

First, the set of emic units is necessarily smaller and more constricted than the set of etic elements. Codification requires that only a few of the large number of etic elements become members of the emic set. This means that no single emic formulation can exhaust all the possible combinations of etic subelements. Chinese has selected one particular set of sounds to constitute its phonemic structure. We interpret a dream using only a few clinical rules and responding only to a few associations.

Second, because iconic representations lack logical operators they cannot achieve self-reference. Consequently they cannot guarantee the accuracy of particular interpretations. Because their structure is not logically secured through arbitrary codification, icons lack internal redundancy: the interpreter cannot tell which part of the icon is "message" and which part is "redundant." Which part of the ceremony is crucial or "meaningful" or which part is happenstance, accident, or repetition of something less obvious? Interpreters therefore import their set of rules. With these they decide which elements of the novel or of the dream are redundant and which critical. They must decide which part of the ceremony is "verb" and which part is "noun," voice, number, mood, and tense. These decisions reflect the set of rules that, ideally, one can articulate and justify by appeal to even more basic rules of inference, evidence, or other rational means.

Responding to Art

Empathy, introspection, and other forms of emotional response to the artifact are not sufficient. Critics should articulate the theory of nature which they consciously or unconsciously employ. Susceptibility to reinterpretation allows iconic forms to persist in a way that articulated utterances cannot. The rite of communion persists. Theological utterances about communion gain and lose importance. In both cases one finds a conflict of interpretations, not a confluence of translations. Translations requires two well articulated systems of logical operators. Each system, or grammar, must have rules to ascertain the "well-formedness" of every item (Frege 1893).

Speakers of natural languages can verify the accuracy of a translation, say from French to English, because they call upon their sense of grammaticalness. A bilingual person can judge the well-formedness of items in French and English. The sentence "10 = 2 times 5" is true only if one has access to the well-defined system of tautologies, called "arithmetic." These rules allow us to translate both sides of the equation into the other side.

This is not true of interpretations in the hermeneutical disciplines. Neither the objects scrutinized nor the rules we use are arbitrary. Translators rely upon the fact that all languages are intertranslatable since they are products of a universal language capacity. Difficulties arise for translators when they attempt to duplicate iconic elements of one language, like imagery and word-play, using the material of another language. When translators become interpreters they find a raft of problems. Because poetry, humor, and drama are rich in iconic elements, one finds them least well-served by translation. A fine translation of Homer in one century becomes inferior in the next because it no longer reflects contemporary taste and style.

Religionists who "reread" religious texts discover new meanings. New Testament scholars continue to find new meanings in a text that is two thousand years old. The "meaning" of the text resides in the exchange between reader and text. Both members of this set, reader and text, change over time, just as culture changes. Therefore, the task of interpretation is endless. There are many ways to stage Shakespeare's plays. There are numerous ways to understand the imagery in Dante's poems. Freud's "texts" can be subjected to similar readings.

These texts, Freud's written works, are distinct from the analytic process and the analytic encounter. For the analytic encounter takes place between actual persons in the here and now of the transference. Regarding the "unreality" of the transference, some say it illustrates the philosophical claim that we can never experience an unconstructed world. Yet transference is a vivid and concrete dimension of a patient's interactions with the therapist. In the moment of a transference storm, for example, when patients revenge themselves upon their analysts for hurts inflicted by their parents, real feelings and real dangers are present.

It is difficult to evaluate interpretative disciplines, like literary criticism or psychoanalysis. The rules which govern how we can carve up the analytic hour are restrictive. Insights derived from such rules are equally vulnerable to deconstruction. One therapist says that patient's sexual fantasies indicate good process because of the rule that unconscious thoughts are always sexual. Another therapist argues that sexual fantasies illustrate a compliant patient because of the rule that the "unconscious" is always unconscious. Hence conscious sexual confession must hide unconscious thoughts, like wishes to please the therapist. (See R. Langs 1985.) Which of these rules is valid? Or, are both valid? Does one rule take precedence over another? In what contexts does the clinician interpret manifest sexual fantasies as nonsexual wishes?

It is far easier to raise legitimate questions in the natural sciences. For example, astronomers note that there is a halo around the sun at 46 degrees. Recently, some scientists have purposed an explanation.[2] Interpreters cannot be so optimistic. Only trivial puzzles yield to a single "best" interpretation. In well-trodden fields of literary criticism, for example, persuasive arguments are made for incompatible readings of the text. Which is better?

Objects in the natural world are material forms or material processes; and, like all material things can be analyzed without remainder. That is, as C. S. Smith (1978) proposes, speaking of the structure of metals, a material object is always "concave inwards." Material objects close in on themselves. We can therefore assess their boundaries with little worry that we will miss a hidden aspect. Objects in the cultural worlds are both material and immaterial; both physical and psychological. They are both concave inwards and connected to other cultural objects. A patient's sexual dream may indicate a sexual wish; or it may indicate and hide a "deeper" anxiety about self-worth.

In his "Copernican Revolution" Freud decentered our belief that we know completely who we are. He proved that no authority, no family, and no religion understands completely human being. The existence of unconscious parts of the self means that we are always incomplete in our self-understanding; we cannot "empty" out the unconscious parts of ourselves.

Self-Understanding and Self-Representations: Emotional Struggles, Logical Quandaries

> After a spell of good spirits here I am now having a fit of gloom. The chief patient I am busy with is myself. My little hysteria, which was much intensified by work, had yielded one stage further. The rest still sticks. That is the first reason for my mood. This analysis is harder than any other. It is also the thing that paralyzes the power of writing down and communicating what so far I have learned. (Freud to Wm. Fliess, August 14, 1897 [1954, pp. 213–214])

It is one task to discuss Freud's Copernican Revolution, to locate him in the "history of ideas," and to talk about psychoanalysis as a science. It is another to do psychoanalysis with a patient or upon oneself. For to do analysis is to take seriously one's mistakes, faults, and nightmares. It requires us to forsake the privileged claim that we know the center of our selves. Analysis proves that even the cleverest person requires on outsider to reveal the person's inner nature. To do this the analyst need not be more intelligent than the patient.

For example, Freud's dream, in which he had Goethe attack Freud's friend, Fliess, is not what Freud said it was: a dream of support for his embattled colleague. Contrary to Freud's self-analysis, the dream shows that Freud identifies himself with the great Goethe and under Goethe's name and authority castigates Fliess's theories. If self-analysis were a sufficient form of analysis and it only required intelligence and courage then Freud should not be wrong about his own dreams.

When Freud says that he is busy with himself as his chief patient, we admire his tenacity and identify with his bad mood. For we also see that the Copernican Revolution encompassed Freud himself; even he could not "know himself" entirely. Knowledge of a self requires one to observe action over time: the "unconscious" is not a region that can be explored entirely from the "inside." It is not a place or location or part of the mind that will yield to introspection alone.

Self-analysis is always partial and incomplete because it is constrained by self-understandings. These are constrained by their origins in systems of self-representation. These systems are constrained by their origins in pictorial memory, in verbal memory, and in "pseudo-emic" systems. Self-understanding is always a kind of theology. It is a set of supreme myths. With them we organize our self-portraits. These self-portraits are always exclusive, one-sided, and apologetic.

Limitations of self-understanding derive from both our emotional resistances to insight and from the logical constraints imposed upon all representations systems. Human beings can exploit these constraints in maneuvers that prevent genuine insight. Clinically, the obsessive, educated patient has no better a prognosis for genuine change than does the less-educated patient. Yet, it may be of some theoretical interest to summarize some of the issues raised above, about the iconic form of self- and object representations. To investigate self-representations is analogous to investigating a painting, or the woodcut of Christ mentioned in the introduction. To say something true about this woodcut, one investigates it. We can use each mode of investigation to examine self- and object representations. For example, one could chemically analyze the paper and ink used in the woodcut. One could analyze the play of lines, the balance of upright with horizontal figures, etc.; one could locate the iconic form historically; one could note where the iconic forms are anatomically incorrect; where the artists chose not to be "naturalistic," etc. Like Steinberg, one could compare this woodcut to the thought world of the period. One could trace the painting's themes to the personal life of the artist. One could speculate how these forms pertain to the artist's internal life and psychological development.

Finally, one could also use oneself as an object of investigation. One could analyze the painting by gauging its effects upon oneself. This would say something about the painting's iconic power. These and other points of view are available. It is hard to integrate what one finds from each into a single, coherent description of the artifact. It is not merely professional jealousies that prevents biologists from saying much to literary critics about emotions. It is the distance that separate one set of scientific models from another set that makes communication difficult. This gap we have already seen in Freud's notion of sublimation and the concepts *quantities* and *qualities*.

Two Kinds of Hierarchy: Material vs. Cultural

C. S. Smith reference to George Kubler's insight that style is like a rainbow, "the phenomenon recedes as we approach the place where we thought we saw it, and is replaced by a previously hidden structure" (1978, p. 21). Rainbows are wonderful but not magical. Thanks to Newton and other scientists we can explain the beauty of rainbows and explain their appearance. Like other material events we cannot perceive them without a proper physical attitude or "point of view."

The style of a certain painter or the style of a certain architecture is similar to the rainbow. We must see elements in relationship to one another before we can say that this building has a "neoclassical" style. In this limited sense one cannot grasp style in the same way one can grasp the object that is stylish because style or quality inheres in the pattern of the subelements that make up the object. To recognize style we have to assume a particular attitude from which we can then perceive the play of diverse elements that together make up the thing in question. If I am not in the correct position or if I lack normal eyesight I will not be able to see the rainbow.

There are limits to what we can see of any natural object. These limits are physical not conceptual, restrictions not absolute barriers.

> In visual perception the angular resolution limit means that the number of things that can be perceived at any one time remains approximately constant while their absolute scale may be altered almost without limit depending on distance or on the use of external instrumentation. Sharp diversity seen as part of a region on one scale becomes mere texture on another and eventually becomes entirely irrelevant except as it contributes to some average property. (Smith, 1978 p. 20)

Physical objects are hierarchical and are made up of smaller entities, and those, in turn, made up of even smaller objects. Natural scientists can, therefore, investigate the interior structure of things. The "angular resolution" limit restricts what we can see with the naked eye. A microscope, set at 100X, breaks that limit. It lets us examine the entities that make up the visible surface. If we wish to examine the entities that make up the surface seen at 100X magnification, we switch to a more powerful lens.

Physics tells us that we will always find smaller elements. These smaller elements, without fail, constitute the surface we see. Because big things are made up of small things science can predict the behavior of big things by understanding how the small things interact. For example, engineers can predict the stress limits of a bridge. They use scientific formula about interactions between smaller elements, like steel griders and cement, and predict how they will interact in the larger structure, the bridge. These formula describe how smaller entities interact when combined into the single, large structure.

This is not true of cultural artifacts, nor of any artifact that is structured according to emic rules. Emic rules impose an arbitrary order upon a set of entities that are, in themselves, interchangeable. The English phoneme /p/ differs from other phonemes, like /b/ and

/v/ by virtue of key physical traits: the use of the tongue, voice box, aspiration, and so forth. In this sense phonemes are "constructed" from sets of distinctive phonal differences. These distinctive features are actual, perceivable differences. Once the emic set is established all other etic elements are excluded from consideration. These excluded elements cannot assume a place on the table of phonemes. These competing sounds are not "smaller" than the phoneme /p/; nonphonemic sounds are not subordinate to /p/. Rules of phonemic occurrence exclude them from the table of phonemes where they would compete with official English phonemes.

To use the terms developed above, emically structured systems reveal a similar set of constraints. It may prove useful to list some of these constraints and then expand upon them. Also, we note that our old problem of quantities vs. qualities reappears. Freud said bare quantities are the real stuff of the universe because he accepted the metaphysics of his day. In doing that he found himself squarely in the midst of the problem of explaining how quantities become qualities. This is precisely the question of how etic elements become emic elements. How do the material particles Freud named "quantities" assume an appearance of "qualities"?

In Freud's language, the problem of quantities evolves into the problem of part instincts. Part instincts derive from the erogenous zones. "Oral" libido is a part instinct. How do part instincts, which are "blind," evolve into human wishes and desires to do things of which culture approves? The gap that separates the natural sciences from the cultural sciences is similar to the gap that separates the "instincts" from the "ego" or etic entities from emic forms. Self-representations and object representations are schemata. Like any iconic image, conceptual restraints apply to them. We can summarize these logical difficulties in seven brief claims.

1. Emically arranged self-representations are rule bound and exclusive: a fixed set, laid down in early parent-child interactions, tends to exclude competing representations.
2. No "higher" magnifying power will reveal a substructure to these self-representations. Self- and object representations are composed of iconic memories. These are not always pictorial: they can be verbal, muscular, etc. (see Rizzuto 1979, chapter 4).
3. "Understanding" the ways in which the icon is used requires one to understand the rules which constrain it. See the example of analyzing the signature of an artist. The microscope reveals more and more details of the ink, but in order to "read" the

script one must know the rules which govern the graphemes that make up written language.

4. External rules, like those of propositional logic, do not govern the operation of these iconic forms. For example, religious texts revered for their truthfulness may reveal logical contradictions.

5. The rules that govern the operation of this system are not usually articulated by ordinary users. Most English speakers cannot and need not articulate the rules of grammar, syntax, and phonemic laws which they obey each time they speak or write.

6. Violating these rules, however, generates anxiety. Contradicting the "truths" of a revealed religion, for example, generates resentment among true believers and danger for the agnostic. Violating a patient's self-representations that make up the personal myth generates acute anxiety.

7. Native or folk understandings of these rules are themselves interpretations, therefore selective, and therefore not complete. Native interpretations are mythical reflections on myth; stories about stories about stories.

A linguist may ask her informants to give explanations of the "meaning and etymology" of certain words. There is no reason to suppose that she will not receive mutually contradictory opinions. Then what? Either one abandons all hope of a consistent, rational theory of semantic operations or one treats all folk analyses with the rigorous distrust usually reserved for fellow scholars. Sperber (1974) points out that native believers will tolerate contradictions not permitted in everyday reasoning: "A Christian to whom one points out a contradiction in the Gospel according to Saint Matthew, between the genealogy of Jesus who descends from Abraham and David through Joseph, and the statement which immediately follows it that Jesus is not the son of Joseph, does not for an instant dream of questioning either of the terms of the paradox and does not doubt that it is resolvable, even if the solution escapes him" (p. 95).

Mythic categories are imposed upon an otherwise seamless whole of experience. Hence, there are always "remainders" and elements ruled out of bounds. Within any phonemic system, there are always sounds that have no status and are therefore "noise." This noise corresponds, structurally, to the contradictions and lacunae that appear in religious accounts of the self. Of course, theologians and other religious authorities can offer ad hoc explanations for these lacunae, but these are not rigorous analyses. They are intelligent rationalizations. They are a retelling of the group's myth with new myths. These rationalizations of the "meaning" of the entity within a given realm are not nonsensical. The group may value them because they help clarify and locate within its symbolic universe elements which would otherwise remain troublesome. However, when the system is challenged by analysis, as when Freud confronted the Eucharist, there is no room for accommodation. Freud wished always to find hidden connections between distinct behaviors. He connects neurosis to dream life and to absent-mindness: "It is easy to recognize a person who is absorbed in day-dreaming in the street, ... by his sudden, as it were absent-minded, smile, his way of talking to himself, or by the hastening of his steps which marks the climax of the imagined situation. Every hysterical attack which I have been able to investigate up to the present has proved to be an involuntary eruption of day-dreams of this kind" (1908a, p. 160). This insight is not compatible with the daydreamer's self-understanding. Freud, the outsider, could see better the underlying unity. Self-analysis and official culture cannot locate this unity. Such observations require a Freud to point them out. Having done that, one can then see the old system from a distance—a distance provided by a foreign system. But one cannot be in two places at the same time. One cannot view the Eucharist as God's presence and as sublimated oral aggression towards the father imago. Many people attempt to amerliorate this kind of conflict of interpretations. They do so by elaborating yet more complex and more abstract meta-emic analyses which assimilate the Christian and the Freudian interpretations into even more universal categories.

These solutions vitiate the arguments of each position. Jung's respect for all religions is also as a covert disregard for their specific truth claims. Freud reduces religious assertions to the flow of vital forces. Jung often desiccates that flow in favor of universal—hence empty—features of the species, the archetypes. Given these conflicts between Freud and Jung many attempt to meld the two into a "higher" theory.

Ludwig Wittgenstein addressed a similar issue in a well-known passage in his *Philosophical Investigations* (1958). He draws a picture of Jastrow's duck-rabbit, which can be seen as either rabbit or a duck. He comments that he can see first the rabbit and then the duck. "But what is different: my impression? My point of view? Can I say? I describe the alteration like a perception; quite as if the object had altered before my eyes" (p. 195). The picture has not changed. The light waves bouncing from the book have not changed. But something is different. Wittgenstein sometimes refers to this as the organization of the perception (p.

196). The way I fit these new experiences into my own conceptual categories (my emic schema) changes. "I meet someone whom I have not seen for years; I see him clearly but fail to know him. Suddenly I know him, I see the old face in the altered one. I believe that I should do a different portrait of him now if I could paint" (p. 197).

Freud and Jung seek to interpret the "same" object, for example, the Eucharist. They do not organize their perceptions of that object in the same way. Consequently each finds that the ideas of the other are necessarily mistaken. This makes the task of the eclectic difficult. One might be a Freudian on Mondays and a Jungian on Wednesdays. One can first see the picture as a duck and then as a rabbit. This solution assumes there are no consequences that follow from adopting either point of view (p. 204).

A linguistic model of interpretation would provide the eclectic a way to accommodate conflicting interpretations. If the interpretation of icons is a kind of translation of "the" message inherent in the object, then all such translations must be structurally homologous; for all languages are intertranslatable (Chomsky 1968).

Then why does one find so many contradictory and mutually exclusive interpretations of the same text? The wholesale application of the linguistic model to the analysis of iconic forms promotes a faith in the eventual equivalence of all "codes." All natural languages are intertranslatable, regardless of their idiosyncratic elements. Then all linguistic structures should be intertranslatable too. One could generate any group of myths, for example, from any other by applying the correct set of rules of transformation.

The conflict of interpretations is finally a conflict of judgments about the actual world. They are conflicts about the external world of qualities which exist in their own right and with their own rules of organization. When the conflict is settled in favor of one party the victors should defend their method. They should attempt to explain more and more novel facts (Lakatos 1976).

Truly original analysis of unconscious sets of self- and object representations requires arduous labor. Novelists, psychiatrists, and sociologists approximate new analyses of social systems. Jane Austen investigated marriage customs, Irving Goffman investigated interpersonal rules in industrial societies. What Freud said of his "little hysteria" seems true of all persons who confront their immersion in a particular system and try to fight their way clear. To do this, to give an accurate account of one's universe, one must be willing to tolerate its imminent destruction and dissolution back into its elementary particles. Confronting earlier versions of the self, through a therapy experience, generates universal fear.[7]

The External World: Source of Self-Object Relationship and Source of Qualities

At the end of chapter 1 I summarized the way I wished to employ recent psychoanalytic theories about infancy to reexamine Freud's notion of sublimation. In chapters 2 and 3 I tried to show how that notion developed in Freud's thought and how it depends upon Freud's basic assumptions, his metaphysics of experience. I have suggested that self- and object representations are structured like other pseudo-emic entities.

In each of these chapters I have criticized Freud's general theory of perception and tried to show how it forces him into speaking of "real quantities" and "illusory qualities." To justify this criticism I suggest, in the following chapters, that J. J. Gibson's theory is more adequate than Freud's. In addition, Gibson's theory of perception grants to the external world an abundance of qualitative differences. Gibson's theory is compatible with both Kohut's fundamental notion of the self-object relationship and with Stern's theory of infant development. When we combine these theories into a single point of view we discover a richer concept of sublimation.

CHAPTER FIVE

PERCEPTION AND EMOTION IN CLASSICAL THEORY AND CONTEMPORARY AUTHORS

> Who alive can say,
> 'Thou art no Poet—mayst not tell thy dreams'?
> Since every man whose soul is not a clod
> Hath visions, and would speak, if he had loved,
> And been well nursed in his mother's tongue.
> John Keats, *The Fall of Hyperion*, 11–15

Theories of Perception

Explaining how human beings perceive their world is a complex task that has intrigued numerous philosophers and psychologists. For example, Kant wished to show how our internal "schemata," or what he termed the "manifold of experience," shape our experience. Thanks to Freud's courage, we, his heirs, can add yet another task to Kant's burden, that of distinguishing to what degree unconscious expectations and unconscious schemata shape all of our experience, including our rational faculties.[1]

The difference between Kant and Freud can be seen daily in analytic work when one listens to an intelligent person reason about a particular inhibition. No amount of such reasoning leads the patient into the deeper, unconscious sources of the inhibition. Rather, only sufficient time, hard analytic work, multiple tests by the patient of the analyst's good will, and other such activities make genuine insights into unconscious motives possible. These insights permit the patient to change. These activities, which always involve the patient's challenging of the analyst's convictions, are not intellectual exercises. Neither a Freud scholar, learned in psychoanalytic language, nor a surgeon, familiar with the intricacies of the body and accustomed to handling life itself, has any special advantage as a patient in analysis. Both must

175

pass through the activities of being in treatment and of confronting his or her personal terrors.

Regarding perception, one can find well-argued treatises that support nearly any theory one might care to pursue. For example, constructivists assert that human beings always construct aspects of their perceptual experience. According to members of this school, no perception occurs without the active mediation of internal schemata. Realists assert that perception is ordinarily immediate and unbiased by internal processes. It seems that the majority of psychoanalytic critics share a "constructivist" opinion as summarized by Rose: "Contemporary psychology assumes that early perception is of the undifferentiated type, diffuse and global, and that a long development must occur before the mind can actively construct an experience of the world in terms of separate, stable objects" (Gilbert Rose 1980, p. 130). I refer to Rose not to refute him but to indicate those elements I believe he overlooks. For example, in a vivid case history, he describes how a young woman, Ariel, responded to a self-prescribed treatment of LSD. She had recurrent psychoticlike episodes, imagined the world as constructed out of giant genitalia, and so forth. Rose says, "These abnormal *perceptions* served multiple functions, both defensive and self-punitive" (p. 46, emphasis mine). But were Ariel's visions perceptions? Strictly speaking, no, for as Rose himself says, "These states could alternate rapidly with normal perception. At no time did Ariel lose the awareness that what she was experiencing were the illusions and hallucinations of a waking dream" (p. 46). It is not correct to say that Ariel's disease was one of impaired perception, in the strict sense of ego functions which orient one in space and time. Ariel was obviously disturbed; but her disturbance was not one of perceptual difficulties and it occurred in the arena that Freud also investigated; the arena of mind in which a disease process operates unaffected by perceptual processes. Rose uses the term *perception* to designate Ariel's sensory experience, her manipulation of those sensations, and her judgments about the likely outcome of one course of action versus another.

Rose articulates the aesthetics implicit in this classical theory of perception and links it to Freud's theory of primary narcissism; a theory born in the "Project's" account of the experience of hallucination. Like Freud and others, Rose assumes that early infancy is marked by a state of primary narcissism in which the "external world" is relatively unimportant and the internal, "primary process" events dominate. Slowly, over time and after many frustrations of primary process wishful thinking, the ego learns to adopt secondary process forms of thought. Rose says the dual nature of human thinking dominates perceptual processes as well: "Our perception of space is likewise double. We see ourselves both in an undifferentiated, fused space and in a focused, delineated space consisting of differentiated, separate objects" (Rose 1980, p. 11; he cites also Anton Ehrenzweig 1953).

Given this classical set of assumptions, Rose proposes an elegant theory of aesthetics: "The recognition by the viewer of the congruence between the outside, harmonious composition of art and his or her own inner, unreconciled struggle leads to responsive participation. The art work externalizes the moment-by-moment activity of the mind in slow motion, magnified and abstracted. This fosters a sense of fusion with the art work" (1980, p. 13).

He reaffirms what I have termed a "constructivist" theory of perception when he adds: "Ego psychology can show that perception and memory do not merely record reality, but *actively* construct it. Perception is not a unitary event which is given, but a cognitive experience abstracted from a framework of contexts. Our sense organs select forms out of William James's (1892) 'big blooming, buzzing confusion' of stimuli. Where sensory input is reduced, the mind may attempt to provide itself with meaning through hallucination and delusions" (pp. 24–25).

Rose draws also upon philosophy, literary criticism, and contemporary notions of reality: "What we carelessly and monolithically call self and reality, however, continue to have endlessly shifting qualities. Psychoanalytic findings, poetic-philosophic institutions, and quantum theory all suggest that reality remains fluid throughout life" (p. 91). Rose does not focus upon the problem of quality and the epistemological questions I raised in chapters 3 and 4. Where shall we locate "qualities," and how shall we explain the organism's capacity to transform quantities into qualities? Rose does not raise these questions because he takes for granted Piaget's basic contentions about the psychological construction of knowledge, processes which are necessarily internal and qualitative. Hence, Rose says that the mind must construct, through arduous development, its experiences of distinct and stable objects.

It might seem that Freud agrees with this general claim. The following quotation, from his beautiful piece on organic and hysterical paralyses, might be read as saying that hysterics manifest primary process forms of perception: "I, on the contrary, assert that the lesion in hysterical paralyses must be completely independent of the anatomy of the nervous system, since *in its paralyses and other manifestations hysteria behaves as though anatomy did not exist or as though it had no knowledge of it*" (1983c, p. 169, emphasis his). Freud's emphasis upon hysteria's "ignorance" of anatomy suggests that hysteria has constructed a notion of the body which is contrary to reality, but this is not so. Freud emphasizes the ignorance of anatomy in order to make his most important point about differential diagnosis: organic lesions always produce malfunctions which obey the rules laid down by the structure of the nervous system.

There is but one nervous system; it follows that similar organic lesions produce similar behavioral disturbances. Pathologists have shown that organic lesions bring about disturbances in associated behavioral systems which can be explained by virtue of the connections between them. So strongly are behavior and organic lesions connected that one can deduce the structure of one from the structure of the other: "In the same way every clinical detail of representation paralysis can be explained by some detail of cerebral structure; and conversely, we can deduce the construction of the brain from the clinical characteristics of the paralyses" (1893c, p. 167).

In other words, Freud describes what happens to accurate perceptions which fall under the sway of primary process thinking. Ariel's accurate perceptions were replayed incorrectly; she could not gain access to them without first reordering her memory processes. This reordering and reorganization took place in the work of analysis. So too, hysterics perceive accurately but remember inaccurately. They cannot access the whole of their memory because part of their memory is tied to painful affects.

An hysteric woman, for example, manifests a paralyzed "arm" when she associates it with frobidden sexual activities, like masturbation. In the language of Freud's prepsychoanalytic article, the conception of the arm "exists in the material substratum, but it is not accessible to conscious associations and impulses" (p. 171) because it is tied to excessively large quotas of affect incurred in a traumatic situation.

Like many other psychoanalytic theorists, Rose wishes to expand the notion of primary process to cover not just modes of thought but modes of perception as well. Freud does not for he held consistently to a theory of veridical perception: that under normal circumstances we perceive in mechanically correct ways. He did not ascribe to the constructivist position which Rose elaborates. But, neither did Freud believe that perception occurs without distortion. On the contrary, the force of his quantity–quality distinction, like its Kantian predecessors, requires him to argue that persons always misconstrue the nature of their real world.

Where we experience a world of subtle qualitative differences, science tells us that there are but variations in quantities of identical particles swirling in the void. Freud's distinct conception of Ananke and its ultimate rule over the lesser, more human gods of the Greek and Christian pantheons, rests upon this belief. For Ananke is the name we give to the laws which these imperceptible particles, these blind quantities, obey and which therefore constrain us. More so, as Freud says in his essay on Leonardo, each of us human beings corresponds to a set of these particles which "force their way into experience" (1910c, p. 137).

This epistemological commitment led Freud to describe sublimation as a mysterious process which occurs within the privacy and darkness of the internal world of blind forces acting upon one another. To remedy this obvious gap in his theory, and to consolidate his speculations about the ultimate biological (nonpsychological) causes of human behavior, he championed the conception of primal energies (*Beyond the Pleasure Principle* [1920g] and *The Ego and the Id* [1923b]). These primal energies are distinguished by their qualitative nature; they represent in themselves tendencies toward specific kinds of actions, erotic and aggressive. They produce specific kinds of feelings, libidinal pleasure, or anxiety, or both (as occurs in states of fusion, like masochism).

To clarify Freud's reasoning and to distinguish it from other positions, I first describe the classical theory of perception and its links to a theory of emotional development, as René Spitz articulated it in his studies of infant communication. Second, I describe an alternative theory of perception implicit in the work of Helmholtz, the mentor of Freud's mentors. I show how Helmholtz's theory of perception, which reflects Freud's values, does not support Freud's radical distinction between qualities and quantities. Since, as I have suggested above, aesthetics deals with *qualitative matters*, and not quantitative, revising Freud's theory of quantity permits us also to revise the received analytic theory of qualities and, therefore, of aesthetic experience.

I suggest that Helmholtz's theory is more compatible with the theory of perception articulated by the American psychologist, J. J. Gibson. Third, I suggest that Gibson's theory of perception matches more closely contemporary theories of the psychoanalytic process. I discuss the work of Joseph Weiss, Robert Langs, and Daniel Stern. These three contemporary authors propose psychoanalytic theories that contradict the basic assumptions of Freud's early theory of perception and the experience of qualities. With these points made, I propose to develop the common links between these three sets of theory. Then, on analogy with Gibson's concept of "visual affordance," I propose that psychoanalytic theory ought to include a notion of "emotional affordance."

Freud and Spitz on Emotional Development

Freud recognized that children must come to grips with the fact that primary love objects, people who constitute its world, are not permanent. Freud describes one such child in a famous passage in *Beyond the Pleasure Principle* (1920g). An eighteen-month-old boy who played the game of "fort" (gone) did so in response to the too frequent absences of mother (1920g, pp. 14–15). Because the boy could not have experienced those absences as pleasurable, Freud concludes that these games, in which the boy repeats his displeasure, manifest tendencies whose motivations are "beyond the pleasure principle." Ricoeur says of this episode that it might better be understood as the "mastery over the negative, over absence and loss, implied in one's recourse to symbols and play" (1965, p. 286).

The game evidently helped the child cope with his mother's frequent absences. It would seem that this kind of play can contribute to adaptation but Freud sees the boy's play as the product of the primary drives and their uncanny ability to reassert themselves. What Freud implies in the main text he seems to deny in the footnote which immediately follows this particular example. In the text Freud suggests that by throwing away the object associated with his mother, the child gained a kind of revenge for the pain she caused him. In support of this rather sinister portrait of the child's mind he adds that the little boy was not displeased by his father's absence; "on the contrary, he made it quite clear that he had no desire to be disturbed in his sole possession of his mother" (p. 16). Freud appends this footnote: "When this child was five and three-quarters, his mother died. Now that she was really "gone" ("O-O-O"), the little boy showed no signs of grief. It is true that in the interval a second child had been born and had roused him to violent jealousy" (p. 16, n.).

This is a remarkable denouement to the innocent story Freud first told when he noted that the child's game was puzzling. There is something uncanny about this innocent child and his game. Although Freud maintains his neutral, descriptive tone, we cannot help but wonder at the viciousness he attributes to the boy and his feelings toward his father. Obviously, Freud means for us to see that the boy's lack of regret over his father's absence is typical of male children during the oedipal period.

There are dozens of similar examples in other Freudian texts: in each he explains that such aggression is the result of the boy's love for his mother and fear of his father's retaliation (e.g., 1900a, pp. 261–266). In these earlier texts the boy's oedipal aggression toward his father is a secondary response to his more primary erotic impulses toward his mother. But when we read that this same child did not grieve the loss of his mother either, the person whom we would expect him to miss most, we are more willing to wonder if indeed there is not some factor operating in him which is more archaic than positive oedipal desires.

Freud does not immediately draw that conclusion for us, but the second sentence in the footnote quoted above reveals he is thinking along that line. Yet, lest he be criticized, he says there were other disappointments in the child's relationship with his mother. These might account for his lack of grief. Only in the last half of the essay does Freud attempt to show how the compulsion to repeat is tied to the death instinct and the individual's impulses to destructiveness (the above summarized from V. P. Gay 1979a, pp. 60–61).

René Spitz considered these issues in *No and Yes: On the Genesis of Human Communication* (1957). He used both psychoanalytic and ethological methods; his famous reports on hospitalism being only one example. Spitz's general argument is that the child's ability to use the semantic category "No" is based upon the Innate Releasing Mechanism (IRM) of rooting, the instinctive behavior that neonates exhibit when they seek out the mother's breast.

I differ with Spitz on three issues: the interpretation of empathic understanding as regressive identification to "archaic forms of thought," transformations of energy, and self. "When the parents imitate the little child's gesture or words, they have to perform an identification on a very primitive level. This is a level which usually is inaccessible to the adult because of infantile amnesia. Trespassing on this territory becomes permissible only because the parents perform this temporary regression in the interest of the child" (1957, p. 41).

This is plausible only in terms of Freud's basic epistemology, to which Spitz refers directly and which he adopts. The metaphors of "deep," "trespassing," and "primitive" derive from an exclusively intrapsychic concept of empathy: that one must engage in "temporary hallucinations" or "regressions" in order to comprehend how another person understands his or her world. At the same time, Spitz notes how the cognitive capacity for empathic understanding must develop slowly (p. 50): "The child distinguishes in the adult partner two affects only. I will call them the affect "for" and the affect "against." In our usual terms the child feels either that the love object loves him or that the love object hates him" (pp. 50–51).

But Spitz's description is strikingly adultomorphic; we are told that upon being told "No, no" as he reaches for a toy, an eleven-month-old child "sits with downcast eyes and an expression of embarrassment and shame as if he had done something terrible" (p. 51). How can the child experience such complex emotions "in himself" if he can perceive only "for and against" in his parents? If, following Spitz, we agree that children acquire empathic capacities through identifying with their love objects, then it would seem that the child cannot really feel ashamed and embarrassed until it has identified those precise feelings in its parents. But Spitz has already said that this is not possible for the very young child. The only way out of this conundrum is to say that Spitz, like Freud in his 1895 essay, and other psychoanalytic specualtions on infantile "feelings," speaks metaphorically. Yet the question is: how can a nonverbal action, the primitive IRM, give rise to a verbal distinction between "yes and no"? As Spitz notes, these semantic and logical capacities constitute secondary process thought. Our question is, then, how do secondary process modes of thought, "reasoning" itself, develop from instincts and IRMs?

A related problem emerges in Spitz's discussion of the process by which a particular IRM (rooting behavior in the neonate) is transformed into a directed act of communication (the symbol of negation). As he says, "a physiologically performed behavior of 'striving toward,' becomes a gestural symbol of 'striving away' " (p. 67). How does this striking transformation occur? In addition to identification with the aggressor (the parent who says "no"), perhaps there is a second factor: "May we assume that regression to the original rooting movement is a second factor in its use for semantic purposes by the fifteen-month-old? After all, we have seen that regression as a consequence of frustration and unpleasure was operative in the reactivation of rooting in the form of pathologic cephalogyric movements" (p. 67). Again, Spitz speculates about the "regressive" shift which underlies the child's ability to draw upon—apparently—its archaic heritage. But such regression occurs only during periods in which secondary process functioning is abandoned. Freud announced, and Spitz recapitulates, that there is no "no," negation, within primary process functioning.

How could the child regress to an archaic IRM and, at the same time, manifest the secondary process functioning which typifies negation? Spitz's answer is that the primary affect of frustrated need (hunger) which instigated the IRM of rooting is evoked in the child's new situation. Hence the child automatically follows the "trace" of that feeling back to an archaic state in which it responded to a similar affect with rooting behavior, that is, it moved its head up and down.

This explanation might be plausible if one accepted a general notion of repetition compulsion (to which Spitz refers in another context, p. 32). Yet the undeniable association of frustration and rooting has the additional element of satisfaction; rooting usually produced feeding and the breast. It seems equally plausible to say that pleasurable affects might as well be traced back to the rooting reflex since it is based on the ubiquitous pleasures of nursing. Hence one should find that the Western gesture for "yes" also has its origins in the nursing situation. Spitz's dilemma is typical of most psychobiological speculations about the relationships which exist between IRMs and later semantic representations. This is no small issue for it pertains to the question of nature and origin of human language. It also pertains to the question of how linguistic artifacts, like poems and novels, evoke emotional responses from human beings whose *primary affective orientation* is toward objects in the external world.

My third difference is with Spitz's description of the self as the "product of intrapsychic processes which take place as a result of the vicissitudes of object relations" (p. 121). Spitz defines the "I" much as Freud did; it is that thing which is opposed to the non-I in the infant's earliest experience. But this means that the "I" is not an actual object in the real world (which Gibson said it was), but the "percipitate of experience" (p. 120). The "self" is even more abstract than the "I." The "self" too is a precipitate but this time of intrapsychic processes. It is the "continuation of the 'I' on a higher level" (p. 121). This metaphor of depth and height is akin to the metaphors of sublimation we investigated in chapter 3. Both sets ignore the person's actual relationship to actual objects, including the visual affordance of the self that obscures a great deal of our visual field (and which is the seat of numerous other sensory experiences).

Spitz recounts Freud's theory of the emergence of a social self out of a physical entity. This parallels the development of secondary processes out of primary, and the development of the dominance of the reality principle over the pleasure principle. As Spitz notes, an infant learning to walk must confront or "evaluate" his or her capacities for locomotion: "in one word, the limitations of the physical self. He is forced to relate one part of his person after the other to the surround, thus expanding the scope of his thought processes and concomitantly of his psychic functions" (pp. 128–129). Gibson lets us modify this traditional claim. The infant does not learn simply the limitations of his or her physical self; he or she learns to perceive the actual structure of the "surround" which is invariant. That is, infants learn to perceive the structure of visual and other sensory affordances. Like Freud, Spitz's insistence upon an intrapsychic theorem of reality testing leads him to connect repetition compulsion with judgment, even if by a tenuous cord of sublimation: "Judgment is a function which can only be applied with the help of constantly reiterated reality testing" (p. 129). (See also Gay 1979a, chapter 8.)

Implied in this view is the claim that reality testing is always subject to dissolution and a regressive restoration of hallucinatory functioning. In other words, because secondary process functions, like judgment, are built upon a "framework" of structured intrapsychic "mentations," they are always liable to collapse. Hence Freud was pessimistic about the permanence of any psychological cure, or any psychological structure which, like the ego, depended upon the constant "reneutralization" of energies which were inherently unstable. The pull toward regression, in the ego and all such structures, produces the need to revert back to earlier modes of functioning; that is, to the regressive hallucinations of dreaming. (See Gay 1979b, pp. 545ff.)

Helmholtz and the Physiology of Perception

Hermann von Helmholtz, one of the great scientists of the nineteenth century, is renown for his contributions to the theory of music, optics, ophthalmology, mathematics, meterology, and physics. An early student of the biologist, Johannes Müller, Helmholtz was a colleague of the renown Ernst Wilhelm von Brücke and Emil Du Bois-Reymond, who in turn influenced Freud's early scientific career in physiology. Although Müller had shown that "deeply incisive difference between the various kinds of sensation" (Helmholtz 1878, p. 119) depends upon the nerves that transmit the sense data, he remained a "vitalist who was convinced that it would be impossible ever to reduce living processes to the ordinary mechanical laws of physics and chemistry" (L. P. Williams 1986, p. 564).

Helmholtz contradicted his mentor's dictum in his own doctoral research on nerve transmissions which, it turns out, are entirely measurable as physiochemical events.[2] In the same spirit Helmholtz refuted the Vitalist claim that animal heat was beyond the ken of natural science. This demonstration was an early and vivid statement of the principle of the conservation of energy (a principle that Freud wished to uphold). A master of many disciplines, Helmholtz also worked on practical matters of medicine, inventing the opthalmascope among other devices. In 1878 he also developed a theory of perception that influenced subsequent generations.

Helmholtz's Argument in 1878

Up to the early nineteenth century most discussions of perception were philosophic. John Locke in the seventeenth century, and Immanuel Kant in the eighteenth, argued for particular theories of perception and from those theories for particular notions of science. To put this issue in a less technical way, the key question has always been: when we perceive the world are we perceiving accurately what is "really there"? Or, are we adding to perception something from our own mind, or does our own mind in fact dominate perception such that we can never really know what the world is like without "mediation" by our subjective categories?

To each of these positions one can assign scores of philosophers: each arguing for his or her version using selected facts. As in political debates, passion can be expended for each position, but one finds no set criteria with which to assess the validity of these opposing claims. This all changed with the advent of the scientific study of perception. Laboratory work could not solve all philosophic puzzles about perception; for some issues are purely conceptual, while others are linguistic. Many others may be unsolvable because they include subtle contradictions made evident only by rigorous, technical dissection of the complex discussions in which they reside.

But laboratory work could establish some new facts that, in themselves, seem to refute some philosophic doctrines. For example, people had long known that a sharp blow to the head caused a person to "see stars" and other bright flashes. Where did these flashes come from? Naively one might say that these bright lights came from either the external world or the internal world. Since no one else, with normal vision, sees the bright stars evident to the prize fighter, many philosophers had concluded that there must be "light actually developing in the eye" (Helmholtz 1878, p. 119). This doctrine was refuted when the German physiologist, Johannes Müller, showed that there is no light source within the eye. Rather, the violent excitation of the optic nerve produces sufficient impulses such that they register as light.

This discovery figures in both Helmholtz's and Freud's deductions about *all* perceptual processes, but, Freud and Helmholtz diverge as to how to interpret these basic laboratory findings. (See also Thoma and Kachele 1986; Snyder 1987.) Their divergence returns us, again, to the issue of qualities and quantities.

Helmholtz on Qualities: Two Forms of Difference

Helmholtz distinguishes two kinds of differences between sensations. One he terms a difference in modality, the other a difference in quality. A difference in modality refers to different senses: blue light belongs to one modality, called vision, while warmth belongs to another modality, called touch. A difference in quality refers to variations within a sensory range: blue light has one quality while red light another; a high pitch sound has one set of qualities while low pitched sounds have another. We can easily make comparisons within a range of qualities. We cannot do this for different modalities. For example, we can say that yellow is "closer" to red than it is to purple but we cannot as surely and easily say that yellow is "closer" to high pitched sounds than it is to low pitched sounds. Of course, poetically and metaphorically people do speak of "heavy colors" or "blue music," or "grey moods," or a "soft pink" color and such. But, by definition, metaphors always require one to mix distinctive categories. The existence of metaphors only emphasizes Helmholtz's point: that modalities are distinctive.

Referring to Johannes Müller's point, Helmholtz notes that the modality of a perceptual experience is determined by which nerves are excited: optic nerves only transmit optic sensations in the visual modality. The "quality" of a perceptual experience is produced, in part, by differences in the exciting agency. The same physical event, a vibrating cello string, can evoke distinctive modalities and within each modality, different qualities. I can see the string vibrate; I can feel the air move around it; I can touch the vibrating cello neck; and I can hear the note it emits. If I am musically educated, I can assess the note's *qualities:* is it flat, too long, or too much vibrato?

In addition, Helmholtz says, if we compare one modality, like vision, against another, like hearing, we discover that they differ radically in their sensitivity to a range of qualities. Using terms from music, he compares the eye and ear: "the ear is sensitive to some ten octaves of different tones, the eye only to a sixth" (p. 120), although science tells us there are vibrations beyond these ranges. Relying upon his musical training, he makes the fascinating comment that the ear can also perceive a "mix" of sounds far more subtly than can the eye perceive a "mix" of colors. "No two chords composed out of different tones ring alike, while yet with the eye precisely the analogue of this is the case" (p. 120). In other words, a musician can hear the difference in consonance produced by notes C and F played together versus D and G, while the painter cannot distinguish one splotch of white made up of greenish blue and red versus another splotch of white made up of greenish yellow and violet.

Are Our Sensations (Conscious Experiencing) of the External World Correct?

Helmholtz avoids many of the usual conceptual difficulties associated with the theory of perception by distinguishing what normal people experience, for example, as color from an objective account of the visible waves emitted by a certain object. One can read Helmholtz as Freud did: as saying that "qualities" per se exist only as functions of the perceiving nervous system:

> The objects extant in space namely appear to us clothed in the qualities of our sensations. To us they appear red or green, cold or warm, to have smell and taste, etc., whereas after all these qualities of sensation belong only to our nervous system and do not reach out at all into external space. (p. 128)

Helmholtz reasserted this claim in another text, his *Handbuch der Physiologischen Optik* (Leipzig, 1867).

> The *properties* of natural objects, despite this name, in truth characterize nothing whatsoever proper to the individual object in and for itself, but instead always a relation to a second object (which includes our sense organs). (Quoted in notes by Moritz Schlick, pp. 168–169)

Few contemporary scientists would argue that "greenness" as a "conscious quality" exists "in the apple," for this would be misusing the words "greenness" and "conscious quality." By definition, qualities in this sense exist only within the consciousness of a perceiving subject. During an operation under deep anesthesia, the patient feels no pain because the quality of "painfulness" that might be present otherwise cannot be present if there is no consciousness in which it can exist. But it is not therefore wrong to say that I "see green" when I pick up my apple. I am not speaking of my "consciousness" when I speak this way: I am speaking of my experience of this apple at this moment. (It might be a red apple shown under a secret light that makes everything appear green. Yet my statement is still valid.)

Helmholtz says that "qualities" do have a relationship to the structure of the objects to which they appear attached:

> Our sensations are indeed effects produced in our organs by external causes, and how such an effect expresses itself naturally depends quite essentially upon the kind of apparatus upon which the effect is produced. Inasmuch as the quality of our sensation gives us a report of what is peculiar to the external influence by which it is excited, it may count as a symbol of it, but not as *image*. (pp. 121–122, emphasis mine)

By the term *image* Helmholtz means an entirely accurate and complete rendition of the thing in itself and an accurate judgment about its nature. Helmholtz argues against a form of naive realism which confuses what we "see" with the way we happen to see it. Naive realists falsely believe that we do in fact have "images" of the external world, images gained by a singular correspondence between conscious acts of perception and the structure of the actual objects which impinge upon us, which produce "effects" in our sensory organs.

Helmholtz argues against this form of naive realism and the "popular opinion, which accepts in good faith the images which our senses give us of things are wholly true" (p. 122). But he does not champion the opposing view which holds that we can have no accurate sense of the external world. For even if we do not have iconic images of the external world, we can have signs of their presence: "The relation between [object and sign] is restricted to the fact that like objects exerting an influence under like circumstances evoke like signs, and that therefore unlike signs always correspond to unlike influences" (p. 122). This claim lets Helmholtz explain how science is possible without falling into the philosophic dead end of naive realism. In order for science to be legitimate, there must be noncontradictory ways to describe lawlike relations in the real world. Evidence from centuries of philosophic argument and decades of scientific work convinced Helmholtz that human perception of the "real world" was not "wholly true" in the way that naive realists claimed.

Yet natural scientists do make claims about the "qualities" of natural objects, claims they hold to be valid and not mere fancy. Helmholtz's notion of sign permitted him to account for valid (scientific) observations of such qualities by noting that there must be some lawful relationship between the structure of things in themselves and things as they appear to us:

> Thus although our sensations, as regards quality, are only *signs* whose particular character depends wholly upon our own makeup, they are not to be dismissed as mere semblance, but they are precisely signs of something, be it something existing or happening, and—what is most important—they can form for us an image of the *law* of this thing which is happening. (p. 122, emphasis his)

Because like causes produce like effects, including like "qualitative experience" in creatures such as ourselves; rational, noncontradictory understanding of the world, that is, science, is possible. Helmholtz agrees that our conscious experience of qualities requires the active mediation of human sensory networks. But he does not conclude therefore, that qualitative experience is unpredictable, capricious, or irrational. Rather, as he says throughout this major address, qualitative differences between sensory experiencing are functions of the interaction between things-in-themselves and the experiencing creature. Because these interactions are predictable and lawful, science can explain more and more about human life, even if our conscious perceptions are shaped wholly by the structure of our nervous system.

Helmholtz on Unconscious Inference

No one can accuse Helmholtz of being either Freudian or fuzzy minded. He was a particularly rigorous scientist who abhorred vacuous reasoning and anything that smacked of the occult. Hence, it comes as some surprise to read him arguing on behalf of notion of "unconscious inference." As he makes clear, Helmholtz does not use this term the way that Arthur Schopenhauer (and later Freud) did.

Again, struggling with Kant's pronouncements about the philosophic grounding of a theory of perception, Helmholtz argues that neither logic nor experimental evidence supports Kant's claim that the rules of euclidian geometry are, as it were, imprinted upon human experiencing by a transcendental source. Kant had explained the power of Newton's physics, which relies upon classical geometry, by arguing that Newton's mind, like all human minds, was constrained by the basic categories of experience, space, time, and causality, as well as number, and other rules of mathematics, such that valid employment of these categories issued in accurate statements about nature.

This brilliant explanation of Newton's success, and thereby of the power of all science, provided Kant his critical method. He could show that science could not transcend limits imposed by the categories of thought itself; science was destined to be constrained for ever. Kant could mark the claims of faith "off limits" to science; for faith pertains to matters beyond the reach of any human reason. Kant justified science by limiting it to the realm of phenomenal experience and, in doing that, he disarmed it as a critic of religion. Kant did not prove that religious claims about God or freedom were correct; he proved that science could never show that they were false. This preserved the possibility of faith.

Kant's term *intuition* suggests how much he wished to maintain his thesis, for "intuitions" are given to us prior to experience: "Kant assumed not only that the general form of spatial intuition is transcendentally given, but that it also contains in advance, and prior to any possible experience, certain narrower specifications as expressed in the axioms of geometry" (Hemholtz 1878, p. 128). These axioms are traditional ones from Euclid, e.g., "Between two points only one shortest line is possible. We call such a line 'straight' " (p. 128).

From these premises Kant went on to argue that ordinary experience of space itself is based on these transcendental givens. But this claim is also a psychological theory, for it asserts that human beings *must* experience space as we do because of the a priori structure of our minds. Helmholtz distinguishes Kant's epistemological arguments from his psychological claims. In contrast to Kant, he shows that post-Kantian developments in mathematics and geometry, particularly topology, were not constrained by Euclid. On the contrary, N. I. Lobachevsky (1792–1856) and G. F. Riemann (1826–1866) created consistent and rigorous geometries whose axioms contradicted those of Euclid.

In addition, Helmholtz notes that other mathematicians developed ways to form "images of metamathematical spaces in parts of Euclidian space..." (p. 130). Hence: "Our attempts to represent [meta]-mathematical spaces indeed do not have the ease, rapidity, and striking self-evidence with which we for example perceive the form of a room which we enter for the first time" (pp. 130–131). Yet, Helmholtz argues there is no logical reason why a person trained in the proper mathematics cannot conceive of non-euclidian space. In fact, this is exactly what non-euclidian geometers accomplish.

Taking a different tack, Helmholtz criticizes Kant's narrow claims about "intuition" as too limiting for, as he asserts, we daily experience subtle intuitions about our psychological space or social context which we recognize as accurate yet which are (1) not given in nature and (2) not susceptible to logical statements. For example, he notes that a child learns to use language and understand sentences such that by adulthood the person can grasp "the finest variations of their sense—often ones where attempts at logical definition only limp clumsily behind" (1878, p. 131).

This capacity to grasp pattern and detail within the millions of potential encounters human beings have within themselves and between themselves and their environment is not reducible to any set of fixed "laws of logic" nor "forms of intuition." Helmholtz adds, "This is precisely the basis of art, and most clearly that of poetry and the graphic arts. This highest manner of intuiting, as we find in an artist's view, is this kind of apprehension of a new type of stationary or mobile appearance of man and nature" (p. 131). (See William Warren [1984] also.) He adds the powerful insight, "That the artist has beheld something true emerges from the fact that it seizes us too with a conviction of its truth, when he presents it to us in an example purified from accidental perturbations" (pp. 131–132).

Unconscious Inferences and a Theory of Fixations

Helmholtz explains the artist's sensitivity, in part, by referring to a process he terms "unconscious inferences" (p. 132). This term he carefully distinguishes from Schopenhauer's notion of the "unconscious" as a peculiar part of the mind, a nonrational part that may oppose the rational part, etc. Rather, Helmholtz speaks about the foundation of *all* reasoning, "an elementary process lying at the foundation of everything properly termed thought, even though it still lacks critical sifting" (p. 132). This process occurs when sensations form "a series of experiences, each of which has long disappeared from our memory and also did not necessarily enter into our consciousness formulated in words as a sentence, but only in the form of an observation of the senses" (p. 132).

Once this has occurred, new sensations that reveal a similar pattern evoke the older set of "connexions": "The new sense impression entering in present perception forms the minor premiss, to which there is applied the rule imprinted by the earlier observations" (p. 132). One can read this as an awkward way of speaking about simple learning. Yet (1) learning is not a simple process and (2) Helmholtz is also describing a basic model of the mind as dedicated to reasoning. From the beginning, according to this model, human mental activity is dedicated to "arguing" from premise to premise to conclusion.

The source of the mind's premises is not the inner world. When Hemholtz says "unconscious," he means neither the Freudian unconscious nor the Jungian unconscious, described in Jung's essays on occult religion. Rather, Helmholtz says consistently that the source of the mind's premises is the interactions that occur between mind and world. In these interactions the mind discovers *new* information by noting changes in the flow of sensations that wash over the person as the person alters his or her body. Like Gibson, Helmholtz notes that persons gain vital information about a thing they "see" by moving themselves, or just their eyeballs, and so varying the angles and shapes of the objects in their perceptual field. It is through these *activities* that human beings, and all other animals, "construct" the most likely representations of their world. But these "most likely representations" are not the product of hallucination; they are the product of actual encounters between an animal and its environment. (See Irvin Rock and D. Smith [1981] also.)

In making these claims, Helmholtz argues against two camps; the nativists and what I have termed the "constructivists" such as Rose and many other psychoanalytic theoreticians. Helmholtz argues against nativists, who claim that human beings "see" the way we do because of innate visual imprints that are not derived from experience. Among his many brilliant points is the interesting observation that if the nativists, including Kant, were correct, we should be able to draw with much more facility than is usual. But "one of the greatest difficulties in drawing, as is well known, is to free oneself from the influences involuntarily exerted by our representation of the true magnitude of objects seen" (p. 134).

In other words, if the nativists were correct it should not have taken many hundreds of years for Western artists to comprehend the laws of perspective and learn to represent on canvas what we see easily and naturally every day, namely that even tall trees appear "smaller" than human beings if the human beings are in the foreground.

I employ Helmholtz to argue also against the constructionist who, as we have seen, always claims that persons must struggle to overcome the inherent tendency toward hallucination.

Perceptions, Qualities, and Affordances

Freud believed what most scientists of his day believed: perception, especially vision, could be best understood on analogy with the numerous machines perfected in his century.[3] Vision must be the activity by which the animal "sees" the retinal image, just as the camera film registers the image passed through the camera's lens and projected back onto the plate. Vision is the processing of sense data, or the bare quantities that Freud described in the "Project."

J. J. Gibson (1979) spent his long career attempting to refute, by experiment and argument, this picture theory of perception. Among his many cogent criticisms one is especially pertinent to our discussion of Freud. By Freud's time, advances in mechanics, as well as in the anatomical study of the visual apparatus, suggested that the brain sees or processes the retinal image. Yet, as we know when looking through a lens taken from an ox, for example, such images are always inverted. This causes no problem for photographers, they simply turn the final print right side up. But what of the brain and our perception of the real world? Most people see the world right side up. Psychologists and neurologists who maintained the camera theory found it necessary to explain how the brain inverts the retinal image.

The key fallacy, Gibson notes, is that this model presupposes that there is an internal observer, some agent within the brain, who "perceives" the retinal image and inverts it before passing it along to the higher brain centers. Of course, this internal observer soon turns into an infinite number of such observers, each of whom must solve the inverted image problem; for if each observer uses a lens, then it too must solve its own inverted image problem. This infinite regress disappears when we abandon the camera model, and with it, the general notion of the machine theory of vision.

In the simplest sense, Gibson says we do not see a retinal image when we see; we see the real, external world. In that world are an infinite number of qualities. One way to summarize Gibson's theory is to compare the traditional, mechanistic, model of perception with the ecological one he advances. The traditional model was championed by Helmholtz, accepted by Freud, and is perpetuated in contemporary computer models. They are all variants of the Kantian theorem that perception is a mediated process. We can summarize this standard model in the following way:

Freudian Model of Perception:

Stages in the Visual Perception of an Object (After Gibson 1979, p 252).

		Various operations on the	Qualitative experience of
		Image in	sensory	the object in
Object ──►	Retinal image ──►	the brain ──►	image ────►	consciousness.

Gibson sets forth a number of objections to this traditional model. Chief among them are: (1) it entails an infinite regress of internal persons who "process" internal images; (2) it predicts that only human lenses will be adequate for vision, while crustaceans, among others, have multilens eyes and yet see just fine; and (3) it cannot account for Ivo Kohler's experimental data (1964) that humans quickly adapt their vision to distortions introduced by reversing lenses. For example, one of Kohler's subjects was able to ski while wearing glass lenses that inverted the light rays entering his eye. Of course, we do not doubt that complex neural processes occur in the brain, and no doubt computer models will help us understand these operations. But such processing is not the human activity of vision. Gibson's model of perception contains no speculations about the internal processing of nerve impulses. Rather, he elaborates a new theory of the relationship between observer and world. He suggests that when we perceive we perceive the way the external world offers us affordances for action in it.

Affordances: From Phenomenology to Ecology

Gibson notes that early gestalt theorists, like Kurt Koffka and

Bertram Lewin, rejected sense data theories which treated the human perceiver strictly as a mechanical entity. Instead, gestalt theorists and other psychologists, especially those associated with phenomenology, described the "invitation character" of objects: a mailbox "invites" the mailing of letters.[5] This "invitation character" was bestowed upon the object by the needs of the viewer. In this sense, the gestalt psychologists held to a constructionist view: a psychological state of need gives rise to a demand character. "The value of something was assumed to change as the need of the observer changed" (Gibson 1979, p. 138).[4]

Gibson's theory differs radically from those of the gestalt writers. To clarify his point of view he coined the term *affordance*. In his terms, "*affordances* of the environment are what it offers the animal, what it *provides* or *furnishes*, either for good or ill.... It implies the complementarity of the animal and the environment. If a terrestrial surface is nearly horizontal (instead of slanted), nearly flat... and sufficiently extended... and if its substance is rigid... then the surface *affords support*. ... It is not sink-into-able like a surface of water or a swamp, that is, not for heavy terrestrial animals. Support for water bugs is different" (p. 127, emphasis his).

Phenomenologists assumed that the external world "looked different" to different animals because these animals differed in their internal states. Gibson reverses this notion and claims it is the animal's relationship to its external environment which permits it to find satisfaction. The flatness and firmness of a piece of land are physical properties that we may measure independent of any animal's use of that land: "As an affordance of support for a species of animal, however, they have to be measured *relative to the animal.* They are unique for that animal" (p. 127, emphasis his). Hence one cannot use a single (etic) standard for measuring affordances as one can for measuring temperature. One must measure "affordances" according to the needs, capacities, and physical characteristics of a particular animal in its particular environment. These ecological characteristics are functions of the real needs of the animal in a real environment.

Gibson's concept of affordances is not identical to "point of view" or to a "phenomenal realm" that can be investigated only via the introspection of an animal's internal states. As Gibson puts it, "an affordance is neither an objective property nor a subjective property" (p. 129). The concept of affordance allows him to define an ecological niche as: "a set of affordances. The niche implies a kind of animal, and the animal implies a kind of niche. Note the complementarity of the two. But note also that the environment as a whole with its unlimited possibilities existed prior to animals. The physical, chemical, meteorological, and geological conditions of the surface of the earth and the pre-existence of plant life are what make animal life possible. They had to be invariant for animals to evolve" (p. 128).

Values, Invariants, and Self

Gibson proposes two seemingly contradictory theses: (1) perceiving an affordance is a value-laden process, and (2) the value perceived is *not* a product of the animal's internal state (which varies) but of the animal's relationship to the perceptible world (which does not vary). Freud says that "qualities," including values, cannot exist "in the world" (because the real world is a realm of bare quantities). Rather, qualities and values must be projected onto it by an internal agency; for example, the needful animal. In pursuing this program, Freud generated many conceptual dualisms. The theory of affordances obviates many of these dualisms and with them many of the traditional problems of body–mind and mind–world interaction. To perceive the world of affordances an animal need only perceive, through a variety of sensory modalities, the structure of its environment as a place of action.

Gibson also says that while affordances are perceived relative to the kind of animal one is, the structure of affordances is not capricious. On the contrary, his theory requires affordances to be invariant. How is this possible? To illustrate an invariant he returns to the postbox. One of the affordances that normal humans perceive as they approach a real mailbox in the real world is the invariant relationship between their distance from it and the visual angle of the object. Gibson uses a sketch to illustrate how this relationship appears to the observer. (See figures on pp. 163, 165, 199 and 288 in Gibson's text.)

When Gibson says animals could evolve only in an environment that was invariant, he means that animals could not orient themselves in a world in which the relationship between observed size and distance, for example, varied in a random way. In such an environment a camera or other mechanism sensitive to light energy could record changes in light patterns, but an animal could not visualize a world. Lacking fixed, invariant relationships between distance and visual angle, one could never be sure if one were approcahing the mailbox or leaving it. Hence our eyes would be useless. They might continue to operate like cameras, but we could not act like persons.

Because his theory is neither mentalist nor reductionist, Gibson can offer a concise definition of what the self is. It cannot be simply the secret, inner, wholly separate agency that Kant designated the Transcendental Ego. Rather, the self must be an aspect of what the observer perceives when he or she recognizes affordances. The self cannot be simply an internal agency for two reasons. First, as we have already seen, it makes no sense to speak of an internal agency, like a self, that resides within the person, busy processing sense data that impinge upon it from the outside world. This just postpones the problem of explaining perception (and all other psychological functioning), since we have to explain how the inner self perceives, thinks, and imagines.[6]

Second, and less obvious, the notion of an inner self is parasitic upon a prior notion that one can "introspect" one's internal states, that one may perceive mental images and examine them in the same way one can perceive and examine "pictures" of the external world. According to this notion, the self or ego or rational faculty is that agency which can turn its direction toward either of these stages of action.

Philosophers like Gilbert Ryle (1949), Ludwig Wittgenstein (1958), and lately, psychoanalysts like Roy Schafer (1976), have attacked this story from the side of logic and intelligibility. Gibson offers additional criticisms. John Locke, David Hume, and many philosophers since, claimed that imagination (or introspection or self-reflection) is the manipulation of "faint images" of real perceptions. The mind operates like a mediator, sitting between the external world and internal theater where it can examine sense data that impinge upon it from either realm. Freud prosecuted this standard thesis in the "Project" when he speculated as to the source of hallucinations.

The theory of hallucination and internal observer are complementary: the mediating ego might well confuse the source of sense data, because there are no qualitative differences between images and perceptions. Freud's speculations on "reality testing" are accounts of the organism's ability to distinguish between external and internal sources of images.

Gibson's theory of affordances offers a simpler explanation of reality testing, one based on actual differences between ideas and perceptions: "A surface is seen with more or less definition as the accommodation of the lens changes; and image does not. A surface can be scanned; and image cannot. When the eyes converge on an object in the world, the sensation of crossed diplopia disappears, and when the eyes diverge, the "double image" reappears; *this does not happen for an image in the space of the mind*" (pp. 256–257, emphasis mine). I have emphasized this last phrase because it satisfied Freud's requirement that a theory of reality testing must refer to behaviors that the ego can carry out. One can walk around a modern painting or scan a movie screen; one cannot walk around a dream image or scan an imaged landscape.

Like Robert Weisberg (1980, chapter 7), Gibson believes that no experimental evidence proves that thinking is the scanning of internal images in the way that one scans the real, external world. Helmholtz made similar observations a hundred years earlier when he tried to refute Kant's doctrine that the truths of euclidian geometry are imposed upon us by transcendental categories. In support of his theory Helmholtz refers to evidence that sightless persons enabled to see could not "perceive" a circle until they touched it. He cites also his own work in non-euclidian geometry which showed that human beings can visualize nontraditional, non-euclidian spaces.

I suggest that Gibson's radical theory of "visual affordances" is a more satisfying theory of perception than its competitors. By using the notion of "affordances," Gibson lets us explain how the same objective thing, say a frozen pond in Mississippi in January, can be different things to different animals such that different animals perceive different affordances in it. For a jackrabbit, the pond surface is "walk-on-able." To a heavy man the surface is "sink-into-able." In both cases, the jackrabbit and the heavy man perceive accurately the same object, but different affordances. Because of these different affordances, each animal adopts a different response: the rabbit bounds ahead, the man goes around (unless he wishes to break through the thin ice).

If the rabbit had been operantly conditioned, by severe shock, say, to avoid ice on ponds, would that make ponds in themselves have different affordances? No. For the pond ice is still traversable as such; the rabbit will not fall through the ice. The experimenters have now added a new feature to walking on ice: severe pain. To avoid that pain the rabbit learns to avoid pond ice. The rabbit may never again bound across a frozen pond, but the pond's affordances have not changed. For consider the reverse; could one train a rabbit to perceive pond water as *not* "sink-into-able"? For the water's quality of "sink-into-ableness" relative to jackrabbits, is not an arbitrary ascription by the rabbit; it is an actual feature of water and jackrabbits.

Experimental Measures of Affordances

Building on J. J. Gibson's work, physiological experimenters have developed ways to measure affordances in human perception. In detailed experiments William Warren (1984) measured human preference for stair riser height relative to leg length. He then compared this ratio to the theoretically optimal energy value for climbing stairs. He found that for any person, tall or short, the preferred riser height is .25 times their leg length, while the optimal energy value (that is, the most efficient riser height) is .26 times leg length. These are remarkably similar numbers. (The subsequent average riser height is, by the way, far higher than the usual step). These findings provide strong evidence for his conclusion, "In selecting a path of locomotion, an actor must in some sense be perceiving 'the work to be done' on various routes to achieve a particular goal" (1984, p. 699).

If this is true, and if other experimental evidence supports Warren's general claims, then we have added reason to carry out Gibson's general research plans regarding affordances; for Gibson stresses the richness of information in the "external world." This information, when matched with the animal's internal sense of its capabilities, yields an accurate judgment about the next course of action. How could an animal carry out such computations? Note that none of Warren's subjects computed, consciously, the ratio of their leg length to the perceived riser height. We doubt that any jackrabbit computes the tensile strength of the ice per se and matches that number against its weight.

An alternative way to assess an affordance is to use the body itself as the unit of measure, a "body-scaled or action-scaled metric" (Warren 1984, p. 700). Given such a body-based metric, the animal then uses it to judge against the optical information pouring into it through its visual apparatus.[5]

Ecological Definition of Self

Where is the self and how should we understand its constitution? According to ecological theory, the self is that thing which is specified uniquely by an animal's perception of its place in its world. In humans it is that real thing which occludes about half of the field of view: "about half of the surrounding world is revealed to the eyes and the remainder is concealed by the head. What is concealed is occluded not by a surface ... but by a unique entity" (p. 112). That unique entity is the self, the physical being which occupies a definite place in the visual field— indeed, it is invariantly unavailable to normal vision. Later concepts of oneself must develop from this kind of experience: "The experience of a central self in the head and a peripheral self in the body is not therefore a mysterious intuition or a philosophical abstraction but has a basis in optical information" (p. 114).[6]

Perception of world and perception of self are two sides of the same act of the perception of affordances. Gibson's analysis of self is much richer than here summarized. However, even a short statement of his position is sufficient to formulate a troubling question. He seems to demonstrate that vision, like the other sensory modalities, is the perception of invariant features of the visual array. If self is specified in the same manner, how does it happen (1) philosophy and religion have agonized over the question of self for many millennia, and (2) many people are not sure that their selves exist, or that their selves are on-going and tangible? Any clinician can document the fact that many patients, especially those termed "narcissistic personalities," experience moments of painful doubt that they are real in any mode. David Winnicott often comments about people like this, people driven to thoughts of suicide precisely because they feel unreal and hopeless. How can the "self" be invariant and yet subject to such distressing questions? In artistic circles, such as occurred in the more lush episodes of Romantic philosophy and Romantic poetry, the self is *not* an invariant object in the real world, perceived in an environment of stability and permanence. Why not? And more pertinent, why is it that such poems, idealist philosophies, and religious rituals, many of which deal explicitly with the elaboration of new roles and understanding of one's self, flourish in an age of reason?

Contemporary Authors and the Theory of Affordances: Weiss, Langs, Stern

Although he does not cite Helmholtz, Gibson's notion of perceptible affordances is compatible with ideas evident in Helmholtz, especially Helmholtz's concept of "unconscious inference." In turn, this concept, advanced prior to Freud, is surprisingly similar to clinical theorems advanced by contemporary psychoanalytic authors, especially Joseph Weiss and Harold Sampson (1986), Robert Langs (1985), and Daniel Stern (1985). Langs focuses upon patients' abilities to perceive the nature of their therapist's unconscious feelings. Weiss and Sampson elaborate a concept of directed, unconscious processing in which patients regulate the appearance of repressed ideas by assessing the treatment situation. Stern develops a theory of self-experience which rejects the notion of primary narcissism, a notion crucial to Freud's theory of hallucination and the origins of reality testing.

I will summarize their claims and then show how each distinctive set of ideas can help me amplify the concept of "emotional affordance."

Unconscious Inferences in Object Relations: Evidence from Psychoanalytic Observations

Helmholtz and Gibson offer theories of how a person gradually learns to operate within the world as we know it. A crucial aspect of both theories is the core idea that the "real world" is full of information. As Gibson puts it, the external world is an infinite source of new perceptions, new vistas, new angles of vision, new tastes, sounds, and other sensations that cannot be reduced to simple formula. Helmholtz amplifies this theme when he says that artists sense the richness of the external world and they represent these discoveries to their audience.

In *The Psychoanalytic Process*, Weiss and Sampson describe with admirable detail their attempt to assess the validity of two competing psychoanalytic hypotheses. These two hypotheses, as elucidated by Weiss, parallel what I have termed the classical theory of sublimation and the theory I argue for in this book. Both hypotheses are Freudian: the earlier of the two, which Weiss terms the "automatic functioning" hypothesis, derives from Freud's early essays on psychopathology and from the metapsychology of *The Interpretation of Dreams* (1900a). The later of the two Weiss terms the "higher functioning" hypothesis derived from Freud's late essays on psychopathology, such as *Inhibitions, Symptoms, and Anxiety* (1926) and his metapsychological texts, such as the *Outline of Psycho-Analysis* (1940) and from many contemporary authors, such as Hans Loewald (1979) and especially S. Asch (1976).

The first clinical hypothesis views the ego as relatively passive vis à vis the power of the drives; the ego must negotiate between drive-based impulses and wishes which impinge upon it from "inside" the mind and external powers, such as parents, who impinge upon it from the "outside." The first hypothesis is the view of the ego I elaborated in my discussion of the classical theory of sublimation. In other words, this *clinical* hypothesis parallels the aesthetic theory Freud advanced at the same time; as we have seen, according to this early theory, the ego basically "lucks into" sublimatory channels which permit the relatively autonomous drives their expression without incurring the wrath of those in power. This element of luck figures in the traditional analytic understanding that sublimation is a mysterious process which happens to a person. It occurs, as the poets said, by the action of a force or demon outside the control and agency of the self.

The second clinical hypothesis is based on the assumption that a person may regulate his or her unconscious mental life "in accordance with his *unconscious* thoughts and beliefs and his assessments of his current reality" (Weiss and Sampson 1986, p. 5, emphasis his). This second hypothesis matches well the theory of perception elaborated in this chapter. Weiss and Sampson say that the ego is not dominated by autonomous or semiautonomous drive elements; rather, it struggles to find a way in which current reality, including the psychoanalytic relationship, can be different from the past. Indeed, Weiss states that persons unconsciously regulate their "unconscious" mind. He summarizes his points as the proposition that patients may unconsciously regulate their use of repression (pp. 6–7).

Weiss does not claim that his theory is wholly original with him, or that other contemporary analysts have not made similar points about the sources of neuroses. For example, Weiss cites Arnold Modell (1965), who also describes how neurotic patients act upon infantile beliefs about their ability to harm their loved ones. Some patients are deathly afraid of being helped by their therapists because then they would become separate from mother or father and violate their parents' pleas to remain attached and maintain the parents' psychic balance (cf. Kohut's insights into the ways parents use their children as primitive self-objects):

> Separation from the maternal object in these people is unconsciously *perceived* as causing the death of the mother. To attain something for oneself, to lead a separate existence, is *perceived* as depriving the mother of her basic substance. (p. 50, emphasis his, citing Modell 1975, p. 330)

Weiss emphasized the word *perceived* in this quotation to underscore his claim that in many cases of survivor guilt, the patient develops a "belief" (p. 50) about the dangerous consequences of separating from mother. This is a belief: *not a perceptual process*. It may be a well-founded belief since mothers and fathers can easily demonstrate to their children how wounded they are by their children's pulling away.

Any clinician can document numerous examples of such manipulation by a depressed mother or father who announces to an anxious and extremely angry child, "So, leave me, get married, get a good job, live a life I cannot control, and I'll die—but feel free to go ahead and be the death of your parent!" Should the parent have lost a spouse, the surviving parent is even more likely to feel bereft of self-object support. Another variation on this theme is the patient whose mother or father severely attacked the patient and who, in turn, identifies with the aggressor and attacks the patient's children with an identical ferocity, disguised with superego propaganda.

Weiss does not deny that children bring their own limited egos to these encounters, their internal worlds, and their projective and identificatory mechanisms. This can distort their parents' ordinary failings into directed, malevolent attacks. Weiss does not reject Freud's insights when he rejects Freud's earliest hypotheses about the automatic functioning of the mind; nor does he ignore the many ways in which such pathogenic beliefs contribute to maladaptive solutions, such as perversions, and so add yet another level of pathology to the patient's total presentation (see pp. 82–83 and 130–131, especially).

Robert Langs and Unconscious Assessment

Robert Langs has written extensively on clinical issues parallel to Weiss's concerns (see his 1985a, b, c). Langs uses his terms derived from intense scrutiny of patients' responses to variations in the psychotherapeutic frame and to "deviations" from an ideal of ego autonomy expressed in the "ideal frame." Among many virtues evident in Langs's work is his emphasis upon validation. Unlike many supervisors in psychiatry and even psychoanalysis, Langs emphasizes the methods by which the therapist can assess the accuracy of his or her interventions and the accuracy of his or her patient's displaced comments about the therapist. I have found Langs's texts extremely helpful, both as supervisor and as supervisee.

He emphasizes that patients typically assess their therapists with keen intensity and surprising accuracy. In numerous illustrations of this process, which he likens to "unconscious" supervision by the patient, Langs demonstrates how patients evaluate their therapist's ability to comprehend the patient's pathology, to contain it, and to not be overwhelmed by it. If the therapist appears overwhelmed by the patient's material, or if the therapist is himself or herself anxious, the patient communicates this fact, via displacements, to the therapist.

Langs terms this form of communication an attempt on the patient's part to "cure" the therapist of the therapist's pathology in order for the therapist to then cure the patient. As odd as this might at first sound, it matches my own experience as patient, therapist, and supervisor. This is only an anecdotal instance and even when added to the hundreds of illustrations that Langs sets forth in his many pieces, this kind of data still remains only suggestive. However, like Weiss and Sampson, Langs's efforts to establish coherent clinical theory promote the possibility of eventual nonclinical validation. Weiss and Sampson (1986) also describe such validation efforts in detail.

Langs emphasizes the interface between patient and therapist and the degree to which patients accurately "read" the therapist's unconscious response to these communications. His core concept of "adaptive context" is that patients respond with their total range of ego functions, adaptive as well as maladaptive, in an effort to situate themselves safely in the two-person context established by the therapist. This context is not a product of patient madness; it is not created by the patient. It is not "transference" per se. Rather, it is created out of the interactions between the two persons. In a telling criticism of traditional teaching, Langs notes that if a patient's pathology is determined by unconscious forces, then no amount of "probing" questions can elicit these unconscious forces directly. Rather, one can only locate unconscious ideas and "forces" by interpreting the manifest disguises of displaced and otherwise distorted thoughts.

Contrary to some models of technique, Langs rejects the notion that the patient's material is determined solely by the unfolding of repressed memories, etc., projected onto the analyst and experienced in transference. Rather, Langs shows consistently that patients shape their responses to the therapist based upon both their own madness and their perceptions of the therapist's madness; that is, how the therapist deals with similar struggles in his or her life.

Weiss makes a similar point. He notes that therapy involves both transference in its classical sense and turning passive into active. The patient experiences the analyst like important persons in the past. The patient also turns passive experiences into active; the patient reenacts the patient's past and so shows the therapist how it felt to be a child in the patient's family. When the patient feels the therapist has passed the test and has not harmed the patient, then using "unconscious control," the patient reveals more about the patient's inner life.

This notion of "unconscious control" may well be Freudian. It derives from Freud's late texts, but it contradicts Freud's original theory of repetition compulsion. As we saw above, when Freud wished to explain why the little boy played a game which must have invoked painful emotions, he admitted that the pleasure principle theorem could not account for the game. Hence, remaining faithful to libido theory required Freud to speculate about instincts that lay even deeper than pleasure and pain, instincts beyond the pleasure principle.

Adhering to these principles forced Freud to judge resistances to therapeutic progress as both the result of these instincts that lay beyond the pleasure principle and as another illustration of the yearning for hallucinatory wish-fulfillment. Weiss and Sampson (1986) cite a passage from an early Freud paper on psychoanalytic technique:

> [Unconscious impulses] endeavor to reproduce themselves in accordance with the timelessness of the unconscious and its capacity for hallucination. Just as happens in dreams, the patient regards the products of the awakening of his unconscious impulses as contemporaneous and real; he seeks to put his passions into action without taking any account of the real situation. (p. 268 [from Freud 1912b, p. 108])

Retaining the metapsychology of the "Project" and the theorem of hallucination, Freud views the therapy as a struggle between three forces: the therapist, the patient, and the patient's "emotional impulses."

For the therapist must compel the patient to submit these impulses "to intellectual consideration" (p. 108). Together, therapist and patient conquer these surging impulses. Freud's language is both martial and grand: "It is on that field that the victory must be won—the victory whose expression is the permanent cure of the neurosis" (1912b, p. 108).

This language and its rhetorical flavor is identical to that of Saint Paul, a Christian moralist, not Hermann Helmholtz, a German scientist. When Freud speaks of the instincts in these early essays his language is rhetorical, persuasive, evocative, and, indeed, theological. Freud's tone matches, in fact, the tone that theologians had struck for millennia when they too addressed the "darker" sides of human beings. In his battles against the dark instincts Freud called upon reason and collegiality; Paul calls upon the power of a transcendental God.

Primary Narcissism: Daniel Stern on Emotional Development

In contrast to early psychoanalytic authors like Freud, who relied upon random observations of children or upon reconstructions of infancy through the analysis of adults; contemporary behavioral scientists elaborate sophisticated theories of child development based on detailed observations of children, beginning with fastidious studies of infant behavior. Daniel Stern (1977; 1985) and other psychoanalysts stand out as both knowledgeable of classic psychoanalytic theory and expert in the scientific (objective) measurement of infant and child behaviors. This dual expertise makes Stern's work appealing; for one cannot accuse him of simple hostility to psychoanalytic truths, avoiding the darker aspects of human nature that Freud saw, and so forth.

Rather, Stern's detailed studies of the infant's sense of self both follow contemporary standards of rigor and reflect psychoanalytic concerns. Chief among these are the infant's sense of others, the sources of emotional stability and related clinical concepts, such as object constancy, core sense of self, narcissistic stability, and "ego identity," etc.

Stern's work is compatible with J. J. Gibson's efforts. In fact, Stern's basic idea of the "invariants" that make up the infant's experience of itself is an idea that echoes Gibson's concept of "visual affordances." They too are "invariant" and this give rise to the possibility of coherent human action. In the next chapter I suggest Stern's discussion of the emerging sense of self and reliance upon a notion of invariance can help us say more about "emotional affordances" and the utility of that concept in the psychoanalytic theory of art.

To sum up this chapter, I refer briefly to Stern's refutations of the Freudian theory of primary narcissism, the theory underlying Freud's theory of all perception and therefore of aesthetic experience. Freud assumed that the newborn, the infant, and the adult in full psychotic "regression" shared a common psychic state: each was a form of primary narcissism. In this mode, which is innate and against which the ego must struggle in order to engage in object relations, there is no "outside" of the self.

Freud elaborated the idea of narcissism partly out of his theory of psychosis, but, as we have seen, primarily out of his theoretical commitments to an epistemology. It decreed that the qualitative richness of the external world was conditioned by our need to impose upon experience a semblance of qualitative differences. Given this developmental schema, Freud concluded that the infant's tendency to "revert" back to a state of nondifferentiation underlies psychotic episodes, institutions like religion, and artistic experience.

Stern finds no evidence for the existence of a phase of "normal autism." Contrary to Freud's assumptions, announced in the "Project," observational research of normal infants yields a portrait of an infant involved with others: "Infants are deeply engaged in and related to social stimuli" (1985, p. 234). Stern's ideas are not new: Sandor Ferenczi developed similar ideas when he rejected the "psychoanalyst as surgeon" metaphor[7], some British Object Relations authors, like Ian Suttie (1952), later Winnicott (1971a), and others challenged the notion of "normal autism."

New is Stern's rigorous, objective evidence against the notion of normal autism. Gained from hundreds of carefully worked out studies, Stern's evidence and that of others contradicts Freud's portrait of the infantile mind which, in turn, has influenced directly the classical psychoanalytic theory of aesthetics. It has influenced every major analytic notion of qualitative experience since. Even Heinz Kohut, who did not fear challenging orthodox opinions, relies upon the theorem of normal autism in his first monograph (1971).

Art and Primary Narcissism: The ARISE Theorem

It is possible to oversimplify Freud and his theory of perception, to reduce his complex account to a strawman whom one then dismisses. I have tried not to do this. I have attempted to present Freud's case fully but without burdening the reader with endless descriptions and qualifications. When this case is presented, and when aesthetic theories which depend upon it are elaborated, we find consistently the central theorem that human beings are *ab origine* hostile to interpersonal relatedness. This core theorem, which Stern refers to as the notion of primary autism, stands up neither to current clinical research, nor to current

behavioral research on infant and child development. I began this
chapter by citing a segment of John Keats's poem, *The Fall of Hyperion*,
which Keats wrote near the end of his life, in 1819:

> Who alive can say,
> 'Thou art no Poet—mayst not tell thy dreams'?
> Since every man whose soul is not a clod
> Hath visions, and would speak, if he had loved,
> And been well nursed in his mother's tongue.
> *The Fall of Hyperion,* 11–15.

Keats feels that any person is capable of writing poetry, if that person
has both loved well and been well loved and has "visions" or "dreams"
to tell others. Are these visions hallucinations, derived from the inner
world alone? One could read Keats as affirming Freud's basic idea of
art, reaffirmed in Rose's learned book, that art is an activity generated
out of regressive moments in which infantile modes reoccur. With
Ernst Kris (1952) Keats could be read as saying that such regressions
occur under some sense of ego control, that poetry is regression in the
service of the ego.[8]

Yet, as plausible as Kris makes his concepts, they rest upon the theorem of primary narcissism, and they require us to place artistic creation in the hallucinatory and regressive mode that Freud first elaborated. An alternative way to read Keats's admonitions in his poem is to
see him as affirming that poets do dream, but their dreams alone do not
constitute poetry. Rather, one should read Keats's best poems, the sonnets written in 1819, as minutely drawn portraits of the actual, external
world, a source of solace, repair, and reconstitution of the self. These
sonnets do not disclose a poetic dreamer, a vision that dominated the
"psychedelic" version of creativity of the late sixties and a vision reflected in the "art as regression" views evident in Kris's and Rose's treatises. Rather, Keats is able to recover for his readers, moments of intense clarity of sight (or smell, or hearing) of the actual, external world.
For example, in *To Autumn* he writes:

> Then in wailful choir the small gnats mourn
> Among the river sallows, borne aloft
> Or sinking as the light wind lives or dies;
> And full-grown lambs loud bleat from hilly bourne.

Astute critics point out that these "naturalistic" lines portray, with
tremendous compression and beauty, an experience that is visual,

auditory, and tactile and evokes a feeling about autumn, the beginning of the end of summer. While Keats ascribes "mourning" to the gnats, he does so with an explicit sense of metaphor; he is not afraid their little hearts are broken. But there is something heart breaking in the suddenness with which he envisions for us the up and down movement of the gnats, their complete dependency upon the wind and the forces which carry us as well, up and down, toward death.

Freud's and Kris's view of art as regression to primary narcissism, the ARISE thesis, even when termed an "adaptive" regression, orients psychoanalytic criticism toward pathography. Kris articulated this theorem most forcefully in his notion that artistic creativity should be understood as "Adaptive Regression in the Service of the Ego," which he summarized as an ARISE event. This concept permitted him to retain Freud's emphasis upon the core concept of regression to primary narcissism and at least recognize that some forms of regression might serve adaptation. As Rose documents, this view requires the analytic critic to focus upon the hallucinatory dimension to aesthetic experience. There may well be such a dimension inherent in aesthetic experience. But to focus exclusively upon such features precludes analytic critics from explaining how works of art may also be accurate portraits of the external world. Some art may be generated out of the ego's struggles with unconscious demons; but other art, works that may revolutionize a culture's self-understanding emerge from interaction, between artists and "reality," between the artist who struggles to discern actual features of the real world and to portray them through the devices at his or her disposal.[9]

Art cannot be restricted to reflections on the inner world alone; art is a human enterprise that knows no restrictions and no boundaries.

CHAPTER SIX

FROM VISUAL AFFORDANCES TO EMOTIONAL AFFORDANCES

Anal Qualities, Anal Character, Sublimation

In 1908 Freud announced that adult character had its origins in infantile sexuality. His general claim seemed harmless:

> Among those whom we try to help by our psycho-analytic efforts we often come across a type of person who is marked by the possession of a certain set of character-traits, while at the same time our attention is drawn to the behaviour in his childhood of one of his bodily functions and organs concerned with it. (1908, p. 169)

His specific claim was more disturbing. The esteemed traits of orderliness, parsimony, and will derive from a period of development in which the anal zone was a source of pleasure. In reaction to excessive anal erotism some people find ways both to derive anal pleasure and to deny its importance. They accomplish this through compromise formations, like the hoarding of money, which disguise the infant's fascination with holding onto its feces. These adult characteristics reveal their origins in anality by the zeal with which they are pursued, the high moral seriousness attached to them, and the anxiety which ensues when they are challenged.

Eight decades of clinical and experimental testing have shown the truth of Freud's claims. Alongside Freud's papers on anal erotism, including his case history of the "Rat Man" (1909), are contemporary monographs, like the work of Shengold (1988). Leonard Shengold demonstrated the many ways in which anality appears in neuroses and in art, especially in the novels of Marcel Proust. Besides many clinical papers on this subject, applied studies show how anality may become typical of national character.

In an argumentative book, *Life is Like a Chicken Coop Ladder* (1984), Alan Dundes describes the ways in which German culture is anal erotic. The title refers to a German folklore saying: life is like a chicken coop ladder, short and shitty.[1] Seymour Fish and Roger Greenberg (1977) reviewed scientific studies of anal character and found strong evidence supporting Freud's claims about the anal qualities of orderliness, obstinacy, and parsimony. Among dozens of studies, they cite G. C. Rosenwald (1972) who found that "the amount of anxiety expressed by persons about anal matters predicted how carefully they arranged magazines that were in disarray" (p. 163). They summarize a vast literature on oral and anal characters ("orals" and "anals"). They report: "that anals were best motivated by giving them pennies and the orals by offering them gumballs" (p. 159).

Much evidence favors Freud's *clinical claims* that anality has qualities which carry over into character development. Little evidence favors his *biological claim* that some people "are born with a sexual constitution in which the erotogenicity of the anal zone is exceptionally strong" (1908, p. 170). Research shows only that mothers with anal character traits will tend to raise children with similar traits. Freud linked his clinical insights into anality with the processes of sublimation and repeats the theory of his *Three Essays on the Theory of Sexuality* (1905d). If there are large quantities of anal excitations (through an inherited surplus or through excessive manipulation) some of the libido is used directly, in anal masturbation for example. Other quantities are "deflected from sexual aims and directed toward others a process which deserves the name of 'sublimation'" (1908, p. 171).

As we saw in chapter 2, this redirection theorem reflects Freud's solution to the quality–quantity problem. Anal *qualities*, like those of holding on, of fascination with things inside a forbidden place, reappear in the anal character type. Freud's entire discussion of sublimation depends upon showing how the sensorial *qualities* associated with a body zone can reappear in an unexpected form. The quantitative theory forced him to conclude that sublimation is a quantitative process. If so, then studies of anal character development should reveal this quantitative factor in operation.

For example, we should find that toilet training determines the presence or absence of adult anal characteristics. There is little evidence in favor of this claim and much evidence against it (Fisher and Greenberg 1977, p. 146). So too, we should find that male homosexuals for example, should show an excess of anal libido in their childhoods. I have found no study that affirms this claim. The quantity theory of sublimation suggests that a man who sublimates his anal erotism into smearing paint should be *less likely to be homosexual* than nonartists, yet sociological and clinical evidence is to the contrary. Male artists of every sort, from sculptors, to designers, to painters, to actors, to dancers, tend to be "inverted" more often than the norm. (See also Janine Chasseguet-Smirgel 1984, pp. 25–30.)

There is no doubt that Freud's clinical discoveries are accurate: infantile modes of intense libidinal pleasure do reappear in adult character types. Yet little evidence favors Freud's quantitative thesis and much evidence argues against it. Can we retain Freud's insights into the ego's origin in the body and offer explanations compatible with research evidence? S. Fisher (1970) found that adults with anal traits focused excessive attention upon the back side of the body. This experiment confirmed the "anal character's" concern with the backside, the hidden, and therefore the anus.

How do anal sensations, regardless of the quantity of libido, become constitutive for object relationships? An immediate answer is to return to Freud and Erikson and focus upon infant and parent interaction. We can make this return trip aided by two major allies: the theory of perception elaborated in chapter 5 and contemporary work in the psychoanalytic theory of infant development. That which links infantile anal pleasures, adult character and "sublimated" forms of anality must be shared *qualitative sensations.* It must be these sensations and their associated fantasies that enter into both perversions and character traits. In other words, there must be a family resemblance between the qualities of anal pleasure and the qualities of sculpture. This brings us back to the notion of affordances.

Visual Affordances as a Model of Emotional Affordances

The notion of affordance lets us reconsider the theory of infant–parent interactions and psychoanalytic theories of empathy and aesthetics. As described above, affordance theory suggests the following points about human perception:

1. The perception of affordances is governed both by innate neural structures and by learning. The physical characteristics of our species determines the boundaries of our sensorial world, that is, limits what we can perceive, and our environment determines what is available to us.
2. In assessing the presence or absence of an affordance an animal uses its own body as a "scaler." Research literature suggests that this scaler is surprisingly accurate.

3. These scalers are based upon a complex and accurate evaluation of one's own body-self, size, mass, height, speed, etc. We then use these scalers to assess our new environment and judge it as an arena of possible action.
4. When the human animal assesses the presence of affordances it uses these idiosyncratic scalers, not an extrinsic set of "etic" measures. (See Lombardo [1987] for a discussion of criticisms of Gibson by adherents of the information-processing paradigm.)
5. Animals carry out these assessments "preconsciously": they need not use conscious reasoning or recall prior experience with this set of environmental structures. (See LeDoux [1989]).
6. Animals can be conditioned against using information from their environment as they interact with it. Animals can be trained to ignore the presence of affordances, but such conditioning does not destroy the actuality of the affordance as the interface between animal and its environment.
7. Keen awareness and response to visual and other sensory affordances have obvious survival value. Natural selection favors animals that derive accurate information from their sensory surroundings and destroys animals that fail. Natural selection favors infants attuned to their parents' tendencies toward violence. It also favors children who can intuit the "kind of child" the parent demands.

Animals (including human beings) use themselves as "scalers" to examine their environment for information about the physical world and its affordances. They also examine it for the presence of emotional affordances (EA). In this sense, emotional affordances are "constant" aspects of the infant–parent interactions. If EA are analogous to visual affordances, then they should be discoverable at some level of observational science. Just as we nonconsciously gauge visual affordances, we must also *nonconsciously gauge emotional affordances.* Hence, to discover what counts as invariant emotional affordances within a particular context, like a family, one cannot rely upon the participants' self-understandings. For example, few of us could say that the optimum height for stairs is .25 times our leg length. Expert architects and engineers do not design stairs with this optimal height. It was discovered by carefully observing how people assess the affordance of "step-up-ability."

To discover what count as EA in a particular person's life one must observe how that person acts and interacts with the person's environment. These observational records and assessments may not match the actor's self-understanding nor the "correct" view of themselves maintained by others.

Structure of Emotional Affordances

Given this brief summary of the theory of visual affordances we can list features that should be true of emotional affordances (EA).

1. If humans perceive EA the way they perceive visual affordances, then humans must have access to emotional scalers. These scalers must be relevant to the task of assessing the presence of EA. They must reflect information about one's internal states, measured through all the sensorial channels available.
2. The experimental literature suggests that persons are accurate in their use of themselves as scalers when they assess affordances. This degree of accuracy, if true of the perception of EA, is another argument against Freud's claim about the ubiquity of hallucination and primary narcissism.
3. Natural selection favors infants who are accurately attuned to their parent's emotional responses, that is, to their parent's attitudes toward their children. A very angry or very rejecting mother produces a dead infant. Hence, natural selection favors infants who can scan their emotional environment, such as mother's mood, and adjust themselves to it. This adjustment to mother's mood, when that mood is variable and hostile, is a key feature in many pathologies. (See C. Bollas, 1987.)
4. Constants present in visual perception emerge in the way animals orient themselves toward their world. Animals do not "learn" them through teaching. Constants present in the perception of EA must emerge in the infant's response to the environment and the environment's response to the infant.

We can contrast this list of features typical of EA by comparing it to a list of features typical of neurotic conditions.

Genesis of Neurotic Psychopathology

1. If they have a choice, human beings should not persist in relationships which are inherently painful. A healthy animal would not continue to attempt to run through a mirror which seemed to reflect the possibility of escape.
2. Yet a defining feature of neurosis is that people persist in harmful relationships. They bang their heads against a wall, make

the same mistake again and again, and end up hurting themselves "against their wills."

3. Following analytic theory and clinical findings, we suppose that such "patterns of failure" stem from early object relationships. Classical insights into transference reenactment and transference testing explain such repetitions in part.

4. But these traditional explanations do not account for the adult who, on leaving home, persists in neurotic actions.

5. If the idea of emotional affordance has any merit it must help us account for the genesis and persistence of neuroses.

6. We examine our world for EA the way we examine it for visual affordances. If we persist in our neurotic actions, then our "neurosis" must be validated by experience. Otherwise, like any animal with a choice, we would learn to avoid the things that hurt us. Yet, as popular music explains, we end up doing the very thing we know will give us pain. A defining characteristic of neuroses is the predominance of self-destructive actions.

7. There are other defining characteristics of neuroses (and neurotic level pathologies). They are not healed by will power (see William James and his struggle with masturbation [Gilman, 1988].) They are not healed by intellect (see Kohut on the reanalysis of psychoanalysts), nor by transcendental means.[2]

8. If frustrating basic needs produces neuroses, then merely symbolic responses to those needs will not cure neurotic illness. Thirst cannot be satisfied, indefinitely, by pictures of water or by training a person to resist the urge to drink.

9. The infant (or child or adult) must find some way to satisfy these basic needs, some way to carry out its basic plans. These psychological needs, like physiological needs, can be matters of life and death. Most clinicians can recall patients who, in the depth of despair and hopelessness, contemplate or attempt suicide.

10. *Emotional Affordances are not the objects that satisfy these needs.* EA are signs of the existence of potential satisfaction. Hence, like visual affordance, emotional affordances indicate that a desired course of action is possible or unlikely or impossible. The visual affordance of "not-sink-into-able" of thick ice only indicates that persons of a given weight can walk there, *if they choose to do so.* Activities of walking or stepping are events that occur within an ecological context defined by the animal's perception of affordances and the choices available to it.

11. Signs of the presence of EA can be faked. The mother's smile is

a *sign* of mother's actual state of mind toward the child; in this sense, her smile can be one form of emotional affordance. The child whose mother fakes a smile and then hurts the child teaches her child to distrust this standard affordance. EA can be faked just as visual affordances can be faked.

This potential for clever fakery does not prove that "It's all a fake!" Some parents can smile and still be villains. This does not invalidate smiles as EA. That magicians can "saw" ladies in half does not invalidate our perception that real saws are dangerous.

It may be helpful to diagram the logic of my argument so far. I first offer this chart and then explain each term in detail. The arrows represent a temporal sequence of basic causes of psychological processes. The chart adopts the standard analytic theorem that there are primary motivators. These, like the "id," influence secondary motivators, like the drives. These, in turn, influence tertiary motives, e.g., wishes, hopes, and ambitions. I use Table 6.1 as a template for additional charts that restate analytic theorems about the genesis of neurosis and neurotic-like institutions, such as religion.[3]

Table 6.1 Flow Chart of Logic of EA Theory

Basic physical and psychological needs must be met, otherwise death occurs.	Primary motivators of action.
	Use internal scalers to measure against external objects.
	Search for EA: match scalers; search for emotional sustenance.
Modify behavior: scan parents, note the presence of distinctive EA (emotional affordances), in response to changes in behavior.	Scan parents and other objects: assess parents' responses and *their* psychological needs, "the exchange rate" operative in that family.
Renegotiate with parents (and other objects): reassess accuracy of originale judgments.	Unconscious processing of the exchange rate: "How will I survive?"

Basic biological needs are fixed by the nature of the animal and its expectable environment (Hartmann 1939, Erikson 1963, John Bowlby 1973). Basic psychological needs appear more variable; they seem shaped both by innate human characteristics and by specific cultural milieus. Hence the range of "good enough" parenting is large. It accounts for the variations anthropologists describe when they compare distinctive cultures. (See Lévi-Strauss 1985; E. O. Wilson 1975.)

Many disciplines attempt to describe "basic psychological needs." Questions about these needs and how they constitute human nature dominate the disciplines of ethics, political science, and theology. Various psychoanalysts define basic needs differently; some study the need to individuate and develop an independent ego (Erikson, 1963), others focus on the search for a responsive enough mothering object (Winnicott 1971, Bowlby 1973, Stern 1985). Others study the need to avoid the "calamities of early childhood": object loss, castration, loss of love, and guilt (Charles Brenner 1982).

To satisfy these basic psychological needs, however defined, the human animal must search for "emotional affordances." The need to eat requires animals learn to walk or swim in order to find food. In order to move around safely and successfully the animal must learn to use the perceptual affordances that suffuse their environments. *Failure to satisfy basic physiological or psychological needs produces disease or death.*

This lets us make the following generalization: the infant, the child, and the adult trains its sensorial aptitudes upon its emotional environment, seeking evidence of EA and then reacting to its presence. The child seeks to find how its parents (emotional caretakers) manifest their own, particular version of caretaking. The parent's availability as affordance varies with the child's behavior. The observant child changes its behavior in accordance.

Emotional Affordances and Self Scalers

If the perception of EA parallels the processes underlying the perception of visual affordances, then the perceiving subject must employ internal scalers. These must reflect accurately the subject's emotional needs. Again, these emotional scalers may not be conscious nor ever enter into consciousness, just as the body scalers described by physiological psychologists may never enter into consciousness. *Conflicts* engendered by errors in judgment or by the lack of fit between internal scaler and available affordance *do* enter consciousness. When obeying a parent requires a child to defeat an ordinary wish, for example, to separate from parental control, neurosis occurs (Weiss and Sampson

1986). It is these neurotic conflicts and associated symptoms that bring patients to therapy.

What are these emotional scalers? Experimental psychology and psychoanalytic infant research suggest some answers which echo Freud's attempts to describe the "experience of satisfaction." They also reflect back upon the issue of "part instincts" and the theory of sublimation derived from instinct models of human behavior. Daniel Stern (1985) reviews many physiological and psychological studies of infant behavior to formulate an idea he terms "affect attunement." It refers to the ways one person perceives the emotional state of another and communicates that perception.

Emotional Scalers and Body Zones

Stern emphasizes the intensity of the baby's experience and the degree to which the mother reflects those emotional intensities or qualities. We can use Stern's discussion to develop the notion of "emotional scaler" in more detail. Stern describes six features of the baby's emotional behavior that the mother could "match" or "attune." He emphasizes the *mother's response* to these six dimensions. I wish to emphasize how each of these dimensions reflects an internal event for the baby and so constitutes an "emotional" scaler for that baby. These six dimensions (cited from pp. 146–147) are:

1. Absolute intensity of behavior, e.g., loudness.
2. Intensity contour: changes in intensity over time.
3. Temporal beat: a regular pulse is matched.
4. Rhythm: set of unequal pulsations is matched.
5. Duration: the time span is matched.
6. Shape: spatial qualities of the action are matched.

Each of these categories uses an abstract name to designate an intensely felt experience evident in both baby and mother (and often shared by the observers as well). Attunement occurs when the mother plays with her baby, when she matches the shape of her baby's emotional state. It does not occur when she mimics her baby's actions. Matching between baby and mother is often cross modal. For example, a parent's voice rises and falls as the baby's level of exertion rises and falls. Stern notes that attunement is not mimicry, nor matching "the other person's behavior *per se*, but rather some aspect of the behavior that reflects the person's feeling state. The ultimate reference for the match appears to be the feeling state (inferred or directly apprehended), not the external behavioral event" (1985, p. 142). Given this understanding, it follows that these six features, and all other features of the infant's experience, can function as emotional scalers. Stern and his colleagues assess the degree to which a mother "matches" her infant's state of arousal. This indirectly assess how the infant gauges its mother's attunements to the infant's internal state. Infants could do this only if they had access, non-consciously, to sets of internal scalers.

Stern supports this claim, as do other baby watchers, when he notes that infants whose mothers are "attuned" to them respond differently than infants whose mother are not attuned. In the well-attuned couple the baby plays easily; only when the attunement is consciously broken does the baby respond, "as if to say, 'What's going on?'" (p. 150). A simple learning theorem, that mother reinforces one behavior, cannot explain the importance of matching the infant's rhythms with mother's rhythms. Babies perceive when their mothers alter their usual pacing: "Many more such individualized perturbations have been performed, all indicating that the infant does indeed have some sense of the extent of matching" (p. 151). (See also pp. 153–154.)

These abilities to perceive the *quality* of mothering afforded one appear early in the infant's development. Infants are better attuned to the "external world" than classical theory allows for they register the pattern of their behavior, like banging a drum, and compare it to their mothers' behaviors. This means that the baby can find *qualitative richness* and unity in otherwise discreet stimuli. In other words, infants and babies are sensitive to the match between their emotional scalers and the world of emotional affordances which surrounds them. The world of emotional affordances is far richer than the internal world of mere fantasy and much richer than described in standard psychoanalytic theories.

Body Zones as Sources of Qualitative Richness

The six dimensions Stern describes are observable features of mother's response to her infant's interior experience. Stern says that infants perceive shifts in their mothers' responses. Then infants must be able to locate and assess these dimensions of their internal experience.

Another source of stimulation for the infant is the workings of its own body, especially those parts of its body associated with pleasure and pain. Infants assess these tensions and qualities with an accuracy similar to that displayed when they assess the external world. This invokes Freud's insights into the sexual zones and their importance to all ego development (Freud 1905d). To return to the issue of anal erotism, infants (and children and adults) must perceive distinctive sensations and *qualities* associated with the anal zone. These distinctive sensations have their own characteristic pattern, a pattern of tension and release that occur in nonanal behaviors. These six dimensions of observable behavior must apply also to these sensations associated with *unobserved behaviors* as well. These hidden, internal experiences and sensations are as real as any other type of sensation. In addition, each of the sense modalities, like taste, is specific to an internal experience. It has its own qualitative richness that yields to the infant a distinctive pattern of tension, pleasure, and pain.

Regarding anal tension states there is a large literature. First are clinical discussions of specific anal erotic modes and their transformations. Second is the less common discussion of anal tension states themselves. Erikson's discussions are well known. Less often cited by American psychoanalysts is H. S. Sullivan's extensive description of anal erotism. Sullivan, whom biographers say was homosexual most of his adult life, elaborates upon the structure of anal sensations.[4] He describes a process "of really staggering importance" (1953, p. 153). By way of a circuitous route, the child retrieves sensations of forbidden pleasures. The example he uses is "the satisfaction of rubbing the anal region with the finger" (p. 153). Because mother forbids this, the infant learns to avoid her anger. Instead, the infant finds an indirect way to manipulate the anus, for example, through a blanket. Sullivan invokes the "good old term" from psychoanalysis, *sublimation* to name this process. In other places, he expands his use of this term. In each case he follows the Freudian model and says that sublimation is an unconscious or "unwitting" (p. 193) process in which zonal pleasure occurs by indirect actions.

Sullivan's elaborate description of anality occurs in his chapter on anxiety generated by mother and her response to her child's body (p. 133). He introduces "into this discussion a group of inferences derived from my own observations" (p. 127) about the "quasi-distance quality" associated with what he terms "anal sentience" (p. 128):

> Now this is the area of data which may be proven by investigation to be erroneous, but about which I believe I have adequate basis for this presentation. It is literally true that the separation of the fecal mass from the contact with the anus is necessary for ordinary completion of the act of defecation. This may seem to you a very trivial matter. (pp. 129–130)

It is not trivial, for in order to achieve this sense of separation from the fecal mass the infant requires the presence of a loving parent. She (or he) wipes the infant's bottom. This action satisfies the "anticontact receptors" which, Sullivan says, congregate in the mucous membrane near the anus. From this early experience the infant (ideally) learns "tenderness which is organized by the infant in his personification of the mother" (p. 130). Or, as Sullivan says, "The anal zone of interaction thus necessarily comes to involve factors of an interpersonal character from very early in life" (p. 133).

Sullivan uses the term *sublimation* in its Freudian sense, but his focus upon the infant's experience of others and his emphasis upon multimodal sensations parallel my efforts to rethink the concept. For Sullivan stresses the complex interactive events that make up the infant's experience of the good mother. These constitute the infant's willingness to seek out new pleasures and to draw upon memories of goodness and hope. He stresses also the forms of anxiety mothers can create in infants: when mother disapproves of the infant's behavior, including the infant's internal sensations, she induces a new form of anxiety. When mother punishes self-stimulation, like anal fondling, she induces what Sullivan termed the "Bad-me." It is "based on this increasing gradient of anxiety and that, in turn, is dependent … on the observation … of the infant's behavior by someone who can induce anxiety" (p. 162).

Consequences of Failure in Positive Attunement

We can link Sullivan to Stern by considering the concept of attunement as Stern develops it. Stern says attunement occurs when the mother (or other loving person) reflects the sensorial qualities of the infant's experience. We might term this "positive attunement," to distinguish it from the "negative attunement" that Sullivan describes as inducing the creation of the "Bad-me." From a distinct point of view, Emanuel Peterfreund (1983) proposes a similar thesis. He compares "heuristic" method in clinical analysis to "stereotyped" applications of theory to patient material. Stereotyped applications mean that the analyst is not attuned to the patient's ebb and flow of affective experience. Rather the analyst uses the patient to decrease the analyst's anxiety. That is, the analyst use the patient as an archaic self-object to decrease the analyst's fear of change or fear of the analyst's internal world.

Analytic theorems, like the notion of the oedipus complex or the concept of self-object, may be useful constructs. When forced upon the patient they make genuine moments of interaction impossible just as the awkward mother who insists upon a cheery infant fails to attune herself to her baby's actual emotional tenor. When the latter kind of failure is intense and chronic, major self-disorders occur; the "Bad-me" dominates the infant's self-experience. Peterfreund describes such an instance, a patient whose mother, according to the patient, "could not hear," and was intolerant of any opposition. "Bad" behavior "killed" her, and she constantly threatened abandonment. She was subject to very rapid mood changes, and very early in life the patient learned to be attuned to these moods, always alert for any sign of breakdown.... She once described her early life as, "This dead mother, this dead house, this dead city." (1983, p. 11)

The last sentence captures with poetic force a world in which emotional affordances cease to appear. This same patient failed to develop a coherent sense of her inner or outer self, "she saw herself as a total 'zero,' and her body as nothing but debris or 'flotsam.' Indeed, she saw her body as made up of totally disorganized, disconnected parts with no apparent central regulatory mechanism" (p. 10). Yet this patient was able to remain in therapy and to benefit, to some degree, from her therapist's good will and skill. The patient's lack of a central regulatory mechanism suggests the absence of what others might term a cohesive self, or a true self, or a coherent ego.

Affordance theory predicts such an outcome. If the maternal object fails to show attunement then the child cannot form additional structures ("ego structures"). Without these the child refuses to take additional chances on new relationships *separate from mother (or father)*. If failures in attunement center on specific issues, such as ambition or narcissistic display, we find ego deficits in those areas. Life is not always as easy as listening to one's favorite music. External conflicts emerge between those who search for happiness, via emotional affordances, and the external world of objects and nature which often fails to supply the affordances desired. Internal conflicts emerge between part instinct derivatives, e.g., oedipal wishes, and other wishes, e.g., to preserve and defend the oedipal opponent. As a result, the infant or child must assess external conflicts and internal conflicts and decrease the psychic pain that results. In more traditional analytic terms, infants and children employ every relevant means, including all their ego skills and modes, to improve their level of comfort. None of these skills, such as repression, is inherently pathological, and none, such as rationalization, is inherently adaptive. Rather all ego functions can be used for defense (Brenner 1982, chapter 5).

Forms of Unconscious Processing

Unconscious processing is the person's assessment of EA and the possibility of attunement. The person can then choose a suitable course of action in response to those perceptions. Assuming that the notion of emotional scalers is plausible, we can say that the infant seeking attunement seeks occasions when another person matches the intensity, rhythm, duration, beat, and shape of the infant's feelings. Unconscious processing refers to behaviors, like perceiving and memory, that the child performs in an instant or over a period of years.

A Gibsonian approach to these processes distinguishes between the child's accurate *impressions* that suffering occurs and erroneous conclusions about why it occurs. The child's restricted fund of experience and limited cognitive abilities limit the child's understanding of why harm occurs and contributes to erroneous judgments. Here many authorities cite Piaget's claims about cognitive stages: because infants and children use prerational modes of thought they cannot comprehend their parents' reasons for inflicting pain on them.

Against these claims some psychologists say children err because they have limited experience, not because they are confined to archiac modes of thought. (See Robert Weisberg 1980.) Also, a growing body of analytic evidence implicates the parents in creating real traumas which have real consequences. By emphasizing the utility of a theory of emotional affordances it may be tempting to reject traditional analytic insights into psychological conflicts. A theory of EA might support a form of environmentalism as a theory of pathology: it is sick parents that make sick children, replace bad parenting with good parenting and we will do away with childhood neuroses. EA theory pertains to the debate between psychoanalysts wary of environmentalism, like Charles Brenner (1959, 1982) and those who favor it, like Robert Stolorow and Frank Lachmann (1980). One might reduce this debate to an issue of differing world views: Brenner represents one school, what Kohut terms the school of "guilty man"; Kohut represents another, what he claims is a school of "tragic man" (1977, pp. 206–207).

A third alternative is to pursue the modified environmentalism implicit in the theory of EA. It is present also in the work of Stern and other baby watchers. I have done this by following out the implications of a psychoanalytic theory of perception that eschews the concept of primary narcissism intrinsic to Freud's theory of reality testing.

For in his more extreme passages, Freud says that the struggle to "test reality" is a constant battle. Fighting against the libido, which seeks to retrieve the lost state of narcissistic pleasures, the ego struggles to retain a sense of reality. Stern's data, like that of many other contemporary child analysts, does not support this extreme portrait. On the contrary, a theory of EA suggests that typical unconscious fantasies, including sexual and aggressive ones, do not reflect primary drives expressed in their nakedness. Rather it reflects products of failure to match primary emotional needs with adequate objects.

These failures may be intrinsic to human development. As the infant matures, the child's internal scalers, based upon biological and psychological tensions, develop at an intensity not matched by its emotional caretakers. For example, the little boy finds intense pleasure in his newly discovered penis. This delight may lead him to wish for his mother to suck it, just as he wishes to fondle her breasts. Both of these actions would yield immediate pleasure to the little boy. Analytic wisdom suggests both would be destructive, though, for both hypersexualize the parent–child bond and make separation and other maturational processes difficult to carry out. Because most cultures restrain sexual play between adults and children these restrictions make sexual fantasies, which are substitute structures, enduring contents of the unconscious.

A distinct kind of unconscious processing, not dominated by primary process thought, one might term "preconscious" calculation. A social scientist, Charles Murray (1984) provides a lucid example of such preconscious calculation. He describes the reasoning process a young couple, the girl pregnant, the boy just out of high school, would undergo in 1960. He compares it to the reasoning process a similar couple make in 1970. In 1960 economic considerations alone made it best for the couple to marry and for the husband to work at a beginning job. Thanks to massive changes in the shift of responsibility and shift in reward structures, by 1970 the women is better off financially having the child and not marrying. Both husband and wife are better off financially if the father seeks work part time and then quits. To a middle-class teacher or social worker, it is abhorrent that a young woman would refuse marriage and get pregnant many times. Murray shows that the woman's decision is reasonable, at least in the short-term economic point of view.

Comprehending the Family's Exchange Rate

Drawing upon these forms of preconscious processing, infants modify their behavior. We all modify our behavior when we feel certain dangers lie in one direction and certain rewards lie in another. One might term this complex interchange between the set of EA offered by the family and the child's internal assessment "learning that family's exhange rate." Which behaviors yield pain, which behaviors yield pleasure, and what do parents want?

Joseph Weiss (1986) says that children infer how they should alter their behavior in order to elicit the responses they require. These interactions teach the child not merely how to act in the sense of comportment, but also how to alter the child's self as experienced by the child.

Using unconscious forms of inference, the child attempts to become the kind of child the parent seems to require to feel better about herself or himself.

Each such form of reasoning may contribute to those processes that promote the child's construction of neurotic patterns. Weiss (1986) focuses upon the centrality of pathogenic beliefs to the construction of neuroses. He gives eloquent testimony to some of the ways in which this occurs:

> One child may infer that if he is clinging and dependent on his parents he will please them; another child, that if he is clinging and dependent on his parents he will drain them; or the same child may infer both ideas. Another child may infer that he must be a bad boy in order to make his parents feel morally superior, or he may assume that he must be bad to protect an unhappy sibling whom the parents, because of worry, wish to perceive as good. As another example, a child may infer that by competing with a parent he will provoke the parent into a dangerous competition with him. Another child may infer that by competing with a parent he will provoke the parent to reject him. (pp. 54–55)

In the face of significant dangers, the right choice spells life, the wrong choice spells death. Here, traditional analytic theory emphasizes ego strengths as built upon positive introjects of loving and beloved figures. Taken to an extreme, this doctrine can be read as claiming that it is the inner world, populated with positive objects, that makes mental health and adaptation possible. But, adaptation is more likely if those introjected images correspond also to a realistic sense of the external world and how *it will treat one.*

Emotional Affordances and the Drives

Our task is to distinguish possible modes of interaction between the child's perception of EA and the child's response to those perceptions. I distinguish an ideal of positive interaction, in which interior body sensations give rise to positive introjects, from nonideal processes. Table 6.2 represents an ideal sequence of zonal pressure (or drive based wish), the child's ego response to that pressure and the ideal parental response to the child's action. Tables 6.3 and 6.4 represent deviations from this ideal of infant–parent interactions.

Table 6.2 Drive seeking and response in normal development

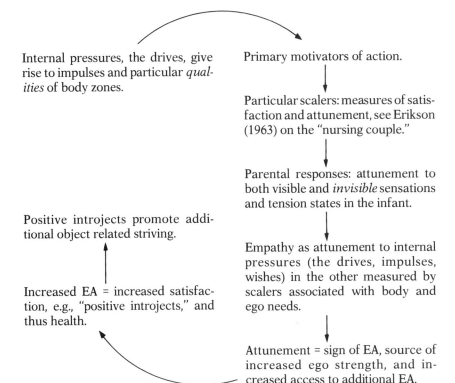

Internal pressures, the drives, give rise to impulses and particular *qualities* of body zones.

Primary motivators of action.

Particular scalers: measures of satisfaction and attunement, see Erikson (1963) on the "nursing couple."

Parental responses: attunement to both visible and *invisible* sensations and tension states in the infant.

Positive introjects promote additional object related striving.

Increased EA = increased satisfaction, e.g., "positive introjects," and thus health.

Empathy as attunement to internal pressures (the drives, impulses, wishes) in the other measured by scalers associated with body and ego needs.

Attunement = sign of EA, source of increased ego strength, and increased access to additional EA.

In Table 6.3, I summarize the theory of perversion discussed in chapter 5. This theory I derive from current psychoanalytic perspectives on perversions. It assumes that perverse sexuality derives from a person's psychological life, not a biological substrate. However, this assumption is not a requirement for if science discovers biological influences on homosexual choice, for example, then these count as "primary motivators of action." This is a vague category because no one has yet shown exactly how these "primary motivators" integrate with "higher level" drives, and the drives with wishes.

Table 6.3 also reflects Janine Chasseguet-Smirgel's book, *Creativity and Perversions* (1984). She traces the subtle links that often bind the idealization of anality in male homosexual persons to a shared passion for aesthetic experience. She stresses the cognitive side of anality; in the anal universe differences of every sort, especially between male and female, are denied. They are homogenized or "analized" into the same substance, feces that defy any effort to maintain distinction.

Oscar Wilde, artist, homosexual prince, and aesthete, struggled to disguise anality with glittering jewels. Chasseguet-Smirgel notes this is most evident in *The Portrait of Dorian Gray*. She also cites Glover's earlier papers (1931, 1964) on the development of fetishism and with Glover notes how the fetishist idealizes objects and requires of them certain aesthetic features, like size and texture. For without these qualities present there can be no sexual excitement, because there is no sexual overestimation.

I wish to stress the values placed upon *qualitative differences* between one object and another in many forms of perversion. From this focus upon differences arises a generalized fascination with the sensory environment: texture, weave, weight, color, fragrance, touch, sound, and other qualities of the admired object are idealized. This, naturally, is part of the reason many significant artists and others devoted to the aesthetic life, such as critics and scholars, are both homosexual and artistic. The homosexual experience is direct and powerful; the aesthetic is indirect and more subtle. It fits a culture which rewards the arduous labor of becoming expert in the details of craft, performance, and criticism.

In my clinical experience, some homosexual men who are unsure of their sexual orientation challenge their own devotion to aestheticism when they experience doubts about their homosexual orientation. A typical dream of such a patient involves him looking at a once-admired object: he examines an antique desk, or aesthetic institution, say the opera, with a new sense of distance. He feels puzzled about its former meaning to him. These dreams often presage a very painful shift in the patient's former idealization of the aesthetic object and of aesthetics itself. This shift is painful because, one learns, the patient has denied his own feelings of worthlessness, of "feeling like shit," by wrapping himself in the sensuous glories of the refined object. Typically, the idealized object appears altered in the dream; it is less grand, less unique, and less special. Often, it becomes ordinary and loses its hallowed status in the patient's environment. For example, the rare eighteenth-century desk, once kept lovingly by the marble fireplace, in the dream sits on the porch loaded down with magazines and umbrellas.

In another case, an esteemed painting, the best in the patient's large collection and admired by his aesthetic friends, appears in a dream washed. It is "cleansed," that is, "deanalised," and so bereft of its aesthetic value. (The shrinking, of course, also reflects diminution of the narcissistic charge attached to the painting, a change instituted by the work of the "shrink.")

Side by side these dreams of diminution of aesthetics, are concrete upsurges in authentic self-esteem. A patient who finds himself less devoted to opera also no longer lets himself be manipulated financially. Or another patient discovers that he is joyful in the presence of an attractive woman. Part of the tragedy surrounding the life of Oscar Wilde centers on his need to design himself, to create a caricature of the high-born aristocrat. His former friend, the young Lord with whom Wilde was infatuated, Alfred Douglas, portrays Wilde's elaborate search for stature. This search led Wilde to submit himself to Douglas, to seduce the young man, for Douglas was a "real" Lord. Using his considerable gifts, Wilde created himself, his character and persona.

Wilde has become a hero to other homosexual men who employ him as part of their own idealized version of homosexuality (cf. André Gide 1949). Many literate and cultured homosexual patients refer to Wilde with mixed feelings. They are fascinated with his sense of style, pomp, disguise, reversal, and wit. His famous sayings, for example, that "Life imitates Art," are, as Chasseguet-Smirgel (1985) notes, about other forms of perversion, inversions of ordinary insights and truisms. This painful shift involves both mourning the loss of the former route toward satisfaction and losing hold of the special fantasies of narcissistic union entailed in the aesthetic encounter. These secondary losses are terrifying and produce fantasies of falling apart or going crazy that resemble other moments of fragmentation anxiety evident in narcissistically vulnerable persons. After they test out a new orientation toward the heterosexual world, with all its new anxieties, such patients are much less fascinated with aesthetic nuances. Such patients do not grow to dislike art or aesthetic objects, but they regret losing access to a concrete source of wonderment.

Articulate patients describe this source of wonderment as an uncanny form of communication that once took place between themselves and the object or between themselves and the object's creator. A large part of therapy centers upon the patient's feelings of identity between himself and the legendary artist with whom he has merged himself. These communions are often the result of wishes to find an absent parent. The artist replaces the mother or father who failed to sustain the child's yearning for real union and real relationship. Direct, sexual expressions of this yearning occur, of course, in homosexual encounters where the body of the same-sexed person is the prize; indirect, aesthetic expression of this yearning occurs in more displaced forms through the exaggerated importance given to sensuous experience.

Table 6.3 Drive seeking and sublimated versions

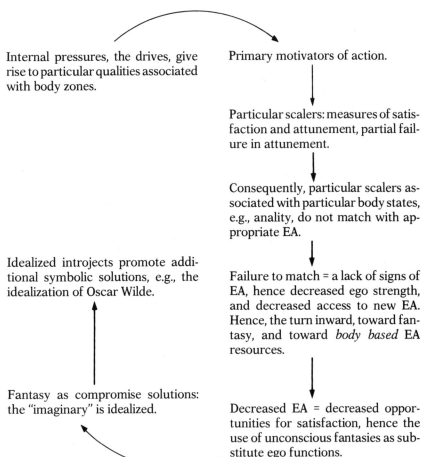

Internal pressures, the drives, give rise to particular qualities associated with body zones.

Primary motivators of action.

Particular scalers: measures of satisfaction and attunement, partial failure in attunement.

Consequently, particular scalers associated with particular body states, e.g., anality, do not match with appropriate EA.

Idealized introjects promote additional symbolic solutions, e.g., the idealization of Oscar Wilde.

Failure to match = a lack of signs of EA, hence decreased ego strength, and decreased access to new EA. Hence, the turn inward, toward fantasy, and toward *body based* EA resources.

Fantasy as compromise solutions: the "imaginary" is idealized.

Decreased EA = decreased opportunities for satisfaction, hence the use of unconscious fantasies as substitute ego functions.

Table 6.4 builds upon the previous three. I include it for the sake of completion and to sketch out the implications of a notion of EA for the received psychoanalytic theory of religion. According to this table we can conceive of religion as "unconscious group fantasy" analogous to the neuroses and to the perversions, yet distinct because validated by social institutions. These group fantasies are compromise formations. They capture both the ethical strivings of a group and the group's desperate wishes to substitute imaginary beings and imaginary companions for missing ego functions. When the ethical dimension weakens and when the group's desperation increases, we find the not-rare event of mass murder. Murder done for religious purposes, like the witch hunts of the Middle Ages and the slaughter of the ideologically impure in communist regimes, remains murder.

Table 6.4 Drive seeking and response in religion

Internal pressures, drives, other impulses with particular qualities from body zones.	Primary motivators of action.
	↓
	Particular scalers: measures of satisfaction and attunement, partial failure of attunement.
	↓
	Failure in attunement to internal pressures (urges, drives, wishes) measured by scalers associated with body needs, e.g. anality.
	↓
Group fantasy as compromise solutions: the "imaginary" is hypercathected and projected into the heavens where it remains "transcendent."	Parental response: nonattunement to both visible and invisible sensations and tension states, hence, substitute self-objects offered.
↑	↓
Decreased EA = decreased opportunities for satisfaction. "Unconscious group fantasy," like religion, in lieu of missing ego structures.	Failure = lack of signs of EA, decreased ego strength and decreased access to new EA. Hence, return to *substitute* self-object entities based on parental teaching.

From Aesthetics to Sublimation

Anyone who has aimed a camera learns how difficult it is to capture the image we wish to preserve. Most of us recognize that we are not artists, we know we lack the "photographer's eye." What is the photographer's eye? This question cannot be answered until one has answered the more basic question, what do we perceive when we perceive the "external world"? I have suggested that Gibson's radical theory of "visual affordances" is a more satisfying theory of perception than its competitors. Implicit in Gibson's theory of visual and other perceptual affordances is the claim that the normal animal is pre-adapted to its usual environment. It is the invariance of the world which gives rise to the invariance of affordances. Freud made similar claims in his speculations on the prehistory of the race (1912–13). But it was Heinz Hartmann (1939, 1964) and his coworkers Ernst Kris and Rudolph Loewenstein, who suggested that human beings are pre-adapted to their physical and emotional environments. From the genetic point of view the most important element within that environment is the infant's mother or mother substitute.

Many studies of parent–child bonding and related conditions like hospitalism (Bowlby 1953; 1973) show that the mothering person must exhibit more than clockwork responses. She or he must love the baby. Loving it means taking authentic pleasure in every little action, in accepting its burps, gas, cries, and other annoyances and—as all parents know—in taking care of the most important baby in the world. How does the infant know that its mother loves it? What in his or her parents' behavior communicates the presence of this vital fact?

The infant must perceive the presence of an emotional affordance. An emotional affordance is an aspect of the environment that offers one access to the satisfaction of a basic need. Perhaps the most obvious example of such an affordance is the mother's smile (Kurt Goldstein 1957; René Spitz 1957; Erik Erikson 1963; Margaret Mahler 1983; Daniel Stern 1977). There seem to be definite, inborn propensities for human infants to move toward stimulus configurations which have the general structure of a smiling, adult face.

The adaptive value of such a propensity and the role it plays in establishing the mother–infant bond are obvious. But trouble enters the world of the mother–infant pair when the mother is absent actually or emotionally, for then the child no longer perceives a crucial feature of its world, the mother's benevolent presence. The real, external world of things does not change in the same fashion: the structure of affordances remains the same. (See also Justin Call, et al. 1983 and L. Stone, et al. 1973.)

As we have seen, Gibson says this constancy is a central requirement of vision. Human action takes place in an environment in which objects come and go out of view, but the relationships between viewer and objects, the affordances, remain invariant. The world of things is in motion, but the structure of those changes is regular: hence it is predictable because the structure of air, earth, water, and sunlight on sand is regular and predictable.

This is also true of primary emotional affordances. That is, because primary emotional affordances are real objects, existing in real time and real space, they manifest all the characteristics of ordinary objects. In addition, they are sources of emotional substenance: ideally, they remain constant enough, during moments and periods of need, for the child or other person to perceive their invariance. However, they *may fail* to meet those needs: people die, parents divorce, and others fail to recognize their children's needs. This means the child must find new ways to locate emotional affordances.

Emotional Affordances versus Representations: The Structure of the Inner World

Emotional affordances cannot be represented. This fact has implications for traditional analytic theories of the "Inner World" as a place of "object and self-representations," for these representations cannot be themselves "emotional affordances." Representations of emotional affordances are, at best, representations of a now-absent "good object." Like paintings, mirrors, and similar surfaces, representations of affordances do not change in response to the viewer's behavior. Gibson, Robert Weisberg (1980), and others assert one cannot walk around a representation and receive from it the "indications" of reality evident in interactions with a real thing. Like other sense modalities, vision is an activity which occurs in mobile animals like ourselves. By walking around the thing or altering our position we increase the chance of noting visual and other perceptual affordances.

Many classic illusions require the viewer to remain immobile. So too, experimenters use chin rests and similar paraphernalia to immobilize the viewer. This prevents him or her from carrying out ordinary modes of "reality testing." One cannot walk around the object and so perceive the presence (or absence) of visual and all other perceptual affordances. Only in relationships with living, three-dimensional persons can one perceive the presence of emotional affordances. For only in such relationships can one experience over time the range of diverse feelings and shifts of emotional view that establish the solidity and aliveness of the other. Psychoanalysts have long held that ideal parents are those who disappoint gradually their children's fixed ideals and fixed demands for an unchanging supply of emotional gratification. These gradual, phase-appropriate, failures "strengthen" the child's ego because they require the child to perceive emotional affordances in persons other than the child's parents.

Portraits are static and, like all icons, are subject to deterioration. Hence one must guard them against any alteration through time. One sees this both in neurotics and in many religious practices. Unlike dream images, mirror reflections, paintings, and recollections, the actual mother is the source of an unceasing number of new "angles" and perceptions. The infant learns about that object over time and in so doing regulates itself by relying upon both her physical and her consistent, good-enough mothering. In Erikson's phrase, children raise their parents. That is, children make severe demands upon their parents and then monitor their parents' response. These demands shape the parents' behaviors and, in turn, the parents modify the child's response. The term *strong ego* denotes a person who understands that his or her parents love their children even when the latter are "bad."

The icon and emblem can preserve only a static element of the loved one. They preserve what can be captured by a photograph or a lock of hair. In this sense they preserve what is least like an actual person: they cannot preserve the interplay between need and satisfaction (Erikson) and the visual interplay between object and viewer (Gibson). The classic concept of emotional fixation is relevant here. Persons avoid new, authentic relationships out of fear of losing hold of the single, iconic elements with which they are tied to the past—now lost—object. Rather, they fixate upon mere representations. These are static and, like dream images, can be manipulated, for example, in masturbation fantasies, but cannot enter into a dynamic relationship between viewer and object (or person and caretaker) because they do not manifest actual affordances.

Consequently, the child loses that crucial ability to define himself or herself in relationship to the invariance of the external world. Similar physiolgical examples of this are persons who are bedridden or astronauts who have been weightless for many months. Both groups of people must learn again how to walk and bear their own weight. They can do so because the earth and its relationship to their bodies do not vary. The landscape varies, but the set of affordances does not. One must lean forward going up steep hills, backwards when running down them, and walk slowly on ice.

I use Gibson's notion of the self as that portion of our world which obscures part of the visual field. Massive alterations in the laws which govern the physical world cause massive alterations in the way we understand ourselves. So too immortality would alter our understanding of human beings—not to mention the way people drive. Erikson's beautiful descriptions of ego-identity are pertinent to this discussion because he holds that among the ego's general tasks is that of preserving both a sense of continuity through time and a sense of place. To accomplish these two tasks the ego must rely upon or come to rely upon the persistence of affectionate relationships with other persons.

Preliminaries to the Analytic Process

A theory of emotional affordances supplements the notion of "real relationship" or "therapeutic bond" as described in the psychoanalytic literature. For a notion of emotional affordance, implicit in both Stern and Winnicott, presupposes that patients cannot enter into transference regressions safely without trusting the analyst and the analytic process. The concept of trust is specific to each patient since each patient brings to the analytic encounter the patient's unconscious fantasies. These produce "pure transference" manifestations. Patients also bring an acute sense of the other person's psychic equilibrium. These latter perceptions do not give rise to transference, but to accurate portraits of the analyst's personality. To focus upon this dimension does not ignore the reality of transference events and the power of transference wishes. Yet, as Weiss (1986) stresses in his study of unconscious perception, patients may regulate the appearance of unconscious material depending upon their assessment of the analytic setting. A patient "ordinarily lifts his repressions and carries out his unconscious plans only if in his unconscious judgment he may safely do so" (1986, p. 6).

Gibson allows us to sharpen this notion by arguing that these are not incidental needs: they are akin to the ego's need for a world of visual and tactile affordances. In Gibson's terms to perceive affordances one must be in a proper (physical) relationship to one's environment. If suddenly sunlight no longer forms shadows when it strikes objects one could not enjoy vistas like the Grand Canyon. Emotional affordances share these characteristics and the additional one of mutuality. In order to see accurately all that need occur is that mailboxes exhibit the usual relationship between the visual angle and my distance from them; the mailbox need not feel or respond to me.

This is not true of emotional affordances. Persons (or animals) to whom I look for emotional affordances must react to me and find in me similar affordances. This is a two-way street or dipolar event, to use Martin Buber's term. I come to trust the ongoing presence of myself to the degree I can believe in the ongoing response of the other. In ordinary terms, this is what most people would call a love relationship; both persons are enhanced by their mutual concern for the other. Parenthetically, that the libido theory cannot account for these experiences is a mark of its limitations.

According to libido theory the quantity of libidinal energies is fixed. In order to love others one must love oneself less. In this schema fixation is an economic event in which large quanta of psychic energy are tied to archaic fantasy images and hence the ego is impoverished. But, as everyone knows, being in love is not necessarily a state of impoverishment. On the contrary, the whole bulk of psychoanalytic research into child development argues the opposite. The capacity to love others is a sign of the ego's strength; self-esteem is enhanced by exercising that capacity, it is not reduced. The self is, in part, constituted by the quality of one's relationship to the external world of objects and other persons. Therefore, errors in the perception of either visual or emotional affordances will impair the self. We see this when human beings find themselves in unpredictable physical or emotional environments. Fixation then occurs because of trauma which, I suggest, is the apparent loss of a virtual emotional affordance. We will see this in the last chapter where we discuss three different responses to the loss of virtual emotional affordances.

We might also view Kohut's theory of the genesis of narcissistic disturbances along these lines. There are phase-specific needs (for initial grandiosity and idealized objects) that require gradual channeling through phase-appropriate relationships to real objects. This process of "reinternalization" cannot occur unless the child perceives the beneficial actions of real persons who can regulate both their own and the child's self-esteem. (As Erikson, again, argues consistently.) Kohut's concept of transmuting internalization is also relevant: "As a result of innumerable processes of microinternalization, the anxiety-assuaging, delay-tolerating, and other realistic aspects of the analyst's image become part of the analysand's psychological equipment" (1977, p. 32). (See also Gill 1963, chapter 3; Schafer 1968.)

Narcissism is failure to regulate self-esteem, failure generated by defects in an average expectable environment of parental empathy (Erikson and Hartmann). According to Kohut, the severity of the defect in parental empathy determines the severity of the resulting pathology. We recall Victor Tausk's paper on "The Influencing Machine" (1919), in which he recounts the sequence by which schizophrenics gradually come to view themselves as controlled by machines, until they themselves become living machines. To be a machine is to be safe from the contamination and danger of actual relationships with both oneself and others. Machines do not vary; they do not interact with one. One cannot be disappointed in them because one cannot love them. In other words, machines offer no emotional affordances and they cannot threaten, therefore, to take any away. A narcissistically vulnerable patient says, "I need a machine to analyze me because I hear too much [referring to the analyst's tone of voice, which might reveal his irritation or his occasional defensiveness when criticized] and it gets you into a mess" (in Arnold Goldberg, ed., 1978, p. 41, interpolation in text). Hearing his therapist's voice frightens this patient because he is aware that he might *correctly* interpret hostility in the analyst's vocal *qualities.*

On the Permanence of Emotional Affordances

Representations of emotional affordances may vary over time as to their ability to evoke the presence of affordances. So too, *representations* of visual and other perceptual affordances vary according to the talent of the artist and our ability to comprehend the artist's communications. If our physical self changes, the world of perceptual affordances also changes; the ice that could once hold us now is unsafe. The stairs that were too tall are now just right (or, if we have arthritis, are too tall). When an infant's emotional status changes and the infant gains ego strength, the features of the person–world interface change. In everyday language, "growing up" means forsaking one kind of emotional affordances for another set of emotional affordances. Neurotics fear insight because they fear altering their last "tangible" link with authentic emotional affordances. (See Pietro Castelnuovo-Tedesco 1984; 1988.)

From Perception to Conception: Reality Testing

Gibson's notion of reality testing contradicts Freud's and that of many subsequent psychoanalysts. For a variety of reasons, Freud believed hallucination was the basic tendency of the mental apparatus. We can restate Freud's thesis, this time using my terms rather than the original and, in that way, reveal the errors I think the original thesis contained. According to the classical theory, the ego acquires the ability to "test reality" and to discover "self and object" boundaries *after* primary process thinking has failed. Freud described this sequence in the "Project." Drive hunger (or "libidinal upsurge" or "drive pressure") evokes genetically based schemata of appropriate need-satisfying objects. For example, the newborn roots around for the nipple. When it succeeds in finding the appropriate object, it is happy. That in turn, leads to a hypercathexis of the iconic representation of the object that satisfied this need. Hence the primitive ego forms the conception of the need satisfying object; this conception represents the original emotional affordance (the generous breast).

When the infant's appetite or need returns, in a circadian or other temporal rhythm, the primitive ego hypercathects the *representation of the breast,* not the breast. It then initiates discharge, waits for gratification that cannot occur and, finally, suffers the painfulness of an increasing appetite unsatisfied by an actual object. This final, painful conclusion makes the ego retrace its steps and examines its ideational contents. The ego must abandon its original, lax style and learn to search for indications of reality. In other words, it must abandon its initial reliance upon primary process thinking and initiate secondary process forms of reality testing.

The ego could make these errors, according to Gibson, only if it were *constrained* from carrying out its usual forms of active "reality testing." That is, the ego would hallucinate and then choose the hallucination over the real object only if it were incapable of assessing the presence or absence of ordinary affordances. Such inhibitions can occur as the result of either infantile, childhood, or adult traumas or because of a daily restriction upon mobility found in sleep. We recall that such inhibitions occur in one daily psychological event: dreaming. As Freud notes throughout *The Interpretation of Dreams* (1900a), dreaming is a psychoticlike process to the degree it replicates the dominance of hallucinatory thinking. But as he also notes, dreaming occurs while the ego is unable to effect actions, the "motor neurons" are not under its control.

This kind of paralysis does *not* typify the infant thrashing around for the nipple. According to Freud's model, both reality-testing and self–other boundaries emerge through time, via suffering and pain, and only in the most precarious way. Regression back to infantile narcissism is a constant and real danger: regression back to the most archaic form being the hallucination of objects. With this theorem in hand Freud advanced his revolutionary views on the essential identity between forms of pathology and normalcy, including cultural institutions. Indeed, if Freud is correct, even in part, we must conclude that normalcy develops out of pathological or protopathological origins. Even the elite and happy among us will manifest "regressive" moments in which we return to that archaic state, e.g., in our dreams (1900a). This latter proposition seems irrefutable: even the elite can regress. But is *all* reality testing a secondary achievement? Does *all* reality testing emerge out of a universal stage of primary narcissism and hallucinatory wish fulfillment? This is no small question.

If Gibson is correct, Freud cannot be right about this general hallucinatory origin of reality-testing. For Gibson argues that the infant, like all animals, is born with a need and capacity to find visual and all other perceptual affordances in the real, external world. The infant learns to perceive the variety of changes and continuities which characterize our world. Neither is the self a mere product of "thought." It must be more than a merely imagined unity, produced by an automatic reflex of the ego which decorates an imagined world with qualities derived from its internal world. Rather, from the beginning, the self and object world are distinct by virtue of the persistence of real visual and all other perceptual affordances. The self is the real thing occluding about half of my vision. Most people perceive it from the beginning of their experience. Hence Gibson says it is not irrational for most people to locate themselves somewhere around their "head" for it is there they perceive their real self to be.

Martin Gardner described one of M. C. Escher's prints, "Escher is seen staring at his own reflection in the sphere. The glass mirrors his surroundings, compressing them inside one perfect circle. No matter how he moves or twists his head, the point midway between his eyes remains exactly at the center of the circle. He cannot get away from that central point: The ego remains immovably the focus of his world" (1966, p. 118). Further, if Gibson is correct, then subsequent hallucinatory behaviors are acquired during states in which the person is immobilized (as in classical vision experiments).

Neurotic and psychotic persons fail to perceive themselves accurately. They constantly misunderstand their social world. They do so not because their perceptual gear is faulty. Rather, they do so because they fear looking too closely at themselves: they prejudge the structure of future and potential emotional affordances. But that does not mean there are none "out" there to be perceived. Rather, neurotogenic symptoms must be products of cognitive fixations.

Neurosis and the Search for EA

Neurotics are unwilling to alter their behavior because they fear (unconsciously) dangerous consequences should they do so. By pursuing the idea of Emotional Affordances and its relevance to child psychiatry we reconsider the standard analytic theory of neurosis. There is no single, dominant opinion perhaps of anything within psychoanalysis. A general claim might be that neurotics suffer mainly from repressed, unconscious ideas, generated out of traumata. These unconscious conflicts produce ego inhibitions and overall ego weakness. These unconscious ideas (or fantasies, or self-representations) the analyst brings to the light of day, primarily through interpreting transferences. The task of understanding the structure of these unconscious ideas has preoccupied analysts from the beginning.

Freud initiated this task about eighty-five years ago in his comments on the cognitive structure of hysterical symptoms. In the last essay in *Studies on Hysteria* he employs various models and similes to describe the peculiar structure of hysteric memories as revealed through psychotherapy. He suggests they are arranged like card files, chains of ideas, foreign bodies, infiltrates, and the like. Finally Freud admits that these similes are incompatible with one another. In other words, they all cannot be correct; they are metaphors. Freud hopes they convey the material uncovered in his psychotherapeutic investigations and which seem fantastic to nonanalysts. Hysteric themes are linked together by both memory and associative contents. The latter are not organized like files or any other physical record, rather, they are aligned according to semantic and accidental associations.

Failure to structure the ego (as defined in classical analytic theory) leads to an excessive reliance upon unconscious fantasies. Fantasies replace ego functions and this, in turn, leads to an excessive reliance upon *representations* of emotional affordances, not actual emotional affordances. Since representations of EA cannot sustain the self, they are always inadequate substitutes for real relationships. But because these representations are vital lifelines to the possibility of relationship, neurotic patients cling to them with ferocity. Hence neurotics are rigid, fixated, and frightened about the possibility of change, for to change is to lose hold of these contrived representations.

In order to preserve these representations and to give the appearance of depth and aliveness, neurotic persons use every means available to them to enhance these unconscious fantasies. To cite Charles Brenner again, persons can use any ego capacity or set of capacities to accomplish these neurotic aims. There is no specific "neurotic" form of defense as opposed to nonneurotic forms of defense. A common resource for elaborating and keeping alive fantasy replacements for actual EA is the imagination. Drawing upon the imagination, the neurotic employs primary process means to keep intact the illusion of spontaneous living.

Clinical Evidence for the Search for EA

Clinical evidence in support of a general notion of EA derives from two independent research efforts. One is a group located on the West Coast, led by J. Weiss. Another is Robert Langs and his colleagues on the East Coast. In their lucid text, *The Psychoanalytic Process*, Weiss and Sampson describe with admirable detail their attempt to assess the validity of two competing psychoanalytic hypotheses. These two hypotheses, as elucidated by Weiss, parallel what I have termed the classical theory of sublimation and that which I argue for in this book. Both hypotheses are Freudian.

The earlier of the two, Weiss terms the "automatic functioning" hypothesis. It appears in Freud's essays on psychopathology and in *The Interpretation of Dreams* (1900a). The later of the two, Weiss terms the "higher functioning" hypothesis. It derives from Freud's late essays on psychopathology (1926d) and texts like the *Outline of Psycho-Analysis* (1940a). The first clinical hypothesis views the ego as passive vis à vis the power of the drives. The ego must negotiate between drive-based impulses and wishes which impinge upon the mind from the "inside" and external powers, such as parents, who impinge upon it from the "outside." In fact, the first hypothesis is the view of the ego elaborated in the classical theory of sublimation, as I discussed in chapter five.

The second clinical hypothesis is based on the assumption that a person may regulate his or her unconscious mental life. He or she does so "in accordance with his [sic] *unconscious* thoughts and beliefs and his [sic] assessments of his [sic] current reality" (1986, p. 5, emphasis his). This second hypothesis matches well the theory of perception elaborated in this chapter. For Weiss and Sampson do not reveal an ego dominated by drive elements. Rather they portray the ego as struggling to find a way in which current reality, including the psychoanalytic relationship, can be different from the past.

Visual Affordances, Empathy and Art

The business of art is to reveal the relation between man and his circum-ambient universe, at the living moment. As mankind is always struggling in the toils of old relationships, art is always ahead of the "times," which are themselves always far in the rear of the living moment. When Van Gogh paints sunflowers, he reveals, or achieves, the vivid relation between himself, as man, and the sunflower, as sunflower, at that quick moment of time. (D. H. Lawrence, "Morality and the Novel," 1936, p. 527)

I cite this passage from Lawrence because it describes an aspect of artistic work that the ARISE theorems, discussed briefly in chapter 5, do not. ARISE (Adaptive Regression in the Service of the Ego) theorems about art emphasize the ways in which the artist must "regress" in ego functioning. From high level, adult "reality testing," the artist regresses to infantile modes of ego organization where fantasy and primary process thought dominate. Lawrence emphasizes a dimension of artistic insight that supplements this traditional analytic theory of aesthetic experience.

For Lawrence says that art is typically ahead of the dictates of official culture, including those of the academy. How could this be possible if art were primarily an exercise in adaptive regression in the service of the ego? If artistic insight were the accidental discovery of a regressed personality, how is it that artists often teach their culture how to see the "external world"?

The ARISE theorem can account for drug hallucinations. It may account for religious trance and some forms of horror writing, such as Poe's stories. But Henry James was not in a regressed ego mode when he documented American and European mores. The ARISE theorem may be useful as an account of some resources for artistic materials—the "unconscious"—but it cannot explain artistic success. The art of the insane is like the Rorschach content of the insane; predictable, trite, "regressed," and stereotypical. Because psychotic persons fix upon a limited number of themes the well-trained clinician can spot psychotic tendencies in Rorschach materials. (See E. Schachtel 1966.)

In claiming a dignity for art equal to that of science I am not equating art with science. Most artists do not research their subject matter the way that scientists do. But artists work just as hard as scientists when they struggle to discover something new about the real world and to communicate that discovery by their art. To do good science one must follow the rules of the academy, rules defined and upheld by the recognized elite of science as it is practiced. The academy's rules are, by this time, well worked out. There are very few such rules for doing good art. If there were, we could all become bona fide artists by just following the rules. Yet we tend to resist applying the title of "artist" to any person, no matter how skilled in craft, who merely follows the rules of a trade.

Lawrence does not claim that Van Gogh's sunflowers are "scientifically" observed artifacts. He does not claim that Van Gogh has made an objective, impersonal survey of the nature of sunflowers in themselves. Van Gogh's painting is not an "objective" metric of sunflowers. On the contrary, Van Gogh explored and then documented the momentary *relationship* between himself and his object. Lawrence counters the scientific value of neutrality with the value of portraying the quality of a relationship *between objects*. In this universe of values Van Gogh's painting can be judged as adequate ("true") or inadequate ("false") to the central task of communication and evocation of similar experiences in another person, the viewer.

Van Gogh's genius was an artistic genius and an observational genius. His talent was not confined to that of recorder of sense data; he was not merely a "pictorial artist." Until one has actually tried to paint, one cannot know how hard it is. Marion Milner made a similar point in a well-known meditation on painting in her delightful book, *On Not Being*

Able to Paint (1950).[5]

In analytic therapy with a novelist or a short story writer one grasps how typical conflicts, oedipal and preoedipal, enter into the patient's artistic works. But one may never see how the artistic patient transforms those conflicts into art full of surprises. An analogous situation is working with novice clinicians. They grasp concepts of psychoanalytic theory and quickly learn to see oedipal themes, or "splitting," or "false self." It takes far longer to learn to discover, in concrete detail, how a particular patient uses a particular defense. To grasp the *aesthetic qualities*, as it were, of a patient's conflicts requires the clinician to empathize with the patient's total experience at the moment, "at the living moment." Beyond that task is the challenge to invite the patient to live through his or her conflicts in the transference relationship to the therapist. This living through makes therapy possible.

Sublimation names creative processes by which persons preserve insights into the human world, a world whose qualities are represented in the work of art. These qualities emerge because the artist uses emotional scalers which permit the viewer to "resonate" with the art object. This resonance is not hallucinatory: Van Gogh's sunflowers do not pretend to be illusions of "real" sunflowers.

Given the psychoanalytic notion of development argued for in this chapter, we can say that there is something fascinating about pretty girls, while portraits of pretty girls are less interesting, and poems about pretty girls are even less compelling, *unless* the poet has genius. In the terms of this chapter that kind of genius is the ability to construct adequate representations of pretty girls. Those representations must evoke the presence of emotional affordances within the ideas and images which make up the poem. These secondary affordances are, though, always disjunctive. They cannot capture the actual feeling of a primary affordance because they are static, while the real thing is dynamic—but unvarying. (Films are the most popular form of iconic representation.)

The classical definitions of sublimation recognize this fact. For they claim that the internal processing which constitutes sublimation is a magical and disjunctive action. An original impulse, aimed at the satisfaction of drives upon actual objects (including one's body), that is upon real objects which persist in time and space, is transformed into an intellectual fixation upon a substitute object, a fantasy object.[6]

Because artists exceed the rest of us in their sensitivity to qualitative differences, our psychological vocabulary will always be stilted and incomplete when compared to the terms available to artists. The vocabulary available to skilled musicians, for example, is far larger than the half-dozen terms used in Stern's text. So too the language of the lover of wine is far larger than that most of us use. The established arts, like painting and sculpture, have developed over many centuries of discovery. Their vocabularies are subtle and may be comprehended only over a lifetime of appreciation. Concert pianists who are masterful in their technique may still spend years preparing to play a Mozart or Beethoven piece. These masters know when their work, their playing, is incorrect. Even if they lack a proper name for the qualitative difference, they hear it. Our ignorance of the subtle, qualitative differences that distinguish one masterful performance from another marks our limitations as critics. It highlights the complexity of musical expression.

In his excellent review of the concept sublimation Kaywin (1966) concludes we ought to measure it by the "distance from the drives" a particular behavior manifests. Here the notion of distance is metaphorical. We have no way of measuring how far away any behavior is from the drives. A sublimated behavior or artifact is one in which qualities of a primary self–other relationship are represented in a new context.[7] In that new context they evoke the presence of the original emotional affordance. Is this more than a metaphor? I attempt to answer this question in the next chapter.

There I examine fictional characters, one drawn from a short story by John Cheever, the other from a Japanese novel by Junichiro Tanizaki. I contrast them with Hamlet and his struggles. Finally, I consider perversions and sublimations in Orson Welles's film, *Citizen Kane*.

CHAPTER SEVEN

EMOTIONAL AFFORDANCES AND THEIR REPRESENTATIONS

> We know that the earliest art works originated in the
> service of a ritual—first the magical, then the reli-
> gious kind. It is significant that the existence of the
> work of art with reference to its aura is never entirely
> separated from its ritual function.
>
> —Walter Benjamin

> The fame of the great names we look up to is im-
> mortal: and shall not we who contemplate it imbibe
> a portion of the ethereal fire, the divine particular
> aurae, which nothing can extinguish?
>
> —Hazlitt, *On the Feeling of Immortality in Youth*

Introduction: Invisible Losses, Visible Repairs

These two quotations are from well-known works on aesthetics.
Walter Benjamin (1936), a philosopher, criticizes reproductions of
original works of art because they cannot retain the original's "aura."
The actual, concrete production of the work, beginning with a ritual
attitude, creates this aura. The "aura" is real; it is part of the relationship
between creator and viewer. This quality is real or else no one would
spend millions for originals and little for reproductions. Its reality must
be safeguarded by knowledge and ritual protection. The piece's lineage
must be known if its aura is to be preserved.

William Hazlitt, a nineteenth-century critic, also speaks of "aura."
Hazlitt, though, speaks of the glow attached to the ideal image of great
authors who preceded him. Like Whitman who balanced sublime
poetry with sublime nature, Hazlitt is devoted to previous artistic
masters. His claim that nothing can extinguish their names and their

power contradicts Benjamin.

I think Benjamin is correct, for many things could extinguish the names of our illustrious forebearers. The destruction of their books and the loss of readers who treasure their thoughts would destroy them and their aura. The " divine aura" is *always* liable to extinction. As Benjamin notes, it must be protected if it is to remain a source of light. The "aura" of a work of art is an invisible quality of the relationship between the creator, the work, and ourselves.

Emotional affordances are invisible but perceptible. That is, emotional affordances are not identical to the particular, three-dimensional person who sits in front of us. Rather, emotional affordances, like self-object relatedness, pertain to the quality of realtionship between the other person and ourselves. Emotional affordances are like the "aura" that surrounds the work of art. We perceive this quality, this "aura," that surrounds a person important to us when we gauge moments of attunement and other moments of empathic awareness that occur between ourselves and the other.

When we lose access to emotional affordances we suffer an invisible but tangible loss. Because this loss is invisible we cannot easily name it. Infants and children are especially vulnerable for they cannot comprehend the adult reasons for the suffering inflicted upon them nor name the source of their hurt. Even sadistic parents must be believed and their actions accepted and even loved. For it is to the parent that the child looks for signs of emotional affordance (EA). Failure to find the sustenance required in the external object promotes the variety of pathology witnessed daily. Because the loss of EA is invisible, and yet the (supposedly good) parent remains visible, the child becomes confused. In their confusion children struggle to repair their losses: they seek concrete representations of the "thing" that is gone. Yet what is lost is a *quality*, not a thing. Therefore, no actual object or action repairs adequately the sense of deficit.

Another response to the loss of EA is to seek idealized systems of thought. This is most obvious in "transcendental religions" and other groups that promise the seeker a direct path to transcendental knowledge. (It figures in many occult experiences as well [Gay 1989].) "Transcendental knowledge" is knowledge about the *invisible forces* or spirits that rule the world. The language of these religious groups, like the language of many scholars devoted to the study of mysticism, reveals a fascination with naming the unnameable.

Regarding "transcendental religions," some scholars write: "Simply stated, our point of view is that mysticism is valid, that human beings can and do attain direct, transcendent consciousness of ultimate reality but that distortions of mysticism abound and can be dangerous" (Anthony, et al. 1987, p. 2). Valid mysticism is mysticism that does not degrade into the horrors of Jim Jones's People Temple and other groups like Synanon. These reveal massive injustices, pathology, and often crime.[1]

I grant the ethical correctness of this point of view. From a clinical perspective, the term *transcendence* suggests that only the select can grasp its hidden truth. This is suspicious for it disguises ordinary yearnings for a happy and trusting relationship. Transcendental teachings project these yearnings away from authentic persons who offer emotional attunement into an external realm "beyond" ordinary experience. One source of this proclivity for projective solutions is the actual invisibility, and therefore the "transcendence," of emotional affordances.

Psychoanalytic clinical work teaches us that the shape of the patient's solutions to his or her suffering reveals the shape of the patient's imagined sense of impairment. This standard formula, made clear by Freud ninety years ago, does not match the patient's self-experience. This clinical formula is alien to the patient's usual modes of thinking about the patient's self. It is also alien to the patient's deep distress over symptoms and, often, secret perversions. This psychoanalytic formula expresses an abstract idea, as does the concept of EA. In Piaget's terms, the concept of EA pertains to the abstract level of intelligence. The notion of "mother as this actual object," pertains to the earlier intellectual level Piaget terms concrete operational.

There is dispute about the reasons for these cognitive differences between young children and older children. Piaget says that there are innate limitations on the infant's capacities. Other authorities argue that infants only lack enough experience; infants lack data, not sufficient intelligence. (See Weisberg 1980.) No one disputes that infants construct their notion of personhood. This construct derives from their life with their family, especially their parents. No infant, no child, and few adolescents could grasp the idea of EA or other concepts like self–object. Similarly, children cannot grasp the concept of empathy for it too assumes that one can abstract oneself from egocentric judgments. This means that when there are deficits in self–object relationships, the infant or child *cannot locate* the source of suffering. Rather the child organizes the child's understanding of pain around concrete experience with this mother or that father or this sibling.

The child may blame another person for the child's problems. Even then the child blames the child's self for wishes about that person. Since Freud's time, we know that children's egocentrism and concrete problem solving causes them to blame themselves for their suffering.

Visualizing the Invisible: Myths

To put this another way, deficits in the self–object milieu, cause the child to find concrete objects and concrete persons to blame. Hence the child blames the child's self and the child's parents. This inability to comprehend why suffering occurs leads the child to rely on primary process thinking. Dan Sperber (1974) calls this "mythical thinking" because it replicates the reasoning processes evident in primitive myths. Primary process thinking generates unconscious fantasies and myths which, in turn, become compromise solutions that both express and deny the sense of guilt attendant to all neurotic fantasy. The child always structures these mythological solutions according to the child's archaic sense of wrongness. There must be a "basic fault," or "sin," which afflicts the child and which caused suffering.

The so-called perversions are sexual actions which represent concretely unconscious fantasies; they reflect the shape of the child's imagined solution to its deficits. Perverse sexual actions match the infantile sense of what "is wrong," and what concrete elements would solve the problem—if only they were present. We discuss perversions in more detail, below, when we consider *Hamlet*, then Orson Welles's famous film, *Citizen Kane*.

A clinical vignette may illustrate how EA are "invisible." An intelligent woman grew up with a mother who exhorted her to be "ethically superior" to all other children. Yet the mother also constantly belittled the little girl's narcissistic yearnings and genuine successes. On learning of the differences between the sexes, the girl explained her mother's apparent praise for ethical values and her mother's anger as her own fault. She concluded that she lacked something which she, the little girl, should have but did not. This something lacking often became symbolized by the penis she observed in little boys and not in herself. Midway in her analysis, she dreamed that she had a penis, "not erect, but definitely bigger than most mens'." Three years into her analysis, the patient noted that she felt that she should "prostate" herself in front of her boss, a woman. She corrected herself and said she meant to say "prostrate," and added she often confused the two terms. The slip revealed both attitudes were present; she felt inadequate and vulnerable to humiliation. As a woman she must either prostrate herself before mother or escape humiliation by having a prostate, a secret, *invisible sign of maleness;* a prostate would undo the sense of damaged self that she felt was responsible for her adult conflicts.

In the following I show how the notion of emotional affordance can enhance psychoanalytic aesthetics. I consider a short story by John Cheever, a novel by a Japanese writer, Junichiro Tanizaki, and related themes from Shakespeare's play, *Hamlet*. Finally, I examine scenes from Orson Welles's film, *Citizen Kane*. In each instance I wish to show how the concept of emotional affordance deepens the received analytic notion of sublimation.

Cheever and Tanizaki describe what they believe are true discoveries about the nature of human beings. They do so by delineating particular qualities of particular environments in which human beings find themselves. Those qualities are actual, not imagined; they may be invisible, but their effects are perceivable features of an environment not mere projections from a sick psyche. These qualities are like the aura of inanimate objects which Benjamin describes.

For Benjamin and his counterpart, William Hazlitt, refer to the aura of a work of art as an actual thing; it is an aspect of thing we perceive. Both authors believe that the aura of a sculpture, for example, is a real feature of its existence. Its aura is not a magical glow projected onto it by the weak minded and gullible. Rather it is a historical feature of the thing. It is part of its authenticity.

Astonishment in John Cheever

> He was always conscious and sometimes mildly resentful of the fact that most of his business associates and all of his friends and neighbors had been skylarking on the turf at Groton or Deerfield or some such school while he was taking books on how to improve your grammar and vocabulary out of the public library. Considering merely his physical bulk, it was astonishing that he should have preserved an image of himself as a hungry youth standing outside a lighted window in the rain. He was a cheerful, heavy man with a round face that looked exactly like a pudding. ("Just Tell Me Who It Was," John Cheever 1979)

Astonishment is a term with a long history. Cheever uses it early in this story and later employs synonyms like *amazement*. The term *astonished* was one of Freud's favorites. The English term derives from the French *astony*, which Webster says is akin to *abolish*. Its original meaning was like the French *etonnement*, one of physical shock. Webster quotes Shakespeare who has a character say, "'Captain; you have astonished him.'" Synonyms are blinded, bewildered, and dazed. According to the *Concordance to the Standard Edition, astonished* or a variant appears 226 times in the English version of Freud's works.[2] Freud employs the term when he wishes to pick out a piece of behavior and subject it to analytic scrutiny. It is not just any bit of behavior, rather it is behavior which appears to confirm what is highly improbable. In a famous association to one of his dreams, Freud recounts how his mother, attempting to refute his religious skepticism, rubbed her hands together. This produced "dirt" and proved that humans were made of earth, just as the Genesis account had said. Freud writes, "My astonishment at this ocular demonstration knew no bounds and I acquiesced in the belief which I was later to hear expressed in the words: "Du bist die Natur einen Tod schuldig" (Thou owest Nature a death) (1900a, SE 4:204).

The psychodynamic sources of astonishment are clear. We are astonished by the verification of an infantile belief or the apparent validation of an unconscious wish. The repressive barrier that separates conscious from unconscious thoughts (and affect from free expression) lifts; suddenly thoughts long denied or surmounted seem validated (1919h). To be astonished is not unpleasant. It connotes an intense, physical sense of vertigo. The French term suggests one feels stunned as if one had drunk too much champagne. Those who see flying saucers or other modern miracles are astonished. The shepherds working in the fields and those who heard Jesus preaching with authority were astonished. As the French version of this New Testament text says, "Ils etaient frappes."[3]

Those astonished may complain about the suddenness of their mood, but we cannot believe the experience is unpleasant. Comic authors, like S. J. Perelman, often use an expression like "he displayed an astonishing degree of perversity" to this effect. It mixes the positive affect of astonishment with the negative one of condemnation. Astonishment is a distant cousin of the uncanny, though it lacks the foreboding quality of the latter term.

I cannot be astonished unless I have formed a decided opinion about the event in question. Radical discoveries in nuclear physics do not astonish me. Discovering gold bars under my basement floor would. To be astonished is to be brought up short: we realize we have misunderstood something. We suddenly see that we must rethink what had appeared to be obvious and clear. Freud capitalizes on these features of the term when he says he was astonished when his mother, rubbing her hands to reveal their "dirt," verified the Genesis story. This makes persons who are astonished liable for reeducation. They are vulnerable to new ideas, including psychoanalytic ones, since they effectively admit that they had misunderstood. Vulgarisms expressing astonishment are often self-deprecatory; "Well I'll be damned" and "dog my cats," are among the more genteel.

Astonishment occurs when one has misconstrued the meaning—

the emotional depth—of either iconic or symbolic representations. The degree of one's astonishment is a function of the degree to which one's fundamental understanding of one's world is challenged. Because Freud often challenged received opinions he used the term frequently. It set the stage for his most radical claims and therefore he uses the term many times in his most radical book, *The Interpretation of Dreams* (1900a).

Mr. Pym, the round-faced hero of Cheever's short story, was self-made and cautious. In demeanor he showed "hardly a trace— hardly a trace of the anxieties of a man who had been through a grueling struggle to put some money into the bank" (p. 370). Cheever does not say to whom Will's self-image would have been astonishing. He speaks to us as if we had just moved in next door and he sympathized with our wish to know our new neighbors. The narrator gives us all the evidence we might require to understand Will and anticipates our psychologizing with a parodied case history. We learn Will's step mother drank sherry out of a coffee cup most of the day, "and what she had to say was usually bitter. The picture she presented may have left Will with some skepticism about the emotional richness of human involvements. It may have delayed his marriage" (p. 371).

We are inclined to feel that these two "mays" are sardonic. The story reveals a man driven to make his wife into daughter, lover, and mother. Cheever treats the traumatic facts about Will's boyhood as if they were incidental to the main story and, instead, focuses upon the apparent fact that Will's wife is having an affair. Of course these early facts are crucial to Will's story.

Cheever's sensitivity to Pym stems, in part, from his own boyhood struggles with his parents, both of whom drank excessively. Recently, we have learned that Cheever's mother drank continuously. On her death bed she asked her son to moisten her lips with her favorite drink, bourbon, which Cheever did, "although I was a little embarrassed" (Rothenberg 1989, p. 15). Rothenberg and others report that Cheever felt excessively attached to his older brother. This attachment horrified Cheever and was partly responsible for his lifelong struggles with alcohol, and later homosexual affairs. Among all the evidence supporting this too intense relationship is the interesting fact that Cheever's brother married one of Cheever's former girlfriends (Rothenberg, p. 17).

In an interview Cheever says about his brother, "I adored him. And then, when he went away to college, I didn't see him. He came back and left . . . I don't know what crossed his mind. I think he saw that I was in trouble; my parents weren't speaking to one another, and he managed to be everything for me. When I was about nineteen, I realized how un-natural this love was and how poignant" (p. 17). Surely the strength of John's yearning for his mother, to pull her out of her stupors, is one source of his "unnatural" attachments to his older brother. For as an older brother he could supply, in part, some glimmer of adult love and protection. Yet, few siblings could meet all these demands. John's brother failed, as most brothers would, to replace the absent mother. Consequently, John also grew up distrusting all forms of nurturing re-lationships with actual persons. Rothenberg suggests that Cheever's major novel, *Falconer*, which is about brother love and brother murder, helped Cheever overcome his alcoholism—at least for a time.

But Cheever also credits Alcoholics Anonymous. AA provides not only a rigorous set of demands on alcoholic patients, with group sup-ports, etc., it also preaches that the alcoholic must give up all sense of private control of self in favor of a relationship to God. This appeal to the divine matches directly the sense of the invisible other, the tran-scendent self-object Person, who, omniscient and forgiving, will give abundantly what Cheever's mother gave only sparingly.

Will's image of himself as a hungry and depressed young man is "astonishing" to those who do not know his story. The psychoanalytic critic seeks to reveal the causes that produce adult character, like Mr. Pym's astonishing self-image. This simple ideal has never been fol-lowed. Early on Freud created the idea of overdetermination to expand the number of causes that produce character. Early traumata shape adult character; they not determine it. Childhood is crucial, as Cheever himself admits by inserting this reluctant bit of case-history. However, when one attempts to use classical theory to explain why the mature man, Pym, continues to imagine (perceive?) himself as a hungry boy, one has to fall back on some version of the hallucination theory.

At some level of perception, Pym's memories are so intense that the energy attached to them "overrides" the ego's normal reality-testing. A moment of partial hallucination ensues for Pym is a fat man. A gap exists between his perceptual system (which should be conflict free) and his memory system (which is vulnerable to surges of instinctual energy). The virtue of the hallucination theory is that it permits us to place instances of self-deception within a spectrum that runs from valid perception to psychotic delusion. Everyday experience and some scientific research confirm that people's images of them-sevles are more complimentary than the assessments others make of them.

A happy child exudes a gentle glow of self-esteem. We hope to see the same in adults. Are both these products of the ego's failure to test reality? Cheever describes another young man in *The Wapshot Scandal* (1964): "Moses was in college and in the last year he had reached the summit of his physical maturity and had emerged with the gift of judicious and tranquil self-admiration" (p. 4). The implication is that if we could see ourselves as "others see us," as Burns says, we would doff our superciliousness. It is difficult to fault this general moralism; but that does not make it valid. Self-deception remains mysterious even if one can assign an instinctual basis to it, most likely the self-preservative instincts. This reclassifies the behavior but does not explain it since the concept of self-preservative instinct is itself defined by the observations of this kind of behavior.

We are astonished at Pym's view of himself because we suppose that people's feelings about themselves are congruent with their appearance to us. This not true of Will Pym, nor is it true of any neurotic. Why not? It is not a matter of hallucination nor of impaired cognitive ability. We assume Pym is able to recognize his reflection in the mirror as he shaves. He would be astonished if he saw a thin young man staring back at him. It is his self-understanding, his self-image, or in the terms used above, iconic representations of himself, that portrays a hungry boy.

Pym's composite self-portrait is static and fixed by his fear of altering his relationship to his actual world. The distrust he learned from watching his mother drink sherry all day and attack him persisted into his adult life. He avoided women who might repeat his mother's treatment of him. Cheever tells us Pym chose to marry a woman, Maria, much younger than himself who calls him "daddy." This reversed his relationship to his mother; he was the wise one, she, Maria, the young one. Her extreme youth also made it less likely that his wife would resemble his mother.

More so, like dream images, Will's image of himself is peculiarly flat. He cannot walk around it just as one cannot walk around one's dream images. The neurotic fails to test current reality. Neurotic persons have a penchant to project previous traumatic expectations upon new experiences. This is not necessarily a failure of secondary process thinking or a regression to primary process ideation. Will fails to perceive authentic emotional affordances because he refuses to "walk around" them and so comprehend their actuality. As Gibson says, neither can we walk around our dream images. Neurotics constrain themselves and limit their actions just as experimenters investigating vision constrain their subjects. In both cases illusions—that is, incorrect interpretations of the visual array—predominate. Experimental constraints reduce the ability of subjects to discover the presence of visual affordances because they cannot alter their relationship to the visual array: they cannot discover invariant relationships which obtain in ordinary situations. The neurotic fails often to discover the presence of emotional affordances. Will Pym cannot bear to see his wife as ordinary nor as an independent being whose actual life is other than the one he ascribes to her. She is to make up for all the deprivations he suffered as a boy. That is, she is to take her place within his private portrait gallery and replace the nightmare vision of his mother sitting in schizoid darkness. Classical analytic theory accounts for such tenacity in terms of the libido's inherent inertia, what Freud sometimes called the libido's adhesion. Later he called these manifestations of the uncanny power of repetition compulsion.

I propose to alter this. I suggest that Will's libido was fixated because Will could not judge the richness of human relationships. Freud's parallel between neurotic characteristics and cultural institutions, reappears here. For if one lacks the ability to perceive authentic emotional affordances in one's real world, one cannot rely upon secondary (iconic and emblematic) representations of them either. In other words, neurotics like Will cannot use culture because they cannot comprehend the logic of secondary emotional affordances.

For the same reason neurotics tend to lack sublimatory capacities. They cannot rely upon cultural institutions, like art and religion, nor can they contribute to those institutions via sublimation. Of course, many artists happen to be neurotic. That does not mean their neurotic condition contributed to their artistic achievements. Sublimation, as defined above, describes a type of achievement. Sublimated artifacts are accurate representations of primary emotional affordances.

Since these representations reveal both iconic and emblematic levels, their "style" will be constrained. The official and unofficial rules which govern art in a particular culture also govern sublimation. African ritual masks are similar to Halloween masks, just as traditional African myths are similar to Western fairy tales. Their dissimilarities are equally striking. What counts as a sublimated (or "powerful" or "magic" or "sublime") artifact in one culture may not enjoy a similar status in another.

John Keats had the strength and the courage to distinguish the beauty of the earth from his hunger for an idealized earth mother. Will Pym cannot accomplish that task, a task which is analogous to that of coming to terms with one's own death. In both cases one must struggle to realize that the pleasures and beauties of the real world, including the beauty of autumn, will persist *after* one ceases to be. The neurotic is not blind to the earth's delights. Like Will, the neurotic casts them only as private pleasures: "It was Maria's youth and beauty that had informed [Will's] senses and left his mind so open that the earth seemed to spread out before his eyes like a broad map of reason and sensuality. It was her company that made the singing of the crows so fine to hear" (p. 372).

As Will ponders these romantic illusions, Maria contemplates supper, "Cold cuts or lamb chops, she wondered ..." (p. 373). We learn Will cannot comprehend that his wife wishes to dress in a provocative costume at the annual ball and to flirt. She does not want to commit adultery. Will is pleased by her tears and weakness. For it meant she was needy and so "his position was more secure." His wife's role is to replace what he had lost; to displace the fixed iconic image of his mother sitting in her craziness, untouchable, and to come under his will. His wife's role and the single task he assigned her was to repair the gaps and rents in his memories of his boyhood. "All that he had ever been deprived of was now his" (p. 372).

Emotional Affordances in a Japanese Novel

I have suggested that sublimation is a process by which the artist creates representations of emotional affordances which resonate with the audience's internal scalers. Cultural rules and specific limitations of each modality shape these moments of resonance. For example, because music has a richer set of rhythms than other arts, music conveys emotional resonances more easily than other arts. In principle, any art that creates patterns, can create sensations that demonstrate attunement to the audience's emotional scalers. So, in principle, architecture might be as emotionally powerful as music or drama—if one were sensitive enough to the rhythm and tensions of volumetric forms.

Artists reveal sublimation when they use culturally sanctioned forms of representation to symbolize the presence of emotional affordances. This may let us account for the religious art we considered in the introduction. The church once authorized pictures of Christ which emphasized his genitals, even, at times, showing an erection. As we noted, these paintings cannot be considered "proper" now, yet for two hundred years they represented official Catholic doctrine.

The automatism that produces dream jokes produces fixations upon single, iconic representations of archaic objects. Freud's patient, the Wolf Man, found himself compelled to fall in love with women he glimpsed bending over. This posture reminded him (unconsciously) of his mother when he glimpsed her in a moment of sexual intercourse. He bound up the whole of his emotional life to this singular, iconic representation.

When Dora, another patient, dreamed of her genitals as a "jewel box" she collapsed her sense of femaleness into a lewd joke. Similar "warmed jewels" appear in Keats's poem *The Eve of St. Agnes.* There Madeline undoes her "warmed jewels"also. Keats's poem evokes the richness of her femaleness and our memories of watching a woman undress. Like the Wolf Man most people have seen their mother in some state of undress. For those not traumatized, these memories fuse with the ineffable feelings of tenderness we feel seeing the body of a loved one. This is true of a body which promises us the real and vivid comfort of happy contentment.

What I have termed "secondary emotional affordances" are necessarily metaphorical in their relationship to primary affordances. They are not merely linguistic. Some people argue that computer-generated verse is poetry if it is grammatical. A computer might produce verse but it could not produce poetry, for unless the computer occupies a place identical to ours, it cannot comprehend either ours perceptual or emotional affordances. To speak about our needs and losses the computer must comprehend what the world offers us as human beings with human bodies. If it did all these things and learned how beauty affects creatures conscious of their death, it would be a fellow being.

To illustrate this issue consider a passage from a novel by Junichiro Tanizaki. A contemporary Japanese couple, on the verge of divorce, debates if they should go out to dinner together:

> Today was not the first time they had been faced with this difficulty. Indeed, whenever they had to decide whether or not to go out together, each of them became passive, watchful, hoping to take a position according to the other's manner. It was as if they held a basin of water balanced between them and waited to see in which direction it would spill. (*Some Prefer Nettles*, 1960, pp. 13–14)

One doubts a computer could have written this. It could do so only if it had had two experiences. First, it had held between itself and another person a large vessel filled with water. Second, if it recognized the subtle connections between those sensations and the experience of moral uncertainty. On reading this short paragraph most adults recognize these features of the relationship between the husband, Kaname, and his wife, Misako. Water in a bowl happens to seek equilibrium. It is also heavy and difficult to control once it has begun to move. This is not a logical feature of water in bowls. A computer could not deduce this feature from abstract physical laws. The computer would need to know the actual feelings of balance and muscular strain that holding a large vessel induces in animals of our size and type. (As Gibson notes, water for water bugs is unlike water for human beings. Water bugs could not balance a bowl of water between them.)

Because water seeks an equilibrium it acts like a level; its surface is always parallel to the line of the horizon. Water forms parabolic lines in a vessel with curved sides, just as a ball thrown into the air forms a perfect parabolic curve as it falls to earth. Having held water in bowls we know that it will reflect the slightest tremor in our hands or in our bodies. Its little waves show as much grace as the largest breakers in the sea. Water in bowls acts like a compass: it seeks out, on its own, the lowest portion of the vessel it occupies. Water in bowls reflects the summation of forces, many of them invisible, that act upon us, and therefore act upon it. So too Kaname and Misako wait for a force larger than themselves to show them the proper direction in their lives.

Which way will the water flow? Which is the "natural" direction of their marriage? Tanizaki suggests the bowl of water will act like a divining rod that seems to pull the water witch after it. Gravity and other natural laws control water. In seeking the lowest level it appears to obey those laws automatically and often contrary to the wishes of humans. Kaname, too, finds himself pulled away from Western affectations and toward Japanese ways he had despised. For like the water he is controlled by forces and needs that surprise and irritate him. Up to that moment he had found the traditional Japanese puppet theatre boring, archaic, and ridiculous. The puppets of the Bunraku Puppet Theatre are large, life-like, representations of human beings manipulated by puppet masters. Kaname struggles to avoid seeing the puppetlike dimension of his life and when he finds himself drawn to such relationships, he is mortified. These issues emerge as the novel progresses toward a final confrontation between the individualism of Western life and the more archaic claims of Japanese traditions.

Kaname's struggle is similar to that of Clem in Thomas Hardy's *The Return of the Native* (1895): both struggle against forces larger and longer-lived than themselves. Kaname's struggle seems particularly Japanese to the degree that the Puppet Theatre is itself so concerned with the issue of personal autonomy versus the claims of the group.

The Bunraku puppet is the antithesis of the Western demigod Prometheus, for the puppet reflects Japanese religious understanding of the cultivation of nature and the dependent status of human beings controlled by forces larger than themselves. Prometheus, on the other hand, represents self-will and the human thirst for power over nature when he seeks insight and "enlightenment." When achieved, both values permit humans to destroy old customs and old patterns. Just as water seeks its own level and exemplifies balance, humans must discover their inner nature and cultivate it.

The metaphor of the bowl of water, which opens the novel's first chapter, touches upon these and other themes. A fuller discussion would take us further along these associative paths, for example, Kaname weighs the pleasures of Western eroticism, exemplified by *The Arabian Nights*, against Japanese sensuality, exemplified by a Japanese maiden. Anality returns as an issue as well. The novel compares Western bathrooms, gleaming with hardware, with the traditional Japanese bath, a wooden house, smelling of the earth and pine trees. The novel's final scene occurs just outside such a house; Kaname has bathed himself, and, as a long delayed rain falls, he sees O-hisa, his mistress, waiting for him in the dark.

The novel is far richer than summarized. Like any such artifact, it cannot be summarized by anything less than itself. As C. S. Smith says in another context, scientific laws are possible only when nature reveals redundant patterns. Scientific laws describe these redundancies in formula from which one can generate the observed complexity. Given that redundancy one can then use Newton's and Einstein's discoveries to describe the behavior of actual systems. That is, because nature is redundant natural sciences can be elegant and precise. This is not true of descriptions of visual and emotional affordances. One cannot describe the fixed rules which govern vision in general. On the contrary, one must comprehend the position in the world which a particular organism enjoys *before* one can comprehend what will serve as affordances for it. A puddle of water is an adequate affordance for water bugs who wish to walk upon it; it is not adequate to animals of our weight and dimensions.

Some Prefer Nettles describes more accurately emotional affordances in Japanese experience than any reductive science. For the novel evokes, through its iconic and emblematic structures, features of life in that culture. What is "ineffable" in Japanese (or American) life is not necessarily the most obscure claims of its religious authorities. The ineffable need not be reduced to the mystical. Rather the ineffable is the countless ways in which Japanese culture has discovered emotional affordances within nature and within itself. The ineffable is the everyday, the commonplace, and even the rituals surrounding the bath.

The Smelly Father in *Hamlet*

Hamlet is a play against which psychoanalysts since Freud have measured themselves and their clinical insights. Freud yearned for his confidant, Fliess, to applaud his insights. Adding yet another essay on *Hamlet* makes one pause. Yet just because the play is so central to European and Western consciousness it attracts continuous attention. I offer the following thoughts only as original to me; among the many thousands of essays on the play, no doubt similar points have been made. When I've borrowed consciously from another author I acknowledge that fact; when I've borrowed unconsciously I must await instruction.

Literary critics chide psychoanalysts for jumping into speculations about Hamlet and the play without a proper sense of play's context and historical setting. Yet Hamlet, the character, is so self-revealing and so lovable that it is artificial to pretend to have no feelings about him. It is tempting to see in Hamlet's character features of Shakespeare's mind, for could an author create a character more noble than the author himself or herself?

Anyone can imagine idealized characters who always do the "correct" thing as dictated by the official rules of a particular culture. It is more difficult for a knave, to use a Shakespearean category, to create a noble character. This would be contrary to laws of economics, physics, and the science of information. In each of these sciences occurs a statement that more developed forms cannot emerge from less developed forms without an organizing principle. "Noise cannot give rise to information." Therefore, whatever is noble and authentic in Hamlet is a product of Shakespeare's mind and spirit.

Historical and critical authorities agree that the play, *Hamlet,* is a complex achievement, written at the height of Shakespeare's enormous powers. The play reveals the vitality of the actor, author, owner; the vitality of a forceful man whom Rowse (1973) says was supremely male: "Altogether [Shakespeare's] pronunciation, with its provincial tones, had a stronger, broader, more masculine sound" than that of other authors of the period (p. 50).

In Rowse's portrait, Shakespeare emerges as a nonpedantic, intuitive poet. He is a man with a remarkable memory, an exquisite observer of human actions, and a consummate actor. He comprehended the weight and texture of words as sensual objects. This is the edge to Shakespeare's robustness: his ability to create entertaining, engrossing action "felt from the inside" not developed out of a bookish environment written for an audience of intellectuals who disdain concrete, specific experiencing. He was a great lyric poet plus a man of action and performance, but he was not apolitical. He observed the royal court at first hand and with that knowledge and sense of tragedy inherent in the workings of the English state, wrote about it in *Hamlet*.

There is a surplus of commentaries on *Hamlet*, yet there are more commentaries on Jesus, whose story is now two thousand years old. Even within the psychoanalytic commentaries about the play, its manifest themes have not been exhausted. (See Edelson 1988, pp. 157–171.) I propose to show how the play remains valuable to us, even as we recede further and further from its original time and place. In considering the play and Hamlet's character, the issue of Shakespeare's preeminent place in English letters arises. Shakespeare's hold upon the title "greatest dramatist of all time" evokes rage and depression in everyone who competes with him. Naturally, there are narcissistic pleasures in identifying with him, in protecting Shakespeare against any assailants, including the psychoanalysts.

The standard analytic way to consider the play's text is to interact with it the way one does with a patient's life story. One imagines oneself in all the main roles, female and male, hero and villain. All psychoanalytic commentaries on *Hamlet* take this obvious tack: to respond to the text as one would to a brilliant patient's account of himself. The analyst responds to the text and its intricacies by responding to the feelings it evokes in the analyst (Winnicott 1971a).

Attempting to do this with *Hamlet* the clinician recognizes a sense of the burden Shakespeare's creativity must have been for him. It is customary to praise Shakespeare and view him from below the stature he has attained. As the greatest of all English authors and perhaps the greatest of all poets, he evokes awe and idealization. One rarely pities him his talent. For most of us who struggle with mediocrity, genius like his is enviable. He is the sibling who always had it easier, the distant colleague whose career sails ahead. He is the Mozart whom we Salieries love and despise. For psychoanalysts, he is the Freud who founded the discipline in which they establish their identities.

To idealize Shakespeare or Freud is to make an empathic understanding of their lives and their works impossible. We cannot comprehend the inner life of a person with semidivine status, any more than the young child can empathize with an idealized parent.

The cost of idealization is that we overlook an aspect of Shakespeare's struggles as they appear in his beloved figure, Hamlet. That aspect is reflected in the famous mystery of Hamlet's character: Why does he refuse to revenge his father's horrible murder, when by all rights he ought to? To the solutions offered to this puzzle I wish to add a note, already stated by Jerome Oremland (1983). Shakespeare struggled to overcome personal losses by composing and working through the character of Hamlet.

Those losses included the death of his son, Hamnet, four years earlier in 1596 at age eleven and the distinct danger of full-scale rebellion against Elizabeth: "The last years of the Queen's reign, around the turn of the century, were dominated by the question of the succession to the throne" (Rowse 1973, p. 161). Hamnet's death harmed Shakespeare doubly: he lost a son and he lost a potential source of immortality. For Hamnet's death meant that Shakespeare would have no male heir and therefore the family name would die out with his own demise. Even then, Shakespeare made extra efforts to obtain a family coat-of-arms in his *father's* name, giving himself "the satisfaction of having been borne a gentleman" (Rowse 1973, p. 133). Shakespeare's personal, narcissistic loss parallels the political disaster created by the Virgin Queen, Elizabeth. She left no heir and therefore threatened the state with anarchy and bloodshed. This potential English disaster is the actual situation Hamlet faces. The state of Denmark is corrupted, its king has been poisoned, and Hamlet himself, the rightful heir to the throne, is abused by his uncle, a usurper.

Hamlet is mainly a play about the death of fathers. Death as a topic of literature is clichéd. Prime time entertainment features deaths by the dozen. In these entertainments, the focus falls upon the intellectual puzzles presented to the audience. Who did what to whom and why and how? The drama does not focus upon the actual, interior, experience of the victim, nor of the fate of the victim's family. It does not because it is disturbing to imagine, to vicariously introspect, the horrors that such violence can evoke. I say can evoke, because even the victim himself or herself may deny the terrors of death. Once, when robbed by men who kept pulling back the hammers on their pistols, I examined the chrome finish of the gun nearest me: it seemed too bright to be real. I did not examine the real possibility of being made dead shortly.

Such denial and intellectualization might serve well enough. If one shared Shakespeare's imaginative capacity then denial might prove inadequate. Shakespeare's supreme intelligence and his capacity to imagine the experience of others, to fabricate Hamlet and Ophelia, is also a source of pain. *Hamlet* is a play about such pain. It is a pain that ordinary people suffer when a child they love is hurt. Then denial may not operate as effectively. Our suffering increases when the dramatic structure makes it impossible to ignore the pain present in another person's life. Shakespeare's artistry and the way he presented his plays forced his viewers to engage with the drama in front of them. A contemporary of Shakespeare describes the effect of his plays upon the audience. The comedies made everyone laugh and crave laughter. Yet

"At a scene of love, 'the beholders rose up, every man stood on tip-toe and seemed to hover over the prey; when they sware, the company sware; when they depart to bed, the company presently [i.e., immediately] was set on fire' " (Rowse 1973, p. 117). To quench this lusty fire the viewers went home to their wives or visited the nearby brothels.

This was Shakespeare's world and his plays, including *Hamlet*, reflected immediate political events, much as an American drama about assassination written after November 1963 would reflect the murder of President Kennedy. That reality, in turn, would deepen the American audience's sense of the play and the evil forces against which the play contends. Again, it is not the mere quantity of pain that disturbs us, it is our empathic nearness to it. Many women suffer intense pain when they deliver their babies; few of them describe this as tortuous. They do not celebrate this pain; they might well seek ways to suffer less, etc., yet they rarely describe it as traumatic. Often women who describe the pain of childbirth do so within the context of deep meaning. They have given birth to another human being, their suffering was not in vain. The dentist who removes a molar may cause us more intense physical pain than being slugged by a mugger but the mugger's violence remains traumatic; it continues long after the face has healed.

Denial of psychic pain occurs in many ways. One is to focus upon an irrelevant aspect of the situation. Another is to seek larger and larger abstract renditions of the situation and its suffering so that only formula remain. Lévi-Strauss (1988) accomplishes this feat in his book *The Jealous Potter* when he reduces the oedipus complex to a "variant" on the idea of procreation.[4]

Denial is not peculiar to academics alone. Most of us cannot maintain empathic immersion in another person's suffering for very long. In *The Destruction of the European Jews* (1961), Hillberg documents how even knowledgeable Jews denied the reality of the Nazi efforts to exterminate them (pp. 652–655, 662–668). A scholar and humanist as wise as Primo Levi employed denial, also, when he contemplated the psychological sources of Nazi crimes, crimes he witnessed at first hand. Speaking about the reasons for the death camps, and on understanding the Nazi hatred for Jews, he writes:

> Perhaps one cannot, what is more one must not, understand what happened, because to understand is almost to justify. Let me explain: "understanding" a proposal or human behavior means to contain it, contain its author, put oneself in his place, identify with him. Now, no normal human being will ever be able to identify with Hitler, Himmler, Goebbels, Eichmann, and endless others. This dismays us, and at the same time gives us

a sense of relief, because perhaps it is desirable that their words (and also, unfortunately, their deeds) cannot be comprehensible to us. They are non-human words and deeds, really counter-human, without historic precedents, with difficulty compared to the cruelest events of the biological struggle for existence. (Levi 1958, pp. 393–394)

He adds, "But there is no rationality in the Nazi hatred: it is a hate that is not in us; it is outside man, it is a poison fruit sprung from the deadly trunk of Fascism, but it is outside and beyond Fascism itself" (p. 394). If Levi means by "outside man," a claim that Nazi atrocities are extrahuman, products of a historical aberration, then he seems wrong. There are plenty of examples of mass murder carried out by each civilization and each "race" in different moments of history. One wishes to agree with Primo Levi, given the lucidity and honesty of his account of life in the death camps; we do not wish to identify with the Nazis. Even if we find the death camps fascinating and horrible we do not wish to empathize with Nazi criminals. We rebel against this assignment and find reason to end it. When we read accounts of the death camps we stop understanding at some point. The story is too upsetting, too dark, and too dreary a set of facts to keep together in mind all at once, which recalls Stalin's famous remark that the death of one is a tragedy, the death of thousands a statistic. This describes ordinary people's inability to comprehend the suffering of more than a few people close to themselves and within their narcissistic realm.

What if we were cursed with Shakespeare's empathy? Would our minds not, by their own accord, continue to imagine the fate of those whom we did not know? By the same token, would not a Shakespearean consciousness, brimming with energy, continue to imagine the fate of our loved ones after death? We would reject folk religious solutions, such as "He sleeps with the angels" because these clichés are another form of denial.

Our thoughts about dead loved ones, about their particular, concrete existence would not cease because they were dead. Our yearning for their presence, to see them again, would not stop when they died. Rather, we would continue to wish them alive. Many of us would have occult moments, and certainly, dreams, in which the dead returned to us. But if we shared Shakespeare's intelligence and empathy, these ordinary devices of denial of suffering would not work.

Sudden death by murder or the death of a child are distressing. For they seem to violate the "natural order" of death. Death should arrive late, after a full life and after one has buried one's parents not one's children. When Hamlet learns of his father's murder his loss is magnified and made horrible for it did not occur according to the rules of Danish (English) life and court. Hamlet's father was slain while asleep, caught and passively impaled by poison, not struck down on the battle field. Added to Prince Hamlet's distress is the awful violence and irrationality of his father's murder. It makes no sense to him, just as we can make little sense of the Nazi war against the Jews.

We cannot locate the meaning of Nazi horrors in a neat set of principles about war or state economy. This is true not just because the Nazis slaughtered so many but because they had such pride in their ability to overcome their feelings of horror. The war against the Jews made little economic sense and, many historians conclude, only impeded the military tasks Hitler assigned his generals.

From analytic perspectives, it is more plausible to see the Nazi campaign as an attempt to project their self-loathing and rage onto the Jews. They turned Jews into vermin and, finally, into refuse: "It became apparent during the first cremations in the open air that in the long run it would not be possible to continue in that manner [burning the corpses]. During bad weather or when a strong wind was blowing, the stench of burning flesh was carried for many miles and caused the whole neighborhood to talk about the burning of Jews, despite official counter-propaganda" (Hoss 1984, p. 122).[5]

Hamlet's Smelly Father: Loss and Recovery

Smell is an impolite topic in American culture, where the body, especially the female body, has become a lucrative marketplace for coverups and repressive traditions for many generations. There is an abundant folklore about smell, odor, perfume, fragrances, etc., but little scientific knowledge about this subject (Engen 1982, pp. 1–5). A major problem is that there exists no recognized method for measuring odor comparable to methods for measuring the intensity of sound or light or air pressure.

An additional problem is that of memory. Both anecdote and clinical evidence (see Kline and Rausch 1985) hold that smells associated with particular events can evoke those events with an intensity far greater than other sensory modes. A variation on this are the famous scenes in Proust's works in which he dramatizes the power of long forgotten and newly rediscovered odors to evoke forgotten experiences.

Another problem is that ordinary language seems deficient in its smell vocabulary (Engen 1982). This makes it difficult to use ordinary means of evocation, such as metaphor and verbal description, to represent smells to the reader or listener. There are many poetic devices that encourage the reader to imagine visual episodes: Homer's "wine dark sea" is an ancient example. Since poetry and music are so similar, poets can employ the sounds, rhythm, and other auditory qualities of speech to evoke other sounds. A famous example is Keats's line in *Ode to a Nightingale*, "The murmurous haunt of flies on summer eves" (1819, line 50).

It is more difficult to evoke the quality of smells (or odors or fragrances). In the same poem, *Ode to a Nightingale*, Keats attempts to describe a moment of intense olfactory sensation:

> I cannot see what flowers are at my feet,
> Nor what soft incense hangs upon the boughs,
> But, in the embalmed darkness, guess each sweet
> Wherewith the seasonable month endows
> The grass, the ticket, and the fruit-tree wild
> (lines 41–45)

Even Keats found it necessary to focus upon the visual aspect of the "soft" incense hanging in the trees, not upon the odors which rise up to the speaker.

Hamlet as Shakespeare: The Struggle against Understanding

This, approximately, was Shakespeare's situation when he wrote *Hamlet*. He had reconciled himself to the death of his son and the loss of his future narcissistic goals. He also faced the threat of political anarchy that could destroy the delicate fabric of English institutions as that nation stood on the brink of its most royal period. His intrapsychic conflicts included the struggle to comprehend his empathic abilities and the suffering they cost him. We can reconstruct some of these conflicts, even without biographical information, because Hamlet encounters them throughout the play.

An even more precise reason to identify Hamlet with Shakespeare is Hamlet's supreme intelligence and his struggles against his capacity for reidentification and empathy. His identification with Claudius—as the oedipal criminal (as Freud notes in his original insights into the play)—weighs on him. So does his identification with his mother and her sexual longings.

Hamlet's identification with his father, the victim of irrational violence, disturbs him because he participates in the ghost's horrors "Alas, poor ghost!" (I, v, 3). This is Shakespeare's struggle also. To adapt the cliché that "to understand all is to forgive all," we might say "to understand all is to suffer all."

A major defense against the suffering of too intense an understanding, against his genius, was Shakespeare's discovery of theatre and the play. For the play is both real and unreal; it is dramatic and painful. Yet it is contained within the safety of the stage and the script fabricated by the author who makes living beings strut and do his bidding. Like a well-conducted analysis, the play evokes destructive conflicts and then attempts to resolve them within the frame of time and space created by the author. So too, analyst and patient share a commitment to the analytic rules which engender the play of transference and with it the possibility of resolution. To use an expression from the nuclear industry, the play is a "containment" building. It permits otherwise destructive drives and wishes expression. Eventually these drives lose their potency. Patients new to analysis do not believe this. They are convinced that talking about unconscious forces will unchain them. The analyst claims that it will make action less likely.

Shakespeare's defense against his intense imagination and so against himself included the act of writing and therefore containment. This is what his alter ego, Prince Hamlet, cannot do even though Hamlet also loves the theatre, has precise critical judgments, and is himself a playwright. To not act is to disobey his father's ghost. To not act, but "act" is to remain the playwright. By not acting Hamlet remains the dramatist who creates alter egos—he remains Shakespeare. For within the realm of memory and fantasy, that is, within the mind, Hamlet is as "real" as any other actor. He "lives" in the same way the dead live, "in memory." He is memorialized, but since he is created within the mind of the playwright, he cannot die the way actual children die. He is therefore immortal. Within the play Hamlet is real and cannot do what he yearns to do: to remain an actor, playing at reality, imagining new worlds.

For as Hamlet's interactions with the players make clear, Hamlet loves the stage. He deeply envies the players who create the fabric of feeling and who "act" on stage with more force than he demonstrates in reality. Shakespeare creates a character who laments his inability to feel as intensely as the actors who act upon the stage seem to feel. To accomplish *his* goals, Hamlet becomes a playwright. He composes the play within the play, his "Mousetrap" version of the Murder of Gonsago, which repeats his uncle's crimes on stage.

Familiar to all analysts is a similar play within the play, the transference. For it is real and holds within it the possibility of new freedom, yet it is also artificial, induced by the rituals of the analytic hour and space. The gratifications made available through a successful analysis are real gratifications, but removed from their infantile origins and only available outside the analytic space.

The Ghost and the Shaman's Return: Concrete Memory vs. the Lie

The Ghost in Hamlet has a task identical to the shaman's task in folk cultures, especially the Siberian circle traditions in which the shaman or medicine expert often speaks out for justice that has gone awry (Kim 1989).[6] *Hamlet* is Shakespeare's longest play and among the most carefully written (Rowse 1985). To describe even one of its many strata requires extensive exposition. Using these principles derived from the two intellectual traditions described above, we focus on a less obvious theme in *Hamlet*. This theme is of "two airs." There is "the good air" of genuine love (heterosexual especially) represented by Ophelia and "the bad air" of regicide and incest represented by the anal, sulphurous air that surrounds the ghost. Later in the play, Hamlet explains to Rosencrantz and Guildenstern:

> ...this most excellent canopy, the air, look
> you, this brave o'erhanging firmament, this majestical
> roof fretted with golden fire—why, it appeareth nothing
> to me but a foul and pestilent congregation of vapors.
> (II, ii, 297–299)

My selection of textual examples is limited; it is not arbitrary. Among the parallel constructions and dense themes that pervade the play is a continuous theme of "good air," versus "bad air," of rank anality versus the sublimation of anality or the opposite of anality, freely given love. These themes emerge in act I when we hear of "strange eruptions in the state" (I, i, 68) and empty graves. The bodies of the dead rise up and reveal the corruption hidden under the King's pretty speeches. These issues come to a point when Claudius reprimands Hamlet for mourning his father:

> Good Hamlet, cast thy nighted color off,
> And let thine eye look like a friend on Denmark,
> Do not for ever with thy vailèd lids
> Seek for thy noble father in the dust.
> Thou know'st 'tis common. All that lives must die,
> Passing through nature to eternity.
> (68–73)

This "passing through" nature is equivalent to the passage of food, which is life giving, through the intestines where after its values have been extracted, it becomes feces, which is putrid matter. From there it passes "into eternity." Claudius's secret crimes against nature have made this natural progression impossible: graves give up their dead. Hamlet cannot throw to earth his unprevailing woe, the air is foul with the smell of carrion and putrefaction. Hamlet must seek his father in the dust and dirt of the grave which has yawned open.

Following his pompous appeal to Hamlet to cease mourning his father, that is, to cease remarking on the passage of life and death, the King causes his cannons to be shot off. His bombast and cruel lies, another form of foul airs, echo the bombast in the heavens. Following the heavenly bombast occurs Hamlet's first soliloquy, "O that this too too solid flesh would melt / Thaw, and resolve itself into a dew."

This speech deepens the theme of the corrupt, the putrid and sullied body which, like the open graves, reveals the hidden corruption in the state. If these signs of disease melted away, like the dew, Hamlet would be spared the tasks in front of him. On learning of the ghost's visitations, Hamlet remarks that "Foul deeds will rise, / Though all the earth o'erwhelm them, to men's eyes" (I, ii, 257–258).

In the exchange between Horatio and Hamlet that follows, Hamlet condenses the manifest improprieties of his mother's hasty marriage to her brother-in-law. He links it again to images of dead bodies and their state.

> Thrift, thrift, Horatio. The funeral baked meats
> Did coldly furnish forth the marriage tables.
> Would I had met my dearest foe in heaven
> Or ever I had seen that day, Horatio!
> My father—methinks I see my father.
> (I, ii, 180–184)

Janine Chasseguet-Smirgel (1984), a French psychoanalyst, describes brilliantly the anal mixing and destruction of difference in the Marquis De Sade's world. De Sade celebrates incest because it undoes difference and boundaries. The same temper emerges in this speech which uses the oral imagery of food. The crimes that have sullied the state make one food—baked to honor the dead—serve as its opposite, festive cake for a wedding party. Claudius's overt passions, to rule in his brother's place and have his wife, are passions to foul the state and destroy order.

The dirty, anal air of crime permeates the scenes with Ophelia and Laeretes and Ophelia and her father. Polonius, the great windbag, sullies Hamlet's love for her. (When Claudius poisons Laeretes's "sporting" blade he again reveals his anal universe. He will poison the young prince with a dirty rapier as he poisoned the King and so the state whose name, "Denmark," he claims for himself.) Hamlet, waiting for the ghost to appear, hears again the King's raucous braying as he drinks. This custom of bombast, Hamlet says, will "soil" the state's collective reputation for it reveals a mole, a basic flaw in the King's temper that will lead to corruption.

Hamlet then sees the Ghost for the first time. The Ghost who lives in "sulph'rous and tormenting flames," in hell which stinks of the anal odors denoted by sulphur because crimes against the state go unpunished. As all folk cultures assert, the ghost of the offended victim cannot rest until justice is served. Therefore the Ghost cannot tolerate the "morning air," which is sweet and unsullied, as was Ophelia's and Hamlet's love for each other. Having given dreadful details of his torments, the Ghost asks Hamlet to remember him. Then follows a fascinating bit of neuroticism. Hamlet declares:

> Remember thee?
> Yea, from the table of my memory
> I'll wipe away all trivial fond records,
> All saws of books, all forms, all pressures past
> That youth and observation copied there,
> And thy commandment all alone shall live
> Within the book and volume of my brain,
> Unmixed with baser matter. Yes, by heaven!
>   (98–109)

Given the Ghost's stupendous revelations, it seems unlikely Hamlet could forget them. Yet he fears he will (wish to) forget; hence he writes them down. The wiping and cleaning of his mind implies that prior to his father's deathly commandment was only "base" matter, that is, anal matters that must be wiped away. This, like all other events in a state made rotten by unnatural crimes (as was Thebes by Oedipus's crimes), is an inversion. Hamlet turns his boyhood's memories, including all his "fond records," into feces that he must now dispose of and replace with his father's demand for revenge. Hamlet rebels against this "analization" of his mind when he struggles against the task to carry out his father's wishes. Hamlet then writes down the maxim, "One may smile and smile and be a villain." He writes this because he wishes to forget what he has just learned, especially about his mother's sexuality. If he forgets these horrible truths, his father's demand will not live "within the book" of his brain.

One way to describe Hamlet's dilemma is to invoke a contemporary term, *father hunger,* to account for his sense of desperation. Father hunger denotes the boy's need for a fathering person who can mediate aggressive fantasies that are otherwise terrifying to the young boy. James Herzog (1982) highlights intrapsychic conflicts that emerge when the boy requires additional self-regulation and the intrapsychic representation of a strong, loving, and resolute father.[7] Such images help the boy establish a sense of maleness and decreases castration anxiety. Without such fathering the boy elaborates fantastic, sexualized solutions to his ego deficits. These fantasies are primitive and triadic. They bridge the gap between self–mother and self–world interactions. They may also be homosexual, for how better to make concrete the wish for merger with a powerful father?

Unconscious Reflections on Death and Fathers

The fate of dead fathers returns as a central theme when Hamlet kills Polonius. He calls him "A rat," an anal animal par excellence, then hides his body (as his father's crime was hidden) and taunts Claudius with a riddle:

> *Hamlet:* A man may fish with the worm that hath eat of a king, and eat of the fish that hath fed of that worm.
> *King:* What dost thou mean by this?
> *Hamlet:* Nothing but to show you how a king go a progress through the guts of a beggar.
>
> (IV, iii, 27–31).

Even the high and mighty return to dust, as the Bible instructs. In Hamlet's imagination, this dust and the substance of the personality do *not* dissolve as they should into mere soil. As Hamlet says in his "To be or not to be" speech, after death one would hope for a transformation of the self. The personality might change into something no longer corporal and no longer tainted by the sins of this world. Because he died without the benefit of confession and remorse and because his murder remains unavenged, Hamlet the king cannot be transformed.

Rather, his personality persists, tormented in the ways he described to his son. When the course of nature is violated, even in death a person receives no rest and no transformation of the self. Rather it is degraded continuously. ("John Brown's body lies a moldin' in the grave.") The self becomes a "living dead." It is a corpse fed upon by worms, and the worms by fish, and the fish by humans, that is, by Hamlet and by Claudius. The noblest of persons, the king himself, is not transformed by death into a transcendent nature. He turns into worms that pass through nature, that is, the guts of a beggar and turns into feces.

The King's Degraded Self

This ultimate degradation is the product of Claudius's crimes. The dead king is also internalized in this archaic manner. For as the ghost scenes make clear, Hamlet now feels his mind, the noblest aspect of a noble prince, filled with his father's vision and requirements. Fish are also "mind food." Murder is an anal action; it turns something sweet into something putrid. This quality appears again when Hamlet visits the graveyard. There we hear repeated Claudius's world view about life passing through nature. In the space near his father's rotting body, Hamlet learns from the grave digger, the Clown, that he was born in the day Hamlet Senior killed Fortinbras Senior. This fact indicates a complex scene. Young Hamlet was conceived not only in an unimaginable act, his father's intercourse with his mother, but, by a violent action, marked by the death of yet another father, Fortinbras. In mythological terms Hamlet replaces the king whom his father killed. He is himself a usurper of whom primitive justice requires, in turn, vengeance at the hands of Fortinbras's son, Fortinbras Junior.

Immediately following this discussion of himself and his remarkable birth, Hamlet asks "How long will a man lie i' the earth ere he rot"? (V, i, 153). This question links together the two fathers, one long dead, the other dead only a few months. Fortinbras ("strong arms") has been rotting for as long as Hamlet has lived; Hamlet Senior is only just dead.

The grave digger replies that the sexually active and deadly syphilitic (which suggests not much difference between the two conditions) rot even before they touch the ground. Then he tosses Yorick's skull to Hamlet. Hamlet's severe imagination, which is part of his and Shakespeare's genius, makes him sick: "And Now how abhorred in my imagination it is! / My gorge rises at it. Here hung those lips I have / Kissed I know not how oft" (175–177). Hamlet's disgust and horror are driven by his father hunger. As he fondles the skull, his wishes to kiss again Yorick's lips. To this homoerotic and regressed yet intense image, he recoils with sarcasm and humor. A more powerful defense than these is philosophizing. To invoke this defense he turns to his comrade, Horatio. Did even the young hero, Alexander the Great, who bettered his father, fall into this state of death and stink? From this anxious question—how did the son, greater than his father, also die and lie stinking in the ground—Hamlet creates a fantasy of stopping a beer barrel:

> To what base uses we may return, Horatio!
> Why may not imagination trace the noble dust of
> Alexander till 'a find it stopping a bunghole?
>
> (190–192)

Horatio's response to this odd question is conventional and shocked, " 'Twere to consider too curiously, to consider so" (p. 193). In his way Horatio is surely correct. There is no reasonable way one can link a dead Macedonian Prince with the cork in an English flask. (In so doing Hamlet links Philip, Alexander's father, Caesar and his assassination, and the dead fathers of the play and their sons.) Hamlet explains his reasoning and his associations:

> No, faith, not a jot, but to follow him thither with modesty
> enough, and likelihood to lead it; as thus: Alexander died,
> Alexander was buried, Alexander re-turneth to dust; the dust is
> earth; of earth we make loam; of why of that loam whereto he
> was converted might they not stop a beer barrel?
> Imperious Caesar, dead and turned to clay,
> Might stop a hole to keep the wind away!
> O, that the earth which kept the world in awe
> Should patch a wall t'expel the winter's flaw!
>
> (194–203)

Since this is the stuff of dreams we are not surprised that Horatio cannot agree to Hamlet's reasoning. Rather, he says his friends thoughts are obviously diseased. The homosexual imagery suggests that alongside positive identifications with Hamlet Senior (and with Claudius), there are deeper identifications with Gertrude, that is, both partners of the primal scene. The themes of oral incorporation and oral impregnation return, with more displacement, when Hamlet says that Alexander's dust is used to stopper a beer barrel.

This degrades King Alexander and it also causes one's gorge to rise since it means that his rotted body lies in the form of a plug next to the liquid one drinks. This fantasy of mixing dead bodies and drink, the absent father and the beer consumed with lusty male friends, undoes the differences in state wrought by death. It is also a fantasy that echoes themes of homosexual coupling. The sequence of association beginning with kisses to Yorick's lips leads to the fantasy that the dead king (who represents Alexander, Caesar, Hamlet Senior, and Hamlet) may stop a bunghole. What is the bunghole?[8] Few analytic commentators reflect upon this singular image. Yet considering other homoerotic elements in the play, one conjectures that it must represent the father's and Hamlet's anuses. We see this within the chain of associations that link Caesar with the stopping up of holes and the wind, which his body, turned to feces, to soil, is to keep away. That winter's flaw is the cold wind and the divine flatus, or "spiritus." It is the product of internal decay and tied to the child's conception of masculine birth (babies are equivalent to feces) and of magical power.

These associations all derive from the poignant moment when Hamlet smells Yorick's skull, for it has the anal smell of death: it is the "bad air," the "sulph'rous," odors that Hamlet associated with his father's ghost and it is the potency of such air, the product of corruption, that sparks off Hamlet's associations to dead generals and kings. For each of these fantastic thoughts concerns the preservation of fathers through some magical (perverse) method of internalization: through the mouth or the anus (Hamlet frequently refers to himself as a "Stallion" which is a male prostitute). To preserve his father, even in the disgusting version of the worm, counteracts Claudius's commonsense version that nature requires the death of fathers.

More so, to preserve his father and to internalize him some way or other is to make unnecessary the action of revenge the Ghost requires of him.[9] For Hamlet is an actor and playwright in every sense of these words: he loves the theatre and its performers just as Shakespeare did. Like Shakespeare, Hamlet has the capacity of genius; his conception is so powerful and his imagination so potent that he can *almost* transform his world of real losses and horror into something else, into the play that mimics the corruption in which he now swims.

But Hamlet the character fails to accomplish what *Hamlet* the play does: transform suffering into art, to "deanalize" crimes into wisdom. Within the world of Hamlet's mind and his lived reality, actual corruption cannot be purged by drama alone.

We recall that Hamlet still did not act against Claudius, even following the "Murder of Gonsago" discoveries and following the attempt on his life engineered by Claudius. Even then Hamlet failed to carry out the Ghost's commands. Only in the "play" of the mock sword fight with Horatio, whose father Hamlet killed, does Hamlet finally act. Even then, it was only after Laeretes exposed the "play" as "real" that Hamlet stabs Claudius. The anal world created by Claudius's crime cannot be purged with words alone; its crimes and the putrefaction they cause are real.

To cleanse the state of these actual evils Hamlet must carry out the very thing that the theatre cannot accomplish, real action. (Just as Claudius could not cleanse himself by prayer when he too attempted to use language alone to bring the pestilence to an end and so undo his actions and cleanse the state.) Hamlet demonstrates again and again that he can imagine every horror and clothe them with tremendous language; he forces Claudius to imagine the fate of kings as they turn into worms and then into a beggar's shit. But these thunderous images and metaphors do not affect Claudius's actions: he remains intent on evil and continues to ruin good persons, as when he persuades Laeretes to cheat in the sword fight.

When Hamlet attempts to stop his mother's incestuous affair with Claudius, Hamlet uses terrifying language. His imagery *almost convinces* her to forsake Claudius (though the Ghost, in his dressing gown, intervenes). In the same way, Hamlet uses his wonderful ability with language to attempt to persuade his mother to reject Claudius outright. When his words fail he lacerates himself with swearing and cursing (which is just more words) just as he lacerates himself when he fails to meet the dramatic standards of the player who can call up tears to match the play.

In his reflections on death, in killing Polonius, and in arranging for the death of Rosencrantz and Guildenstern, Hamlet shows that he is not afraid of death nor of the dead. Hamlet does not deny that horrors, suffering, and loss punctuate human life. In this sense Hamlet is not neurotic. Rather he is afraid of something else: of losing his mystery. For to act in reality and not via the theatre and the play, Hamlet must forsake his inmost genius, his mystery, his mind's eye, or, one might say, his Shakespearean consciousness.

Sublimation and Perversions in *Citizen Kane*

Orson Welles's film *Citizen Kane* (1941), portrays both the story of Charles Foster Kane and the American class structure in the first half of this century. The film is a dramatic achievement, filled with psychological insights about the effects Kane's boyhood had on his subsequent development into a publisher, modeled on the much-feared William Randolph Hearst. In brief, the movie shows us how a poor couple, the Kanes, happen upon a huge fortune. The mother decides to send her son, Charles, who is five, away for a proper education. Charles becomes a fearless, heedless, and often cruel tycoon who eventually destroys himself.

From the outset, Welles and the film company, RKO, publicly rejected identifying the film's protagonist with Hearst. The original film script derives from biographies of Hearst, at that time, a legend in American capitalism. With equal intensity Welles and many of his critics dismissed the "dollar book Freud" theme of the young boy's suffering represented by the famous "Rosebud" sequence. Because "Rosebud," the young boy's sled, represents his lost relationship to his mother, sophisticated viewers have avoided pursuing that theme for it seems too obvious and unrelated to the film's technical achievements. Yet the film does reflect Hearst's life and the "dollar book Freud" theme is crucial to the film's story.

I wish to show how the film reveals both Kane's traumatic origins and hints at the perverse structure these traumata forced upon his character. More so, as we see in the film, Charles Kane attempts to solve his character pathology with an appeal to culture; he piles up "great art," by the dump load. In so doing he reverses the course of sublimation and culture; he turns art into refuse.

In her lengthy study, *The Citizen Kane Book* (1971), Pauline Kael says *Citizen Kane* "isn't a work of special depth or a work of subtle beauty. It is a shallow work, a shallow masterpiece" (p. 4). She adds, "*Citizen Kane* is a 'popular' masterpiece" (p. 5) and she is especially critical of the Rosebud "gimmickry" (p. 5) that she feels makes the film's central mystery largely a fake issue, suited better to cheap novels and popular theatrics. The film is shallow, she says, because the director telegraphs so often the characters' internal states. Its theatrics derive in large measure from Orson Welles's bravado style, already made famous in his New York productions where he had astounding successes in both classical and contemporary theatres. In addition, Welles had produced and starred in the infamous Mercury Theatre broadcast of "War of the Worlds" on Halloween night of 1938. He so frightened his radio audience that he became famous all over again.

Kael reserves her bitterest comments for three scenes in the movie and for its use of the Rosebud theme. This theme originates in the first spoken words of the film. In this scene the elderly Charles Foster Kane stares at a little glass ball with a snow scene, gasps out the name "Rosebud" and dies, alone in his castle. A second scene Kael dislikes follows immediately. As Kane topples over he drops the little glass ball, containing the snow scene. The ball rolls to the floor, shatters, and through the shattered glass fragment we see Kane's nurse enter the room. Kael calls this scene "empty virtuosity" (1971, p. 54).

The third scene Kael dislikes is the moment Kane meets Susan, a young naive woman whom Kael feels is inappropriate to the film. She is a "dumb girl" (p. 54) who does not match the powerful personality of Kane. The Rosebud theme and these three scenes, which Kael finds offensive, I find to be crucial to the film. Our disagreement is not accidental. For Kael does not like the "Freudian" stuff, while I do. Where she finds shallowness I find themes linking each of the scenes she dislikes to one another and to the central conceit of "Rosebud."

Kael focuses upon the making of the movie and the personalities of those who created it; she does not focus upon the interior experience of the young boy, Charlie. If she did, she would find that the irrelevant scenes, especially Kane's first meeting with Susan, elucidate Charlie's unspoken and unspeakable losses. Those experiences of loss parallel important elements in Welles's life story. For both the fictional little boy and Orson Welles suffered disruptions in their relationship to both parents.

Citizen Kane is not a naive autobiography of Welles, nor was it Welles's project alone. Yet the film's core issue—the development of Charles Kane the man—revolves around the forced and cruel separation Kane's mother effected when she "saved" him by sending him away from her and her husband to live with the odious banker, Mr. Thatcher. In doing so Mrs. Kane robbed her son of his real father and gave him a poor substitute. This accelerated, if not initiated, Kane's tragedy for it created a permanent fault line in the young boy's psyche. That is, the boy's expulsion from his parents' home is not merely sad, it is tragic. It stamped permanently his capacity to become fully human, that is, to become a self.

Kael is a sophisticated writer, associated many years with *The New Yorker*, as was the hero of her book, Herman Mankiewicz. Like John Cheever, another *New Yorker* author, Kael knows all about psychoanalysis since she has read about it and no doubt has many friends who are analysts or who have been analytic patients. Like yet another *New Yorker* author, Woody Allen, Kael chooses to write about analysis with a studied tone of humor; analysis is no longer the rage and Freud's struggles to uncover heretofore hidden truths are common knowledge.

For we have all heard about this stuff, like oedipal conflicts; it is no longer satisfying to point out oedipal themes in a movies because anyone can do it. The obvious "Freudian" stuff in *Citizen Kane* fails to galvanize sophisticates because it leaps out at one; it is no longer subtle and no longer, therefore, worthy of comment by them. It is true that *Citizen Kane* is prone to half-baked criticism. Some say it is the most studied film in history (Carringer 1985).

Like *Hamlet*, *Citizen Kane* lends itself to multiple interpretations and invites the forays of the novice. But in the film's favor is the fact that it is a popular film and a popular art form. It is therefore accessible to many people who have little daily contact with the more prestigious forms of art, such as paintings hidden in distant museums or architecture hidden in distant cities.

When we examine *Citizen Kane* and its obvious symbolism, we find that contemporary analytic theory, especially the theory of the formation of sexual perversions, illuminates those moments Kael most disliked.

The Development of Perversions

According to contemporary psychoanalytic theory of perversion, Mrs. Kane carries out the basic recipe for producing a child driven to perversions of one sort or another. Out of complex motives she destroys her son's ability to remain in childhood. (I use the word *perversion* in a classic Freudian sense to refer to sexual actions which have other than a heterosexual, genital focus and aim.) Instead, as key scenes make clear, young Charles becomes astute at reading the lowest motives of those around him. This stands him in good stead to become a master of yellow journalism where the lowest common denominator wins the rating war and the successful publisher is one who gratifies the public's yearning for blood, guts, sex, and more sex.

To produce a child fascinated by these elements and who makes them his career one must attack the young child's sense of physical and psychological integration. Some contemporary analytic studies of perversion outline this recipe in detail. To use some of these insights I comment on the work of Charles Socarides (1988), Robert Stoller (1975), and Masud Khan (1979). For a compelling and clinically detailed critique of Socarides and the point of view I here utilize, see Isay (1989).

Socarides (1988) summarizes his many years of work with "perverse" patients and amalgamates drive theory of sexuality, the so-called classical theory, with object relations theory. The latter type, broadly conceived, ranges from Melanie Klein (1957) and to Khan (1979), and Selfpsychologists from Kohut (1979) to Stolorow and Lachmann (1980). I cannot summarize Socarides's subtle and lengthy discussion in a way that adequately represents his reasoning. The few comments that follow do not validate Socarides's points, nor do they reveal Socarides's extensive efforts to document his clinical sources. His case histories are poignant samples of human experience and his basic claims are persuasive. The latter reflects his efforts to distinguish two classes of perversions: those deriving from preoedipal stage traumata and those deriving from oedipal stage traumata.

While perverse acts may appear identical, for example, homosexuality in two male patients, origins in distinctive epochs of ego development means that their internal organizations also differ. As Socarides puts it, and using language that reveals his efforts to match classical theory with contemporary theory, "The underlying unconscious motivational drives are distinctly different" (1988, p. 71). In cases of distinct perversion, Socarides argues that the patient manifests ego deficits caused by failures in the patient's earliest relationships with caretakers: perversion is the compulsive need to engage in sexualized relationships. Like other neurotic actions, perverse acts reflect unconscious demands to act with no heed given to moral, legal, or reality constraints. One may define compulsive heterosexual intercourse as a neurotic symptom, just as one may define pedophilia, some forms of homosexuality, and transvestism as perversions.

Unlike the ideal of heterosexual intercourse, clearly perverse actions always include a large measure of hatred, often disguised but always detectable. Drawing upon his work with perverse patients and upon the analytic wisdom of other practitioners, Socarides notes that the goal of the perverse action is to achieve sexual satisfaction with an object (a person or a nonperson) that represents, during the moment of orgasm, a magical union with the person whom the patient has lost and without whom he or she is incomplete.

However, the object of the perverted sexual attack is never a complete person whose entire personality the pervert desires. Rather he or she represents a class of persons whom the patient feels has the idealized characteristics the patient requires. For example, a male homosexual may require his conquests to be strong, working men of a certain build or color. The remaining characteristics of his sexual partners are unimportant. Of course, this compulsive focus upon a fixed set of objective features in the sexual partner occurs in nonperverted sexuality as well.

Because orgasm is an intense pleasure and induces, momentarily, an altered state of consciousness, it is an extremely powerful method for creating a hallucinatory moment of wish-fulfillment. The wishes fulfilled in this manner always include a reunion of self and lost objects; of self and persons who have failed to perform their tasks of maintaining the security of the self that is now threatened with fragmentation. This magical infusion is temporary: "The effect is transitory, leading to an insistent need for multiple and frequent sexual contact. In those requiring multiple and frequent encounters, boundaries between self–object representations may be quite fragile. The greater the capacity of orgasm to restore the patient's sense of self, the more difficult it becomes to remove the perverse need" (1988, p. 16).

In addition, Socarides notes that the basic principle of overdetermination discovered by Freud and made clear by Waelder (1936) rules the life of patients with perversions, as it rules all lives. The particular perverse act helps preserve the self and counter depression. It draws to itself additional functions. "It is not the erotic infantile experience per se which is sought in the perverse act; it is the reassuring and reaffirming function of the erotic experience which is reanimated and pursued" (1988, p. 17). This means that the perversion itself becomes an organizing experience and so becomes valuable to the patient who chances upon this mode of ego consolidation.

Referring to the compulsive quality of perversions, Socarides cites Khan (1965) who describes the fleeting euphoria that perverse actions bring. This euphoria and temporary cessation of anxiety make the perverse action addictive. New bouts of anxiety drive the patient on to seek new partners to provide another moment of temporary relief. The perverse action and objects associated can become the core of existence to the person who depends upon them exclusively.

Disruption and The Child's Conception of Reunion

Socarides summarizes his theory of the traumatic origins of preoedipal perversions (1988, p. 41). Because of overwhelming traumata suffered at the hands of a caretaker, the child sexualizes ego functions normally consolidated during the period of separation-individuation, roughly one and one-half to three years of age. The perverse actions which result represent, therefore, the child's conception of the action that would reunite the child with the child's parent from whom all good things flow. This is a useful formula and it accounts for the dramatic, ritualized form that perverted acts always display: as reenactments of conceptions of action, perversions are already symbolic events.

Socarides's formula also permits us to clarify a point crucial to psychoanalytic aesthetics. The process of separation–individuation is a *process*, and not a thing: it is invisible. Rituals, perverse or not, that refer to it are abstract and "symbolic" for they have no concrete referent. These ritual actions have, rather, an invisible and nonintellectual referent: the quality of the relationship that obtains between parent (usually mother) and infant.

Perverted actions, carried out in a stylized manner, refer to the child's conception, which, in turn, refers to the subtle qualities of parenting present in the child's environment. An analogy is the horrible monster portrayed in children's stories who represents, unconsciously, the child's portrait of the interactions that occur between parent and child. When "Dad is a bear" and "Mother is a bitch" and "Junior is a little monster" each has totemic referents, linked to the unconscious images these names evoke. In the nightmare these images are given new life.

In some forms of public nightmare, these images are fully expressed. For example Gregory Bateson and Maragret Mead (1942) illustrate such a nightmare in their famous photographic analysis of

Balinese ritual dances. In addition, following Winnicott (1971a) we note that a feature common to many intense forms of parenting is the "preoccupation" typical of the mother when she tends her infant. This mode of consciousness, of fascination, is visible in the new mother, but also in the child at play or the fortunate adult who can also play. In ordinary, wide-awake consciousness, we are aware of our posture and of time passing. But during a moment of fascination we are engrossed, taken out of ordinary experience, and possessed by the event. We are out of our ordinary frame of consciousness and therefore free.

Of course, if one feels that one's environment is hostile one does not enter into this state easily. Patients new to analysis observe how scary it is for them to "regress," that is, to stop controlling their experience by focusing upon the passage of time or by "analyzing" themselves as they scan every word and gesture they make. To avoid psychoanalytic regression some patients keep a running tab of the minutes passed in analytic sessions. They are ready to bolt at any moment and vigilant against the dangers of becoming fascinated by the analytic process and so dominated by the unconscious wishes that animate their unconscious thought processes.

Perversions and Symbolic Reenactment

Because perverted actions are symbolic reenactments of lost, preverbal relationships, they are doubly removed from ordinary discourse and representations. This double distance from ordinary objects makes it difficult to perceive the real core of perversions. One must undo two levels of symbolic representation; the perverted action itself represents a prior, now repressed, traumatic occurrence and the traumatic occurrence itself represented the loss of a relationship between parent and child.

The relationship lost can be described differently. Kohut and other Selfpsychologists would describe it as primary self/self–object relationship in which the parent performed ego functions for the child such that the child (or infant) experienced these functions as under the infant's control. Stern (1985) would use similar concepts to describe the infant's sense of self that is vulnerable to failures in the parents' "instinctlike" response to the infant's needs. (See also Erikson [1963] on "the nursing pair.")

Common to all these accounts is the insight that the infant and young child cannot comprehend the pain the child suffers when such failures occur except in the egocentric and primary process concepts that dominate infantile intelligence. No matter how massive the parents' failure, the infant considers the pain inflicted as due to its own actions. The child's wishes and unconscious fantasies must be responsible for the child's suffering.

Concrete images and representations, typical of childrens' thinking cannot comprehend the invisible processes between self and mother. In a similar way it is difficult to reduce the processlike core of psychoanalytic psychotherapy to simplistic images and representations. Both patients and analysts may wish to find a single formula that defines psychoanalysis. Yet in its depths, analysis too is a process which takes place over ritualized time and space (Peterfreund 1983).

In the language of Self Psychology, perverse actions denote failures in self–object realtionship between parent and child. But, again, since the self–object relationship is itself a measure of the quality of relationship between persons, no single, concrete object is sufficient to capture it entirely. In the sentimental language of American musicals, "How do you hold a moonbeam in your hand?"[10] In the more sober language of cognitive psychology and perception theory, because the child's caretakers have failed to provide sufficient regulation of the child's total self through adequate responses, the child turns to concrete actions and concrete objects that, in their mundane reality, seem to promise the immutability and permanence now lost.

Socarides, like many authors who deal with the genesis of borderline personalities, emphasizes the parents' active and persistent attacks upon the child's developing sense of self-cohesion. Like Stern (1985), whom I discussed at length in chapter 4, Socarides emphasizes that parental attacks upon the infant and the child erode the child's basic ability to find reliable self–objects.

In this sense it is interesting to compare evidence from children raised within concentration camp conditions with the childhoods of adults with severe perversions. Socarides proffers lengthy, beautiful accounts of a range of perversions, from some forms of male homosexuality to masochism and voyeurism to pedophilia. Each story begins with an account of overwhelming traumata suffered at the hands of hostile parents. Following that trauma, the child attempts to cope with the anxiety which now floods upon the child and with the child's subsequent rage at the parent who perpetuated these horrors. For example, a man in his late twenties, whom Socarides describes as a narcissistic pedophile, felt the compulsive need to seduce young boys two or three times a week, often jeopardizing himself with arrest and humiliation. The patient was the oldest of a large family. His father was cruel to his mother, barely supported the family, and both mother and father abandoned the children to an orphange, when he was five years old, "on the pretext that the mother would return for them the next day" (1988, p.

451). After two or three years of waiting for that day the boy developed a terror of white mice, for he heard stories that the mouse mother eats her young that cannot take care of themselves: "He often had fantasies of all the children in his family returning to the mother's womb, suppressing this when the fantasy of a frightful tearing-apart of his mother began to intrude" (1988, p. 451). When he seduced the young boys, during an altered state of consciousness, the patient felt identified both with his lost mother and with the little boy. He was, in other words, both the little boy who found his mother suckling him (her breast became his penis) and he was the "good mother" who suckled her child (the child his parents abandoned). (See below Stoller's patient, a young woman whose burglary symbolized in detail her symbolic stealing back into her mother's womb [1975, chapter 9].)

Socarides describes another patient, a thirty-nine-year-old man who was a heterosexual transvestite. At age four, his mother placed him in a home for six months. This horrible experience became the center of his life. Even though the boy became a successful academic, "inwardly he experienced himself as having a ratlike complex, wandering around like a rat in a maze, not knowing what to do next" (1988, p. 375).

Upon analysis, each intricate ritual surrounding his cross dressing revealed its origins in the young boy's attempt to comprehend his dilemma and to exact from it some momentary relief and satisfaction. To put on women's clothes was to identify himself with women, especially with mother, and therefore to merge with them. By using the costume to emphasize his penis he displayed the fact that he was male, a person with a penis, and in this way felt safe from castration. Orgasm, brought about by ritualized and compulsive masturbation, brought relief from the disturbing sense of fragmentation, experienced first when his mother abandoned him. (See Khan 1979, as well.)

Representations of Ego Consolidation: Recalling the Unremembered and Unnameable

The child prone to perverse solutions reveals massive deficits in ego consolidation. In the presence of an attacking, vicious self–object the child sets upon a course of action that is bound to fail. We can see this from three distinct points of view: cognitive and developmental, affect and self–other differentiation, and the absence of sufficient structuralizing. It is to specific (fetishistic) objects and sensations that the patient attaches the magic of ego consolidation.

Therefore, analyst and patient examine the specifics of the patient's erotic life. Some of the linkages between the perverted act and the massive traumata suffered at the parents' hands are clear. For example, a patient can have erections and orgasm only if he wears a stocking that matches the color of his mother's stockings. Some linkages are less clear. Like manifest dream images, they can be established through detailed analytic scrutiny. For example, Stoller (1975) discovered that the "iceman" who figured in one patient's memories, represented the icy, dead mother (p. 171) who had too little to give anything to her daughter. The daughter, in turn, became a thief who broke into family houses and stole from them everyday objects, like music boxes, that linked mother and child.

When Kael dismisses the "Freudian stuff" about loss and suffering in *Citizen Kane*, she does so with little reflection upon the suffering children undergo in such circumstances. She resembles anthropologists who record "just the facts" about a culture's attacks upon its children in initiation rituals, for example (De Mausse 1989; Gregor 1985). Other social critics affirm the political claim that sexuality is merely life-style. They do not see the rage that underlies perverse actions. But, all these issues become manifest in *Citizen Kane.*

Overt Traumata in Citizen Kane

Traumata in *Citizen Kane* are visible and well documented, perversions occur in disguise, at latent levels. We can establish the existence of such perversions by arguing backwards and, judging from the horrible, deathlike existence that Kane exhibits in his later life, we can infer the representations of perverse actions and fantasies that always underlie them.

Kane suffered many hardships. At age five his mother sends him away to be raised by the obsessional banker, Mr. Thatcher, tearing him away from his father whom she openly despises. Thatcher's devotion is to the money Mrs. Kane has settled upon her son, not to the boy himself. As a grown up Kane fails in each dimension of adult life. He fails to find authentic love in his new household; he fails to secure a professional identity other than that of yellow journalist, and he fails to create an adequate marriage. He destroys his chances for political success, ruins his relationship to his new wife, then destroys her. He humiliates himself in front of his servants and dies unloved, amidst the mountains of art he collected and turned into junk.

I term these events "traumatic" in the sense that Anna Freud used the term: "shattering, devastating, causing internal disruption by putting ego functioning and ego mediation out of action" (1967, p. 242, cited in Rothstein, ed., 1986, p. 51). Such events may include physical pain, as that induced by a psychotic parent upon a child's genitals, or it may be unadulterated psychical pain, as that induced by the parent who threatens to abandon a "bad" child. Such events always induce a sense of powerless and the inability to comprehend the suffering now taking place. The ego cannot "mediate" the intense pain the child suffers and there is no adult present who can carry out that task for the child. So, the child is left to the child's resources, which include regression to perverse sexual actions.

The Unremembered in Charlie's Life: Representations of Representations

Forgotten traumata are important to Charlie Kane's story. We can recover their origins by using principles derived from clinical psychoanalysis: traumata always leave indicators in the person's total behavior. Greenacre (1956) observed that a key clinical indicator of the existence of hidden traumata is the dream within the dream, or its equivalents, the joke within the dream, or the play or movie within the dream. (See Rothstein 1986, p. 2.) With this principle we can investigate *Citizen Kane* and seek there evidence of these forms of convoluted messages.

As soon as we ask this question we see that the entire film replicates the structure of dream within dream and story within story that Greenacre says typifies accounts of patients who have no direct memory of their suffering. For, from the opening scene, in which the camera pans past the "No Trespassing" sign to the final scene, in which Charlie's sled is burned, we follow a skein of stories within stories and dreams within stories and stories within dreams.

Of course, many films prior to *Citizen Kane* used the convention of the story within the story. It is an ancient literary convention as well; to engage the reader's interest, a character within the story tells another story. However, *Citizen Kane* differs from these literary examples by the intensity with which the film pursues these conventions and by the self-conscious, dreamlike style which dominates many of these moments of story within story. The most celebrated story within the film's story is the short newsreel, "News on the March!" a brilliant mock documentary, complete with "authentic" footage from the silent-film era up to 1940, the year in which *Citizen Kane* was shot. "News on the March!" is itself a homage and parody of the news films of the day. It conveys the basic outline of Kane's life and so prefigures for us the story that follows.

But prior to the "News on the March" sequence is the stylized opening which bothered Pauline Kael. Without warning, the screen shifts from showing us Kane, aged and dying in his huge bed, to a snow scene, "An incredible one. Big impossible flakes of snow, a too picturesque farmhouse and snowman" (Mankiewicz and Welles 1971, p. 95). As Kane utters the single, famous word, "Rosebud," the camera pulls back and we see that what we had thought was an "actual" scene takes place in a toy glass ball that the old man grasps in his hands. For the first-time viewer this odd sequence states the film's manifest mystery: what did Kane mean by the word "Rosebud," and how is this word connected to the "incredible," that is, unbelievable, snow scene in the glass?

For the veteran viewer this scene prefigures Kane's boyhood trauma. For he was wrenched away from his mother and father during a snowy day when he played on his sled, "Rosebud." We know also that Kane had taken the toy from his second wife, Susan, who had it on her mantle when she first met Kane. Added to the "too picturesque" toy and Kane's longings for his mother and for Susan, is the shot which ends this scene: as Kane dies he loses grip of the toy ball, it bounces down the steps in dreamlike slow motion and shatters. The original shooting script makes the meaning of this sequence clear; the glass ball with it idealized world "breaks, the fragments glittering in the first ray of the morning sun" (Mankiewicz and Welles 1971, p. 97).

Welles unites the drama of the moment of death with the moment of sunrise. Both are transitional events. In other films, like the vampire story in F. W. Murnau's film, *Nosferatu* (1921), evil men die when pierced by the morning light. (We recall the Ghost in *Hamlet* also feared the morning air.) The camera then shoots through the broken glass, toward the opening door where we see a nurse in white uniform come toward the dead man's bed. In effect, the camera thus pulls the nurse into the "incredible" world, the too-perfect fantasy world of "Rosebud," and places her there, uniform and all, with the farmhouse and snowman which represented Kane's lost boyhood.

This is more than a clever shot for it encompasses the nurse with Kane's inner world symbolized by the round glass globe and its incredible picture of home. In dynamic sense this brief scene expressed Kane's deepest wish, to have a nursing, caring mother break through his glassy world. Having seen the film's conclusion, we recall the deathly cold face the old man showed the world and the quality of rigor mortis that characterized his inability to feel. This scene also captures a portion of Kane's tragedy, for the nurse comes too late, after the ball is shattered, after Kane has died. The nurse, with all her motherly duties failed, arrives too late, except to cover the corpse, a task she does in icily correct fashion, mocking the way parents tuck in a beloved child for the night.

As Greenacre noted about other "dreams within dreams," this scene and dream within a scene contains the elements which make up

Kane's private tragedy and his actual traumata. We conclude that his mother also failed in her duties and that the boy felt exiled and bereft, as if he were dying. His little world, the sense of perfection and completion which marks the naive happiness of childhood, was shattered. The too-perfect house and snowman reflects the too-perfect, that is, childish hopes which the young boy had. The manifest symbols of snow and snowman make this clear: the boy was sent away during a snowy time.

The Recollection of Trauma

A second story within a dream sequence occurs when Thompson, a newsman sent out to solve the mystery of Kane's last word, "Rosebud," goes to read Thatcher's diary. (From the "News on the March" sequence we have already come to know Thatcher, understood that it was he who took the young boy away from his mother, and seen him denounce Kane as nothing more or less than a Communist.) In a grotesquely cold and Kafakesque "library" done with "all the warmth and charm of Napoleon's tomb" (Mankiewicz and Welles 1971, p. 133), Thompson reads how Thatcher took the boy away. From the white of the diary's pages the scene dissolves into a field of white snow and a distant figure, Charles at age five (which contradicts Thatcher's statement that the boy was age six. In the real world, such an error bespeaks an unconscious desire on Thatcher's part to age the boy, thus making his cruelty less severe).

In this scene, lasting only a few minutes, we see enacted the drama of Charlie's family and the grotesque errors carried out "for the child's own good." In a series of sparse, choreographed movements, three adults, mother, father, and the banker, decide the boy's fate while the boy plays in the snow. To make this scene work, Welles and his cameraman, Gregg Toland, had to keep each of the four players in constant contact with one another visually, on a line of sight that appears, to the viewer, to be fifty or sixty feet long.

As in the opening scene, where a lighted window in a dark castle draws our eyes to it, our eyes are drawn to the young boy cavorting in the snow. This scene parallels the previous scene of the nurse captured in the glass ball. Welles makes the viewer assume the boy's location in space and in a psychological portrait as well. We see, at first, only the boy at play in a vast field of snow, just as we saw, at first, only the picturesque house in an unreal snow storm.

As the camera pulls back we see that we are looking through a window, from the perspective of Mrs. Kane. She calls out to her son, "Be careful, Charles!" When the aged Kane peers at the glass ball and recalls the sorrow it evokes in him, he replicates his mother's feelings when she peered out at her son as she prepared to give him away to Mr. Thatcher and the bank. Thatcher's voice breaks this spell as he hurries Mrs. Kane along to the legal paperwork. The camera pulls back again, to reveal Mr. Thatcher, a very "stuffy young man" (Mankiewicz and Welles 1971, p. 137). Then we hear the father's voice, "You people seem to forget that I'm the boy's father." Once more, the camera pulls back further and we see Mr. Kane, a folksy character who complains but does not fight for his boy: "If I want to, I can go to court. A father has the right to."

In the father's compact speech we learn that a boarder in Mrs. Kane's rooming house had given her stock (or deed) certificates to an abandoned gold mine. The boarder, Fred Graves—a name that echoes his job as a miner and his death—thus makes Mrs. Kane sole owner of a fortune and with that power she divorces her son from his father. Mr. Kane loses the battle with his wife and Mr. Thatcher to whom the law and money are absolutes.

This scene, reproduced below, shows the two men struggling for control of the boy's fate. It reverberates with the future tragedy of Charles and it echoes, also, one of Orson Welles's losses. For just as Kane Senior and Mr. Thatcher struggle for control of the young boy, Welles's father struggled with another man, a dazzling Jewish doctor, Maurice Bernstein, who insisted upon becoming the protector and mentor of the young Orson Welles. The doctor so insinuated himself into the Welles household that Orson quickly came to calling him "Dadda" (Brady 1989). Bernstein retained his mentor–caretaking role even into the production of the movie. When Welles broke his ankle, Bernstein was flown cross country to Hollywood where he tended Welles constantly (Brady, pp. 257–258).

But Kane Senior is impotent. Even though his intuition is correct, that the boy should remain home, he fails to protect his son. His language, homespun and awkward, "I don't hold with signing my boy away to any bank as guardeen," marks him as intellectually weaker than Mr. Thatcher, who oozes correctness and superiority. When Kane Senior repeats his complaint, his wife, now steely with purpose, cuts him off: "I want you to stop all this nonsense, Jim." This is how one might discipline a rowdy dog.

Mr. Thatcher intones again that since Mrs. Kane is the sole owner of the Colorado Lode (the magical, anal stuff given to her by an underground personage) she has *unlimited and absolute power* to dispose of her son the way she wishes. Kane Senior tries one last time: "anyone'd think I hadn't been a good husband and a good father." Mrs. Kane silences him again and signs the documents which will force Charles away from his home. As she does so Mr. Kane walks toward the win-

dow, through which we can still see Charles playing.
Just before the window closes we hear Charles cry out, "If the rebels want a fight boys, let's give it to 'em! The terms are unconditional surrender. Up and at 'em The Union is forever!" This line, "The Union is forever," derives from the Civil War, which ended the year Charles was born. (The year being 1870 and Charles being five years old.) The "Union" effected by his birth made the couple a family, just as the "Union" effected by the North's victory in the Civil War made the country whole. A new civil war, between husband and wife, takes place in the boy's house, except this time the union between child and parents is dissolved.

A commodity, the "mother lode" of gold, destroys authentic mothering and makes authentic fathering impossible. Charles' father, Kane Senior, did not fight to the end. He surrendered his son to the power of filthy lucre and so turned him into another commodity, just as slaves were human beings turned into commodities by their owners. Kane Senior closes the window; the glass separates child and father, just as the glass ball separates Kane's isolated moments of joy from himself.

Then Mrs. Kane goes back to the window and opens it; for this brief moment she undoes the consequences of her actions. She has secretly packed the boy's trunk, tells Mr. Thatcher that and leads the two men out into the snow where Charles continues to play in blissful ignorance. Mr. Thatcher introduces himself, and then Kane Senior calls to his boy, "Charlie." The boy runs toward his father, who has squatted down to receive the boy into his arms. Before the boy can reach his father, Mrs. Kane calls him back: "Mr. Thatcher is going to take you on a trip with him tonight, Charles."

In a battle prefigured in "News on the March!" Charles strikes his new, pseudofather with his sled, "Rosebud," kicks his ankles and asks: "Why aren't you comin' with us, Mom?" To this question the movie gives a partial answer: Kane Senior, seeing his son attack a guest, says, "What that kid needs is a good thrashing!" Mrs. Kane says that is why the boy must be raised "where you can't get at him." On one level Mrs. Kane protests that she sends her boy away because she loves him; she doesn't want her husband to thrash him. Yet, there is no evidence that Kane Senior is a violent man; he does not drink, for example. Nor is his son afraid of him; as the previous scene made clear, Charles adores his "Pop." The young boy's play is that of a robust male child: he fights for just causes (the "Union"), identifies with heroes (he tells his imaginary enemies, "You can't lick Andy Jackson! Old Hickory, that's me!"), and he is creative (describing his snow man, "See, Mom? I took the pipe out of

Mrs. Kane signs away her son, Mr. Kane complies.

his mouth. If it keeps on snowin', maybe I'll make some teeth and whiskers").

These are all signs of a happy, contented child who identifies easily with men, especially his father. We are as much puzzled by Mrs. Kane's reasoning as is the boy. Here the conceit of Kane's dying word, "Rosebud," gains more stature. For it is puzzling in a way that Mrs. Kane's actions are puzzling. At the film's manifest level, Mrs. Kane appears worried and affectionate toward her son. Yet, at the film's latent level is the undeniable message that her actions are cruel. In response to this singular fact, movie critics, like Pauline Kael, dismiss this core theme as maudlin and pandering to the prejudices of American audiences who wished to see the very rich destroyed by their wealth. This may be true, but Kael does not reflect upon the actual suffering wealth can inflict upon children. Many clinicians have treated someone who inherited a fortune, or treated someone close to such a person. There, in the secrecy of the consultation, one hears in detail how a large trust fund, for example a few million dollars to be given to a young man at his twenty-fifth birthday, destroys his sense of competency and power. The money becomes the organizing center of his life. All his plans for marriage, career, education, indeed all his relationships center around the day the cash is his. In the meantime, he has not matured emotionally and has not achieved the psychic distance necessary between himself and his parents. Many such men turn into what Thatcher calls Kane, "a lucky scoundrel, spoiled, unscrupulous, irresponsible" (Mankiewicz and Welles, p. 148).

Kane's fate was much worse than the child born into money. For the latter child, money is an ordinary part of life. While money may become constitutive of all relationships between the child and the child's environment, for example between the child and the governess hired to be kind, money does not separate the child from the child's parents. But this is exactly what the gold mine did to Kane: the "good fortune" visited upon his family became the single reason (or excuse) his mother used to tear him away from his home.

Perverse Actions and Their Representations

Because the movie had to pass the film censors, one never sees actual perverse sexual actions (though the original script contains numerous references to perverse activities). Charlie's perversions are symbolized in his profession, Yellow Journalism, and in the story's dreamlike sequences. Yellow Journalism deals exclusively with crime, sexuality, and criminal perversions; in all such publications are stories about every variety of perversion, including homosexuality, fetishism, telephone perversions, transvestism, transsexualism, masochism, voyeurism, pedophilia, exhibitionism, and coprophilia.

The sled denotes the last moment the boy was loved apart from his money. It represents a state of being for which he searches throughout the film. Losing that state evokes rage and desolation for mother has turned her child over to an institution, a bank, that makes live things dead. The bank turns mothering into anal objects; the gold lode, the sixth-largest fortune in the world. Charlie's rage is split: he wishes to make all others do his will, to shame and attack the bankers, especially "Mr. Thatcher," and to relocate the idealized image of love as conceived by a five-year-old child.

The third scene Kael disliked shows Charles meeting Susan, a twenty-one-year-old woman who will become his second wife. In an occult mood (Gay 1989) Kane searches for his lost youth, something missing since his childhood. Spurred on by his yearning he looks for something that will be given to him from out of the blue. We learn that just before he met Susan he was on his way to visit one of his warehouses, containing his mother's belongs and, we surmise, the sled, "Rosebud." Kael calls this scene Hollywood "Meet cute." The genre is a variation on the theme of "somewhere there's a special person," that "love is fate," that "this love was meant to be," that it was "made in heaven." "Meet cute" scenes, with endless variations, are always "chance" meetings dictated by the characters' internal needs and by the conventions of theatre. They are not trivial. Such meetings are fated and occult. They represent long-repressed yearnings to receive from heavenly powers, from the idealized mother, ceaseless love, flowing from what Keats called the "millioned pleasured breast."

Through the magic of identification, they evoke similar yearnings in the viewer. In *Citizen Kane* the occult moment occurs at the end of a rain storm, when Susan emerges from a drug store and sees Kane standing on the street corner, without a taxi or his limousine. She arrives in time to see him splashed by a passing carriage: he is a waif, lost and puzzled by the big city. She rescues the lost boy—magically— since her apartment is right next to the drug store.

As Kane struggles to clean his expensive coat, Susan offers him hot water to clean his face, the way all mothers do. She suffers from a toothache and yet rescues him from the outdoors. Kane treats her childhood ailment, the toothache, in school-boy fashion: he will get her mind off from it (rather than pay for a late night dentist). In this mood (made nonsexual by Susan's insisting that Kane not shut her apartment door) they play children's games: Kane makes shadow figures and charms Susan out of her toothache.

In a sharp transition from this mood, Kane learns that Susan's mother wished Susan to be a singer of "grand" opera. Susan says "You know how mothers can be," and Kane replies, "Yes, I know." He mumbles these words with a far away look and then turns toward Susan his "maternal" affection: that is, he will treat Susan the way his mother treated him. He will "love" Susan the way he was loved. He will give her the very things she does not want or need.

On the manifest level all is sweetness and light. But on hearing of her mother's plans for Susan's life, which parallel his mother's plans for his life, Kane's mood changes and he takes up where her mother left off. He will transform Susan, an ordinary, normal woman, into a work of art, an opera star. He will magnify himself and her; she will *become* someone worthwhile, an opera singer. She is not lovable in herself, just as the little boy was not lovable in himself; money determined everything. Susan tries to protect herself from this awful repetition when she states honestly that her voice is not that good and she does not share her mother's grandiose hopes.

Under the guise of love but with the intention of torture, Kane exposes Susan to as much humiliation as possible, in retribution for the horrors his mother visited upon him. He both identifies with the aggressor (his mother) and identifies his protégé with mother: she will be destroyed with "love." Just as the pedophile may identify himself both with his target and with his mother whose love he receives through the fantasy of the perverted action, Kane parents the way he was parented. As Susan says later, Kane gives her anything she *might* want, such as her own opera house, but nothing she really *does* want. Kane learned at age six that he could have anything he might want—like expensive toys or a new sled—but not what he needed: to remain at home with his family where "the union is forever." Kane duplicates his suffering and destroys Susan. He drives her to attempt suicide and to destroy herself with alcohol, having lost all the money that was once hers. Because he explained his own torturous childhood as the result of his inner badness, Kane struggled to find a career that counteracted his "wrongness." He wasted as much of his inheritance as possible, and chose careers that seemed to proclaim his humanitarian impulses; his newspapers would expose corruption, he would become the governor who cleaned up the state.

Unable to fathom the depth of his guilt, he sabotages his efforts. With great skill the film shows us Kane, strutting in front of a huge poster showing his face, promising to destroy corruption in the state as soon as he becomes governor. Peering down at him is Boss Jim W. Geddes, Kane's target. Peering up at him is his son by his first wife, a niece of the president. His son (indeed his entire camp) is sure of his success and asks if he is governor yet. This repeats Kane's boyhood struggle to persuade his father to become powerful and protect him. But just as Kane's father was humiliated by Mr. Thatcher, who "stole" the boy away from his home, so too Kane is humiliated by Boss Geddes (who protests that Kane's newspapers have offended his mother). Kane's son will discover that Kane is a weakling and is forced to abandon his high hopes for reform. To round out the tragedy, Kane loses his boy who is whisked away because of the scandal that surrounds Kane's affair with Susan.

Emotional Affordances in Citizen Kane

When he grew up Kane learned that "art" was valued and proper: so he bought as much as he could. He plundered other peoples' holdings, just as he plundered castles and other noble buildings to construct his grotesque house, Xanadu. Plundering is another perversion of desire, the desire to hold and to collect. To plunder is to destroy art, to take it away from others who might find in it actual affordances for emotional growth and communication. Kane collects art in order to hold it, keep it in boxes, to dump it into a vast warehouse of stuff and to prevent others from enjoying it.

Just as King Claudius destroyed Hamlet's world, Kane seeks to turn the fine arts into detritus, into junk. Early versions of the *Citizen Kane* script contain detailed exposés of Kane's perversion. In those versions when Kane reaches his twenty-fifth birthday Thatcher visits him to terminate the bank's guardianship. Kane receives him in an elegant Italian ballroom. There he conducts a party filled with "pimps, Lesbians, dissipated army officers, homosexuals, nymphomaniacs and international society tramps" (Brady 1989, p. 240). Kane assembles these assorted perverts in order to shock Thatcher and to waste his fortune all the more quickly. When he takes on the *Inquirer* newspaper he notes how even losing a million dollars a year he can continue for sixty more years. These few comments on the film only touch on one aspect of the story and the theme of irreconcilable loss. The film's story is more complex than this. The film's artistic merits, especially its pace and emotional excitement, cannot be reduced to its themes. Among the acknowledged "classic" films, *Citizen Kane* remains a provocative experience. The brilliance of its editing, sound overlaps, dissolves, casting, music, staging, and pace is rightly celebrated and studied fifty years after its appearance.

Because it is a classic and widely known I have referred to it in this study of aesthetic experience and emotional affordances. I have tried to show that the concept of emotional affordance lets us amplify traditional analytic concepts of the lost object and the process of sublimation. In classical formulations, sublimation refers to the fate of instinctual forces, especially sexual drives. Perversions were explained as alternatives to sublimation. This was a valuable theorem, for it let Freud unite his theory of culture with his theory of neurosis. Yet it made the process of sublimation mysterious: it was an event that occurred to the instincts, it had little to do with conscious experience.

The invisible aspects of sublimation, I suggest, should be linked with the invisible qualities of infant–parent interactions. Specifically, I have suggested that benign self and self–object relationships rest upon invisible exchanges between parent and child or between any two persons who love each other. It is not mother's claims of love that provide emotional sustenance. It is her preconscious ability to communicate back to her child that the child's emotional state resonates with her own. These subtle forms of communication make possible the perception of emotional affordances.

Just as human beings can calculate instantaneously the ideal structure of visual and other affordances, so too we calculate the presence or absence of emotional affordances. To be near such an affordance is to be connected, understood, and therefore protected from the terrors of schizoid loneliness. Art that does this, through the numerous sensory modes available to it, accomplishes the same task. We see Kane's life and pity him and ourselves. As Aristotle said two thousand years ago, art renews us because it arouses terror and then pity. Art invokes our losses and threats, and then, by the act of communicating these worlds to us, provides a moment of reconciliation. Artists understand something true but invisible about being a conscious human being and communicate that insight through their art.

Conclusion

Emotional affordances refer to tangible, real, intense, and memorable features of interactions between ourselves and others. They are the antithesis of perverse actions. For perverse actions symbolize intangible, fantastic, and compulsive efforts to fabricate real affordances. The memory of such an affordance appears in a delicate scene in *Citizen Kane*. Mr. Thompson, the newsman sent out to investigate the meaning of the word "Rosebud," asks Bernstein, Kane's lifelong friend (whose name is that of Welles's "Dadda") what Bernstein thinks it means. Bernstein responds, perhaps "Rosebud" refers to a girl? Thompson responds that it is hardly likely Kane would recall the name of a girl he met fifty years ago.[11]

Bernstein, sitting in a huge CEO office with a rain storm pounding against the giant windows, says that Mr. Thompson is pretty young. (The rain storm recalls the rain storm which brought Susan and Kane together originally.) People remember the small parts of life too. He adds: (shooting script directions in brackets)

> You take me. One day, back in 1896, I was crossing over to Jersey on a ferry and as we pulled out there was another ferry pulling in [slowly]—and on it there was a girl waiting to get off. A white dress she had on—and she was carrying a white parasol—and I only saw her for one second and she didn't see me at all—but I'll bet a month hasn't gone by since that I haven't thought of that girl. [Triumphantly] See what I mean![Smiles] (Mankiewicz and Welles, pp. 153–155)

This fine moment, which Welles said was the best thing in the movie (Brady 1989, p. 275), underscores Kane's loneliness, for it is Bernstein who can recall this moment of loveliness and promise, not Kane. The pristine girl—woman, white dress and white parasol, is coming in, while Bernstein is pulling out. Therefore they cannot meet. But Bernstein is able to recall this one second of feminine, virginal, sexual beauty as an affordance that continues to sustain him. His triumph is over the brash young reporter searching for the clue to the "Rosebud" mystery. Pursuing a "hard nosed" thesis, Thompson misses entirely the answer contained in Bernstein's speech: "Rosebud" refers to the lost parent, that is, to the lost mother and father who did not sustain their boy the way that Bernstein is sustained by a single glimpse of earthly beauty.

Freud pursued the thesis that sublimation must be something that occurs within the mind, that is, within the mental apparatus as it struggles against the instinctual drives, especially those which lead to perverse sexual actions. Psychoanalysts who followed refined this thesis and claimed that sublimation is also an ego achievement in which the ego uses its archaic heritage of fantasy as a resource for solving old problems in a new way. I have suggested yet another layer to this notion of sublimation and proposed that the words "perversion" and "sublimation" refer neither to modes of sexual congress nor intimations of sexuality, but to forms of object relatedness. It is premature to conclude that there can be no mature homosexual love, for example, because the sex organs employed are not those of heterosexuality. Rather, our task is to examine empathically the emotional texture of a person's life and assess how that person perceives the vitality of other persons, other beings, and nature. In perversion the self closes down upon itself and seeks incorrectly sustenance from its archaic fantasies. In sublimation the self opens up toward the horizon of emotional affordances and discovers there ways to make the unseen ties that link self to self visible in the work of art.

NOTES

Introduction

1. *The Sexuality of Christ in Renaissance Art and Modern Oblivion.* New York: Pantheon/October. The book raises many questions about the cult of Mary and her divine station in folk religion as well. See Steinberg's arguments against cover ups and see his documentation of the evasions of many scholars about this form of art on pp. 8–9. See also his extensive notes in the last third of the book. Is there evidence from history of childhood studies about the practice of manipulating an infant's penis and its use in the period? See de Mausse et al. (1974). What do we know of the history of the sixteenth-century child-rearing practices? Why did taste in religious art change? What relationships exist between this celebration of the body and the baby (and Mary's breast) with other socialpolitical structures of the period? One might say that these paintings focus upon Christ's penis and therefore the phallus, yet it is difficult to see them as phallocentric or as displays of male dominance. First, these paintings, depict the penis, not the erect penis, (except in the few sketches that Steinberg describes). Second, these paintings are not attacks on femininity, at least not on mothering, nor on the female breast, nor on Mary's perfection. Third, these paintings, at least on the surface, celebrate the infant–maternal bond to the detriment of neither person.

2. He retrieves the term *humanation* from seventeenth-century English to parallel the theological term *incarnation.*

3. See Mary's canopy over the genitals of the sleeping infant, on p. 43, 44, and many other illustrations in the text as well.

4. See his note on p. 81

5. What historical resources are available regarding this question? Answers to these questions will not be simple. Steinberg notes that even during this two-hundred-year period of the undisguised representation of Christ's sexuality (or any sexuality?) there were efforts to repress them "even while these works were created" (1983, p. 180). The disfiguring of these paintings and sculptures continues into our time. Steinberg says that many esteemed scholars failed to inform their public readers that restored paintings, for example those of Madonna and Child, had suffered obvious mutilations.

6. For a rigorous attempt to meld Freud's "classical" theory of the instincts with contemporary object relations theory, see Otto Kernberg (1976). Kernberg does not focus upon the issues of "qualities" and "quantities" as I do. Rather he retains Freud's language about the process of sublimation. I discuss Kernberg's important work in chapter 4.

7. Under the umbrella of *structuralist* one may place the fundamental works of Claude Lévi-Strauss and Jean Piaget, and those of numerous contemporary authors who employ multidisciplinary points of view to elaborate complex descriptions of social and psychological structures. For example, see Blau and Merton (1981). In addition to the extensive, technical literature in philosophy and phenomenology, one will find a rich tradition in the scientific study of religion. It ranges from Eliade's essays on myths, through Carl Jung's essays and those of his students, to the work of many contemporary authors, e.g., Howard Harrod (1982).

Chapter 1. Art and the Organization of the Self

1. "Degas's Brothels: Voyeurism and Ideology," *Representation* (1987) 158–185. See also Greenacre's own essays in applied psychoanalysis, *Swift and Carroll: A Psychoanalytic Study of Two Lives*. New York: International Universities Press, 1955.

2. On primary process thought and film, see Christian Metz, *The Imaginary Signifier: Psychoanalysis and the Cinema*, Bloomington: Indiana University Press, 1977. For the views of a practicing psychoanalyst see Harvey R. Greenberg, *The Movies on Your Mind*, New York: Saturday Review Press, 1975. For an excellent history of the horror film in all its variations understood in classical psychoanalytic forms, see James B. Twitchell, *Dreadful Pleasures: An Anatomy of Modern Horror*, New York: Oxford, 1985. For a series of thoughtful articles on the relationship between fantasy, especially cinematic fantasy, and political structure, see *Formations of Fantasy*, eds. Victor Burgin, James Donald, and Cora Kaplan, London: Methuen, 1986. Among many excellent articles see Carol J. Clover, "Her Body, Himself: Gender in Slasher Films," *Representations*, (1987) 20:187–227. Also see Robert S. Parigi, "Reading the Entrails: Splatter Cinema and the Post-Modern Body," (1982) *Art Criticism*, vol 4. no. 2:1–18.

3. See Eric Auerbach's noted essay on this theme in *Mimesis* (1953), especially his comments: "The Homeric poems conceal nothing, they contain no teaching and no secret meaning. Homer can be analyzed... but he cannot be interpreted" (p. 13). For a related discussion see Thomas R. Martland's study (1981) on religion and art as foundational experiences, prior to science in all its foms (*Religion as Art: An Interpretation*. Albany: SUNY Press).

4. On the Rat Man see Freud, 1909d.

5. See also Kohut on self–object transferences, in his 1977, 1979, 1984.

6. Shengold derives this from Steegmuller, 1972, p. 109.

7. See Fraiberg's classic papers (1980). See also Stern's discussion (1985), pp. 112 ff. On the ubiquity of adults harming children see also Lloyd deMause (1982) especially his short note, "What Incest Barrier?" (1988). This topic includes the deep issues surrounding child abuse and the genesis and

persistence of the archaic superego which one finds alive and well in contemporary patients.

8. These accounts, these private myths, do not show "meaningfulness" in the strict sense of that term. See Sperber, (1974) who argues that the term meaning is best ascribed to utterances which show both "paraphrasability and analyticity."

9. See structural studies of Rotinese mythology using the principles of Claude Lévi-Strauss in Fox (1988).

10. In his review article, Kaplan (1988) summarizes well many of the difficulties inherent in "applied psychoanalysis." He cautions against a too programmatic view of applied psychoanalysis and cites approvingly Kenneth Burke's (1967) vigorous and metaphorical reflections on psychoanalysis and art. In one sense Kaplan's point is irrefutable, since art always entails a notion of creativity and creativity always entails a notion of unpredictability. Therefore there can be no "theory" of art since there can be no rigorous theory of the unpredictable. But if Kaplan were entirely correct, the clinician could not rely upon the applied study of art to contribute to psychoanalysis. Following Freud's lead, Ernst Kris (1952), trained both in art history and clinical psychoanalysis, advanced an ego psychology of artistic creation as did Heinz Hartmann in his programmatic essays (1964). Contemporary ego psychologists have also addressed themselves to the "ego qualities" inherent in the sensuous surface. Among these authors are Noy (1973), Rose (1980), and Kaplan (1988).

Chapter 2. Freud and The Location of Values

1. For example, see Jones (1953) and Ellenberger (1970).

2. For example, Harold Bloom (1973) and Francesco Orlando (1971). See also Andrew Brink (1977).

3. The Concordance to the SE lists one reference only to Freud's use of the term *nostalgia.* It occurs in the phrase *nostalgic dream,* which translates the German *Sehnsuchtstraum,* SE 5:624; GW 17:22. On the "oceanic feeling" see Freud 1930a, pp. 64–68, 72. Also see J. M. Masson (1980).

4. See F. Deutsch (1957) and Erik Erikson (1962).

5. For example, see Frederick Crews, ed. (1970) and his next book (1975).

6. Private communication, I. Schiffer, MD, Toronto, Ontario.

7. It is interesting to compare these typical examples with young men and horses. In some literary works the horse's phallic characteristics are used to set off the boy's own phallic striving and his anxious response to those dangerous wishes. His fascination with horses seems to cover up deeper feelings about the dangers of the father. In D. H. Lawrence's story "The Rocking Horse Winner" and in Peter Schafer's play *Equus,* boys are overwhelmed by horses. Self-destruction and castration anxiety dominate both stories. Lawrence seems concerned to describe the former. In his story, the element of the fantastic predominates. The young boy employs his furious, masturbatory, rocking to induce an altered state of consciousness, and then, like a shaman, divines the outcome of events not yet taken place. Castration wishes and anxieties are more obvious in Schafer's play about a

boy compelled to puncture the eyes of horses, just as Oedipus put out his own eyes upon learning of his oedipal crime.

8. Feffer (1982) argues the opposite point of view. He criticizes Freud for remaining too Cartesian, for assigning some qualities to the external world. Instead, Feffer seeks to expand the constructionist elements in Freud's thought. Under this revised formula, psychoanalysis would include theorems about the child's "construction" of space and time as elucidated by Piaget and his disciples.

9. The "Project" was not intended for public considerations. Hence Freud's nomenclature is often untidy and confusing. In the handwritten text he used the Greek letters whose Latin names are Phi, Psi, and Omega. Freud refers often to the latter as the "w" system since the lower-case German letter resembles the Greek lower-case Omega. I follow him in this.

10. The extensive work of Lacan and his followers is relevant to this aspect of Freud's thought. However, I am not convinced by the general mode of attack that seeks to replace Freud's much criticized economic metapsychology with one based on linguistics. I think Freud is a structuralist, but not a linguistic one. On the contrary, I believe his is more a "biogenetic" structuralist whose fundamental assumptions and hopes are closer to those of sociobiology and psychobiology, especially the work of Wilson (1975; Lumsden and Wilson 1981). I consider this at length in chapter 4. See also Gay 1982, "Semiotics as metapsychology", and d'Aquili, et al. 1979.

11. I distinguish "structure" from "form." Structure refers to the abstract relationships that exist between distinct elements of the text or artifact. It is demarcated by hierarchical theorems. In this sense both traditional and transformational grammars are structural; each aims to give an account of the small number of sentence types out of which the infinite number of actual sentences are composed. Parsons's attempts to rank types of societies (1966), as well as types of social theories, are also structural in this sense, for he wishes to reveal the hidden patterns that underlie the seeming diversity of societies and social theory. Indeed, this is a common element of most contemporary sciences; their practitioners seek to find the simple patterns and elements that underlie the oddities and confusions on the surface, which ordinary mortals perceive as real. (See Simon 1977 and van Gigch 1974.)

"Form" may refer to the object's actual appearance, to its particularity, or its "aura," as Benjamin (1936) described it. Gilbert Rose's excellent essay on psychoanalytic aesthetics (1980) is noteworthy because it stresses the formal qualities of a work of art. For these features distinguish mediocrity from genius. It is the nuance and shading of a soprano's voice that distinguishes her from all other sopranos, for good or ill. We expect a good critic to have a good ear, or a good eye, or a good nose. All these gifts are gifts of the senses, not the mind. Of course, the more a critic knows about the particular art and its history, the better. Noy (1973) also considers the issue of form and formal qualities of the work of art in his many important pieces on psychoanalytic aesthetics.

Chapter 3. Sublimation and the Mystery of Transformation

1. Quotation from Bertram 1974. See additional issues of the "sublime" in New

Testament texts as the control of hubris and other narcissistic dangers. See also Bertram 1974, "Hupsos" in Kittel 1974, Vol. 8, pp. 602–620.

2. For substantial reviews of the concept see Jones 1916; Glover 1931; Levy 1939; J. C. Flugel 1942; Hart 1948; Lichtenberg 1949; Kris 1952; Arlow 1955; Kaywin 1966. For descriptive studies see Sharpe 1930 and 1935; Roheim 1941; Schmideberg 1947; Segal 1952; Benveniste 1953–55; Odier 1954; Marcuse 1955; Brown 1959; Baudoin 1950; Sandler and Joffe 1966; Oremland 1975.

3. Arieti illustrates this in his book, *Creativity: The Magic Synthesis* (1976). Although he uses terms derived from Freud and from cognitive psychology, his notion of a "tertiary" process which underlies creative thinking repeats pre-Freudian theories which also isolated "creative" (or veridical) thinking from ordinary thinking. His title denotes his major claim: creativity is a magical process. The deep ambiguity of the term *sublimation* is similar to the ambiguity one finds surrounding key terms in Marx. Robert Heilbroner (1980), no enemy of Marxist thought, noted that the central concept of "labor value" remains undefined and probably undefinable within classical Marxist treatises. Since labor value is that worth which the worker imparts to an object or product and which the capitalist is said to expropriate unfairly this ambiguity remains a serious difficulty for Marxists.

4. The total number includes variations of the term.

5. Religion is the earliest form of sublimation according to Nunberg and Federn 1967, p. 149.

6. Theoreticians who followed him, particularly Hartmann, Kris, and Loewenstein, developed the idea of fusion and its relationship to the mysteries of sublimation.

Chapter 4. Origins of Complex Behavior and Sublimation

1. Pike, *Language in Relation*, p. 41, also quoted in L. Fisher and O. Werner, "Explaining Explanation: Tension in American Anthropology," *Journal of Anthropological Research* 34 (1978): 194–218. They debate Marvin Harris on the usefulness of the terms *emic/etic* and rightly criticize him for assigning to the latter alone the rank of "true science." But wrongly conclude the term is but another version of the insider/outsider distinction and should therefore be laid to rest (p. 197). They argue, "harmful bacteria exist in some culturally defined worlds, but not in others" (p. 202). Some native medical traditions may not use the concept bacteria; it hardly follows that the lack of a name is adequate to refute a general truth claim, i.e., that there are tiny plants which cause infection and disease in all people. Fisher and Werner collapse the distinction between things and their names; just as many others confuse a difference in color terms with a difference in the ways distinct peoples "perceive" the spectrum. See also Alan Dundes (1963) and S. Lindenbaum (1979). The latter studied how a New Guinea tribe created mythic explanations of a major crises: the sudden death of young women. Scientific research yielded an answer contrary to the tribe's spiritualist explanation: a virus remained living in the brains of dead human beings whom the tribe ate. Since the Kuru women ate more brain tissue than the men they tended to contract the viral disease more frequently.

2. Robert G. Greenler, et al., "The 46 Degree Halo and Its Arcs," *Science* 206 (1979); 648–649. St. Thomas Aquinas amplified the difference between the natural and the hermeneutic sciences in his famous discussion of the two kinds of truths of Scripture:

> Any truth can be manifested in two ways: by things or by words. Words signify things and one thing can signify another. The Creator of things, however, can not only signify anything by words, but can also make one thing signify another. That is why the Scriptures contain a twofold truth. One lies in the things meant by the words used—that is the literal sense. The other in the way things become figures of other things, and in this consists the spiritual sense. (Thomas Aquinas 1926, p. 275)

3. We esteem those who articulate crucial features of our social system from within and so tell everyone what they always knew but had not recognized. Thus Aristotle's "discovery" of the existence of tense, like Plato's earlier elaboration of the noun–verb distinction, is counted as one of his major philosophic achievements. See John Lyons, *Introduction to Theoretical Linguistics* (Cambridge: Cambridge University Press, 1968), pp. 10–11. Great novelists, like Jane Austin and Henry James, are esteemed as creative artists because of their uncanny ability to record exquisite facts of social life. Many of Freud's most brilliant formulations elucidate structures which had lain embedded in the matrix of social conventions. For example, his basic concept of *resistance* is, in part, an intrapsychic analogue of a social interaction in which one person resists the entreaties of another:

> I now became insistent—if I assured them that they did know it, that it would appear to their minds—then, in the first cases, something did actually occur to them. . . . After this I became still more insistent; I told the patients to lie down and deliberately close their eyes in order to "concentrate". . . . I then found that without any hypnosis new recollections emerged which went further back and which probably related to our topic. Experiences like this made me think that it would in fact be possible for the pathogenic groups of ideas, that were after all certainly present, to be brought to light by mere insistence; and since this insistence involved effort on my part and so suggested the idea that I had to overcome a resistance, the situation led me at once to the theory that *by means of my psychical work I had to overcome a psychical force in the patients which was opposed to the pathogenic ideas becoming conscious (being remembered).* (S. Freud and Josef Breuer, *Studies on Hysteria* (London: Hogarth Press, 1955 [1895], SE 2: 268, emphasis his)

4. Raffael Scheck, "Did the Children's Crusade of 1212 Really Consist of Children? Problems Of Writing Childhood History" in *The Journal of Psychohistory,* 1988 (vol. 16, no. 2), pp. 176–182. He cites Ernst Bloch, *Aufklaerung und Teufelsglaubae.* Rede [sic] in Salzburg 1971. Cassette ex libris, Zuerich.

5. Lamrack: see E. Jones, 1955 vol. 2, pp. 194–195

6. This logical feature of emic analyses has led the critics of emic analytic methods, like form criticism or psychoanalysis, to demand a complete confession of the "scientific" suppositions which undergrid their methods. Such defenses are difficult to make since they require one to elucidate ever more fundamental, hence ever more obscure, emic systems, e.g., the a

priori structure of one's language or the nature of scientific inquiry. Religious forms, like theologies and rituals, have similar tasks: to protect the arbitrary codes with which distinct cultures define themselves. Religion joins the struggle against entropy and against the dissolution of meaning. Anthony Wilden says in his critique of Lévi-Strauss (1972), to understand why one set of mythic operators, e.g., dominant males, occurs in a culture's myth we must know for whom—what classes—they were composed and who maintained them. One need not adopt a Marxist attitude to assert that while it seems true that mythic thought can use any set of objects as it operators, e.g., honey and ashes, it also seems true that some groups will benefit more from some myths, e.g., Eve emerging out of Adam's rib, than they will from others. Mythic thought (and unconscious thought) operates with a potpourri of artifacts and symbols and so appears undetermined. Lévi-Strauss claims he has discovered the laws which govern the production of myths. However, in contrast to the phonemes, "mythemes" are rich in content and meaningful elements in their own right. That mythic thought requires contrasting pairs, etc., may be a universal feature of human cognition; that women are portrayed as secondary help-mates is a feature peculiar to male-dominated societies. I said earlier it was wrong to assume that because language incorporates an emic system, all representational systems are essentially linguistic or that psychological or cultural systems are structured like a language.

Theology, art criticism, and psychoanalysis do not permit their practioners the luxury of simply translating a message from one language to another. Following Wilden (1972) we note that their susceptibility to reinterpretation makes religious stories and other myths the bane of authoritarian regimes. When the once untouchable Bible became available to the masses revolutionary interpretations of papal authority were suddenly made possible.

A well-formed system that incorporates distinctive features permits translation. The following chart from Singh and Singh (1976) arranges English consonants according to the presence or absence of seven distinctive features:

A feature-by-consonant matrix showing seven distinctive features and twenty-four consonants

	Consonant*																							
Feature	p	t	k	b	d	g	f	v	θ	ð	s	z	tʃ	dʒ	ʃ	3	m	n	ŋ	j	r	l	w	h
Voicing	0	0	0	1	1	1	0	1	0	1	0	1	0	1	0	1	1	1	1	1	1	1	1	0
Nasality	0	0	0	0	0	0	0	0	0	0	0	0	0	0	0	0	1	1	1	0	0	0	0	0
Continuancy	0	0	0	0	0	0	1	1	1	1	1	1	0	0	1	1	0	0	0	0	0	0	0	1
Sibilancy	0	0	0	0	0	0	0	0	0	0	1	1	1	1	1	1	0	0	0	0	0	0	0	0
Front	1	1	0	1	1	0	1	1	1	1	1	1	0	0	0	0	1	1	0	0	1	1	0	0
Sonorancy	0	0	0	0	0	0	0	0	0	0	0	0	0	0	0	0	1	1	1	1	1	1	1	0
Liability	1	0	0	1	0	0	1	1	0	0	0	0	0	0	0	0	1	0	0	0	1	0	1	0

*1, feature present; 0, feature absent.

This matrix is also a translation device. For if the chart is valid, it lets us designate exclusively each consonant using a binary name. For example, we could designate the phoneme /p/ as "0000101." We could designate the phoneme /h/ as "0010000."

7. On the fear of change see Castelnuovo-Tedesco 1984; 1989.

Chapter 5. Perception and Emotion in Classical Theory and Contemporary Authors

1. "I am conscious of myself, not as I appear to myself, nor as I am in myself, but only that I am. This representation is a thought, not an intuition" (Kant 1781, p. 168). "Although my existence is not indeed appearance (still less mere illusion), the determination of my existence can take place only in conformity with the form of inner sense, according to the special mode in which the manifold, which I combine, is given in inner intuition. Accordingly I have no knowledge of myself as I am but merely as I appear to myself" (p. 169). Hume expressed a similar sentiment when he argued that "I never can catch myself at any time without a perception, and never can observe any thing but the perception. When my perceptions are remov'd for any time, as by sound sleep; so long am I insensible of myself, and may truly be said not to exist" (*Treatise*, 1739–40, p. 252). See Chisholm 1976, pp. 38–41 for a review of Hume's argument.

2. Single labels like "materialist" or "Darwinian" do not apply consistently to the subtle differences in thought between Helmholtz and his colleagues, such as Brücke and Du Bois-Reymond, or between Darwin himself and continental thinkers who more rigorously reject nonmaterialist theories of neurology: for example, Meynert, according to Amacher 1965, pp. 36–37, did not accept Darwin's own theory that human beings could pass on through some as yet unspecific mechanism of inheritance-learned emotions. In this sense Darwin was Lamarckian. Yet, "The difference between Darwin and Meynet was typical of the difference between the study of the organism in England and in Germany. The English were no less materialistic, but they did not tend to describe behavioral phenomena in terms of nervous mechanisms with precise anatomical locations as did the Germans" (p. 37).

3. Both the magic lantern and later the camera provided useful models of consciousness. Goethe employed the former to describe the way young Werther experienced the world—a world of bare quantities—when he had lost his love: "Wilhelm, what is the world to our hearts without love? A magic lantern without light. But as soon as you put the little lamp inside, the most colorful pictures shine on your white screen. And even if it were no more than that, no more than fleeting phantoms, it always makes us happy to stand before them like naive boys and delight in these marvelous sights" (1774, p. 27). Meynert used a camera analogy to explain how consciousness was the product of the "projection" of intercellular excitation (Jones 1953, pp. 375–376). On the magic latern and "projection" see also Lee Baily 1986, 1988.

4. He refers to Koffka 1935, and to Marrow's (1969) book on Kurt Lewin.

5. Another example of an affordance is the "rule of even spacing." "This equivalent to the rule of equal amounts of texture for equal amounts of terrain.

The fact can be stated in various ways. However stated, it seems to be a fact that can be seen, not necessarily a concept of abstract space including numbers and magnitudes. Ecological geometry does not have to be learned from textbooks" (1979, p. 162).

6. It is not accidental that some Freudians are uneasy with theories that include major hypotheses about a "self" or even ego-identity. Jung's championing a doctrine of noumenal Self, around which the psyche revolves, was only an early example of heterodoxy. Eissler (1971) lambasted Erikson's "virtuology," in part, because it emphasizes a rational, autonomous, and consciously functioning self that can "freely pledge" its loyalties.

7. See Ferenczi's letters to Freud and his letters and technical diary reported in Peter Gay 1988, pp. 577–587.

8. See also many other contemporary researchers who have contributed important findings, see Klaus et al. (1972); Klaus and Kennell (1982), Kennell and Klaus (1983), and Stern (1985). The latter authors summarize current research from a psychoanalytic point of view. See also Emde and Sorce (1983) who develop the notion of "emotional availability" along lines similar to my much more abstract notion of "emotional affordance." John Bowlby's important studies on attachment and loss prefigure many of Stern's basic objections to classical Freudian theory, see Bowlby 1973, his appendix II.

9. Freud had noted in the "Project" that sleep was characterized by paralysis of the will or motor paralysis (SE 1:337, 340). However, he did not link this fact to the concomitant increase in hallucinatory thought. He expanded his discussion in *The Interpretation of Dreams* (1900a) in the chapter on dream psychology. First he recapitulates the "Project's" theory of hallucination: "As a result of the link [between mnemic image of breast and the experience of satisfaction] that has thus been established, the next time this need arises a psychical impulse will at once emerge which will seek to re-cathect the mnemic image of the perception and to re-voke the perception itself" (1900a, pp. 565–566). He links the motor system not to the activity of perception, as Gibson argues, but to the diversion of excitation (or Qh in the "Project") away from primary process tendencies toward hallucinatory wish-fulfillment. Because motor functions are inhibited by the state of sleep, wishes from the system Ucs. may "prance upon the stage" (p. 568) with no danger, since they cannot gain access to motility.

Chapter 6. From Visual Affordances to Emotional Affordances

1. Variations on the "life is like a chicken coop ladder" include "because it's shitty from top to bottom," "a person can't get ahead because of all the shit," and "because each rung is shittier than the preceding one" (Dundes 1984, pp. 9–11). Dundes cites authorities such as Borneman (1971) who "claims that no other European people use anal erotic terms in their slang as the Germans do" (p.17).

2. See "repetition compulsion" in Freud (1920; 1927) and in others who describe the manifest features of such behavior. But it is not an explanation for such actions, other than to rename it "compulsion." For an "Object

Relations" point of view that parallels Weiss and Sampson (1986), see J. H. Rey "That which patients bring to analysis" *International Journal of Psycho-Analysis,* 1988, 69:4, pp. 457–473.

3. I derive part of this chart from Langs 1985c, p. 261. See Douglas 1914, pp. 36 ff, on Wilde's efforts to appear constantly as "elegant correctness," etc., and wearing elaborate clothing "designed subtly to convey the impression that he owned at least ten thousand acres somewhere or another" (p. 37). For a fascinating study of the grotesque in the visual arts of the same period, see Ewa Kuryluk, *Salome and Judas in the Cave of Sex.* Evanston, Ill.: Northwestern University Press, 1987. Kruyluk focuses upon the work of Aubery Beardsley's erotic and obscene drawings. Her third section, on the technique of the grotesque, parallels Janine Chasseguet-Smirgel's [(1984), *Creativity and Perversion.* New York: Norton] insights into the central place of reversal, separation, duplication, multiplication, elongation, and other means of distorting the normal body (pp. 301 ff).

4. Sullivan's lectures contain much of value, especially his focus upon the richness of the infant's experience and upon the multiple ways in which sensation of other and self enter into self-understanding. (See pp. 133–149.) I find that Stern (1985) refines these insights in his text as well. On the "anal distance" receptors see contemporary texts on urology and proctology regarding these claims. On Sullivan as a precursor to contemporary object relations theory, especially with regard to his focus upon the infant–maternal bond, see Mitchell and Greenberg 1983.

5. See citations of Milner also in Peter Fuller, *Art and Psychoanalysis* 1980. London: Readers and Writers, pp. 130–135. Fuller describes experiences with art books and medical texts that parallel those I describe from my boyhood in the introduction.

6. See Hans Sachs (1934) on the delay of the machine age.

7. On violence toward children see de Mause (1988). More subtle forms of controlling violence involve what Bollas (1987) terms "normotic illness." Parents treat the child as a "commodity in a world full of physical objects" (James 1988, p. 560). See C. Bollas, *The Shadow of the Object: Psychoanalysis of the Unthought Unknown.* London: Free Association Books, 1987. For a sensitive summary and critique see also D. Colin James's review of the book in *International Journal of Psycho-Analysis,* 1988, pp. 558–561.

Chapter 7. Emotional Affordances and Their Representations

1. See many other citations from this text: *Spiritual Choices: The Problem of Recognizing Authentic Paths to Inner Transformation,* eds. Dick Anthony, Bruce Ecker, and Ken Wilber. New York: Paragon, 1987.

2. Freud's fondness for the term *astonishment* is not an isolated feature of his thought. On the contrary, the *Concordance to the Standard Edition* offers us a valuable way to measure an aspect of Freud's style. For example, we learn that aside from the usual propositions and connecting words, Freud's most frequently used term is *dreams.* It appears 6,113 times (plus many more times in variations like "dreams and dreaming"). But the second and

third most frequent terms are *only* (5,634) and *all* (5,557). This is a bit astonishing since that places them well ahead of words which one would have guessed would be more important, e.g., *ego* appears only 2,671 times, *unconscious* 2,070, and *neurosis* 1,576 times. One way to understand this fact is to note that *all* and *only* are antithetical pairs. Together they mark off the entire realm of semantic space. They sharpen a rhetorical point by creating, when used separately, a brilliant comparsion between a singular, individual point of view and the majority opinion. Most experts were too little astonished by the ubiquity of infantile amnesia. Only psychoanalysis pierced through the veil of cultural illusions. Freud's penchant for the unique sample and his active dislike of statistical measures, the beloved of American social sciences, also figures into his affection for *all* and *only*. Freud's recurrent need for an alter ego, like Fliess and Jung, and his concomitant need for a vivid enemy are dramatic instances of an all-or-nothing stance. Or, as Jesus said, he who is not for me is against me, at least with regard to the vital question of protecting a singular and unique truth against the forces combined against it and against those who discovered it. On the dramatic myth of origins and its relationship to official psychoanalytic history, see H. Ellenberger, *The Discovery of the Unconscious* (1970), and Hannah S. Decker, *Freud in Germany* (1979). On issues of Freud's style and its rhetorical forms see Patrick Mahoney, *Freud as Writer* (1982) and French psychoanalytic essays on style and its relationship to psychoanalytic thought.

3. French translation of Mark 1, 22. Paris: Editions du Cerf, 1975.

4. See *The Jealous Potter* (1988) (Chicago: University of Chicago Press): Lévi-Strauss likens Oedipus Rex to detective stories. Like primitive myths, all these forms of drama reveal intellectual struggles to find a symmetry that seems to operate in human life as it does in science and philsosphy (p. 202). "I do not contest the existence of impulses, emotions, or the tumultuous realm of affectivity, but I do not accord primacy to these torrential forces; they erupt upon a structure already in place, formed by the architecture of the mind." And, "A primitive schematism is always there to impose a form on the turmoil of emotions" (p. 203).

5. See the *Autobiography of Hoss*, p. 122. In *KL Auschwitz Seen by the SS: Hoss, Broad, Kremer.* New York: Howard Fertig, 1984. Hoss's zeal and ethical standards are revealed in his lament about German guards whom some Jews were able to bribe: "Jewish gold was a catastrophe for the camp" (p. 132). Prisoners used it to buy special privileges and so disrupted camp discipline. See also Primo Levi (1958) *Survival in Auschwitz* and *The Reawakening: Two Memoirs.* New York: Summit Books, 1985.
On the smells of Auschwitz, see Richard L. Rubenstein, *After Auschwitz: Radical Theology and Contemporary Judaism.* Indianapolis: Bobbs-Merril, 1966: "God was dead, hell—the anus mundi—was established on earth, and yet even hell had lost its fine savor. All that remained, then, as well as now, was an ineradicable stench. Nothing real had been gained; even the SS had won only the fantasy war against the Jews while losing the real one against the Allies" (p. 44). He adds, "As we have noted, the Nazis referred to the camps as the anus mundi and they were entirely willing to permit the corpses to deteriorate in large numbers unburied. The smell of carrion is terrible, but there is little or nothing to distinguish it from a strong smell of

feces. While the Nazis could not without incontinence give free rein to their own anal obsessions, they could and did turn the Jews, whom their folk-culture regarded as the satanic murderers of the dead God, into feces" (p. 38). "The basic project of the death camps was to turn the Jews into feces, the Devil's food, gold, and weapons" (p. 34).

6. S. N. Kim, "Lamentations of the Dead: The Historical Imagery of Violence in Cheju Island, Korea" (1989) *Journal of Ritual Studies*, 3:251–285. See other articles on shamanism and memory: M. Taussig 1984b: "History as Sorcery," *Representations*, 7:87–109 and 1984a, "Culture of Terror—Space of Death: Roger Casement's Putomayho Report and the Explanation of Torture." *Comparative Studies in Society and History*, 26/3:467–487.

7. Herzog, James (1982). Father Hunger. In *Father and Child: Developmental and Clinical Perspectives*, eds. S. H. Cath, A. R. Gurwitt, J. M. Ross. Boston: Little, Brown 1982. On the Mousetrap play and mice and anality, see L. Shengold, *Halo in the Sky: Observations on Anality and Defense*. New York: Guilford Press, 1988.

8. "Bung" still appears in what the OED calls pugilistic slang, where it means to punch one's opponents' eyes. Eric Partridge, in *Shakespeare's Bawdy* (New York: Dutton, 1969), reviews all the plays and poems but does not discuss this passage. He does note that bunghole is slang for anus (1969, p. 73). E. A. Colman (*The Dramatic Use of Bawdy in Shakespeare*. New York: Longman, 1974) mentions neither term. In addition to these speculations, one may add that the term *bunghole* appears only once in all Shakespeare's works, in this play written around 1601. The term was common enough in the early seventeenth century so that one author could write, in 1611, that a certain animal was "a small and ouglie fish, or excrescence of the Sea, resembling a mans bung-hole, and called the red Nettle" (*OED*, 1933, I, p. 1178). On the "rotten state" see H. D. F. Kitto (1956) for a brilliant exposé of Hamlet's actual circumstances.

9. Regarding "revenge" is the point-for-point comparsions between Laertes and Hamlet evident throughout the play. For example, Laertes believing that Claudius has killed his father, Polonius, surges forth for revenge. In support of the Oedipal reading of the play, the citizens proclaim him king when he announces his intention to kill Claudius. (Act IV, v, 98–108.) Learning that it was Hamlet who killed his father, Laertes conspires with Claudius, as did his father, Polonius. Claudius and Laertres plot to poison Hamlet Junior the way Claudius poisoned his father. Indeed, Claudius insists on having two poisoned sources: one being Laertes's sword, the other the cup of wine (one a male object, the second a female object). Some of these points grew out of a conversation with Dr. E. J. Frattaroli at the annual winter meeting of the American Psychoanalytic Association in New York City on 17 December, 1988.

10. From a conversation with Mark Houglum, Ph.D. candidate at Vanderbilt University.

11. See Robert L. Carringer (1985), *The Making of Citizen Kane*. Berkeley, CA: University of California. Also, see Ronald Gottesman, ed. (1971) *Focus on Citizen Kane*. Englewood Cliffs, N.J.: Prentice-Hall.

GLOSSARY OF TECHNICAL TERMS

The following are technical terms used in this text. I define them here briefly and more extensively in the text. See the Index references in this book. Regarding all major psychoanalytic terms, consult the following excellent reference works:

The Language of Psycho-Analysis. (1967). By J. Laplanche and J. B. Pontalis. Trans. D. Nicholson-Smith. New York: Norton.

Psychoanalytic Terms and Concepts. (1990). Ed. Burness Moore and Bernard Fine. New York: The American Psychoanalytic Association. These authors define central psychoanalytic terms and locate them in either Freud or later psychoanalytic authors and within specific texts.

For help with general psychiatric and psychological terms see:

American Psychiatric Glossary. (1988). Ed. Evelyn Stone. Washington, D.C.: American Psychiatric Press.

A Dictionary of Psychotherapy. (1986). Sue Walrond-Skinner. London: Routledge & Kegan Paul.

Lexicon of Psychiatric and Mental Health Terms. (1989). Geneva: World Health Organization.

Glossary

Abandonment anxiety: According to clinicians who work with infants and young children, the anxiety—both conscious and unconscious—one feels when one contemplates losing access to an important person or to that person's internal representation. (See also "Self–object.")

Adhesion of the Libido: A term from Freud's classic theory, pertaining to his notion that, once they are formed, "libidinal" or "erotic" ties between oneself and another (or images of the other) adhere tenaciously. Hence, the "work" of psychoanalytic therapy entails struggling against this tendency. (See also "Regression.")

*Affects:*In general, a feeling, positive or negative, tied to an idea, which, in turn, is the product of instinctual wishes.

Affordances: A term from the psychologist, J. J. Gibson, they are those invariant features of the relationship between a perceiver and the perceiver's expectable environment such that the perceiver comprehends that environment as a place of action. An affordance is thus an actual aspect of how a particular animal situates itself in a particular environment.

Aggressive instincts: In Freud's "classical theory" (which see) those innate impulsions, based in the germ plasm, that push one toward aggressive instincts. (See also "Death instincts.")

*Anal instincts:*In classical libido theory, those innate impulsions which give rise to wishes and pleasures associated with the anal–urethral area of the body. Often associated with aggressive instincts, especially, in so-called anal rage.

*Ananke:*Freud's use of the Greek term for fate or "The Fates" which control even divine powers and which determine the shape of all human instincts and, therefore, of human fate as well.

Antisexual instincts: From the classical theory, those instincts later associated with ego defense, especially repression, which impel one to resist sexual wishes, themselves driven by sexual instincts.

Anxiety: In Freud's early theory, a painful, conscious state of fear caused by the damning-up of libidinal impulses. In his later theory, anxiety includes both conscious and unconscious forms and is traced to unconscious defensive efforts by the ego to elicit defense against an anticipated danger.

A priori structures of the mind: Terms from Immanuel Kant's treatises on the philosophy of science; those structures of mind which Kant says are prior to any experience and which determine the structure or form by which rational thinking takes place.

Association: A term developed especially in Freud's major text on dreams, *The Interpretation of Dreams* (1900a); an idea (thought, wish, feeling) elicited spontaneously by a mental stimulus. (See "Free association.")

*Attunement:*From Object Relations Theory especially; the concept that an empathic caretaker or therapist comprehends the inner experience of the other rather as one "tunes" one's instruments when playing music with another.

Cathected Neurone: In classical theory, especially the "Project" of 1895, a hypothetical element in the brain which is "filled with" (cathected with) various forms of energy.

Censorship: From *The Interpretation of Dreams* (1900a) and related texts; the agency in the mind which operates both consciously and unconsciously to suppress wishes the expression of which might endanger the ego.

Classical Theory: Generally refers to all of Freud's corpus, which spans a period of roughly 1893 to 1939. More narrowly, it refers to his Instinct Theory and the metapsychology associated with that theory in papers he wrote between 1909 and 1920. After 1920 his work is better described as Ego Psychology because in those papers he focused upon the eog and its "energies" and less upon the "instincts" which ultimately determine human experience.

Complex: A term derived from both Freud and Carl Jung; a fixed set of behaviors and psychopathological actions that persists and commonly occurs with such regularity that it appears in most cultures and cultural forms, hence "Oedipus Complex" refers to a child's struggles with triangular relationships to its parents.

Compromise formations: From Ego Psychology especially, refers to both minor and major forms of behaviors that simultaneously express and suppress, liberate and repress, instinctual wishes. The resultant behavior, e.g., neurotic fears that a loved one might die, is a compromise between the two competing wishes.

Compulsion to repeat: From classical theory, behaviors that manifest directly the primary instincts' tendency toward repetition and return to archaic states of being.

Construction: From clinical theory, the joint effort by analyst and patient, using current transference events, to conceptualize the patient's early emotional environments. In cultural critiques, Freud "constructed" portraits of human prehistory as well.

Containment: From clinical theory, the analyst's effort to elicit and then "recognize" the patient's archaic feeling states which the patient had previously disowned, usually through projection.

Counter-transference: From the clinical theory; the analyst's conscious and unconscious experience of the patient as if the patient *were a person from the analyst's past.* (See "Transference.")

Defense: From the clinical theory; a person's conscious and unconscious efforts to avoid psychic pain, e.g., shame or guilt. In classical theory repression was typically the defense most often discussed; in more recent theory any ego activity, including insight, can serve defensive purposes.

Deficit in the ego: The lack of a major and definable skill or so-called ego function, like judgment or reality-testing, which operates in a well-developed personality.

Delusion: From general psychiatry, a belief strongly held and defended even when contradicted by reality-testing and social norms.

Denial: A major ego defense in which one unconsciously perceives a truth about the self and then consciously denies it.

Depression: A general psychiatric term for negative moods (and affects) commonly associated with deficits in self-esteem, pessimism, somatic complaints, sleep, and other disturbances, some of which are obvious and some of which are hidden.

Deprivations: From Object Relations Theory (which see); actions by parenting persons which actively deprive the infant and child of emotional nurture and sustenance.

Depth psychology: A general term, usually referring to Freud's thought and the many schools of thought influenced by his theories, which conceives of the layers of the mind, ranging from "superficial" to "deeper" strata.

Developmental point of view: From classical theory, Freud's claim that all complex behaviors, especially psychopathologies, have their origins in prior interpersonal and intrapsychic events.

Displacement: From classical theory, a major ego defense in which one directs attention away from an area or feeling that might provoke psychic pain to another that seems safer.

Distinctive feature: From linguistics, any perceivable aspect of speech or language that permits one to distinguish one minimal unit from another, e.g., phonemes are distinguished from one another according to the presence or absence of distinctive auditory features.

Economic point of view: From classical theory, Freud's claim that all complex behaviors, especially psychopathologies, have their origins in the flux of primary instincts, e.g., love and hate.

Ego: From classical theory and later ego psychology, that agency that theory tells us is, or should be, unitary in the psyche and which is the seat or source of adaptation and survival, therefore, the seat of all defensive operations as well as all ego functions, e.g., consciousness, judgment, reality testing. (Compare to the "Self.")

Ego defense: Narrowly defined, any activity by the ego which serves to decrease psychic suffering and increase psychic balance or pleasure at the cost of reality-testing.

Emic and etic: From linguistics, especially the work of Kenneth Pike (1962), who, using linguistics as a paradigm, argued that one can find phon*emic* and phon*etic* differences in human behavior that parallel these linguistic structures. "Emic" structures are thus rule bound, arbitary, culture specific, and based on distinctive features, while "etic" structures are the opposite.

Emotional affordances: From this text, on analogy to visual affordances (which see); those aspects of the other or symbols of the other, as in art, the presence of which informs me that they are sources of emotional sustenance.

Empathy: From classical theory and later; the ego capacity to comprehend the intrapsychic experience and world of another person.

Epistemology: From philosophy, a theory of how knowledge is possible and how science develops and evolves.

Fantasy: From classical and all later analytic theories; conscious and unconscious personal narratives that express (and conceal) archaic ego states and archaic solutions to psychic suffering. (See also "Perversion.")

Fixations: From classical libido theory; Freud's claim that infants and children, in the process of ego and libidinal development, may become mired in a particular phase (e.g., in the oral, anal, or phallic state) and not progress beyond it.

Frame: Primarily from the work of Robert Langs (1985); the set of boundaries, expectations, and responsibilities that therapist and patient agree upon that provide the "space" in which all therapy is to take place, e.g., a fixed time, place, fee, and therapeutic goal.

Genital sexuality: From classical theory; the most developed form of human sexual development in which a sexual relationship with another is focused primarily upon mutual genital sexual expression and in which both partners find in the other avenues for self-coherence as well.

Gibsonian Theory: Referring to the theories of perception, especially the notion of affordances, advanced by J. J. Gibson (1970: 1979) and by E. Gibson as well.

Guilt: From classical theory; a negative affective state in which the ego feels responsible for criminal actions and awaits punishment (from the superego).

Hypercathected: From classical theory; the state in which a neurone is overfilled with psychic energy and therefore disturbs psychic equilibrium which, when expressed, appears as neurotic fixations.

Hypersexual: Extreme, neurotically driven, sexual expressions.

Hysteria: In classical theory, a neurosis more common in women, though appearing in men, in which a body part is hypercathected with sexualized energy, and hence impaired. (See "Dora," in the Index.)

Icon, Iconic: From aesthetics, representational objects, like signs or gestures, whose structure parallels that of the item to which they refer, e.g., holding one's nose is iconic for "this smells bad."

Id: From classical ego theory, the third part of Freud's tripartite theory of mind; the original matrix of psyche and soma which is the seat of the instincts and the source of later instinctual manifestations, like sexual and aggressive wishes, and which is foundational to the ego and superego.

Idealization: From classical theory and Self-Psychology: an ego defense and developmental process by which one ascribes to others images of greatness and perfection which stem from one's own narcissistic tensions.

Identification: From all psychoanalytic authors, that profound, unending, and deep process by which personal identity is formed and maintained through becoming like, in part, persons one admires and wishes to "take into the self."

Illusion: In classical theory, a belief driven by a wish with little or no reality support, e.g., religious beliefs in heaven. In ORT, especially David Winnicott, an unending process by which persons generate a sense that there is an intermediate space between their inner selves and the inner selves of other beings in which they may meet.

Infantile neurosis: In classical theory, a neurotic condition in infants and children, which may disappear but to which any complete adult analysis must penetrate and resolve by resolving its reincarnated form, the adult transference neurosis.

Inner world: In general analytic parlance, the set of conscious and unconscious images and feelings about self and others which take place within the mind of an individual.

Instincts: In Freud, the original biological forces which undergrid and predate all later psychological structures. (See "Id.")

Intrapsychic point of view: A general analytic orientation toward self and others: that they and we have inner worlds from which spring many of our actions, especially neurotic actions.

Introjection: Classical theory and all later theory: an imagined process by which a person takes in or "introjects" desired attributes of another, often in an "oral" or "anal" manner. (See also "Perversion.")

Invariances: From Gibson (1979), those relational features between self and the external world which remain unchanging, e.g., the pull of gravity upon one's body is an invariant feature of life on this planet.

Isolation: A major ego defense in which one consciously or unconsciously avoids psychic pain by severing the link between one's feelings about an event or person and one's recognition of those feelings.

Latent content: From Freud, especially *The Interpretation of Dreams* (1900a), the set of feelings and ideas hidden from conscious awareness "beneath" the manifest content.

Libido: From Freud, all energies that aim to unite one thing with another, one person with another, and one body with another. (See also "Anal" and "Oral.")

Magical thinking: See Primary process; thinking in which the ego's ability to judge, test reality, and postpone action (or discharge) is overcome by wishful impulses as occurs in dreams.

Manifest content: From Freud, especially *The Interpretation of Dreams* (1900a), the set of feelings and ideas which appear immediately and on the surface, e.g., the dream text as reported spontaneously by a patient.

Masochism: In all analytic theory, an action which while painful also yields libidinal discharge and therefore pleasure, even if unconscious pleasures. (See also "Perversion.")

Metapsychology: From Freud, his general and highly abstract theory of the mental apparatus and its functioning. Metapsychology is "beyond" psychology proper because it aims to explain psychological findings using "more basic," and nonpsychological concepts like energy and structure.

Mourning: From one of Freud's greatest essays, "Mourning and Melancholia" (1917e): a psychological task, or labor, in which the ego must accept the loss of a beloved (libidinized) object and disentangle its hopes and securities tied to that object slowly, over time by "hypercathecting" memories, discharging the affect there accumulated, and so forsaking one's infantile wishes toward the object.

Narcissism: In classical theory, the original state of self-love, like the Greek mythological character, Narcissus, in which one perceives no other objects worthy of sharing love. In later theory, especially the work of Heinz Kohut (1971; 1977), narcissism is seen as a line of development and fundamental to any form of bona fide maturity.

Neurone theory: Freud's earliest metapsychology, using abstract models of the neural structure of the brain to explain psychological functioning.

Neurosis, Neurotic: In all analytic theory, a long-standing form of psychic suffering in which a patient's ego is basically intact (is not submerged in unconscious processes as are psychotic persons) but severely confined by unconscious conflicts, stemming from infantile and adolescent crises not resolved fully.

Noumena: From the German philosopher, Immanuel Kant: those fundamental aspects of reality which lay beyond the scope of direct human perception and manipulation. (See also "Phenomena.")

Nuclear conflict: From Freud, the oedipal conflict in its fullest measure.

Object: In all analytic theory the actual, external person, thing, or other being important to one.

Object representations: Our conscious and unconscious images of an external object.

Oedipal complex: The nuclear complex, according to Freud, of all human families and all human cultures. The triangular conflict that emerges when a child enters the phallic period, about ages three to five, and discovers that adults of both sexes have sexual lives and "secrets" and "powers" denied to the child.

Omega Neurones: In Freud's earliest metapsychology; the hypothetical set of neurones responsible for consciousness.

Ontogenetic: In Freud, the ways in which an individual develops over time, opposed to the development of a species or group.

ORT, Object Relations Theory: In general, contemporary schools of psychoanalytic thought, often stemming from British authors like Melanie Klein and David Winnicott, which focus attention upon the ways in which relationships, "object relations," between parent and child influence deeply the intrapyschic realm. Other ORT authors, like Kernberg (1976) integrate these concerns with classical ego psychology.

Perversion: In the classical theory, and action or fantasy leading to orgastic discharge which is not focused primarily upon the genitals of self and the other (of the opposite sex). In Freud, perversions are expressions of primary sexual instincts, like oral and anal impulses, that have not succumbed to organization under the "higher" genital aims. In post-Freud authors, especially ORT, perversions are seen as symptomatic expressions of efforts to repair a psyche, through magical means, and to overcome deficits in emotional environment.

Phallocentric: In classical theory, a perversion that focuses upon and idealizes the erect penis.

Phenomena: From Kant, those aspects of the world as perceived and subject to scientific inquiry; dominated by a priori principles of thought and opposed to the world of noumena.

Phenomenology: In general terms, a philosophic and scientific orientation toward manifest and immediate given experience; the exploration of the experience without prejudging its sources and its meanings or its ultimate nature, its "ontology."

Phi Neurones: In Freud's earliest metapsychology, those hypothetical neural structures responsbile for perception in all forms.

Phylogenetic: In Freud, the ways in which an entire species or distinct group developed over time, as opposed to ontogenetic.

Pregenital: In Freud, libidinal impulses and wishes associated with them deriving from sexual organs that develop prior to the genital stage, e.g., oral and anal sexual actions.

Preoedipal: In Freud, psychological and intrapsychic events that occur prior to the oedipal stage. In general, all those events that occur within the infant's mind and between infant and parents prior to the oedipal period.

Primary process: In Freud's metapsychology, the original mental set of the infantile psyche, revealed nightly in dreams and in all other regressed moments where the adult psyche reverts from secondary process thinking to magical forms of thought.

Projection: A basic and primitive ego defense in which one ascribes negative aspects of the self to others external to the self and then, typically, responds to those aspects with aggression.

Psi Neurones: In Freud's original metapsychology, those hypothetical neurones responsible for memory and many other ego functions.

Psychic pain: Any form of suffering whose origin and locus is mental.

Psychodynamic: In general, a theory and point of view that sees the human psyche, or mind, as organized, in part, in response to the pressure of various "forces" or "dynamics," many of which are unconscious and therefore hidden from ordinary inspection.

Psychosis: For Freud, a severe form of mental illness in which ordinary reality-testing is not available to a person, in which primary process thought dominates, and in which the person cannot distinguish between fantasy and reality. "Hallucinatory" thought during dreams is, Freud says, a form of controlled psychosis.

Qh: Typescript shorthand for Freud's Greek symbol with which he designated a quantity of psychic energy in the "Project" of 1895.

Reality-testing: In Freud, a central task of the ego; to distinguish internal stimuli and thoughts or fantasy from external thoughts and stimuli. Reality-testing develops slowly over time, as other secondary process functions do, and is subject to regression, as in neurosis, or disappearance, as in psychosis.

Regression: In general, a state in which a person's ego functioning has reversed and operates at a prior developmental state, e.g., in dreams we "regress" to primary process thinking in which wishes and anxieties are given hallucinatory reality. In clinical practice, regression occurs when the transference neurosis sets in and the patient experiences the analyst as if the analyst were a person from the past.

Repression: A basic and primitive defense mechanism by which the ego denies attention cathexis to ideas which, if expressed, would cause psychic pain. Repression thereby causes breaks or gaps in the ego's conscious experience; hence the common experience of forgetting is typically a product of repression.

Secondary process: All those mature ego functions, like reality-testing, that develop after the child matures and which are liable to regression when the ego faces severe strain.

Self-object: A term central to Heinz Kohut (1971; 1977); a person (for example, a mother) who performs ego functions for another person who cannot perform them for himself or herself. In benign circumstances, a positive self-object relationship is one in which the self-object soothes, helps, loves, and nurtures the one in need. In hostile self-object realtionships, a person with power, say an adult, demands self-object responses from a person with less power and less freedom, say the adult's child.

Self-preservative instincts: From Freud, those ego-based instincts that aim to preserve the self and which oppose the death instincts.

Sexualization: A complex ego defense in which one imagines sexual pleasure with another person or thing in order to avoid feelings that would otherwise threaten to overwhelm the ego with suffering.

Splitting: A major and ubiquitous ego defense in which one "splits" images of another or of oneself into acceptable parts (the "good" images) and unacceptable parts (the "bad" images). Freud first spoke of splitting per se with regard to male perversions in which the patient found sexual pleasure with a fetish object with which he denied the existence of female differences and so denied his horrible fear that he too might be "castrated." An excellent and complete discussion occurs in James Grotstein's *Splitting and Projective Identification* (1981).

Structural Theory: Freud's last and most famous metapsychological theory; the theory of ego, superego, and id "structures" which make up the mature mental apparatus. From 1921 on, Freud and others, especially the school associated with "Ego Psychology," elaborated detailed theorems as to how each of these structures was energized, developed, altered through internalization, and interacted with the other two agencies and the external world.

Superego: The last agency of the structural model to develop, originally amalgamated with the notion of ego ideal. After 1923 Freud ascribed to it the voice of morality and other conscious and unconscious modes by which it silently controlled the ego. Typically, guilt and shame are ascribed to a punitive superego as are other self-attacking and self-destructive urges.

Transference: The central feature of psychoanalytic therapy, an unconscious set of events and fantasies in which the patient reexperiences the analyst as if the analyst *were* a person important in the patient's past and responds to the analyst with feelings and impulses first experienced toward that earlier person.

Transference Neurosis: The central target of interpretation in classical psychoanalytic work: when a patient is fully "in" analysis, Freud said that the patient's original neurosis was now transformed into a new, transference neurosis. Hence, in the here and now of the analytic hour, patient and doctor could see precisely how the prior neurosis occurred and why it persisted. By curing the patient of the transference neurosis, one cures the patient entirely.

Tripartite Theory: Another name for the structural theory of ego, super-ego, and id mental agencies.

❄

BIBLIOGRAPHY

Abraham, Karl (1909). Dreams and myths. In *Clinical Papers and Essays on Psychoanalysis*, pp. 153–209. New York: Basic Books.

Abraham, Karl (1916). The first pregenital stage of the libido. In *Selected Papers*, chapter 12. London: Hogarth Press, 1927.

Abraham, Karl (1927). *Selected Papers*. London: Hogarth Press.

Abraham, Karl (1965). *Selected Papers of Karl Abraham, M.D.*, trans. Douglas Bryan and Alix Strachey. London: Hogarth Press.

Aeschylus. *Aeschyli: Septem Quae Supersunt Tragoediae*, ed. Gilbert Murray. Oxford: Clarendon Press, 1937.

Amacher, Peter (1965). *Freud's Neurological Education and Its Influence on Psychoanalytic Theory*. New York: International Universities Press.

American Psychiatric Association (1980). *Diagnostic and Statistical Manual of Mental Disorders*. 3rd ed. Washington, D.C.

Anthony, Dick, Ecker, Bruce, and Wilber, Ken, eds. (1987). *Spiritual Choices: The Problem of Recognizing Authentic Paths to Inner Transformation*. New York: Paragon.

Apfelbaum, B. (1965). Ego psychology, psychic energy, and the hazards of quantitative explanation in psycho-analytic theory. *International Journal of Psycho-Analysis*, 46:168–182.

Aquinas, Thomas, (ND). *Quaestiones Quodibetales*, ed. P. Mandonnet. Paris: Lethielleux, 1926.

Arieti, Silvano (1976). *Creativity: The Magic Synthesis.* New York: Basic Books.

Arlow, J. A. (1955). Report on panel on sublimation. *Journal of the American Psychoanalytic Association* 3:515–527.

Arlow, J. A. (1961). Ego psychology and the study of mythology. *Journal of the American Psychoanalytic Association* 9:371–393.

Arlow, J. A. (1969). Fantasy, memory, and reality testing. *Psychoanalytic Quarterly* 38:28–51.

Arnheim, Rudolph, ed. (1971). *Entropy and Art.* Berkeley: University of California Press.

Asch, S. (1976). Varieties of negative therapeutic reaction and problems of technique. *Journal of the American Psychoanalytic Association* 24:383–407.

Ashby, W. Ross (1956). *An Introduction to Cybernetics.* London: Chapman & Hall Ltd.

Auerbach, E. (1938). Figura. *Archivum Romanicum* 22:436–489.

Auerbach, E. (1953). *Mimesis: The Representation of Reality in Western Literature,* trans. Willard R. Trask. Princeton: Princeton University Press.

Austen, John (1939). *The Story of Don Juan.* London: Martin Secker.

Austin, J. L. (1962). *How To Do Things with Words.* New York: Oxford University Press.

Austin, J. L. (1964). *Sense and Sensibilia.* New York: Oxford University Press.

Bailey, Lee. (ND). "Skull's Lantern: Psychological Projection and the Magic Lantern," ms.

Bailey, Lee. (ND). "Projection and Unmasking the Gods," ms.

Balint, Michael (1968). *The Basic Fault: Therapeutic Aspects of Regres-*

sion. London: Tavistock.

Barnard, John, ed. (1973). *John Keats: The Complete Poems.* London: Penguin Books.

Barros, Carlos P. (1973). Thermodynamic and evolutionary concepts in the formal structure of Freud's metapsychology. In *World Biennial of Psychiatry and Psychotherapy,* ed. Silvano Arieti. Vol 2, pp. 72–111. New York: Basic Books.

Bate, Walter Jackson (1964). *John Keats.* Cambridge, Mass.: Harvard University Press.

Bate, Walter Jackson, ed. (1964). *Keats: A Collection of Critical Essays.* Englewood Cliffs, N.J.: Prentice-Hall.

Bateson, Gregory (1967). Style, grace, and information in primitive art. In *Steps to an Ecology of Mind,* pp. 128–156. San Francisco: Chandler, 1972.

Bateson, Gregory (1972). *Steps to an Ecology of Mind.* New York: Ballantine.

Bateson, G. and Mead, M. (1942). *Balinese Character: A Photographic Analysis.* New York: New York Academy of Sciences.

Baudouin, C. (1950). La sublimation des images che Huysmans lord de sa conversion. *Psyche* 5:378–385.

Bellak, L., et al. (1973). *Ego Functions in Schizophrenics, Neurotics and Normals.* New York: John Wiley and Sons.

Benjamin, Walter (1936). The work of art in the age of mechanical reproduction. In *Illuminations,* ed. Hannah Arendt, pp. 217–267. New York: Schocken, 1969.

Benveniste, Emile (1953–1955). Remarques sur la fonction du langage dans la decouverte freudienne. *Psychanalyse* 1:3–16.

Beres, D. (1957). Communication in psychoanalysis and in the creative process: a parallel. *Journal of the American Psychoanalytic Association* 5:408–523.

Bergler, Edmund (1945). On a five layer structure in sublimation. *Psychoanalytic Quarterly* 14:76–97.

Bergler, Edmund (1950). *The Writer and Psychoanalysis.* Garden City, N.Y.: Doubleday.

Bernheimer, Charles (1987). "Degas's Brothels: Voyeurism and Ideology." *Representations* 20:158–185.

Bertram, Georg (1974). "Hupsos." In: *Theological Dictionary of the New Testament,* eds. G. Kittel and G. Friedrich, trans. G. W. Bromiley. Grand Rapids, Mich.: Eerdmans.

Bibring, E. (1941). The development and problems of the theory of the instincts. *International Journal of Psycho-Analysis* 22:102–131.

Bieber, Irving (1980). *Cognitive Psychoanalysis.* New York: Jason Aronson.

Bird, Brian (1972). Notes on transference: universal phenomenon and hardest part of analysis. *Journal of the American Psychoanalytic Association* 20:267–301.

Black, Max (1962). *Models and Metaphors.* Ithaca: Cornell University Press.

Blau, Peter M. and Merton, Robert K., eds. (1981). *Continuities in Structural Inquiry.* London: Sage.

Bloch, Ernst (1971). Aufklaerung und Teufelsglaubae. Read in Salzburg 1971. Cassette ex libris, Zurich.

Bloom, Harold (1963). *The Visionary Company: A Reading of English Romantic Poetry.* New York: Anchor.

Bloom, Harold (1973). *The Anxiety of Influence: A Theory of Poetry.* London: Oxford Press.

Boden, Margaret A. (1972). *Purposive Explanation in Psychology.* Cambridge, Mass.: Harvard University Press.

Bollas, Christopher. (1978). The aesthetic moment and the search for transformation. *Annual of Psychoanalysis* 385–394.

Bollas, Christopher (1987). *The Shadow of the Object: Psychoanalysis of the Unthought Unknown.* London: Free Association Books.

Borneman, Ernest (1971). *Sex im Volksmund: Die Sexuelle Umgangsprache des deutschen Volkes.* Reinbek bei Hamburg: Rowohlt Verlag.

Bourke, J. G. (1891). *Scatalogic Rites of All Nations.* Washington: Lowdermilk.

Bowlby, John (1953). *Child Care and the Growth of Love.* London: Pelican.

Bowlby, John (1969). *Attachment and Loss: Attachment,* vol. 1. London: Hogarth Press.

Bowlby, John (1973). *Attachment and Loss: Separation, Anxiety and Anger,* vol. 2. London: Hogarth Press.

Brady, Frank (1989). *Citizen Welles: A Biography of Orson Welles.* New York: Sribners.

Braun, Bennett, ed. (1986). *Treatment of Multiple Personality Disorder.* Washington, D.C.: American Psychiatric Press.

Brenner, Charles (1959). The masochistic character: genesis and treatment. *Journal of the American Psychoanalytic Association* 7:197–226.

Brenner, Charles (1982). *The Mind in Conflict.* New York: International Universities Press.

Breuer, Joseph and Freud, S. (1895d). *Studies on Hysteria.* London: Hogarth Press, 1955.

Brink, Andrew (1977). *Loss and Symbolic Repair: A Psychological Study of Some English Poets.* Hamilton, Ontario: The Cromlech Press.

Brody, S. (1980). Transitional objects: idealization of a phenomenon. *Psychoanalytic Quarterly* 49:561–605.

Brody, S., and Axelrad, S. (1970). *Anxiety and Ego Formation in Infancy.* New York: International Universities Press.

Brody, S., and Axelrad, S. (1978). *Mothers, Fathers, and Children.* New York: International Universities Press.

Brown, Norman O. (1947). *Hermes the Thief: The Evolution of a Myth.* Madison: University of Wisconsin Press.

Brown, Norman O. (1959). *Life Against Death.* Middletown, Conn.: Wesleyan University Press.

Bunker, H. A. (1934). The voice as female phallus. *Psychoanalytic Quarterly* 3:391–429.

Burgin, V., Donald, James, and Kaplan, Cora, eds. (1986). *Formations of Fantasy.* London: Methuen.

Burke, Kenneth (1967). *The Philosophy of Literary Form: Studies in Symbolic Action.* Baton Rouge: Louisiana State University Press.

Burnshaw, Stanley (1970). *The Seamless Web: Language-Thinking. Creature-Knowledge, Art-Experience.* New York: George Braziller.

Busch, F., Nagera, H., McKnight, J., et al. (1973). Primary transitional objects. *Journal of the American Academy of Child Psychiatry* 12:193–214.

Buxbaum, E. (1941). The role of detective stories in child analysis. *Psychoanalytic Quarterly* 10:373–381.

Cairns-Smith, A. G. (1971). *The Life Puzzle.* Edinburgh: Oliver and Boyd.

Caldwell, James Ralston (1945). *John Keats' Fancy: The Effect on Keats of the Psychology of his Day.* Ithaca: Cornell University Press.

Call, J. D., et al., eds. (1983). *Frontiers of Infant Psychiatry.* New York: Basic Books.

Calow, Peter (1976). *Biological Machines: a Cybernetic Approach to Life.* London: Edward Arnold.

Campbell, John D. (1967). Studies in attitude formation: health orientation. In *Attitude, Ego-Involvement and Change*, eds. C. Sherif and C. Sherif, pp. 7–25. New York: John Wiley.

Carnap, Rudolph (1955). Foundations of the unity of science, In *Toward an International Encyclopedia of Unified Science*, eds. O. Neurath, R. Carnap, and C. Morris. Chicago: University of Chicago Press.

Carringer, Robert L. (1985). *The Making of Citizen Kane*. Berkeley, Cal.: University of California Press.

Castelnuovo-Tedesco, Pietro (1984). Fear of change as a source of resistance in analysis. In *The Annual of Psychoanalysis* 14:259–272.

Castelnuovo-Tedesco, Pietro (1989). Change and Therapeutic Effectiveness in Psychoanalysis and Psychotherapy. Special issue of *Psychoanalytic Inquiry* 9:1.

Chasseguet-Smirgel, Janine (1984). *Creativity and Perversion*. New York: Norton.

Cheever, John (1964). *The Wapshot Scandal*. New York: Harper and Row.

Cheever, John (1979). *The Stories of John Cheever*. New York: Knopf.

Chisholm, Roderick M. (1976). *Person and Object: A Metaphysical Study*. La Salle, Ill.: Open Court.

Chomsky, Noam (1966). *Cartesian Linguistics: A Chapter in the History of Rationalist Thought*. New York: Harper.

Chomsky, Noam (1968). *Language and Mind*. New York: Harcourt, Brace and World.

Churchman, C. West (1971). *The Design of Inquiring Systems: Basic Concepts of Systems and Organization*. New York: Basic Books.

Clarke, Charles, and Clarke, Mary Cowden (1878). *Recollections of Writers*.

Clippinger, John Henry (1977). *Meaning and Discourse: A Computer*

Model of Psychoanalytic Speech and Cognition. Baltimore: Johns Hopkins University Press.

Clover, Carol J. (1987). Her body, himself: gender in slasher films, *Representations* 20:187–227.

Cohen, E., Namir, L. and Schlesinger, I. M. (1977). *A New Dictionary of Sign Language.* The Hague: Mouton.

Colby, K. M. (1955). *Energy and Structure in Psychoanalysis.* New York: Ronald Press.

Colby, K. M. (1974). *Artificial Paranoia: A Computer Simulation of Paranoid Processes.* New York: Pergamon.

Colby, K. M. (1976). Clinical implications of simulation model of paranoid process. *Archives of General Psychiatry* 33:854–857.

Colman, E. A. (1956). *The Dramatic Use of Bawdy in Shakespeare.* New York: Longman.

Coltera, J. (1965). On the creation of beauty and thought: the unique as vicissitude. *Journal of the American Psychoanalytic Association* 13:634–703.

Crews, Frederick, ed. (1970). *Psychoanalysis and Literary Process.* Cambridge, Mass.: Winthrop.

d'Aquili, Eugene, et al. (1979). *The Spectrum of Ritual: A Biogenetic Structural Analysis.* New York: Columbia University Press.

Darwin, Charles (1959). 6th ed. *The Origin of Species by Means of Natural Selection, or The Preservation of Favoured Races in the Struggle for Life.* New York: Collier Books.

Dawkins, Richard (1976). *The Selfish Gene.* Oxford: Oxford University Press.

Decker, Hannah S. (1979). *Freud in Germany.* New York: International Universities Press.

deMausse, Lloyd, ed. (1974). *The History of Childhood.* New York: The

Psychohistory Press.

deMausse, Lloyd (1982). *Foundations of Psychohistory.* New York: Creative Roots.

deMausse, Lloyd (1988). What incest barrier? *Journal of Psychohistory* 16, 4:273–277.

De Rivera, J. (1977). *A Structural Theory of the Emotions.* New York: International Universities Press. (Psychological Issues, Monograph No. 40.)

Derrida, Jacques (1972). Freud and the scene of writing. *Yale French Studies* 48:73–117.

Deutsch, F. (1957). A footnote to Freud's "Fragment of an Analysis of a Case of Hysteria." *Psychoanalytic Quarterly* 26:159–167.

Devereux, George (1956). Normal and abnormal: the key problem of psychiatric anthropology. In *Some Uses of Anthropology.* Washington, D.C.: Anthropological Society of Washington.

Dickey, James (1958). *Drowning with Others.* Middletown, Conn.: Wesleyan University Press.

Dittmann, Allen T. (1972). *Interpersonal Messages of Emotion.* New York: Springer.

Douglas, Lord Alfred (1914). *Oscar Wilde and Myself.* New York: Duffield & Company.

Dubos, René (1965). *Man Adapting.* New Haven: Yale University Press.

Dundes, Alan (1963). From etic to emic units in the structural study of folk-tales. *Journal of American Folk-Lore* 75:95–105.

Dundes, Alan (1984). *Life is Like a Chicken Coop Ladder: A Portrait of German Culture Through Folklore.* New York: Columbia University Press.

Edelheit, H. (1969). Speech and psychic structure. *Journal of the American Psychoanalytic Association* 17:381–412.

Edelson, Marshall (1988). *Psychoanalysis: A Theory in Crisis.* Chicago: University of Chicago Press.

Edgcumbe, F., ed. (1937). *Letters of Fanny Brawne to Fanny Keats.* New York: Oxford University Press.

Ehrenzweig, Anton (1953). *The Psycho-Analysis of Artistic Vision and Hearing: An Introduction to a Theory of Unconscious Perception.* London: Routledge and Paul.

Eidelberg, L., et al. (1962). Panel report, Narcissism. *Journal of the American Psychoanalytic Association* 12:593–605.

Eigen, M. (1981). The area of faith in Winnicott, Lacan, and Bion. *International Journal of Psycho-Analysis* 62:413–433.

Eissler, Kurt (1963). Tentative notes on the psychology of genius, In *Goethe: A Psychoanalytic Study* (2 vols.) Detroit: Wayne State University Press.

Eissler, Kurt (1971). *Discourse on Hamlet and HAMLET: A Psychoanalytic Inquiry.* New York: International Universities Press.

Eliade, M. (1958). *Patterns in Comparative Religion.* New York: World Publishing.

Eliade, M. (1964). *Shamanism: Archaic Techniques of Ecstasy.* New York: Random House.

Ellenberger, Henri F. (1970). *The Discovery of the Unconscious.* New York: Basic Books.

Ellis, Havelock (1897). *Studies in the Psychology of Sex.* Philadelphia: F. A. Davis.

Ellul, Jacques (1965). *Propaganda.* New York: Knopf.

Emde, Robert N., and Sorce, J. F. (1983). The rewards of infancy: emotional availability and maternal referencing. In *Frontiers of Infant Psychiatry*, ed. J. D. Call et al., pp. 17–30. New York: Basic Books.

Ende, Stuart A. (1976). *Keats and the Sublime.* New Haven: Yale University Press.

Engen, Trygg (1982). *The Perception of Odors.* New York: Academic Press.

Erikson, Erik H. (1950). *Childhood and Society.* New York: Norton.

Erikson, Erik H. (1962). Reality and actuality. *Journal of the American Psychoanalytic Association* 10:451–473.

Erikson, Erik H. (1963). *Childhood and Society,* 2d ed. New York: Norton.

Feffer, M. (1982). *The Structure of Freudian Thought.* New York: International Universities Press.

Fekete, John (1977). *The Critical Twilight: Explorations in the Ideology of Anglo-American Literary Theory from Eliot to McLuhan.* London: Routledge & Kegan Paul.

Fenichel, Otto (1945). *The Psychoanalytic Theory of Neurosis.* New York: W. W. Norton and Company.

Ferenczi, S. (1913). Ein kleiner Hahnemann. Trans. as "A little chanticleer" in *First Contributions to Psycho-Analysis.* London: Hogarth Press, 1952.

Ferguson, Eugene S. (1977). The mind's eye: nonverbal thought in technology. *Science* 197, no. 4306:827–836.

Fisher, L., and Werner, O. (1978). Explaining explanation: tension in American anthropology. *Journal of Anthropological Research* 34:194–218.

Fisher, S. (1970). *Body Experience in Fantasy and Behavior.* New York: Appleton-Century-Crofts.

Fisher, S., and Greenberg, R. P. (1977). *The Scientific Credibility of Freud's Theories and Therapy.* New York: Basic Books.

Fiske, D. W. (1979). Two worlds of psychological phenomena. *American Psychologist* 34:733–739.

Flew, A. (1978). Transitional objects and transitional phenomena. In *Between Fantasy and Reality*, ed. Grolnick et al., pp. 485–501. New York: Jason Aronson.

Flugel, J. C. (1942). Sublimation: its nature and conditions. *British Journal of Educational Psychology* 12:10–25; 97–107; 162–166.

Foucault, Michel (1976). *The History of Sexuality, An Introduction*, trans. Robert Hurley. New York: Pantheon Books.

Fox, James J. (1988). *To Speak in Pairs: Essays on the Rituals and Languages of Eastern Indonesia*. New York: Cambridge University Press.

Fraiberg, S. H. (1980). *Clinical Studies in Infant Mental Health: the First Year of Life*. New York: Basic Books.

Frank, A., (1969). The unrememberable and the unforgettable. *Psychoanalytic Study of the Child*. 24:48–77.

Frege, Gottlob (1893). *Translations from the Philosophical Writings of Gottlob Frege*. Trans. Peter Geach and Max Black. Oxford: Blackwell, 1952.

Freud, Anna (1967). Comments on psychic trauma. In *The Writings of Anna Freud*, vol. 5, pp. 221–241. New York: International Universities Press, 1969.

Freud, Sigmund. Unless otherwise noted, all Freud references are to volumes in *The Standard Edition of the Complete Psychological Works of Sigmund Freud*, 24 volumes (London: Hogarth Press and The Institute for Psycho-Analysis). I use the *Standard Edition* date and notations for volume and initial page number. References to James Strachey, the general editor of the *Standard Edition*, are also to these volumes.

(1888b) "Hysteria" and "hystero-epilepsy," *Standard Edition*, 1, 39.

(1891b) *On Aphasia*. London and New York, 1953.

(1893c) Some points for a comparative study of organic and hysterical motor paralyses. *Standard Edition*, 1, 157.

(1895a) "A project for a scientific psychology." In *The Origins of Psycho-Analysis*, trans. Eric Mosbacher and James Strachey. New York: Basic Books, pp. 347–445. Revised and reprinted in *Standard Edition*, 1, 175.

(1895d) Studies on Hysteria, *Standard Edition*, 2.

(1900a) The Interpretation of Dreams. London and New York, 1955; *Standard Edition*, 4–5.

(1901b) The Psychopathology of Everyday Life. London, 1966; *Standard Edition*, 6.

(1905c) Jokes and their Relation to the Unconscious, *Standard Edition*, 8.

(1905d) Three Essays on the Theory of Sexuality, *Standard Edition*, 7, 125.

(1905e) Fragment of an analysis of a case of hysteria, *Standard Edition*, 7, 3.

(1907a) Delusions and Dreams in Jensen's "Gradiva," *Standard Edition*, 9, 273.

(1907b) Obsessive actions and religious practices, *Standard Edition*, 9, 3.

(1908a) Hysterical phantasies and their relation to bisexuality, *Standard Edition*, 9, 157.

(1908b) Character and anal erotism, *Standard Edition*, 9, 169.

(1908d) "Civilized" sexual morality and modern nervous illness, *Standard Edition*, 9, 179.

(1909b) Analysis of a phobia in a five-year-old boy, *Standard Edition*, 10, 3.

(1909d) Notes upon a case of obsessional neurosis, *Standard Edition*, 10, 155.

(1910a) Five lectures on psycho-analysis, *Standard Edition*, 11, 3.

(1910c) Leonardo da Vinci and a Memory of his Childhood, *Standard Edition*, 11, 59.

(1912a) Postscript to a case of paranoia, *Standard Edition*, 12, 80.

(1912b) The dynamics of transference, *Standard Edition*, 12, 99.

(1912c) Types of onset of neurosis, *Standard Edition*, 12, 229.

(1912–13) Totem and Taboo, *Standard Edition*, 13, 1.

(1913f) The theme of the three caskets, *Standard Edition*, 12, 291.

(1913i) The disposition to obsessional neurosis, *Standard Edition*, 12, 313.

(1914b) The Moses of Michelangelo, *Standard Edition*, 13, 211.

(1915e) The unconscious, *Standard Edition*, 14, 161.

(1916–17) Introductory Lectures on Psycho-Analysis, rev. ed., *Standard Edition*, 15–16.

(1917c) On transformations of instinct as exemplified in anal erotism, *Standard Edition*, 17, 127.

(1917d) A metapsychological supplement to the theory of dreams, *Standard Edition*, 14, 219.

(1917e) Mourning and melancholia, *Standard Edition*, 14, 239.

(1918b) From the history of an infantile neurosis, *Standard Edition*, 17, 3.

(1919g) Preface to Reik's *Ritual: Psycho-Analytic Studies*, *Standard Edition*, 17, 259.

(1919h) The "uncanny," *Standard Edition*, 17, 219.

(1920g) Beyond the Pleasure Principle, *Standard Edition*, 18, 7.

(1921c) Group Psychology and the Analysis of the Ego, *Standard Edition*, 18, 69,

(1923a) Two encyclopaedia articles, *Standard Edition*, 18, 235.

(1923b) The Ego and the Id, London, 1962. *Standard Edition*, 19, 3.

(1924c) The economic problem of masochism, *Standard Edition*, 19, 157.

(1925d) An Autobiographical Study, *Standard Edition*, 20, 3.

(1925h) Negation, *Standard Edition*, 19, 235.

(1925j) Some psychical consequences of the anatomical distinction between the sexes, *Standard Edition*, 19, 243.

(1926d) Inhibitions, Symptoms and Anxiety, *Standard Edition*, 20, 77.

(1927c) The Future of an Illusion, *Standard Edition*, 21, 3.

(1928b). Dostoevsky and Parricide, *Standard Edition*, 21, 175.

(1930a) Civilization and its Discontents, *Standard Edition*, 21, 59.

(1932a) The acquisition and control of fire, *Standard Edition*, 22, 185.

(1933a) New Introductory Lectures on Psycho-Analysis, London, 1971; *Standard Edition*, 22, 3.

(1937c) Analysis terminable and interminable, *Standard Edition*, 23, 211.

(1939a) Moses and Monotheism, *Standard Edition*, 23, 3.

(1940a) An Outline of Psycho-Analysis, *Standard Edition*, 23, 141.

(1950a) *The Origins of Psycho-Analysis*, London and New York, 1954. Partly including "A Project for a Scientific Psychology," in *Standard Edition*, 1, 175.

(1954) *The Origins of Psychoanalysis.* M. Bonaparte, A. Freud, E. Kris, eds. New York: Basic Books.

Freud, Sigmund (1960). *Gesammelte Werke.* 18 vols. in 17. Frankfurt am Main: S. Fischer.

Fromm, Erich (1950). *Psychoanalysis and Faith*. New Haven: Yale University Press.

Fromm, Erich (1959). *Sigmund Freud's Mission: An Analysis of His Personality and Influence*. New York: Harper & Brothers.

Fuller, Peter (1980). *Art and Psychoanalysis*. London: Readers and Writers.

Gardner, M. (1966). The eerie mathematical art of Maurits C. Escher. *Scientific American* 214:110–121.

Gathorne-Hardy, J. (1972). *The Rise of the British Nanny*. London: Hodder & Stoughton.

Gay, Peter (1988). *Freud: A Life for Our Time*. New York: Norton.

Gay, V. P. (1978). Reductionism and redundancy in the analysis of religious forms. *Zygon* 13:2, pp. 169–183.

Gay, V. P. (1979a). *Freud on Ritual: Reconstruction and Critique*. Missoula, Mont.: Scholars Press.

Gay, V. P. (1979b). Against wholeness: the ego's complicity in religion. *Journal of the American Academy of Religion* 47:539–555.

Gay, V. P. (1982). Semiotics as metapsychology—the status of repression. *Bulletin of the Menninger Clinic* 46:489–506.

Gay, V. P. (1989). *Understanding the Occult: Fragmentation and Repair of the Self*. Minneapolis: Fortress Press.

Gay, V. P. (ND). "Expert System in Psychiatry," ms.

Gedo, John M. (1979). *Beyond Interpretation: Toward a Revised Theory for Psychoanalysis*. New York: International Universities Press.

Gedo, John M., and Goldberg, A. (1973). *Models of the Mind*. Chicago: University of Chicago Press.

Gedo, John M., and Pollock, George (1976). *Freud: The Fusion of Science and Humanism, The Intellectual History of Psychoanalysis*.

New York: International Universities Press.

Geertz, C. (1973). *The Interpretation of Cultures.* New York: Basic Books.

Gibson, J. J. (1950). *The Perception of the Visual World.* Boston: Houghton-Mifflin.

Gibson, J. J. (1970). On the relation between hallucination and perception. *Leonardo* 3:425–427.

Gibson, J. J. (1979). *The Ecological Approach to Visual Perception.* Boston: Houghton-Mifflin.

Gide, André (1949). *Oscar Wilde: In Memoriam (Reminiscences) De Profundis,* trans. B. Frechtman. New York: Philosophical Library.

Gill, Merton M. (1963). *Topography and Systems in Psychoanalytic Theory.* (Psychological Issues, Monograph No. 10). New York: International Universities Press.

Gilman, Sander L. (1988). *Disease and Representation: Images of Illness from Madness to AIDS.* Ithaca, NY: Cornell University Press.

Giovacchini, P. (1960). On scientific creativity. *Journal of the American Psychoanalytic Association* 8:407–426.

Girard, Rene (1972). *Violence and the Sacred,* trans. Patrick Gregory. Baltimore: Johns Hopkins University Press, 1977.

Gittings, Robert (1954). *John Keats: The Living Year.* Cambridge, Mass.: Harvard University Press.

Gittings, Robert (1964). *The Keats Inheritance.* London: Heinemann.

Gleason, H. A. (1955). *An Introduction to Descriptive Linguistics.* New York: Winston.

Glover, Edward (1931). Sublimation, substitution, and social anxiety. *International Journal of Psycho-Analysis* 12:263–297.

Glover, Edward (1933). The relation of perversion formation to the development of reality sense. *International Journal of Psycho-*

Analysis 14:486–504.

Glover, Edward (1964). Aggression and sado-masochism. In *Pathology and Treatment of Sexual Deviations*. London: Oxford University Press.

Goethe, J. W. (1774). *The Sufferings of Young Werther*, trans. Harry Steinhauer. New York: Norton, 1970.

Goldberg, A., ed. (1978). *The Psychology of the Self: A Casebook*. New York: International Universities Press.

Goldberg, A., ed. (1980). *Advances in Self Psychology*. New York: International Universities Press.

Goldenweiser, A. (1934). *Anthropology: An Introduction to Primitive Culture*. New York: F. S. Crofts.

Goldstein, Kurt (1957). The smiling of the infant and the problem of understanding the "other." *Journal of Psychology* 44:175–191.

Gombrich, E. H. (1960). *Art and Illusion: A Study in the Psychology of Pictorial Representation*. Princeton: Bollingen.

Gombrich, E. H. (1972). *Symbolic Images: Studies in the Art of the Renaissance*. London: Phaidon.

Gottesman, Ronald, ed. (1971). *Focus on Citizen Kane*. Englewood Cliffs, N.J.: Prentice-Hall.

Greenacre, Phyllis (1955). *Swift and Carroll: A Psychoanalytic Study of Two Lives*. New York: International Universities Press.

Greenacre, Phyllis (1956). Re-evaluation of the process of working-through. In: *Emotional Growth*, pp. 641–650. New York: International Universities Press, 1971.

Greenacre, Phyllis (1957). The childhood of the artist: libidinal phase development and giftedness. *Psychoanalytic Study of the Child* 12:47–72.

Greenberg, Harvey (1975). *The Movies on Your Mind*. New York: Saturday Review Press.

Greenberg, Jay, and Mitchell, Stephen (1983). *Object Relations in Psychoanalytic Theory.* Cambridge, Mass.: Harvard University Press.

Greenler, Robert G., et al. (1979). The 46 degree halo and its arc. *Science* 206:643–649.

Gregor, Thomas (1985). *Anxious Pleasures: The Sexual Lives of an Amazonian People.* Chicago: University of Chicago Press.

Grolnick, S., et al., eds. (1978). *Between Fantasy and Reality: Transitional Objects and Transitional Phenomena.* New York: Jason Aronson.

Grotstein, James (1981). *Splitting and Projective Identification.* Northvale, N.J.: Jason Aronson.

Habermas, J. (1968). *Knowledge and Human Interests,* trans. J. L. Shapiro. Boston: Beacon, 1972.

Hamilton, James (1969). Object loss, dreaming and creativity. *Psychoanalytic Study of the Child* 24:488–531.

Hanly, Charles (1977). An unconscious irony in Plato's Republic. *Psychoanalytic Quarterly* 46:116–147.

Hanson, N. R. (1976). *Perception and Discovery: An Introduction to Scientific Inquiry.* San Francisco: Freeman, Cooper and Company.

Hardy, Thomas (1891). *Tess of the d'Urbervilles.* London: Macmillan.

Hardy, Thomas (1895). *The Return of the Native.* London: Osgood, McIlvaine.

Harris, M. (1968). *The Rise of Anthropological Theory.* New York: Thomas Y. Crowell.

Harris, Zellig S. (1951). *Structural Linguistics.* Chicago: University of Chicago Press.

Harrod, H. (1982). *The Human Center.* Philadelphia: Fortress Press.

Hart, H. (1947). Narcissistic equilibrium. *International Journal of Psycho-Analysis* 28:106–114.

Hart, H. (1948). Sublimation and aggression. *Psychiatric Quarterly* 22:389–412.

Hartmann, E. (1927). Understanding and explanation. In *Essays on Ego Psychology,* pp. 369–403. New York: International Universities Press.

Hartmann, H. (1939). *Ego Psychology and the Problem of Adaptation.* New York: International Universities Press, 1961.

Hartmann, H. (1955). Notes on the theory of sublimation. In *Essays on Ego Psychology,* pp. 215–240. New York: International Universities Press.

Hartmann, H. (1960). *Psychoanalysis and Moral Values.* New York: International Universities Press.

Hartmann, H. (1964). *Essays on Ego Psychology.* New York: International Universities Press.

Hartmann, H., E. Kris, and Loewenstein, R. M. (1964). *Papers on Psychoanalytic Psychology.* New York: International Universities Press.

Hartnett, William, ed. (1977). *Systems: Approaches, Theories, Applications.* Dordrecht: D. Reidel.

Hauptman, William (1977). Ingres and photographic vision. *History of Photography: An International Quarterly* 1, 2:117–127.

Hazlitt, William (1778–1830). *Essays,* ed. Charles H. Gray. New York: Macmillian.

Hauser, Arnold (1951). *The Social History of Art,* vol. 1. New York: Alfred A. Knopf.

Heilbroner, Robert L. (1980). The labor theory of value revisited. *Dissent* 27/1:91–99.

Helmholtz, Hermann von (1867). *Handbuck der Physiologischen Optik.*

Leipsig: L. Voss.

Helmholtz, Hermann von (1877). *On the Sensations of Tone as a Physiological Theory of Music,* trans. Alexander J. Ellis. New York: Dover, 1954.

Helmholtz, Hermann von (1878). The facts in perception. In *Hermann von Helmholtz: Philosophical Writings,* pp. 115–163, eds., Robert S. Cohen and Yehuda Elkana. Boston: D. Reidel.

Herzog, James (1982). Father hunger. In *Father and Child: Developmental and Clinical Perspectives,* eds. S. H. Cath, A. R. Gurwitt, J. M. Ross. Boston: Little, Brown.

Hilberg, Raul (1961). *The Destruction of the European Jews.* Chicago: Quadrangle Books.

Hildebrand, Adolf von (1893). *The Problem of Form in the Figurative Arts in Painting and Sculpture.* New York: G. E. Stechert, 1907.

Holland, Norman (1975). *5 Readers Reading.* New Haven, Conn.: Yale University Press.

Holt, Robert R. (1962). A critical examination of Freud's concept of bound vs. free cathexis. *Journal of the American Psychoanalytic Association* 10:475–525.

Holt, Robert R. (1965). A review of some of Freud's biological assumptions and their influence on his theories. In *Psychoanalysis and Current Biological Thought,* ed. Greenfield and Lewis, pp. 93–124. Madison: University of Wisconsin Press.

Holt, Robert R. (1972). Freud's mechanistic and humanistic images of man. In *Psychoanalysis and Contemporary Science,* ed. Robert R. Holt and E. Peterfreund, 1:3–24.

Holt, Robert R. (1976). Freud's theory of the primary process—present status. *Psychoanalysis and Contemporary Science* 5:61–99, ed. T. Shapiro. New York: International Universities Press.

Holt, Robert R. (1978). Ideological and thematic conflicts in the structure of Freud's thought. In *The Human Mind Revisited: Essays in*

Honor of Karl A. Menninger, ed. S. Smith, pp. 51–98. New York: International Universities Press.

Hong, M. and B. Townes (1976). Infants' attachment to inanimate objects: a cross-cultural study. *Journal of the American Academy of Child Psychiatry* 15:49–61.

Hopper, S. R. (1965). Wallace Stevens: The sundry comforts of the sun. In *Four Ways of Modern Poetry,* ed. N. A. Scott, Jr. Richmond, Va.: John Knox Press.

Horowitz, M. (1967). Visual imagery and cognitive organization. *American Journal of Psychiatry* 123:938–946.

Horton, P. C. (1974). The mystical experience: substance of an illusion. *Journal of the American Psychoanalytic Association* 22:364–380.

Hoss, Rudolf (1984). *Autobiography of Hoss.* In *KL Auschwitz Seen by the SS: Hoss, Broad, Kremer.* New York: Howard Fertig.

Howson, Colin, ed. (1976). *Method and Appraisal in the Physical Sciences: The Critical Background to Modern Science, (1800–1905).* Cambridge: Cambridge University Press.

Isay, Richard A. (1989). *Being Homosexual: Gay Men and Their Development.* New York: Farrar, Straus, Giroux.

Jack, Ian (1967). *Keats and the Mirror of Art.* Oxford: Clarendon Press.

Jacobson, E. (1964). *The Self and the Object World.* New York: International Universities Press.

James, William (1892). *Pyschology.* New York: H. Holt and Co.

James, William (1902). *The Varieties of Religious Experience.* New York: Collier Books.

Jones, E. (1912). The value of sublimating processes for education and re-education. *Journal of Educational Psychology* 3:241–256.

Jones, E. (1916). The theory of sublimation. In *Papers on Psychoanalysis,* pp. 87–144. London: Bailiere, Tindall and Cox, 1948.

Jones, E. (1931). The problem of Paul Morphy. *International Journal of Psycho-Analysis* 12:1–23.

Jones, E. (1953). *The Life and Work of Sigmund Freud*, vol. 1, *The Formative Years and the Great Discoveries, 1856–1900*. New York: Basic Books.

Jones, E. (1955). *The Life and Work of Sigmund Freud*, vol. 2, *Years of Maturity, 1901–1919*. New York: Basic Books.

Joyce, James (1916). *Portrait of the Artist as a Young Man*. New York: Viking Press, 1964.

Jung, C. G. (1952). Answer to Job. In *The Portable Jung*, ed. Joseph Campbell, pp. 519–650. New York: Viking Press.

Jung, C. G. (1961). *Memories, Dreams, Reflections*. New York: Random.

Kael, Pauline (1971). *The Citizen Kane Book*. Boston: Little, Brown.

Kant, Immanuel (1781). *Critique of Pure Reason*, trans. Norman Kemp Smith. New York: St. Martin's Press, 1965.

Kant, Immanuel (1796). *Groundwork of the Metaphysic of Morals*, trans. H. J. Patton. New York: Harper and Row, 1964.

Kant, Immanuel (1798). Anthropology from a Pragmatic Viewpoint. In *Analytic of the Beautiful*, pp. 59–78, trans. Walter Cerf. Indianapolis: Bobbs-Merril, 1963.

Kantorowicz, E. H. (1957). *The King's Two Bodies: A Study in Mediaeval Political Theology*. Princeton: Princeton University Press.

Kaplan, Donald M. (1988). The psychoanalysis of art: some ends, some means. *Journal of the American Psychoanalytic Association* 36:259–293.

Kaywin, L. (1966). Problems of sublimation. *Journal of the American Psychoanalytic Association* 14:313–334.

Kennel, John H., and Klaus, M. H. (1983). Early events: later effects on the infant. In *Frontiers of Infant Psychiatry*, ed. J. D. Call et al., pp.

7–16. New York: Basic Books.

Kepes, Gyorgy, ed. (1965). *Structure in Art and Science.* New York: George Braziller.

Kerenyi, K. (1956). The trickster in relation to Greek mythology. In *The Trickster,* ed. P. Radin (1956).

Kermode, Frank (1963). *Romantic Image.* New York: Chilmark Press.

Kernberg, Otto (1976). *Object Relations Theory and Clinical Psychoanalysis.* New York: Jason Aronson.

Khan, Masud (1965). Intimacy, complicity and mutuality in perversions. In *Alienation in Perversions.* New York: International Universities Press, 1979, pp. 18–30.

Khan, Masud (1979). *Alienation in Perversions.* New York: International Universities Press.

Kim, S. N. (1989). Lamentations of the dead: the historical imagery of violence in Cheju Island, Korea. *Journal of Ritual Studies* 3:251–285.

Kittel, G., ed. (1967). *Theological Dictionary of the New Testament,* vol. 4. Ann Arbor: Wm. B. Eerdmans.

Kittel, G., ed. (1974). *Theological Dictionary of the New Testament,* vol. 11. Ann Arbor: Wm. B. Eerdmans.

Kitto, H. D. F. (1956). *Form and Meaning in Drama.* London: Methuen.

Klapp, Oren (1978). *Opening and Closing: Strategies of Information Adaptation in Society.* Cambridge: Cambridge University Press.

Klaus, M., et al. (1972). Maternal attachment: importance of the first post-partum days. *New England Journal of Medicine* 286:460–463.

Klaus, M. and Kennel, J. H. (1982). *Parent-Infant Bonding.* St. Louis: C. V. Mosby.

Klein, M. (1948). *Contributions to Psycho-Analysis, 1921–1945.* London:

Hogarth Press.

Klein, M. (1957). *Envy and Gratitude.* New York: Basic Books.

Klimar, E. E., and Bellugi, U. et al. (1979). *The Signs of Language.* Cambridge, Mass.: Harvard University Press.

Kline, Neal, and Rausch, Jeffrey (1985). Olfactory precipitants of flashbacks in posttraumatic stress disorder: case reports. *Journal of Clinical Psychiatry,* 46:383–384.

Koffka, K. (1935). *Principles of Gestalt Psychology.* New York: Harcourt Brace.

Kohler, Ivo (1964). *The Formation and Transformation of the Perceptual World.* New York: International Universities Press.

Kohut, Heinz (1965). Autonomy and integration. *Journal of the American Psychoanalytic Association* 13:851–856.

Kohut, Heinz (1966). Forms and transformations of narcissism. *Journal of the American Psychoanalytic Association* 14:243–273.

Kohut, Heinz (1968). The psychoanalytic treatment of narcissistic personality disorders. *The Psychoanalytic Study of the Child* 23:86–113.

Kohut, Heinz (1971). *The Analysis of the Self.* New York: International Universities Press.

Kohut, Heinz (1977). *The Restoration of the Self.* New York: International Universities Press.

Kohut, Heinz (1979). The two analyses of Mr. Z. *International Journal of Psycho-Analysis* 60:3–27.

Kohut, Heinz (1984). *How Does Analysis Cure?* ed. A. Goldberg and P. Stepansky. Chicago: University of Chicago Press.

Kordig, Carl R. (1971). The theory-ladenness of observation. *The Review of Metaphysics* 24:448–484.

Kris, E. (1952). *Psychoanalytic Explorations in Art.* New York: International Universities Press.

Kris, E. (1955). Neutralization and sublimation. *Psychoanalytic Study of the Child* 10:30–46.

Kris, E. (1956). The personal myth: a problem in psychoanalytic technique. In *Selected Papers of Ernst Kris.* New Haven, Conn.: Yale University Press.

Kroeber, A. (1948). Seven Mohave myths. *Anthropological Record* 11, No. 1.

Kubie, Lawrence S. (1934). Body symbolism and the development of language. *Psychoanalytic Quarterly* 3:430–444.

Kubie, Lawrence S. (1948). Instincts and homeostasis. *Psychosomatic Medicine* 10:15–30.

Kubie, Lawrence S. (1953a). The central representation of the symbolic process in psychosomatic disorders. *Psychosomatic Medicine* 15:1–7.

Kubie, Lawrence S. (1953b). The distortion of the neurotic process in neurosis and psychosis. *Journal of the American Psychoanalytic Association* 1:59–86.

Kubie, Lawrence S. (1954). The fundamental nature of the distinction between normality and neurosis. *Psychoanalytic Quarterly* 23: 167–204.

Kubie, Lawrence S. (1956). Influence of symbolic processes on the role of instincts in human behavior. *Psychosomatic Medicine* 18:189–208.

Kubie, Lawrence S. (1958). The neurotic process as the focus of physiological and psychoanalytic research. *British Journal of Psychiatry* 104:518–532.

Kubie, Lawrence S. (1962). The fallacious misuse of the concept of sublimation. *Psychoanalytic Quarterly* 31:73–79.

Kuryluk, Ewa (1987). *Salome and Judas in the Cave of Sex*. Evanston, Ill.: Northwestern University Press.

LaBarre, W. (1954). *The Human Animal* Chicago: University of Chicago Press.

LaBarre, W. (1970). *The Ghost Dance, Origins of Religion*. New York: Dell.

Lacan, J. (1949). Le Stade du Miroir comme formateur de la fonction de je. *Ecrits*. Paris: Editions du Seuil, 1966.

Lain Entralgo, Pedro (1970). *The Therapy of the Word in Classical Antiquity*. New Haven: Yale University Press.

Lakatos, Imre (1976). History of science and its rational reconstructions. In *Method and Appraisal in the Physical Sciences: The Critical Background to Modern Science, 1800–1905*, ed. C. Howson, pp. 1–39. Cambridge: Cambridge University Press.

Lakatos, Imre (1978). Mathematics, Science and Epistemology. *Philosophical Papers*, vol. 2, ed. John Worral and Gregory Currie. Cambridge: Cambridge University Press.

Langer, S. (1962). *Philosophy in a New Key*, 2d ed. New York: Mentor Books.

Langer, S. (1967). *Mind: An Essay on Human Feeling*, vol 1. Baltimore: Johns Hopkins University Press.

Langs, Robert (1985). Making interpretations and securing the frame: sources of danger for psychotherapists. *International Journal of Psychoanalytic Psychotherapy* 10:3–23.

Langs, Robert (1985a, b, c). *Workbooks for Psychotherapists*, in 3 vols. Emerson, N.J.: Newconcept Press.

Laplanche, J., and Pontalis, J. B. (1967). *Vocabulaire de la Psychanalyse*. Paris: P.U.F.

Laughlin, Charles D., and d'Aquili, Eugene G. (1974). *Biogenetic Structuralism*. New York: Columbia.

Lawrence, D. H. (1936). *Phoenix: The Posthumous Papers of D. H. Lawrence*, ed. E. H. McDonald. New York: Viking.

Leach, E. (1964). Anthropological aspects of language: animal categories and verbal abuse. In *New Directions in the Study of Language*, ed. E. H. Lenneberg, pp. 23–63. Cambridge, Mass.: MIT Press.

Learning Designs, Inc. *Recognition Assessment—Empathy. Administrator's Manual.* Toronto, Ontario.

LeDoux, Joseph (1989). Emotions may be triggered before conscious thought. In *The Nashville Tennessean*, 27 August 1989, by Daniel Goleman, p. 10 E.

Levi, Primo (1958). *Survival in Auschwitz* and *The Reawakening: Two Memoirs*. New York: Summit Books, 1985.

Lévi-Strauss, Claude (1955). The structural study of myth. In *Myth: A Symposium*, ed. T. A. Sebeok, pp. 81–106. Bloomington: Indiana University Press.

Lévi-Strauss, Claude (1961). *Tristes Tropiques: An Anthropological Study of Primitive Societies in Brazil.* New York: Atheneum.

Lévi-Strauss, Claude (1972). The raw and the cooked. In *Mythology*, ed. P. Maranda, pp. 251–298. London: C. Nicholls.

Lévi-Strauss, Claude (1988). *The Jealous Potter*, trans. B. Chorier. Chicago: University of Chicago Press.

Levy, Harry B. (1939). A critique of the theory of sublimation. *Psychiatry* 2:239–270.

Lichtenberg, P. (1949). Sublimation. *Persona: Intercollegiate Journal of Psychology* 1:2–9.

Lichtenstein, H. (1964). The role of narcissism in the emergence and maintenance of primary identity. *International Journal of Psycho-Analysis* 45:49–56.

Lindenbaum, Shirley (1979). *Kuru Sorcery: Disease and Danger in the New Guinea Highlands*. Palo Alto: Mayfield.

Locke, John (1690). *An Essay Concerning Human Understanding*, 2 vols. New York: Dover, 1959.

Loewald, H. W. (1975). Psychoanalysis as an art and the fantasy character of the psychoanalytic situation. *Journal of the American Psychoanalytic Association* 23:277–299.

Loewald, H. W. (1979). The waning of the oedipus complex. *Journal of the American Psychoanalytic Association* 27:751–775.

Loewald, H. W. (1988). *Sublimation: Inquiries Into Theoretical Psychoanalysis.* New Haven, Conn.: Yale University Press.

Lombardo, Thomas J. (1987). *The Reciprocity of Perceiver and Environment: The Evolution of J. J. Gibson's Ecological Psychology.* Hillsdale, N.J.: Lawrence Erlbaum.

Longinus (ND). *On the Sublime*, trans. W. Hamilton Fyfe. Cambridge, Mass.: Harvard University Press.

Lorenz, Konrad (1966). *On Aggression*, trans. M. Latzke. London: Methuen.

Lukes, S. (1970). Some problems about rationality. In *Rationality*, ed. Brain Wilson, pp. 294–313. New York: Harper and Row.

Lumsden, Charles J., and Wilson, E. O. (1981). *Genes, Mind, and Culture: The Coevolutionary Process.* Cambridge, Mass.: Harvard University Press.

Lyons, John (1968). *Introduction to Theoretical Linguistics.* Cambridge: Cambridge University Press.

McLuhan, Marshal (1966). The emperor's old clothes. In *The Man Made Object*, ed. Gyrogy Kepes, pp. 90–95. New York: George Braziller.

Mahl, George F. (1969). *Psychological Conflict and Defense.* New York: Harcourt Brace Jovanovich.

Mahler, M. (1983). The meaning of developmental research of earliest infancy as related to the study of separation-individuation. In *Frontiers of Infant Psychiatry*, eds., J. D. Call et al., pp. 3–6. New

York: Basic Books.

Mahoney, Patrick (1982). *Freud as a Writer.* New York: International Universities Press.

Mankiewicz, Herman, and Welles, Orson (1971). Script to Citizen Kane. In *The Citizen Kane Book* by Pauline Kael. Boston: Little, Brown.

Marcuse, H. (1955). *Eros and Civilization.* Boston: Beacon.

Marrow, A. J. (1969). *The Practical Theorist: The Life and Work of Kurt Lewin.* New York: Basic Books.

Martland, Thomas R. (1981). *Religion as Art: An Interpretation.* Albany: SUNY Press.

Masson, J. Moussaief (1980). *The Oceanic Feeling: The Origins of Religious Sentiment in Ancient India.* Boston: Keuwer.

Mead, G. H. (1925/1926). The nature of aesthetic experience. *International Journal of Ethics* 36.

Meissner, W. W. (1978). Psychoanalytic aspects of religious experience. *Annual of Psychoanalysis* 6:103–141.

Menninger, W. C. (1943). Character logic and symptomatic expressions related to the anal phase of psychosexual development. *Psychoanalytic Quarterly* 12:161–193.

Metz, Christian (1977). *The Imaginary Signifier: Psychoanalysis and the Cinema.* Bloomington: Indiana University Press.

Miller, G. A., Galanter, E. and Pribram, K. H. (1960). *Plans and the Structure of Behavior.* New York: Holt, Rinehart and Winston.

Milner, Marion (1950). *On Not Being Able to Paint.* New York: International Universities Press.

Minsky, Marvin (1981). Profiles (Marvin Minsky). *The New Yorker.* 14 December 1981, pp. 50–126.

Mischel, Walter (1979). On the interface of cognition and personality:

beyond the person-situation debate. *American Psychologist* 34: 740–754.

Modell, A. (1965). On having the right to a life: an aspect of superego development. *International Journal of Psycho-Analysis* 46:323–331.

Morrison, Claudia (1968). *Freud and the Critic.* Chapel Hill: University of North Carolina Press.

Muensterberger, W. (1978). Between reality and fantasy. In *Between Reality and Fantasy,* ed. Grolnick, et al., pp. 3–13. New York: Jason Aronson.

Muir, Kenneth, et al. (1958). *Keats: A Reassessment.* Liverpool: University Press.

Murray, Charles (1984). *Losing Ground: American Social Policy 1950–1980.* New York: Basic Books.

Murray, J. M. (1964). Narcissism and the ego ideal. *Journal of the American Psychoanalytic Association* 12:477–511.

Nagera, H., ed. (1969a). *Basic Psychoanalytic Concepts of the Libido Theory.* New York: Basic Books.

Nagera, H. ed. (1969b). *Basic Psychoanalytic Concepts on the Theory of Dreams.* New York: Basic Books.

Nagera, H., ed. (1970). *Basic Psychoanalytic Concepts on Metapsychology, Conflicts, Anxiety and Other Subjects.* New York: Basic Books.

Nietzsche, Friedrich (1872). *The Birth of Tragedy from the Spirit of Music.* In *The Philosophy of Nietzsche,* pp. 947–1088. New York: Modern Library.

Noy, P. (1973). Symbolism and mental representation. *Annual of Psychoanalysis* 1:125–158. New York: Quadrangle Books.

Noy, P. (1979). Form creation in art: an ego-psychological approach to creativity. *Psychoanalytic Quarterly* 48:229–256.

Nunberg, H., and Fedren, P., eds. (1967). *Minutes of the Vienna Psychoanalytic Association*, vol. 2. New York: International Universities Press.

Ober, W. (1968). Drowsed with the fume of poppies: opium and John Keats. *Bulletin of the New York Academy of Medicine* 44:862–880.

Odier, C. (1954). Essai sur la sublimation. *Revue Suisse de Psychologie Pure et Appliquee* 13:97–113.

O'Flaherty, W. (1973). *Asceticism and Eroticism in the Mythology of Siva.* London: Oxford University Press.

Olden, C. (1953). On adult empathy with children. *The Psychoanalytic Study of the Child* 8:111–126. New York: International Universities Press.

Olden, C. (1958). Notes on the development of empathy. *The Psychoanalytic Study of the Child* 13:505–518. New York: International Universities Press.

O'Malley, John W. (1979). *Praise and Blame in Renaissance Rome: Rhetoric, Doctrine, and Reform in Sacred Orators of the Papal Court, c. 1450–1521.* Durham, N.C.: Duke University Press.

Oremland, J. D. (1975). Analysis of a talented musician. *The Psychoanalytic Study of the Child* 30:375–408.

Oremland, J. D. (1983). Death and transformation in *Hamlet. Psychoanalytic Inquiry,* 3:485–512.

Orlando, Francesco (1971). *Toward a Freudian Theory of Literature, with an Analysis of Racine's Phedre,* trans. Charmaine Lee. Baltimore and London: The Johns Hopkins University Press, 1978.

Osgood, C. E., May, W., H. and Miron, W. S., (1975). *Cross-Cultural Universals of Affective Meaning.* Urbana, Ill.: University of Illinois Press.

Oxford Annotated Bible. Revised Standard Version. New York: Oxford University Press.

Parigi, Robert (1982). Reading the entrails: splatter cinema and the post-modern body. *Art Criticism* 4, No. 2, pp. 1–18.

Parsons, T. (1966). *Societies: Evolutionary and Comparative.* Englewood Cliffs, N.J.: Prentice-Hall.

Partridge, Eric (1969). *Shakespeare's Bawdy.* New York: Dutton.

Paul, Robert A. (N.D.). Linguistic inadequacy and the characterization of emotions. Unpublished manuscript.

Pederson-Krag, Geraldine (1951a). "O poesy! For thee I hold my pen." In *Psychoanalysis and Culture,* ed. G. W. Wilbur and W. Muensterberger, pp. 436–452. New York: International Universities Press.

Pederson-Krag, Geraldine (1951b). The genesis of a sonnet. *Psychoanalysis and the Social Sciences* 3:163–176. New York: International Universities Press.

Peterfreund, E. (1983). *The Process of Psychoanalytic Therapy.* New York: Analytic Press.

Peterfreund, E., and Schwartz, J. (1971). *Information, systems, and psychoanalysis. Psychological Issues* no. 25/26. New York: International Universities Press.

Pierce, J. (1961). *Symbols, Signals and Noise.* New York: Harper.

Pike, K. (1954). *Language in Relation to a Unified Theory of the Structure of Human Behavior,* vol. 1. Glendale: Summer Institute of Linguistics.

Pike, K. (1962). *With Heart and Mind, A Personal Synthesis of Scholarship and Devotion.* Grand Rapids, Mich.: Eerdmans.

Pribram, Karl H., and Gill, Merton M.(1976). *Freud's Project Reassessed.* London: Hutchinson.

Pruyser, Paul (1973). Sigmund Freud and his legacy: psychoanalytic psychology of religion. In *Beyond the Classics,* ed. C. Glock and P. Hammond, pp. 243–290. New York: Harper.

Radin, P. (1956). *The Trickster: A Study in American Indian Mythology.* New York: Philosophical Library.

Raine, Kathleen (1967). *Defending Ancient Springs.* London: Oxford University Press.

Rank, O. (1924). *The Don Juan Legend,* ed. and trans. David G. Winter. Princeton: Princeton University Press, 1975.

Rapaport, David (1950). *Emotions and Memory.* New York: International Universities Press, 1971.

Rapaport, David (1955). Seminars on Psychoanalytic Ego Psychology held at the Western New England Institute of Psychoanalysis, ed. Stuart C. Miller, typescript.

Rapaport, David (1960). *The Structure of Psychoanalytic Theory.* New York: International Universities Press.

Rappaport, Roy (1968). *Pigs for the Ancestors: Ritual in the Ecology of a New Guinea People.* New Haven, Conn.: Yale University Press.

Rappaport, Roy (1971). Ritual, sanctity, and cybernetics. *American Anthropologist* 73:59–76.

Rawson, P. S. (1966). *Indian Sculpture.* New York: Dutton.

Reader's Digest Fix-It Yourself Manual. Pleasantville, N.Y.: Reader's Digest Association, 1977.

Rey, J. H. (1988). That which patients bring to analysis. *International Journal of Psycho-Analysis* 69:457–473.

Reynolds, Reginald (1946). *Godliness and Cleanliness.* New York: Harcourt Brace and Jovanovich.

Ricoeur, Paul (1965). *Freud and Philosophy.* New Naven, Conn.: Yale University Press, 1970.

Ricoeur, Paul (1967). *The Symbolism of Evil.* Boston: Beacon Press.

Rieff, Philip (1959). *Freud: The Mind of the Moralist.* New York: Doubleday.

Rizzuto, Ana-Maria (1979). *The Birth of the Living God: A Psychoanalytic Study.* Chicago: University of Chicago Press.

Roazen, P. (1975). *Freud and His Followers.* New York: Knopf.

Rock, Irvin, and Smith, D. (1981). Alternative solutions to kinetic stimulus transformations. *Journal of Experimental Psychology, Human Perception and Performance* 7:19–29.

Rogers, Robert (1967). Keats's strenuous tongue: a study of "Ode on Melancholy." *Literature and Psychology* 17:2–12, 41–43.

Roheim, G. (1941). The psychoanalytic interpretation of culture. *International Journal of Psycho-Analysis* 22:147–169.

Rose, Gilbert J. (1980). *The Power of Form: A Psychoanalytic Approach to Aesthetic Form.* New York: International Universities Press.

Rosenwald, G. C. (1972). Effectiveness of defenses against anal impulse arousal. *Journal of Clinical and Consulting Psychology* 39:292–298.

Rothenberg, Albert (1989). Psychoanalysis and creativity: John Cheever's greatest novel. *Psychologist-Psychoanalyst* 9:15–19.

Rothstein, Arnold, ed. (1986). *Reconstruction of Trauma: Its Significance in Clinical Work.* Madison, Conn.: International Universities Press.

Rousset, J. (1978). *Le Mythe de Don Juan.* Paris: A. Colin

Rowse, A. L. (1973). *Shakespeare the Man.* London: Macmillan.

Ryle, Gilbert (1949). *The Concept of Mind.* London: Hutchinson.

Sachs, Hans (1934). The delay of the machine age. *Imago* 20:78–94.

Sachs, Hans (1945). *Freud, Master and Friend.* Cambridge, Mass.: Harvard University Press.

Sampson, G. (1980). *Making Sense.* Oxford: Oxford University Press.

Sandler, J., and Rosenblatt, B. (1962). The concept of the representational world. *The Psychoanalytic Study of the Child* 17:128–145.

Sandler, J., and Joffe, W. G. (1966). On skill and sublimation. *Journal of the American Psychoanalytic Association* 14:335–355.

Schachtel, Ernest G. (1966). *Experiential Foundations of Rorschach's Test.* New York: Basic Books.

Schafer, Roy (1968). *Aspects of Internalization.* New York: International Universities Press.

Schafer, Roy (1976). *A New Language for Psychoanalysis.* New Haven, Conn.: Yale University Press.

Scheck, Raffael (1988). Did the Children's Crusade of 1212 really consist of children? Problems of writing childhood history. *The Journal of Psychohistory* 16, no. 2, pp. 176–182.

Schimek, J. G. (1975). A critical reexamination of Freud's concept of unconscious mental representation. *International Review of Psycho-Analysis* 2:171–187.

Schlick, Moritz (1921). Notes and comments on Helmholtz. Originally in *Schriften zur Erkenntnistheorie,* Berlin. Reprinted in Helmholtz, Hermann von (1878).

Schmideberg, M. (1947). On sublimation. *Samiksa* 1:97–118.

Schon, Donald A. (1963). *Invention and the Evolution of Ideas* (originally published as *Displacement of Concepts*). London: Tavistock, 1967.

Scimecca, J. A. (1979). Comments on E. Becker and culture hero. *Review of Religious Research* 21(1).

Segal, H. (1952). A psycho-analytic approach to aesthetics. *International Journal of Psycho-Analysis* 33:196–207.

Shands, Harley C. (1970). *Semiotic Approaches to Psychiatry.* The Hague: Mouton.

Shannon, C. E., and Weaver, W., (1949). *The Mathematical Theory of Communication*. Urbana: University of Illinois Press.

Sharpe, Ella F. (1930). Certain aspects of sublimation and delusion. *International Journal of Psycho-Analysis* 11:12–23.

Sharpe, Ella F. (1935). Similar and divergent unconscious determinants underlying the sublimations of pure art and pure science. *International Journal of Psycho-Analysis* 16:186–202.

Shaw, C. G. (1928). Culture. *Encyclopaedia of Religion and Ethics*, ed. James Hastings, 3:358–363.

Shaw, George Bernard (1903). *Man and Superman*. New York: Brentano's, 1914.

Shengold, Leonard (1988). *Halo in the Sky: Observations on Anality and Defense*. New York: Guilford Press.

Shevrin, Howard (1973). Brain wave correlates of subliminal stimulation, unconscious attention, primary and secondary-process thinking, and repressiveness. In *Psychoanalytic Research: Three Approaches to the Experimental Study of Subliminal Processes* (Psychological Issues, Monograph No. 30), ed. M. Mayman, pp. 56–87. New York: International Universities Press.

Shevrin, Howard (1978). Semblances of feelings: the imagery of affect in empathy, dreams, and unconscious processes—a revision of Freud's several affect theories. In *The Human Mind Revisited*, ed. Sydney Smith, pp. 263–294. New York: International Universities Press.

Simon, B. (1973). Plato and Freud: the mind in conflict and the mind in dialogue. *Psychoanalytic Quarterly* 42:91–122.

Simon, B. (1978). *Mind and Madness in Ancient Greece: Classical Roots of Modern Psychiatry*. Ithaca: Cornell University Press.

Simon, Herbert A. (1969). *The Sciences of the Artificial*. Cambridge, Mass.: MIT Press.

Simon, Herbert A. (1977). *Models of Discovery and Other Topics in the*

Methods of Science. Dordrecht: D. Reidel.

Simon, Herbert A. (1979). *Models of Thought.* New Haven, Conn.: Yale University Press.

Singh, Sadanand, and Singh, Kala S. (1976). *Phonetics: Principles and Practices.* Baltimore: University Park Press.

Smith, C. S. (1978). Structural hierarchy in science, art, and history. In *On Aesthetics in Science,* ed. Judith Wechsler, pp. 9–53. Cambridge, Mass.: MIT Press.

Smith, Darrell (1982). Trends in counseling and psychotherapy. *American Psychologist* 37:802–809.

Synder, Douglas (1987). On Freud's adoption of the objective view regarding psychological phenomena. *Psychoanalysis and Contemporary Thought* 10:129–153.

Socarides, Charles (1988). *The Preoedipal Origin and Psychoanalytic Therapy of Sexual Perversions.* Madison, Conn.: International Universities Press.

Spence, Donald (1987). *The Freudian Metaphor: Toward a Paradigm Change in Psychoanalysis.* New York: Norton.

Sperber, Dan (1974). *Rethinking Symbolism,* trans. A. L. Morton. Cambridge: Cambridge University Press, 1975.

Spiegel, L. A. (1966). Affects in relation to self and object: a model for the derivation of desire, longing, pain, anxiety, humiliation, and shame. *The Psychoanalytic Study of the Child* 21:69–92.

Spitz, René A. (1946). Anaclitic depression. *The Psychoanalytic Study of the Child* 2:313–342.

Spitz, René A. (1957). *No and Yes: On the Genesis of Human Communication.* New York: International Universities Press.

Spitz, René A. (1969). Aggression and adaptation. *Journal of Nervous and Mental Diseases* 149:81–90.

Steegmuller, F. (1972). *Flaubert in Egypt: A Sensibility on Tour.* Boston: Little, Brown.

Steinberg, Leo (1983). *The Sexuality of Christ in Renaissance Art and Modern Oblivion.* New York: Pantheon.

Sterba, R. (1930). Zur problematik der sublimierungslehre. *Internationale Zeitschrift für Psychoanalyse* 16:370–377.

Stern, Daniel (1977). *The First Relationship: Infant and Mother.* Cambridge, Mass.: Harvard University Press.

Stern, Daniel (1985). *The Interpersonal World of the Infant: A View from Psychoanalysis and Developmental Psychology.* New York: Basic Books.

Stillinger, Jack, ed. (1978). *The Poems of John Keats.* Cambridge, Mass.: Harvard University Press.

Stokes, Adrian (1958). *Greek Culture and the Ego: A Psycho-Analytic Survey of an Aspect of Greek Civilization and Art.* London: Tavistock.

Stokes, Adrian (1973). *A Game that Must Be Lost: Collected Papers.* Cheadle Hulme: Carcanet Press.

Stoller, Robert (1975). *Perversion: The Erotic Form of Hatred.* New York: Pantheon Books.

Stolorow, Robert, and Lachmann, Frank M. (1980). *Psychoanalysis of Developmental Arrests: Theory and Treatment.* New York: International Universities Press.

Stone, L. J., et al., eds. (1973). *The Competent Infant.* New York: Basic Books.

Strachey, J. (1957). Editor's Introduction to "Papers on Metapsychology," pp. 105–107, by S. Freud. In *Standard Edition*, vol. 14, London: Hogarth Press. All references to Strachey cite his comments throughout the *Standard Edition*.

Sullivan, Harry Stack (1953). *The Interpersonal Theory of Psychiatry.*

New York: Norton.

Sullivan, Harry Stack (1964). *The Fusion of Psychiatry and Social Science*. New York: Norton.

Suttie, Ian D. (1952). *Origins of Love and Hate*. New York: Julian Press.

Swanson, Don (1977). A critique of psychic energy as an explanatory concept. *Journal of the American Psychoanalytic Association* 25:603–633.

Swanson, Guy E. (1960). *The Birth of the Gods*. Ann Arbor, Mich.: University of Michigan Press.

Tanisaki, Junichiro (1960). *Some Prefer Nettles*, trans. E. G. Seidensticker. Tokyo: Tuttle.

Tausk, V. (1919). On the origin of the "influencing machine." in schizophrenia. *Psychoanalytic Quarterly* 2:519–556.

Taussig, Michael (1984a). Culture of terror–space of death: Roger Casement's Putomayho report and the explanation of torture. *Comparative Studies in Society and History* 26/3:467–487.

Taussig, Michael (1984b). History as sorcery. *Representations* 7:87–109.

Thoma, Helmut, and Kachele, Horst (1986). *Psychoanalytic Practice*, trans. M. Wilson and D. Rosevare. New York: Springer Verlag.

Thompson, S., ed. (1955–58). *Motif-Index of Folk Literature*, 6 vols. Bloomington: Indiana University Press.

Tillich, Paul (1951). *Systematic Theology, Vol. I, Reason and Revelation, Being and God*. Chicago: University of Chicago Press.

Tillyard, E. M. W. (1946). The Elizabethan world order. In *Shakespeare: The Histories*, pp. 32–41. Englewood Cliffs, N.J.: Prentice-Hall.

Trilling, Lionel (1951). *The Selected Letters of John Keats*. New York: Farrar, Straus and Young.

Twitchell, James B. (1985). *Dreadful Pleasures: An Anatomy of Modern*

Horror. New York: Oxford University Press.

Udy, Stanley H. (1964). Cross-cultural analysis: a case study. In *Sociologists at Work,* ed. P. E. Hammond, pp. 186–212. New York: Basic Books.

Updike, John (1979). Sublimating. In *Too Far to Go.* New York: Fawcett Crest.

Upton, A., and Samson, R. W. (1963). *Creative Analysis.* New York: E. P. Dutton.

van Gigch, John P. (1974). *Applied General Systems Theory.* New York: Harper and Row.

Vayda, A. P., and Rappaport, R. (1963). Island cultures. In *Man's Place in the Island Ecosystem,* ed. F. R. Fosberg. Honolulu: Bishop Museum.

Waelder, Robert (1936). The principle of multiple function: observations of overdetermination. *Psychoanalytic Quarterly* 5:45–62.

Waelder, Robert (1960). *Basic Theory of Psychoanalysis.* New York: International Universities Press.

Waelder, Robert (1962). Psychoanalysis, scientific method, and philosophy. *Journal of the American Psychoanalytic Association* 10:617–637.

Wallace, Anthony F. C. (1966a). *Religion: An Anthropological View.* New York: Random.

Wallace, Anthony F. C. (1966b). Ritual: sacred and profane. *Zygon* 1:60–81.

Wangh, M. (1957). Reporter: the scope of the contribution of psychoanalysis to the biography of the artist. *Journal of the American Psychoanalytic Association* 5:564–575.

Ward, Aileen (1963). *John Keats: The Making of a Poet.* New York: Viking.

Warren, William (1984). Perceiving affordances: visual guidance of stair climbing. *Journal of Experimental Psychology, Human Perception and Performance* 10:683–703.

Weisberg, Robert W. (1980). *Memory, Thought and Behavior.* Oxford: Oxford University Press.

Weiss, Joseph, and Sampson, Harold (1986). *The Psychoanalytic Process: Theory, Clinical Observation, & Empirical Research.* New York: Guilford.

Weyl, Herman (1952). *Symmetry.* Princeton: Princeton University Press.

Whitman, Walt (1889). *Leaves of Grass.* New York: Norton, 1965.

Whyte, Lancelot L. (1951). *Aspects of Form.* London: Humphries.

Whyte, Lancelot L. (1954). *Accent on Form.* New York: Harper and Row.

Whyte, Lancelot, Wilson, L., A., and Wilson, D., eds. (1969). *Hierarchical Structures.* New York: American Elsevier.

Wilden, Anthony (1972). *System and Structure.* London: Tavistock.

Williams, A. Hyatt (1966). Keats' "La Belle Dame Sans Merci": the bad-breast mother. *American Imago* 23:63–81.

Williams, L. P. (1986). Helmholtz. *The New Encyclopedia Britannica,* 15th ed. Chicago: Encyclopedia Britannica.

Wilson, E. O. (1975). *Sociobiology: The New Synthesis.* Cambridge: Belknap Press.

Wilson, E. O., and Lumsden, C. J. (1981). *Genes, Mind, and Culture.* Cambridge, Mass.: Harvard University Press.

Wimsatt, W. K. (1954). *The Verbal Icon: Studies in the Meaning of Poetry.* Lexington: University of Kentucky Press.

Winnicott, D. W. (1953). Transitional objects and transitional phenomena. *International Journal of Psycho-Analysis* 34:89–97.

Winnicott, D. W. (1971a). *Playing and Reality*. London: Tavistock.

Winnicott. D. W. (1971b). *Therapeutic Consultations in Child Psychiatry*. New York: Basic Books.

Wittgenstein, L. (1958). *Philosophical Investigations*, 3d ed., trans. G. E. M. Anscombe. New York: Macmillan.

Wormhoudt, Arthur (1956). *Hamlet's Mouse Trap. A Psychoanalytical Study of the Drama*. New York: AMS Press.

Zweig, Paul (1968). *The Heresy of Self-Love: A Study of Subversive Individualism*. New York: Basic Books.

INDEX